"I welcome *Defending Black Faith* [as a resource] for the ongoing dialogue with respect to the mean... of Christianity for blacks. This book ought to be enthusiastically embraced by critical thinkers of all ages within the body of Christ, and especially by students in colleges and seminaries."
CHERYL J. SANDERS
Senior Pastor
The Third Street Church of God
Washington, D.C.

"For years African-American Christians have been attacked for our commitment to Christ. In the streets, schools, barbershops, beauty salons, college campuses, jails and prisons, African-American Christianity has taken a beating. *Defending Black Faith* provides all Christians with Christ-centered, biblically based, theologically sound answers to the most blistering attacks upon the faith. It equips and empowers the reader to boldly reclaim lost people and lost areas of the community for Christ. The book is a must read!"
FRANK M. REID III
Senior Pastor
Bethel African Methodist Episcopal Church, Baltimore

"This thorough, exhaustive and relevant work should prove to be an invaluable resource for those who endeavor to 'contend for the faith,' that saints would be able to intelligently present the gospel of Jesus Christ in such a way that souls would be won for the Kingdom of God."
JACQUELINE E. MCCOLLOUGH
Associate Pastor
Elim International Fellowship, Brooklyn

"Craig Keener and Glenn Usry have done it again! *Defending Black Faith,* the sequel to *Black Man's Religion,* is a must read for every Christian on the North American continent. The book will be of immense value for college students and for Christians who are incarcerated. These two populations are under the heaviest attack from the Nation of Islam, and the work that Keener and Usry have done will give them more than adequate tools not only for answering, but for silencing all of the preposterous claims of those who attack the Christian faith."
JEREMIAH A. WRIGHT JR.
Senior Pastor
Trinity United Church of Christ, Chicago

Defending
BLACK FAITH

Answers to
Tough Questions
About
African-American
Christianity

CRAIG S. KEENER
& GLENN USRY

≋
IVP

InterVarsity Press
Downers Grove, Illinois

InterVarsity Press® is the book-publishing division of InterVarsity Christian Fellowship®, a student movement active on campus at hundreds of universities, colleges and schools of nursing in the United States of America, and a member movement of the International Fellowship of Evangelical Students. For information about local and regional activities, write Public Relations Dept., InterVarsity Christian Fellowship, 6400 Schroeder Rd., P.O. Box 7895, Madison, WI 53707-7895.

Scripture quotations, unless otherwise indicated, are the authors' own translation.

ISBN 0-8308-1995-9

Printed in the United States of America ∞

Library of Congress Cataloging-in-Publication Data

Keener, Craig S., 1960-
    Defending Black faith : answers to tough questions about African-
American Christianity / Craig Keener and Glenn Usry.
        p.   cm.
    Includes bibliographical references (p.   ).
    ISBN 0-8308-1995-9 (alk. paper)
        1. Afro-Americans—Religion.   2. Afrocentrism—Religious aspects—
Christianity—Controversial literature.   I. Usry, Glenn.
    II. Title.
    BR563.N4K44   1997
    270'.089'96073—dc21   96-29819
                                                                                        CIP

20	19	18	17	16	15	14	13	12	11	10	9	8	7	6	5	4	3	2	1
14	13	12	11	10	09	08	07	06	05	04	03	02	01	00	99	98	97		

To the memory of
Glenn's late brother,
Gregory Keith Usry,
who inspired him to be real,
zealous and radical

Introduction

Our first book, *Black Man's Religion,* responded to White as well as Black objections to African-American Christianity.[1] In this book, however, we primarily respond to some Afrocentric writers who have challenged the historical credibility of the Christian faith. Because this book was originally intended to be a training manual for African-American Christian students, we have retained our original objective of answering particular questions that often confront our students. We nevertheless encourage readers to reapply the information here to other worthy projects different from our own. Such projects could include teaching apologetics (defending the faith), history or evangelism in churches.

The Plan of This Book

We start by rehearsing the points covered in our first book which are most important to our case here. Thus we trace our African and African-American Christian heritage and respond to claims from some Islamic groups that Christianity is inherently racist or proslavery. Some say Christianity is a White man's religion; our first book responded by claiming that it is a "Black religion" too. The first three chapters here provide a relatively concise, "free" review of these points from *Black Man's Religion* (for further detail, consult that volume), plus a small amount of new information.

Those who have read *Black Man's Religion* recently may skip immediately to chapter four, where we respond to claims by various Afrocentric authors that all Christian doctrines originated in Africa. Chapters five through seven respond to three writers against Christianity whose works have circulated in some African-American circles, one a leader in heterodox Islam, one an orthodox Muslim and one propounding a view more akin to Eastern mysticism. Readers should keep in mind that in all three cases we are responding to these writers' claims, not attacking them or responding to all people who share elements of their worldview.

Most of this book simply responds to objections to Christian faith, but the heart of our own argument appears in the final two chapters. In chapter eight we turn to the question of truth—not just whether Christianity's detractors are wrong, but whether the biblical message about Jesus is *right*. Did the first witnesses of Jesus report about him accurately? What historical evidence remains that would be adequate to invite an open-minded skeptic to faith in Jesus? Our final chapter addresses the most disputed doctrine of the Christian faith today: Jesus is the only rightful Lord and Savior of humanity. Many Christians find themselves struggling with this doctrine, yet it is at the heart of the faith taught by the apostles and witnesses who knew Jesus best. The Black church, given its sensitivity to oppression, rightly provides a bastion of tolerance toward all, but tolerance and kindness do not necessarily mean that we *agree* with all. Not unexpectedly, the affirmation of Jesus as Lord will never be popular among those who are not Christians, but if Jesus is the true Lord (as chapter eight argues), then we must embrace the full implications of that claim.

We close with two appendixes. The information in them is important for those who wish to pursue matters further, although readers can catch the main substance of the book without them. Because we respond to an imbalanced use of African backgrounds in chapter four, we provide one sample of a more balanced approach in appendix A, illustrating how ancient Israel freely learned from and influenced other cultures, both in northeast Africa and in western Asia. Although appendix B is at best a brief example of what could be done, it responds in some detail to an objection raised by Ahmed Deedat against the first five books of the Bible for which we lacked adequate space in chapter six.

What This Book Includes
It should be noted that we are responding here to writers who challenge African-American Christianity itself, not to those who dispute particular traditions preferred by many African-American Christians. For instance, we will not expend space defending the King James Version of the Bible against its detractors; neither of the authors depends on that translation, because we do not think it is the most accurate.[2]

Further, we cannot address every possible objection to Christianity, and so we offer merely a sample response to some of the works we have found circulating on the popular market. (Other issues are, however, widely addressed elsewhere. Those concerned about scientific issues, for instance, should contact Reasons to Believe, P.O. Box 5978, Pasadena, CA 91117-0978, a reputable organization headed by astrophysicist Hugh Ross.[3])

The arguments we address here do not always represent the best arguments against our faith, but these are the sorts of issues we have most often confronted. We trust that our discussion will remind Christians that we have a much stronger and more credible case for our position than those who oppose the Christian message have considered. As in our first book, Craig was responsible for most of the research, and Glenn for the overarching Afrocentric perspective.

A Brief Apology

This book is an "apology" in the sense of an *apologia,* the Greek word for a defense. But here we also pause to offer one apology in the more traditional English sense of the term. Responses to *Black Man's Religion* have varied from favorable (including postpublication endorsements by Jeremiah Wright and Jawanza Kunjufu of Chicago and Charles Copher of ITC in Atlanta) to unfavorable (so far indicated particularly by a death threat even before the book's publication). The death threat was predictable and requires little response here. Based on past experience we also expect that some people who dismiss Afrocentrism will criticize our book without reading it; others who uncritically accept all proposals by Afrocentric writers may likewise disregard us because we differ from some non-Christian Afrocentric perspectives. We do not wish to expend space trying to refute objections that would be refuted if critics simply *read* the book.[4]

One negative observation received so far, however, deserves a more serious response, and that is a complaint some have raised concerning the word *man's* in the title *Black Man's Religion.* Although many readers liked the title—including some women friends who approved it before publication—others have felt that the title excluded women. Thus we pause to explain that the title did not reflect our own choice of language (as one may gather from the rest of that book) but alluded to Elijah Muhammad's phrase "white man's religion" now heard widely on our streets. We toyed with "Black People's Religion" and other variations on the title, but none preserved the essential allusion to "white man's religion" we sought to counter.[5] Nevertheless, concerned lest anyone misinterpret our intention, we explained the title both on the back cover and in the book's opening paragraph. In that first paragraph we further explicitly disavowed sexism (as well as racism). We trusted that those who knew something about us or chose to read the book further would understand our intention.[6] Although gender prejudice is not the focus of either that book or this one, we reaffirm our commitment to justice across gender as well as racial lines, and our commitment to our highly esteemed sisters in their labor for justice.

Acknowledgments

Special thanks are due to friends, both professors and graduate students, who graciously reviewed parts of our manuscript outside our discipline: especially James Hoffmeier, John Lamoreaux and Rodney Sadler. Thanks are also due our editors at IVP, Rodney Clapp and Ruth Goring. For information and promotional support we thank also Dr. Greg Moss, moderator of the Rowan Baptist Association (North Carolina); Brian Keith Williams, pastor of Body of Christ Tabernacle (Columbus, Ohio); Dr. Frank Madison Reid, pastor of Bethel A.M.E. (Baltimore); Dr. Jeremiah Wright, pastor of Trinity United Church of Christ (Chicago); and Dr. Johnny Youngblood, pastor of St. Paul Community Baptist Church (Brooklyn). Craig also thanks Brian Harvey for rekeying Craig's manuscript on the tabernacle (originally written in his graduate-school days, before he could afford a computer).

The danger of further acknowledgments is that once one begins it is difficult to know where to stop. Glenn thanks his wife, Ruta Marie Usry, for being the embodiment of a spiritual partner and best friend; and his mother, Ora Lee Usry, who epitomizes the strengths of Black womanhood, not to mention motherhood; his late father, Oscar Caswell Usry, who encouraged him to read the Scriptures; and other members of his family. He also thanks his mentors in ministry, especially Bishop Clarence Carr of the A.M.E. Zion Church, and also Bishop Ruben L. Speaks and the late Bishop William Smith. Craig thanks his mentors in the Black church, especially Pastor Nilous Avery, Mount Zion Missionary Baptist Church (Salisbury, North Carolina); Pastor Carl Kenney, Orange Grove Missionary Baptist Church (Durham, North Carolina);the Reverend Jacqueline Reeves of the A.M.E. Church (Elizabeth, New Jersey); Dr. Frank Madison Reid III, of Bethel A.M.E. Church (Baltimore); and Dr. Jeremiah Wright, Trinity United Church of Christ (Chicago).

We also must acknowledge those whose suggestions started us on the research path that led to these two books: most importantly, New Generation Campus Ministries in Atlanta (especially Bryan Crute, Dean Nelson, Howard and Tecla Sanders, and Louis Williams); also Dr. Darrel Rollins, dean of Shaw Divinity School (Raleigh, North Carolina); and Dr. James R. Samuel, then dean of Hood Theological Seminary (Salisbury).

1

A Black Religion

What Do You Say When Someone Claims That Christianity Is a White Religion?

The white race's false religion called Christianity . . . gives you no desire or power to resist them. The only way and place to solve this problem is in the Religion of Islam. . . . In the religion of Christianity the white race has had us worshiping and praying to something that actually did not even exist.[1]

Philip . . . encountered a Nubian court official of Candace, queen of the Nubians, who was her royal treasurer. He had just journeyed to Jerusalem to worship God. As this man was sitting in his chariot, on his way back to Nubia, and reading the book of Isaiah the prophet, the Spirit told Philip, "Go over and meet this chariot." . . . So beginning from Isaiah, Philip explained Jesus to him. And as the chariot continued on its way they passed some water; and the official exclaimed, "Here is water! Should anything keep me from being baptized?" (Acts 8:26-36)[2]

Especially beginning in the nineteenth century, Western Protestant missions made a significant impact in Africa. African Christians themselves spread this impact more than Western missionaries could have done, however, and the African church grew hundreds of times over, to currently more than half of Black Africa's population. But less known is the fact that many Africans had embraced Jesus and the Bible long before European missionaries came—in fact, before Britain and Germany had opened to Christianity. Because this chapter largely retraces ground covered in greater depth and with fuller documentation in the second chapter of *Black Man's Religion,* readers most familiar with that book may wish to fast-forward to chapter four.

North Africa and Early Christian History

After the fall of Carthage, the Roman Empire encompassed a sophisticated and flourishing civilization in North Africa as well as southern Europe. Historians often credit the North African theologian Tertullian with creating what became the traditional form of Latin Christianity.[3] By the end of the second century, North Africa was so thoroughly Christianized that Tertullian could protest to the emperor, "We have left nothing to you but the temples of your gods!"[4] Christianity developed earlier and spread faster in North Africa than in most other parts of the Empire; Latin Christianity originated there, ultimately shaping the thought of the Roman Church.[5]

Even in the nineteenth century, European scholar Theodor Mommsen acknowledged that "through Africa Christianity became the religion of the world."[6] Nearly half of the most prominent church leaders in the first few centuries (such as Origen, Cyprian, Athanasius and Augustine) were North African,[7] and probably a fair number of these were dark in complexion.[8] Christianity spread in Egypt so widely that that country remained majority Christian into the tenth century,[9] and to this day at least 10 percent of its population remains Christian.[10]

North Africa was one of the gospel's securest homes. As African scholar John S. Mbiti puts it,

> Christianity in Africa is so old that it can rightly be described as an indigenous, traditional and African religion. Long before the start of Islam in the seventh century, Christianity was well established all over north Africa, Egypt, parts of the Sudan and Ethiopia.[11]

But shortly after Rome fell to northern European barbarian hordes, the barbarians streamed into North Africa, devastating its civilization (c. 429).[12] By the time Islam began its conquests, the North African church was so disunited that much of it readily succumbed.[13] In fact Egypt, tired of Byzantine rule,[14] welcomed the Arabs in A.D. 641; the initial treaty promised Christians religious freedom provided they paid a poll tax.[15] But in the intermittent persecutions of the eighth and ninth centuries, Muslims destroyed centuries of Coptic art; heavy financial pressures also made life difficult for the Copts.[16] From 1250 the Mamelukes repressed the Copts even more harshly, till by the fourteenth century they had become only a small portion of Egypt's population.[17]

In time, all of North Africa, which had been mainly Christian, fell to Islam. Preceding centuries of internal strife (the Donatist schism), repression over secondary doctrinal issues by others who claimed the same Christian faith (Rome and Byzantium) and repression from more serious distortions of the Christian faith (the Arians) had rendered the North African Christians weak and susceptible to collapse.[18] In a very real sense, professing Christians rather than Muslims undermined Christianity in North Africa; to some extent the Arabs simply cleaned up after them. Some of us may wonder whether history is not repeating itself in many of our cities today.

Under Islamic law, Christians were given the status of second-class citizens and made to bear a tax that many peasants could not afford to pay. Muslims converting back to Christianity could be tortured or killed.[19] Some local groups of Christians persisted for many centuries, but outside of Egypt, most were eventually violently stamped out.[20] Thus most of North Africa became Muslim in faith and came to be dominated especially by Arab peoples and civilization.[21]

Nubia

Farther south in Africa, however, Christianity continued to grow—as it had for some time, indeed, from the very beginning of the Christian mission. According to the Bible, the very *first* Gentile Christian (the first Christian who was not Jewish) was an Ethiopian, a Black African official of Queen Candace (*kan-dak'e*—Acts 8:27).[22] The author of Acts probably intends this account to symbolize the great spread of Christianity in Africa which he expected, and which has in fact happened.[23]

This first non-Jewish Christian in the New Testament was plainly from Africa. Greek writers used "Ethiopians" to refer to all Black Africans, who became the standard by which the Mediterranean world defined blackness.[24] Other texts mention Nubia's queen, whose dynastic title was the Candace.[25] This kingdom was an ancient and powerful Nubian civilization with its capital in Meroe, which had continued since around 750 B.C.26

The official's witness might have proved more significant in African history, but the empire of Meroe was declining by the mid-first century A.D., "almost certainly" because of "the rise of a rival trading empire, with its centre at Axum" in East Africa.[27] Yet Christianity spread southward into Nubia again in the 300s and 400s, this time from Egypt, till Nubia became predominantly Christian.[28]

Unlike many other peoples, Nubia adopted Christianity without coming under the sway of Roman law;[29] having done so, Nubia clung to it fiercely.

Despite organizational weaknesses of Nubian Christianity, the church survived the Islamic conquest of much of North Africa. Whereas Egypt's Christians virtually invited their Arab conquerors in to liberate them from the Eastern Roman Empire, the Black Nubians refused submission. Unable to conquer Nubia after taking Egypt in 641, the Arabs made an unusual treaty (Arabic *Baqt*) in 652,[30] a compromise of peace in return for an annual tribute of 360 Nubian slaves.[31] Yet the Arabs were looking out for their own interests; besides the slaves acquired under the treaty, the Arabs took other Nubian slaves by trade.[32]

Eventually the Arab rulers repressed the Egyptian Christians who had welcomed them. They forced the Christians to pay tribute and prohibited them from building "new churches or monasteries" or from any public signs "of Christian practice."[33] Chancellor Williams recounts the intervention of the Nubian kingdom of Makuria on behalf of the now-persecuted Christians of Egypt in 745, when Omar, initiating a de facto holy war, imprisoned the patriarch and began "destroying churches or converting them into mosques." Once Nubia marched against the Arab governor, the latter quickly backed down from his policy of repression.[34] The Nubian king on various occasions protected the patriarch of Alexandria, but Arab rulers also sometimes grew suspicious of the Coptic Egyptian Church's African ties.[35]

From reading Arab reports from the seventh through fifteenth centuries about the Black civilizations to the south,[36] one might think that Christianity was Africa's indigenous religion and wonder how aware these Arabs were of Christianity elsewhere. But this African civilization, more prosperous than that of the Arabs, invited their conquest.[37] Arab Egypt implemented policies designed to erode Nubia's strength, hoping to make it a vassal kingdom.[38] Far less united than Arab Egypt, Nubia could not provide a long-term response. The Arabs finally crushed Nubia in 1270, and even then Nubia regained its freedom and remained free until the sixteenth century.[39]

The Nubian church perished only in the late fourteenth or early fifteenth century, its influence declining as that of hostile Islamic neighbors increased.[40] Invading Arab nomads finally brought medieval Nubian civilization to an end.[41] Once the Arabs placed a Muslim king on the throne, he immediately turned a church in the capital into a mosque, indicating Nubia's new direction.[42] Christianity lingered, but eventually Islam prevailed, "sustained by the influx of marauding Arab tribesmen."[43]

Abyssinia

The East African land of Abyssinia (ancient Axum, modern Ethiopia) also holds a very significant place in Christian history; Christianity became the religion of that land at roughly the same time that it became the religion of the Roman Empire. Abyssinia's Axumite king Ezana (also spelled Aezanas) converted sometime around 333 and made Christianity the state religion; many Christians had long lived in Axum before that time.[44] In contrast to the Roman Empire and the barbarians of northern Europe, Ethiopia converted to Christianity without martyring Christians. It may have been the most open and ready soil in which Christianity ever took root.[45]

Inscriptions from Ezana's time state that his empire stretched across much of central Africa into Arabia and on the Nile as well.[46] After the rise of Islam, this East African empire became the primary defender of oppressed Christian minorities in Muslim lands. As William Leo Hansberry, founding scholar of Howard University's African history program, explains:

> An appeal . . . was also dispatched to Egypt by the Ethiopian king Amda Tseyon, warning the sultan that unless the repressive measures being imposed on the Egyptian Christians were revoked, he would institute a similar program of proscriptions against the Muslims in Ethiopia. In addition, the Ethiopian king threatened to divert the course of the Nile, which would have had the effect of transforming much of Egypt into a desert.[47]

Amda Tseyon's threat worked, but in the reign of his successor (Newaya Krestos, 1344-1372), the sultan had Abba Mark, the Alexandrian Christian patriarch, imprisoned. Newaya Krestos again threatened the sultan, who quickly "abrogated his harsh measures against his Christian subjects."[48] Both medieval Europe[49] and this solidly Christian African empire's own literature testify to its continuing commitment to Christ.[50] In contrast to some other faiths, then, Christianity began in Africa without conquests or force of arms.[51]

African Christians had originally been kind to Arab Muslims, providing them refuge.[52] But relations changed over time, and Arab Muslims were exerting severe pressure on Axum in the tenth century.[53] In time the Arab regime in Egypt "blocked attempts by Christian Ethiopia to establish contacts with the outside world," because Arabs feared that Ethiopia might make common cause with professedly Christian medieval Europe.[54] In the sixteenth century the forces of Islam stepped up their imperialistic advances southward. Ethiopian scholar Ephraim Isaac mourns that "the Ethiopian Church lost not only many of its great teachers, writers and leaders but also many of its treasures of literature and art. It was this second phase of Moslem onslaught that brought the golden age of monastic life in Ethiopia to a close."

But the Ethiopian church "regained internal stability" in the mid-seventeenth century, establishing itself against both Arab and Portuguese influences; from this point Ethiopia remained strong.[55]

Western Missions and Africa

Perhaps because most African Christians, like most medieval European Christians, did not evangelize much or engage in missions, God used Western missionaries to bring the gospel to parts of Africa. These missionaries often came in alongside Western colonialism, sometimes with Eurocentric attitudes. While they brought the truth of Christ and the Bible, they often brought many cultural untruths mixed up with the truths.

Yet nineteenth-century evangelical missions were not simply the product of colonialism.[56] Indeed, even in the European colonial period relations between pragmatic colonial authorities and more committed Christians were sometimes quite strained. The authorities were often at odds with Protestant missionaries[57] and worked to suppress African Christian revival movements when these threatened Europe's economic advantage. For example, colonial authorities arrested Prophet Braide in 1916; he preached, healed and caused rain to fall in the name of the God of Israel. They arrested him for the same reason rioters opposed the apostle Paul in Acts 19:25-27: his ministry was affecting their income. Prophet Braide denounced liquor and hence cut into colonial profits on the three-million-gallon-a-year rum and gin industry in West Africa.[58] Because the majority of European traders in the colonial era were irreligious, they tended to turn Africans *away* from Christianity rather than toward it.[59]

Colonial authorities in Africa often opposed missionaries, both African-American and White.[60] Uncomfortable with evangelical Christians' morally conservative lifestyle, "many British administrators were critical of the missionaries, and hostile to Christian-educated Africans."[61] Many colonial authorities in West Africa therefore preferred Muslims over Christians as well as over those practicing traditional religions; they discriminated against Christians in hiring practices.[62] And though Western missionaries were usually culturally insensitive, they tended to be less insensitive than other Europeans.[63] It was their culture, not their faith, that generated their insensitivity.[64]

Even so, African Christians quickly learned to read the non-European Bible for themselves; they were not solely dependent on the missionaries. After massive revival movements (like the indigenous East African revival, independent from mission churches), African churches were often more radical than the Western missionaries. Even some of the missionaries seemed threatened by the Africans' intense devotion to Christ.[65] But as we noted above, Christianity had come to Africa long before the presence of Western missionaries. In fact, some African peoples converted to Christianity before the ancestors of those European missionaries did!

Conclusion

While Ethiopian Christianity endured, it did not exert much missionary vision to expand elsewhere in Africa or beyond.[66] Nubia had likewise exerted little missionary vision beyond its borders, and in time, dependent on Alexandria for trained clergy, it lacked teachers to continue instructing its own people in the Christian faith.[67] In military terms, no matter how strong one's defense, defeat is nearly inevitable when an army has no offense. If European missionaries stirred up the gospel anew in Africa, it was not because no African Christians existed before their arrival. It was because in that period only the European Christians had discovered Christ's command to evangelize all nations (Mt 24:14; 28:18-20; Acts 1:8). Yet they merely brought Africa a gift that had been Africa's birthright long before, a birthright that some African Christians, especially in Egypt and Ethiopia, had continued to embrace.

As one writer points out, no one would even think of calling Christianity a "white religion" today if more Egyptian, Ethiopian and Nubian Christians had spread the gospel to the rest of Africa.[68] Still, history testifies to the ancient churches of Africa and shows that Christianity was never solely a "white religion."

2

What Do You Say When a Muslim Says Christians Were Proslavery?

[Allah, a.k.a. Wallace D. Fard] said that Christianity was a religion organized and backed by the devils for the purpose of making slaves of black mankind. I also bear witness that it certainly has enslaved my people here in America, 100 per cent. . . . The greatest hindrance to the truth of our people is the preacher of Christianity. . . . He is the man who stands in the way of the salvation of his people. (Elijah Muhammad)[1]

[Islam, on the other hand, is purely] a religion of peace, freedom, justice and equality. (Elijah Muhammad)[2]

The Son of Man's mission was not for others to serve him, but for him to be the servant of others, and to offer his life as a ransom-price for the people. (Mk 10:45)

You masters do the same things to them, and do not threaten them any longer, knowing that in heaven dwells the Master of yourself as well as of them, and he is an impartial judge. (Eph 6:9)

Because Jesus calls Christians to love all people, when we respond to Muslims it is important to make clear that we are not attacking them. Christians obedient to Christ's example and teaching ought to befriend Muslims, not attack them! We are distressed by the fact that many Americans mistreat members of minority religions or (in the case of foreign Muslims) foreigners. Our purpose in this chapter is not to attack Muslims but to respond to the claim by some Muslims that Christians' involvement in the slave trade or colonialism makes Christianity anti-African.

We respond first of all by pointing to Muslims' involvement in the same practices and suggesting that Muslims therefore act unethically when they use this objection to recruit former Christians into their ranks. Some would argue that Christianity and Islam are both anti-African,[3] but a more reasonable conclusion is that members of both faiths have lived in ways contrary to their own best teachings.[4]

Second, we will respond by showing what true Christians did to combat slavery. This is the subject of chapter three. As noted in our introduction, these first three chapters summarize salient points from Black Man's Religion, so those who have read that book recently may wish to begin in chapter four.

Arab Expansionism

When Muslims attack Western colonialism, they often speak the truth. Muslim peoples, however, were no less colonialistic when they conquered their way across North Africa. In contrast to Christianity, which in its first centuries was a religion of the oppressed, Islam quickly grew into an international empire shaped by "the experience of power and domination."[5] In time Muslims brought down many of the great empires of African history, although before the fall of those empires they had often contributed to their culture as well.[6]

Egypt. Arab domination transformed Egypt, as we noted in the preceding chapter. Molefi Kete Asante, a well-known Afrocentric scholar, points out that the Arabs who controlled Egypt from 641 on had

little respect or appreciation for the classical civilization they found in the Nile Valley. Having destroyed the organic structure of the African society they found in Egypt [and] reinstituted the ban on the Egyptian language . . . the Arabs created the perfect opportunity for the distortion of the African heritage of Egypt.[7]

Coptic peasants had maintained much of the language of ancient Egypt until the Arab period,[8] but by the twelfth century Arabic was replacing Coptic as the primary language.[9] As throughout Islam's medieval expansion, Islamization inevitably produced Arabization.[10] (Although Arabs constitute under one-sixth of the world's Muslims, Islam has retained a strong Arab coloring focused on the Arabian sanctuary and Arabic Qur'an; "unlike Christianity, it did not break with the milieu in which it was born."[11])

West Africa in general. West Africa had first known Islam as a religion of foreign traders. From around 1100 to 1600, Islam maintained itself in West

Africa through "the patronage of the older African traditions" that hosted it, and only a minority elite were truly Islamized. (This undoubtedly suited some Berber and Arab Muslims. Because Islam taught that those who were already "true" Muslims should not be enslaved, many propagators of Islam in Africa avoided proselytizing too much, lest they reduce "the potential reservoir of slaves."[12]) Even in later times, slave raiders conveniently assumed all West Africans to be idolaters, therefore subject to enslavement.[13] Thus the slave trade spread along with the armies of Islam, and by the nineteenth century Africa was providing the "overwhelming majority of slaves used in Muslim countries."[14]

Ghana. The West African empire of Ghana "was old when the Arabs first mentioned it in A.D. 800";[15] a primary source of gold for North Africa and Europe, the kingdom was so wealthy that the Arab geographer El Bekri reported in 1067 that Ghana's army comprised 200,000 men.[16] This empire flourished until it was crushed in 1076 by Sanhaja Berbers who had been converted to Islam.[17]

Songhay. Similarly, Muslim invaders destroyed the mighty West African civilization of Songhay. Songhay had advanced communication, literature, roads and so forth.[18] Its leading city, Timbuktu, with about 100,000 inhabitants, was one of the greatest intellectual centers of medieval times.[19]

Sunni Ali, who became ruler in 1464, "became a nominal Muslim for the same economic reasons that influenced other black kings": the Arabs controlled all trade northward to Europe and to Asia. Most of his people, however, maintained their traditional African religions and resented Islam. The Arabs recognized Sunni Ali's "real loyalty . . . to the traditional religion of the Africans,"[20] for he destroyed many Muslim scholars and forbade "the observance of Islamic law among members of his court."[21] His paradoxical stance reflected both political and trade realities on the one hand and traditional African pluralism on the other: African society could tolerate Islam, but Islam claimed civil authority over the state and the right to forbid all other religions, and Sunni Ali feared for Songhay's sovereignty.[22] Under Sunni Ali, Timbuktu launched a counteroffensive, directed not against individual Muslims but "against the influence of the ideology they professed which was regarded as incompatible with traditional African values."[23]

But the Arabs quickly deposed Ali's successor for his unwillingness to accommodate Islam and replaced him with a strong Muslim.[24] The sultan of Morocco invaded Songhay in 1582, equipped with cannons from the north; eventually Songhay collapsed under the pressure.[25] The Arab-Berber conquerors deported the last Black president of the university, Ahmad Babo (1556-1627), to use his learning for the Moors, but they destroyed all his works.[26] Contrary to Islamic law, non-Black Muslims enslaved Black Muslims as well as Black non-Muslims, leaving mulattos furiously protesting that they were White.[27] Chancellor Williams finally mourns, "The armies of Islam continued their triumphant march in Africa, destroying its basic institutions wherever they could do so."[28] W. E. B. Du Bois thinks that had the nominally Christian civilizations of Europe and Ethiopia not been separated, Ethiopia might have "rescued the Songhay culture"; but as it was, a once great culture fell into oblivion.[29]

Zimbabwe. The southern African empire of Zimbabwe also encountered Arab imperialism.[30] As soon as the empire was divided at the death of a key ruler, Arabs advised and funded both sides, pitting them against one another to weaken them and gain power for themselves.[31] They might have succeeded in their plan had not the Portuguese arrived before the Arabs could reap the benefits of their own tactics.[32]

Slavery in the Arab World

Most empires throughout history held slaves. What surprises many people today, however, is how widespread hard-core slavery remains in modern times. The last region to officially abolish slavery was the Arabian peninsula in 1962,[33] but even then official proclamations seem to have had little effect.[34] In the mid-sixties it was still being estimated that Saudi Arabia alone held a quarter of a million slaves.[35] Many, though by no means all, regions that still practice slavery are predominantly Muslim countries. This does not mean that slavery is inherent in Islam; it does, however, again undercut some Muslims' claim that Christianity is proslavery whereas Islam is not.

We first examine Arab slavery in history, then Arab racism and finally attempts to abolish slavery. After this we will turn to examining slavery and other kinds of oppression elsewhere in the contemporary world, before returning to the question of slavery and religion in the United States.

Arab slavery in history. Apart from the Western slavery with which African-Americans are familiar firsthand, the largest enslavement of Africans in history involved the Arabs. This is not to imply that Arab slavery was harsher than other kinds of slavery.[36] But the Arab slave trade in Africans introduced significant aspects of oppression into human history. Despite the prevalence of slavery in the early Roman Empire,[37] it had mostly vanished from Europe in the early Middle Ages;[38] it was the Arabs' slave trade that paved the way for Western slavery of Africans. The Arabs' slave trade has a much longer history than the Europeans' slave trade, although its geographical distance from the New World has made that history less known in North America. Under Arab leadership, slavery moved from a local or regional level to a much wider geographical area.

The Arab world's involvement in expanding the slave trade was not purely coincidental. As one specialist in the field notes, "Islam, by sanctioning slavery, gave tremendous impetus to its growth and, as a consequence, sparked the development of the slave trade along transcontinental lines."[39] That Muhammad himself held slaves[40] made the institution impossible to challenge, and through subsequent centuries of Islamic law, slavery came to be regarded as required by the Qur'an itself.[41] These assumptions about Islamic law made the abolition of slavery more difficult; Muslims objected that "to forbid what God permits is almost as great an offense as to permit what God forbids."[42]

Thus the Arabs' slave trade in East Africa was increasing even as the British and French finally began working to abolish the slave trade on the seas; most slaves from East Africa were sent to Arabia and the Persian Gulf area.[43] Indeed, because Arabs, Berbers and Persians pioneered the long-distance slave trade to begin with,[44] and because "the importation of Black slaves into Islamic lands" over twelve hundred years may have involved more slaves than the European slave trade did, some African writers have suggested that not only the West but also the Middle East should pay reparations to Africa.[45] The Arab world had slavery for a thousand years before the Europeans used slaves in the Americas and continued it over a century after the West abolished it; Arabs retained as many as eleven million slaves during this period.[46]

The Arab slave trade was vicious. Though the march across the Sahara desert was briefer than transport in cargo holds across the Atlantic, the death rate may have been as great; stragglers, weakened by malnutrition, were either killed or left to die on their own.[47] But in contrast to Western slavery, the Arab market usually preferred young women and girls, who generally sold for higher prices than male slaves did. Women were used especially as household servants and concubines.[48] By contrast, Arabs often neutered male African slaves to become eunuchs in prestigious households, a practice that grew with the Turkish sultans.[49] As is often found in history, slavery involved a sexual double standard: Arab men slept with Black women slaves, but their wives dared not sleep with male slaves. Arab male fears helped produce the stereotypes of Africans in medieval Arab literature "as creatures of immense sexual appetites and powers."[50]

Judaism and Christianity, which had earlier existed in cultures practicing slavery (albeit often on a smaller scale), had opposed the sexual use of slaves (Christian law mandated excommunication from the church for this offense). Islam, however, did not consider slave concubinage morally objectionable. Arab masters regularly kept and sought slave concubines.[51] An Islamicist observes that mating with Black slave women was sanctioned by Islamic law "and indeed by the Qur'an itself."[52]

Racism and Arab slavery. Although some Muslims in the West have exploited the notion that Islam historically escaped the curse of racial prejudice, nineteenth-century Western thinkers created this idea merely as a foil to challenge Western racism.[53] The notion was never more than propaganda, as scholars trained in medieval Arab literature have shown.[54] Given the widespread respect for Africa in Greek and Roman sources,[55] Western prejudice against Africans may itself have derived in significant measure from attitudes of Arab slave traders.[56] Certainly early Christianity emphasized the equality of all, specifically including Africans, and, like a few other groups such as the cult of Isis, swept aside racial distinctions in its common fellowship.[57] Islam can function and sometimes has functioned as a multicultural brotherhood as well, but the economic temptation involved in slavery led to a period with many examples of Arab prejudice.

Arab prejudice did not begin with color;[58] its slavery began as multiracial, and Arabs favored White slaves.[59] Nevertheless, they came to associate slavery especially with Blacks.[60] One writer concludes that, for whatever reasons, "the Arabs had always considered Africans as especially suited to be their servants."[61] Although exploited later by White racists,[62] the tradition transferring the curse of Canaan's subjugation to all Hamite, hence (on their reading) African, peoples predates its abuse by Europeans. Ninth-century Islam associated the tradition of Ham's blackness with the thesis that Ham was "cursed" with blackness.[63] Many Muslims used this "curse" to justify enslaving Africans, even when they were fellow Muslims.[64] Although Genesis speaks of Canaan's rather than Ham's enslavement, Arabs transferred the curse of slavery to all of Ham's descendants, whom they took to be Black Africans.[65]

We should pause to emphasize that this tradition about the cursing of Ham bears little resemblance to what the biblical text *says!*[66] In the Bible itself neither Ham nor his other sons (including clearly African ones like Africa-

Cush and Egypt-Mizraim), apart from Canaan, were cursed.[67] The curse on Canaan was fulfilled in the time of Joshua and his successors and ceased to be applicable later as descendants of the Canaanites assimilated into other peoples.[68]

But given a racial theory, despite the southward advance of Islam into West Africa in the 1300s, "the perception remained, disputed but widespread, that African Muslims were somehow different from other Muslims and that Africa was a legitimate source of slaves."[69] Nineteenth-century Muslim reports, similar to those of American slaveholders, claimed that Blacks were *happy* to be Muslim slaves; this had made them human beings.[70]

Arabs paid much higher prices for White women (whom they obtained from areas like Turkey and southern Russia near the Black Sea) than for Black women.[71] Yet once the Russians had cut off the supply of most White slaves, the Muslim nations increased their enslavement of Blacks from East and West Africa.[72] Color also affected one's social mobility. Until the supply of White slaves was reduced in the nineteenth century, Blacks "were most commonly used for domestic and menial purposes, often as eunuchs," and to work the salt and copper mines of the south.[73] White slaves regularly became generals, officials and rulers, but Black slaves only rarely rose this high in the central Muslim lands.[74] And while Arab masters slept with concubines of any complexion, their racially mixed servant armies became a source of tension, leading to racial segregation.[75]

Because slaveholders can depersonalize their slaves, they develop stereotypes about them quickly. Thus Arab texts often report Africans to be stupid, dishonest, unclean and stinky, and sometimes call their women ugly[76] and people of either gender "distorted" or "monstrous."[77] Ibn Qutayba (828-889), for example,[78] explains that Blacks "are ugly and misshapen, because they live in a hot country. The heat overcooks them in the womb, and curls their hair."[79] Those with dark complexion are said to suffer "insult and humiliation," whereas other Arab texts speak of Whiteness "as a mark of superior birth."[80]

As in many cultures,[81] though non-Arab converts were equal in theory, in practice they "were regarded as inferior and subjected to a whole series of fiscal, social, political, military, and other disabilities."[82] A good Black slave was not without hope, however; in one tale a good Black slave was allowed to turn White at his death as a reward![83]

Attempts to End the Slave Trade
After Christian abolitionists gained political influence in Britain and the British Empire abolished slavery, growing abolitionist sentiments led the

British to oppose slave trade in the Arab world as well.[84] Britain urged Arab leaders to abandon the trade,[85] but Arab leaders warned that their societies depended so heavily on it that attempts at abolition would jeopardize their thrones and possibly their lives as well.[86] Convinced that Islamic law permitted and therefore established slavery, "the most conservative religious quarters," especially in Mecca and Medina, opposed the reforms most fervently.[87]

Thus when the British persuaded the Turkish Empire to reduce the slave trade,[88] Shaykh Jamal issued a *fatwa* from Mecca in 1855 declaring the Turks now apostate from true Islam; as a consequence, he declared, it was "lawful to kill them without incurring criminal penalties or bloodguilt, and to enslave their children."[89] Arabs revolted, attacking the Ottoman authorities, who finally agreed to permit the slave trade in the Hijaz.[90]

Nevertheless, abolitionism gradually made some progress. The sultan of Morocco insisted that abolition was unrealistic, since slavery was part of Islamic religion as well as regional culture;[91] but Britain succeeded in most of North Africa except Morocco and with the Ottoman Empire except the Hijaz.[92] Iran outlawed slavery in 1906, although the prohibitions were enforced only by laws that were enacted later.[93] In time, many Muslim leaders also concluded that the spirit of Islam did not support slavery.[94]

Official decrees were helpful, but the struggle to end the slave trade was far from ended. Egypt's ruler enlisted a British explorer to help shut down the slave trade in the Upper Nile region, where "5000 Arab slave traders . . . were shipping some 50,000 slaves a year down the Nile," but the attempt proved mostly unsuccessful.[95] The slave trade in the Sudan was heavy in the 1850s and 1860s. The new ruler Khedive Ismail outlawed it, but his employment of non-Muslim Europeans to help him only provoked Muslim resentment.[96]

The sultan of Oman and Muscat found the slave trade particularly profitable. From 1818 on, the sugar plantations of the Mascarene Islands required a continuing supply of slaves; in the decade following 1835, Omani businessmen there controlled large estates of two to three hundred slaves each.[97] To better control his profitable and growing empire in East Africa, Omani sultan Seyyid Said actually moved his seat of authority from Oman to Zanzibar.[98] The Arab slave traders were from Oman, not Zanzibar, so they also exploited Zanzibar, kidnapping its citizens if too few slaves were available.[99]

The English, meanwhile, were horrified by accounts of dead and live slaves crammed together as tightly as possible in Arab cargo holds, "one mass of smallpox." When the British learned that Seyyid, who by now controlled much of the East African coast and the Arab slave trade there, was shipping slaves to India, they quietly objected to him.[100] After realizing that the British could not intercept most of the ships, the Omanis continued breaking the treaty, until finally Seyyid needed British help too much not to cooperate. In the end, Britain forcibly shut down the East African slave trade, closing it down in Zanzibar in 1897 and in Kenya in 1907.[101] The British finally succeeded in Zanzibar by a show of force, but the Arab plantations there were able to survive into the twentieth century anyway, since most ex-slaves remained as tenants working plots of land on their former masters' estates.[102] (African-Americans may recall the similar American practice of sharecropping.)

Thus Chancellor Williams, an African-American historian especially proficient in this part of African history, expresses his concern over the confusion of many U.S. youth, who "are dropping their white western slavemasters' names and adopting, not African, but their Arab and Berber slavemasters' names!" He laments that "Blacks are in Arabia for precisely the same reasons Blacks are in the United States, South America, and the Caribbean Islands—through capture and enslavement."[103] He notes that many African historians, still reacting to more recent European colonialism, have emphasized the evils of

> European imperialism in Africa while ignoring the most damaging developments from the Arab impact before the general European takeover in the last quarter of the nineteenth century, a relatively recent period. . . . From the earliest times the elimination of these [African] states as independent African sovereignties had been an Asian objective, stepped up by Muslim onslaughts after the seventh century A.D.104

"The Islamic advance was three-pronged," he reports: "proselytizing missions claiming one brotherhood; widespread intermarriages and concubinage with African women, due to the Muslim system of polygamy; and forceful conversions at sword point."[105] North African mulattos called themselves White and helped Arab slave traders enslave Black peoples, fearful of the consequences of being considered Black by the traders.[106] Further,

> as Arabization spread among the Blacks so did slavery and slave raiding. The Arabs' insatiable and perpetual demands for slaves had long since changed slavery from an institution that signaled a military victory by the number of captured prisoners to an institution that provoked warfare expressly for the enslavement of men, women and children for sale and resale.[107]

The Ottoman Turks in early-nineteenth-century Sudan were no less repressive than the Arabs; their leader Muhammed Ali massacred more African men, women and children than any ruler before him—so much "that even the white world protested."[108] Although some today have glossed over the earlier period,

> very simply . . . Arab screams against Western imperialism are the screams of outrage against Western imperialists for checking and subduing Eastern imperialists in the very midst of the Blacks they had conquered. There are still countless thousands of Blacks who are naive enough to believe that the Arabs' bitter attack on Western colonialism shows their common cause with Black Africa.[109]

Sometimes Western and Arab colonialists actually made common cause; most European colonial governors in the 1800s were financially encouraging Islam as an alternative to traditional religions and practices in Sierra Leone.[110] Not only colonial governors and companies but also many early Christian missionaries viewed Islam favorably and worked with Muslims where possible.[111] In some sense both Western and Arab powers thus joined forces in a manner that—whether intentionally or not—exploited Africa.

Slavery Today

Outright slavery, whether of Africans or others, continues to occur in many Muslim nations today. One example is Pakistan (where Christians and lower-caste Muslims are particular targets); some have estimated that as many as twenty million Pakistanis are held in bondage.[112] Unofficial slavery also includes child labor; about half of the fifty thousand children forced to work in Pakistan's carpet industry die by the age of twelve.[113] Former Pakistani slave Iqbal Masih, who spoke out against this oppression, was gunned down by an assassin at the age of twelve in April 1995.[114]

In the Sudan, the Arab Muslims of the north have been systematically starving the Black African adherents of traditional African religions and Christianity in the south, who rebelled because the north imposed Islamic law over the whole land.[115] The conflict and the inflexibility of the northern rulers led to as many as two million deaths between the mid-1980s and the mid-1990s.[116] Meanwhile, six to eight million Blacks have lost their homes; Christians (mostly Black) are often executed, boys are drafted to fight for the north, and slaves are forced to convert to Islam.[117] Government troops have begun "ethnic cleansing" among the Nuba mountain people, especially the Christians there.[118] In the wake of this civil war, raiders have been taking slaves, a practice the Sudan had once abolished.[119] Many of the enslaved are "children between the ages of eight and fourteen who are forced to march from their native lands to the North where they are sold into slavery."[120] "Some who have tried to escape have been branded, or have had their Achilles tendons cut; some have been castrated. Many, both male and female, are regularly raped."[121]

Although the tragedy easily rivals that of Bosnia, North American media have given Bosnia much more attention. Bosnia in Europe deserves attention, but African-Americans will not be surprised at the media's relative neglect of Black African suffering.

Besides thousands of extrajudicial executions in government raids on villages, Amnesty International reports the enslavement of many women and children for domestic use in the Sudan.[122] Likewise, a Sudanese professor reports that Arab militias burn villages, killing the men and seizing women and now-orphaned children to do chores and as concubines; slaves are also shipped to other Muslim lands.[123] A Sudanese lawyer noted that northern armies recruit children to convert them to Islam so they can join in fighting their homeland; enslaved children are also kept as "a living blood bank," routinely "rounded up to donate their blood" to wounded northern soldiers.[124]

In the Islamic republic of Mauritania, Arab-Berber Muslims from the north hold many Black African slaves from the south.[125] As *Newsweek* reports,

> More than 100,000 descendants of Africans conquered by Arabs during the 12th century are still thought to be living as old-fashioned chattel slaves. Aside from the shantytowns and a strip of land along the Senegal River, virtually all blacks are slaves, and they are more than half the population.[126]

Others estimate more specifically that, despite denials, the Arab-Berbers (called "Beydanes," "white men") hold ninety thousand chattel slaves ("reportedly sold for as little as $15, given as gifts, or traded for cars, camels, or other goods"), plus 300,000 economic slaves.[127] One slave interviewed declared, "Naturally, we blacks should be the slaves of the whites."[128]

In Bangladesh, slave traders kidnap three- to six-year-old boys or buy them from parents for the equivalent of twenty years' wages and empty promises of hope for the boys. The boys are then used as camel jockeys in races patronized by gamblers in Persian Gulf nations. Each boy is tied to a camel's back, and his screams make the camel run faster; many die or are maimed. Gulf nations buy twelve- to twenty-five-year-old Bangladeshi females at auctions as well. Those considered particularly beautiful may fetch as much as two thousand dollars from sheiks; brothels employ those considered less attractive, who typically bring a price of two hundred dollars.[129]

One Gulf nation, Saudi Arabia, a U.S. ally, is a strict Islamic state that represses its own 10 percent Shiite Muslim minority and has arrested many practicing Christians as well, including hundreds of workers from developing countries.[130] In earlier decades a high-level witness reported that some Saudis, most of them African-born and pretending to be missionaries, were sent to the Sudan and West Africa. There they promised to take fellow Africans to Islamic holy sites "so that they may make the pilgrimage and teach them the Koran in Arabic." Once in Saudi Arabia, these pilgrims were being enslaved.[131]

The Injustice Continues

Amnesty International has documented other deadly injustices besides slavery in many Islamic lands. In Mauritania,

> government troops killed hundreds of unarmed villagers, shooting some of them dead simply because they were fishing during curfew hours. As tensions escalated between black and Arab-Berber communities in Mauritania, hundreds of blacks taken into custody "disappeared."[132]

A later Amnesty report documents that the government tortured and killed at least 399 political prisoners, Black men from the southern part of the country.[133] Arab Islamic fundamentalists are gradually working to expand their own influence (and ultimately, they hope, control) in East Africa.[134]

Many believe that one positive effect of Islamic law is that it applies ethical principles to societal conduct in a way that most world religions, including Christianity, do not. A negative effect, however, is that a state backed by the absolute moral certitude offered by religion can often exploit those religious certainties in ways that violate human rights. In recounting some examples, we do not claim that all Muslims would support the following practices; most of our Muslim friends, in fact, would not do so, and many predominantly Muslim nations would not do so.[135] Yet it is noteworthy that under Shari'a, Islamic law, only Muslims are qualified to testify in court; a Muslim who renounces Islam and cannot be persuaded to recant is executed, in accord with the words of Muhammad in the *Hadith Al-Bukhari:* "Kill him if he changes his religion."[136] Even in freer states like Egypt, "charges of blasphemy against writers, printers and publishers have drawn eight-year prison sentences."[137]

Some have reportedly appealed to Black Americans to challenge the Arab slave trade, but with mixed success. When Muslim and former Mauritanian diplomat Mohammed Athie, now a political refugee, sought Black political leaders' help in publicizing the situation, the NAACP supported him, but many others reportedly told him they needed to avoid the issue lest they offend "the Nation of Islam, which has dismissed the allegations of slavery as propaganda, an attempt by Jews in the United States to discredit Arabs and Islam."[138] It seems fair to say that to be truly supportive of the African-American experience, more Muslims in the United States should openly condemn African slavery, even where it is perpetrated by fellow Muslims.

Conclusion

Examples could be multiplied further, but the point should now be established. Muslims cannot cite "Christian" complicity in the slave trade without also indicting themselves. This does not, of course, absolve professed Christian slaveholders from guilt. Did most Christians respond to the slave trade the same way most Arab Muslims did? To this question we turn in the following chapter.

3

What Do You Say When Others Complain That Christians Did Not Oppose the Slave Trade?

Unfortunately, the Christian doctrine to which the behavior of some professed Christians testifies best is the doctrine of human sinfulness. Many, perhaps most, people who claim to follow Christ have never really submitted their lives to him and hence are not truly his followers. Many of those who do follow him have yet to understand all the areas of their lives in which his lordship demands radical change. But that is not the end of the story. Many vocal Christians did take a firm stand against slavery, even though they lived in a culture that more often ignored it.

Slaves, Slaveholders and Christ

Slavery generally did not serve to promote Christianity; through most of U.S. history slaveholders "did little to promote the evangelization of blacks."[1] For the first century and a half of North American slavery, until religion gained a stronger hold in the southern colonies,[2] slaveholders saw to it that most slaves heard little about Christianity.[3] During this period, the Black church was strongest among free Blacks in the North.[4]

The first American slaveholders did not want their slaves to hear about the Bible, because they feared that the slaves would understand that Christianity made them their masters' equals before God.[5] Slaveholders "feared that Christianity would make their slaves not only proud but ungovernable, and even rebellious."[6] History shows that they sometimes turned out to be right—slaves frequently assumed that Christianity did make them their masters' equals.[7] Some slaves who became Christians also became abolitionists, quickly challenging Western churches' complacent acceptance of—and at times complicity in—slavery.[8]

But many more slaves heard about Christianity in the time of the Great Awakening, an evangelical revival that "fostered an inclusiveness," treating all as equals, and that was available to all regardless of class or education.[9] As Lerone Bennett Jr., historian and senior editor of *Ebony* magazine, points out concerning the late 1700s, "Baptists and Methodists strongly condemned slavery," and Blacks "like Joshua Bishop of Virginia and Lemuel Haynes of New England pastored white churches."[10]

Black authority and interracial ministry disturbed supporters of the status quo who had no personal commitment to Christ.[11] Sometimes Black ministers were persecuted for their Christian preaching.[12] Thus in 1788 former slave Andrew Bryan, baptized by the Black Baptist minister George Liele, joined forces with a White and another Black Baptist minister to start Savannah's Ethiopian Church of Jesus Christ.

Slave owners eager to clamp down after the more liberal treatment of the British . . . harassed . . . Bryan . . . and in 1790 he was imprisoned along with about fifty members of his congregation. As their white friend Abraham Marshall reported, ". . . they were imprisoned and whipped. . . . *Andrew* . . . told his persecutors that he rejoiced not only to be whipped, but *would freely suffer death for the cause of Jesus Christ.*"[13]

Bryan was still a slave at the time, but he purchased his freedom and that of his wife after his master died. By 1800 his church had seven hundred members, he was often baptizing between ten and thirty people, and other Baptist churches sprang up from his own. The White Baptist churches of Savannah praised him for his work.[14] Other Black Baptists in the South "participated in the rapid growth of legal biracial congregations," some of which belonged to local Baptist associations.[15] By 1844, just under one-quarter of U.S. Baptists may have been Black, yielding around 170,000 Black Baptists.[16]

After slave insurrections motivated by Black preachers, however, southern Whites often feared slaves' religious meetings, and many southern states passed laws restricting such meetings.[17] Northern Blacks, very many of whom had practiced Christianity since the 1700s free from slavery,[18] found a strong Christian population among southern Blacks when they sent missionaries to evangelize them after the Civil War, but the numbers of Christians jumped dramatically after the end of slavery through northern Black Christians' efforts.[19] The greatest growth of the churches thus came after slavery, from the impetus of African-Americans who had already been free.[20]

Slavery and Free Readers of the Bible

People in power often use any tools available—including the Bible—to justify their power or rationalize their abuse of power. Others, however, approach the Bible with an ear and a heart for justice. We treat biblical arguments for justice more fully in *Black Man's Religion*, but here rehearse how some nineteenth-century Christians understood biblical teachings on slavery while it was a divisive issue in the United States.

Northern Black Christians issued calls for emancipation[21] and noted that the Bible obligates Christians to oppose slavery.[22] It was in fact a fiercely committed Black Christian, David Walker (not Elijah Muhammad over a century later), who in 1829 first called hypocritical White Christians "devils,"[23] though he also praised the Whites who had genuinely joined Blacks in the cause of freedom.[24] Predominantly northern Black churches like the A.M.E. and the A.M.E. Zion were strongly abolitionist.[25] The Scriptures proved essential in the Black church's battle against slavery.[26]

But Black Christians were not alone in their fight, as one African-American scholar points out:

> For the most part, northern black Christians adhered to the Protestant revivalist doctrines of the antebellum period. Those doctrines tended to brand slavery a sin, thereby making opposition to slavery a sign of holiness and a Christian duty. . . . The American antislavery and reform movements were directly related to the evangelical movement of the early nineteenth century.[27]

Already in the 1700s some Quakers, Anglicans and others were denouncing American slavery.[28] With much more significant impact, John Wesley and all the other early Methodist leaders vehemently opposed slavery;[29] Bishop Asbury noted North Carolina slaveholders' consequent fear concerning Methodist influence over the slaves.[30] Reports in 1827 indicate that the Methodists and Friends were the most active antislavery denominations, but many Baptists,[31] Presbyterians[32] and others were also involved in the work.[33]

History and contemporary accounts alike provide ample testimony of the gospel's power to transform its followers to transcend racial prejudices.[34] But the gospel's transforming power does not prevent many who falsely profess faith in it from compromising it to accommodate their culture. Nominal Christians are more apt to interpret the Bible in light of their own culture than to read their culture in light of the Bible. Churches in the nineteenth century, like churches today, generally welcomed all who came, hoping to improve their moral condition through biblical instruction. But then as today, the reticence to demand a moral transformation upon conversion proved danger-ous: unchanged churchgoers can quickly become the majority in a church, corrupting it with non-Christian values.

Well into the middle of the nineteenth century, most Americans viewed abolitionists as supporters of an extremist, hence unpopular, cause.[35] Some Methodists made initial compromises in the early 1800s because slaveholders, mistrusting Methodists' antislavery reputation, allowed them no access to the slaves.[36] At the same time, the highly evangelistic and rapidly growing Methodist Church once led by Francis Asbury was becoming somewhat more traditional and bureaucratic, as large move-ments usually eventually do, losing some of its earlier fervor.[37] Despite continuing antislavery efforts, White Methodists began to water down their earlier demands for immediate freedom for slaves to favor a policy of merely gradual abolition.[38] As Dennis Dickerson, historiographer of the A.M.E. Church, points out, Black Methodist movements preserved Wesley's spirit more closely on this point.[39] Meanwhile proslavery senti-ment became so strong in the South[40] that many southern ministers who were advocating immediate abolition were forced to emigrate northward to the free state of Ohio, sometimes taking their congregations with them.[41] In time, many denominations split along northern (abolitionist) and southern (slaveholding) lines.[42]

Abuse of the Bible

Those who favored slavery often simply cited the practice of slavery through-out history, including in Bible times, to support the idea that slavery is natural; they avoided grappling with whether the biblical writers actually favored or disapproved of the institution.[43] Although abolitionist preachers soundly refuted the proslavery arguments slavery supporters did offer from the Bible,[44] opponents of abolishing slavery had economic incentives to disre-gard them (in this their moral commitment resembled that of most North Americans today, who ignore most injustices practiced in the contemporary world). Thus slaveholders allowed some preachers access to the slaves, once they developed ways to leave out parts of the Bible that sounded as if they made the slaves equal.[45] "The master class understood, of course, that only a carefully censored version of Christianity could have this desired effect.

Inappropriate biblical passages had to be deleted; sermons that might be proper for freemen were not necessarily proper for slaves."[46]

Thus preachers would quote Ephesians 6:5: "Slaves, submit to your masters," out of context.[47] Yet a few verses down, in verse 9, Paul says, "And you, masters, do the same things to them, because you also have a Master in heaven." In antiquity, only very few people said that slaves and masters were equal before God; those who went as far as Paul generally believed that slavery was immoral.[48] Paul's words were some of the most radical antislavery words of his time, yet by quoting out of context a verse that in context meant something quite different, slaveholders made slavery sound more acceptable.[49]

The slaveholders severely misrepresented Paul. First, Paul was addressing nonracial Roman household slavery, a situation quite different from the slavery practiced in the Americas. Household slaves had greater opportunities for freedom, status and economic mobility than did the vast majority of free peasants in Paul's day; one wonders whether the same term should apply to both U.S. slavery and Roman household slavery.[50] Second, Paul's surviving letters are not essays addressing all moral issues of his day (which would have included the oppression of rural peasants, empires' suppression of indigenous peoples, and other issues generally removed from his urban audiences); instead they are pastoral letters addressing needs in specific congregations.

Third, Paul wrote to first-century Christians, who were few in number and persecuted, and at that point could exercise little influence to change the wider social situation. Finally, as we have pointed out, Paul's words suggest that he regarded slavery as an evil, not a blessing. Why didn't he advocate a more activist response to slavery? Apart from changing public opinion, the only abolitionist method previously attempted in the Roman Empire was slave wars—which had always proved costly and never succeeded.

Most nineteenth-century Black abolitionists did not advocate a slave war any more than Paul did; only modern armchair revolutionaries can afford to condemn both Paul and nineteenth-century Black abolitionists while remaining silent on many issues of desperate current concern. Thus one leader in Nation of Islam has denounced Christians for not standing more forcefully for justice, yet when he met with leaders of Islamic countries he reportedly failed to speak against the sins of his "Muslim brothers" who routinely enslaved African Christians.[51] What Paul did write undermined the moral foundation of slavery, and nineteenth-century abolitionists could make ready use of his teaching.[52]

Many abolitionists also complained about the popular *distortion* of Christianity;[53] the Bible is hardly the cause of its own abuse.[54] Yet counterfeits cannot keep the true Christian faith from emerging to challenge them. Abolitionism has distinctively, perhaps uniquely, arisen in societies directly influenced by Christianity; most other societies and philosophers in history have merely taken the institution for granted.[55] The slaves quickly recognized "that the Bible had more to say about Jesus lifting burdens than slaves obeying masters," and thus they "discovered a secret their masters did not want them to know."[56]

The Bible and Abolitionism

At the same time that southern slaveholders were exploiting the Bible and twisting Christianity for their own purposes, a revival movement was sweeping through the North. As people began to actively believe the Bible's teaching, they began to recognize its declarations against injustices such as kidnapping and enslaving people. These abolitionists could follow the example of William Wilberforce and the Clapham Sect in Great Britain; fueled by the Wesleyan revival movement surrounding early Methodism,[57] the British abolitionists had lobbied Parliament until finally slavery was abolished in the British Empire. Thus "in the 1790s the evangelical was marked out as much by a desire for the abolition of the slave trade as by an interest in missions."[58]

That some ministers defended maintaining the status quo[59] is not surprising; most people in most cultures support the prevailing sentiments of their societies. What is more significant, however, is how Christian faith became a driving force for abolition, a moral cause that societies without Christian influence have rarely birthed. Preachers like La Roy Sunderland wrote angry tracts demanding the abolition of slavery and promising God's swift judgment against the nation if it were not done;[60] many denounced slavery as a sin, in works bearing titles like "God Against Slavery . . . the Duty of the Pulpit to Rebuke It as a Sin Against God."[61] The evangelical humanitarian Lewis Tappan explained that abolitionists "hold that no slaveholder professing to be a Christian is entitled to Christian FELLOWSHIP, *because* slaveholding is a sin, and should subject the offender to discipline."[62] The only appropriate remedy for slavery was therefore repentance.[63]

The evangelical revival in western New York, Pennsylvania and Ohio, especially through Charles Finney's revivals, became a primary source of antislavery workers.[64] Lyman Beecher, one of the most prominent clergymen of the day, tried to steer a safe course between traditional scholars and the radical new revivalists crusading for salvation and social reform. When ministerial student Theodore Weld began agitating for the antislavery cause, the trustees of Beecher's Lane Seminary tried to force the students to leave the issue alone. Weld and forty students—mostly converts of Finney's revivals—then withdrew from the school, leaving it empty.[65] The students ended up at Oberlin and, led by Finney and Weld, precipitated another national revival—this one for the abolition of slavery.[66] Beecher was enraged, but most of his own children, including Harriet Beecher Stowe, eventually went over to the revivalists' abolitionist cause.[67]

White abolitionists worked to end slavery, but Black Christians voiced still stronger convictions.[68] Various Black churches served the Underground Railroad;[69] "the most vigorous organizers of networks 'to freedom' were black churchmen."[70] During the Civil War, Black Union troops marched into Charleston, South Carolina, singing Methodist hymns.[71]

Slaves and Bible Interpretation

Black and White abolitionists understood the Bible correctly on slavery, but they were not alone. Our few records of what the slaves believed show that slaves knew from the Bible stories they did hear that their preachers weren't telling them the whole story, and they reconstructed a more just version of Christianity on their own. As Cheryl Sanders, a womanist theologian at Howard Divinity School, summarized her findings in her Harvard dissertation, "Conversion introduced the slave to a gospel of freedom which contradicted the gospel of submission they were taught by whites."[72]

Some slaves were able to learn to read before Nat Turner's rebellion and discovered the truth directly from Scripture itself: "When my master's family were all gone away on the Sabbath, I used to go into the house and get down the great Bible. . . . There I learned that it was contrary to the revealed will of God, that one man should hold another as a slave."[73] Many slaves who could not read nevertheless understood more of Christianity than the slaveholders intended. They learned to fathom the message of "harmless" Bible stories like those of Moses and Samson better than the White preachers did. The slaves then lifted their voices in prayer to the God of the Israelites. "Oh, Mary, don't you weep, don't you moan," they sang; "Pharaoh's Army got drownded."[74] Gabriel Prosser, leader of a major slave revolt, saw himself as a new Samson called to battle the White Philistines and liberate his people.[75]

Of course, even those White preachers who, to gain access to the slaves, preached submission to masters recognized that the parts of the Bible they did preach were "potentially subversive to the institution of slavery."[76]

Sometimes they avoided altogether the stories about God smiting Pharaoh to lead his people out of slavery.[77] But even these preachers could not evade pervasive themes of human dignity in the Bibles they used; preaching about Adam and Eve, they found it necessary to declare that all humans ultimately shared the same ancestors, that all were sinners, that God demanded submission from masters as well as slaves, and that Jesus became a servant himself.[78] They likewise had to preach that all people come to God on the same terms, whether they are Black or White.[79]

These White preachers were trying to preach a religion that was never built to accommodate slavery or oppression, but as the Bible points out, sinful people readily twist the truth so they can fit it into the way they and their peers are already living (Jer 17:9-11; Jas 1:21-27). In Jesus' day, it was often the most religious people who opposed him. One need not agree with all of Marcus Garvey's proposals to appreciate his stinging critique of professing Christians who ignore Jesus' values:[80]

> a form of religion practised by the millions, but as misunderstood and unreal to the majority as gravitation is to the untutored savage. We profess to live in the atmosphere of Christianity, yet our acts are as barbarous as if we never knew Christ. He taught us to love, yet we hate. . . . If hell is what we are taught it is, then there will be more Christians there than days in all creation. . . . If our lives were to be patterned after the other fellow's all of us, Bishop, Priest and Layman would ultimately meet around the furnace of hell, and none of us, because of our sins, would see salvation.[81]

Or as Frederick Douglass put it,

> I love the pure, peaceable, and impartial Christianity of Christ: I therefore hate the corrupt, slaveholding, women-whipping, cradle-plundering, partial and hypocritical Christianity of this land. Indeed, I can see no reason, but the most deceitful one, for calling the religion of this land Christianity.[82]

Leaders of slave revolts—including Nat Turner, a Baptist preacher;[83] Denmark Vesey, with help from fellow African Methodist Episcopal conspirators;[84] and Gabriel Prosser, the "new Samson"[85]—found strength in their faith.[86] White slaveholders often recognized the danger; for instance, hostility toward Methodism, toward missionaries working among slaves, and toward anyone suspected of wishing to improve conditions for slaves grew in the wake of Vesey's revolt.[87] Religious assemblies of slaves without White supervision became illegal.[88]

Many Bible believers advocated less violent forms of resistance, disobeying their oppressors to meet for worship and to pray and work for freedom.[89] But in each case models from the Bible and Christianity provided slaves with ideological equipment for their resistance. Northern figures prominent in the resistance, including Harriet Tubman, the "Moses of her people,"[90] and preacher Sojourner Truth, were motivated by their understanding of the gospel of Christ.[91]

Even after slavery, it was their faith that sustained African-Americans in the face of unrelenting trials.[92] As one Black theologian puts it, "The Christian faith gave the black man a sense of 'somebodiness' in spite of circumstances to the contrary."[93]

In the 1960s historian Lerone Bennett Jr. pointed to various strands of resistance before the middle of the twentieth century and observed, "In 1955, Martin Luther King fused these elements and added the missing link: that which has sustained and bottomed the Negro community since slavery—the Negro church."[94]

Conclusion

As a Jewish Christian writer points out:

> Those who most strongly fought slavery in America were religiously committed. This included the evangelist Charles Finney, whose Oberlin College became a bastion of slave liberation, and Jonathan Blanchard, whose Wheaton College participated in the underground escape network. The civil rights movement of Martin Luther King derived its inspiration from the biblical Exodus.[95]

The Bible and its message of salvation and liberation brought hope to the slaves and became a powerful resource among Christians fighting for the abolition of slavery. Whatever other resources may have been valuable under other circumstances, it remains significant that the primary religious voice raised against slavery was that of the Christian tradition. It is therefore hypocritical for adherents of religions that practiced slavery (and that lacked significant abolitionist movements except those influenced by Christian sources) to charge Christianity with being proslavery.

4

What Do You Say When Someone Claims That All Christian Doctrines Began in Africa?

Some Afrocentric writers claim that all Christian beliefs began in Africa. While Africa was certainly part of the world in which the biblical faith began and developed, as Afrocentric Christian writers have long argued,[1] those who claim that Africa was the cradle of all Christian beliefs overstate the case.[2] Yet some Afrocentric writers go still further, claiming that Christianity is simply an inferior copy of traditional African religions, just as some have claimed the entire mantle of Greek philosophy for Egypt. Writers who go this far often contend that African-Americans should abandon Christianity in favor of more original African religions.

One writer complains that Judaism, Christianity and Islam are simply "carbon copies of African religions."[3] Yet given the great diversity of traditional African religions,[4] one wonders how any religion could be a carbon copy of African religions as a whole.[5] Whereas "revisionism" sometimes means revisiting historical data from a less biased perspective, this writer's account is revisionism in the negative sense: distorting history by an unfairly tendentious (biased) reading of the evidence.

Cultures and Christianity

We should state our own understanding of culture up front. First, we believe most accusations of wholesale borrowing regarding any culture are overstated. It is certainly reductionistic to suppose that ancient Israel (or any other culture for that matter) never made any original contributions! But second, we also believe that God often works through culture, and that he even provides redemptive analogies in many cultures.[6] At some points, then, Egyptian and other backgrounds will suggest where Israel learned particular ideas or practices (some positive, some negative, some neutral). At other points Egyptian background will shed light on the general culture in which Israel moved. We cannot simply assume, however, that everything important in Israel's faith is borrowed, or that when an element is borrowed, it is borrowed from a single source. Instead we must critically evaluate each comparison—something that some who attribute everything in the Bible to African sources have not done.

Eastern Africa and western Asia both played important parts in biblical history, and biblical writers responded positively and negatively to various aspects of those cultures. That writers would respond to the issues of the cultures around them is not surprising. Our book, for example, responds to particular issues relevant in our day; had the questions been different, our answers would have formed a quite different book (if we had written it at all). In the same way, cultural settings in biblical times provided the questions the Bible's writers had to answer. Yet the biblical writers did not simply uncritically adopt the views prevailing in Egypt or in Babylon; often the biblical writers even went against the grain of their own Israelite culture, when it was shaped too much by religions conflicting with what God had taught them. God can and does work through cultures; but God is not limited to culture.

Other cultures. Others have claimed aspects of the Bible for different cultures. Thus, for example, one writer on Persian history, explaining the beliefs of the Zoroastrian religion in Persia, suggests that Zoroastrianism affected the Judeans exiled there before the time of Christ. The writer insists that under Zoroastrian influence,

> Semitic belief in existence after death was illuminated by true immortality. Satan the Accuser became the Devil. Egyptian apocalypse imported into Jerusalem was transformed into genuine eschatology, the doctrine of the *last* things, resurrection and the last judgment.[7]

But such claims, like the claims for massive borrowing from African culture, can be pressed too far. While Persian thoughts about a future day of judgment amplified tendencies in that direction already found in the earlier biblical prophets (such as Is 2:1-22; 26:19-21; Amos 5:18-20), this may be a case where the dominant culture's questions forced a minority to grapple with the implications of its own beliefs. The exile in Babylon and Persia led Israel's sages to discuss personal immortality in deeper ways. What did God's justice mean, not only for Israel as a whole, but for the individual? For bodily beings whose bodies had died, how could God provide an ultimate future hope in the good world he had created?[8]

It is not surprising that the Israelites would have believed in an afterlife; most cultures do. What is surprising is how rarely the Hebrew Bible comments on the afterlife. Yet the Israelite teaching of bodily resurrection (Is 26:19; Ezek 37:12-14; Dan 12:2) remains consistent with other aspects of Israel's faith. The ultimate test of the teaching's truth cannot be whether it has "parallels" in other cultures, but whether or not it happens; and, as we shall argue later in this book, some strong historical evidence supports the thesis that bodily resurrection has already happened once. Further, some Persian influence does not imply that every Jewish belief in this period developed only from Persian roots. The Jews in Persia did not simply borrow every aspect of Zoroastrian thought;[9] while these Jews recognized a more personal role for Satan than earlier Israelites had, they never embraced any sort of cosmic dualism like that taught in Persia.[10] Nor did they embrace the particular vision of the future taught by Zoroastrianism, despite the overlap of some elements.[11]

By contrast, another writer, an African-American scholar, complains about Greek influences in early Christianity.[12] The New Testament reflects a Jewish worldview, but Judaism by this period was very much affected by Greek thought.[13] Yet as we noted above, God can work through cultures, and when writers address their own culture, this does not necessarily make them incorrect—it means only that they addressed the issues at hand, just as many of us seek to do today.

It is true that we must "retranslate" the gospel message to reveal its relevance to contemporary culture, including African-American culture. Our cultural setting differs from that of the earliest Christians, and had biblical writers been writing to us, they would have used our language and addressed issues in our culture. But how far does one go in translating from one culture to another?[14] In our view, reliable translation requires faithfulness to the *meaning,* which requires a closer analysis of the earliest Christian texts (in our New Testament) than the critic of Greek influences provides.[15] He redefines Christianity, opening the parameters of early Christianity too wide without paying enough attention to the testimony of the earliest Christians or their concern for theological and moral boundaries.[16]

A universal God. Although Africa plays an important role in the biblical narrative, God's original purpose in calling Israel was to bless *all* the peoples of the earth; he chose one nation merely as a vehicle for enlightening all nations (Gen 12:3). If ancient Israel and modern European Christians have erred by making their own cultures the norm for human history or God's purposes, we also err if we appropriate the Bible for ourselves alone and repudiate other peoples instead of recognizing God's universal purposes. If he did not allow Israel to depend on its chosen status (Amos 3:2; 9:7), there is no point in trying to elevate our own ethnic status before him. Can we really suppose that the God who formed the universe is God of only one people, whether that be Israel, Europe or Africa (Rom 3:29-30)?

Most Afrocentric biblical literature (for instance, that written by William Dwight McKissic and Walter McCray), while rightly emphasizing the role of Africans in the biblical story, is careful not to exclude other peoples. Yet some writers have gone overboard in their eagerness to produce African roots of the faith. In practice, some have played down what God revealed through his prophets in history in favor of aspects of African culture that sometimes parallel but sometimes contradict those revelations, and usually do not reflect direct borrowing from either source.[17]

All religions and ideologies (including Afrocentrism) were birthed in specific historical settings, and such origins need not invalidate what these ideologies say. An American may say something biased by his or her American perspective, but simply being an American or speaking English or Spanish does not necessarily mean that one is speaking untruth. The Bible came to us in specific historical settings, and the possibility of specific African backgrounds is as worthy of consideration as any other.

Yet some advocates of this approach merely *assume* that God has worked through their ancestral continent's cultural evolution (rather than any other continent's), while dismissing out of hand the proposal that he revealed himself through one people's prophets who openly owned him and some-times died for him. Some justify this approach by claiming that White people have followed the same practice for a long time, but this justification is hardly the same thing as proving that our claim is true; after all, we know that the White claim is false. A Black claim is no more necessarily true, simply because those who wish to believe it are Black.

As Christians, we believe that the God of history revealed himself to some extent in the history of all peoples, but we affirm that all peoples must also acknowledge his right to speak as he will, and Jews, Christians and Muslims acknowledge that he spoke in a special way through Israel's historic prophets. They teach, of course, that from the outset God's mission was ultimately for all peoples (as in Gen 12:3, cited above).

In other words, those who ask why we should start from the assumptions of religions that began in the region of Egypt, Mesopotamia, Palestine or Arabia also start with cultural and intellectual assumptions forged in some specific geographical area, whether African, European or otherwise. Humans do well to decide the truth of claims attributed to an eternal God on grounds more substantial than appeal to geographical preferences; wherever God chose to reveal himself, he is greater than geographical boundaries, and we should evaluate claims to speak for him on the basis of their consistency with reality. Unless one argues for simply a pantheon of different tribal gods, we recognize that a supreme God must be the God of all humanity; thus the specific cultures that have spread the message of that God are less important than the message he sent through them.

Other writers have argued elsewhere, however, for the truth of the Christian faith, and we offer our own case in the next-to-final chapter of this book. For now we want to respond to objections raised in some non-Christian Afrocentric circles, rather than giving a sustained argument for the truth of Christianity.

No neutral language or culture exists in which God could reveal himself; the influence of various cultures and languages on the world of the Bible therefore does not need to challenge its inspiration. Here we respond to some imbalanced claims for biblical cultures; in appendix A we offer a sample of what we hope is a more balanced approach, comparing Israel's tabernacle with the various forms of temple structures throughout both Egypt and the Near East.

Ethics and Wisdom

Rather than debating about generalizations, we will examine some specific claims about African/Egyptian backgrounds to biblical ideas, although our responses can at most be samples. For instance, some writers have claimed that the "Negative Confessions" of the Egyptian Pyramid Texts provide our closest moral parallels for the Ten Commandments.[18] (The "Negative Confessions" are lists of statements that one has not engaged in various forbidden behaviors.)[19] This particular claim is probably correct; the Negative Confessions are the closest parallels to the Ten Commandments we know of in ancient society. Yet in this case the parallel does not say very much; it just means that no other parallels are closer.

The overlap between the Ten Commandments and the Negative Confessions reflects some nearly universal human values (such as societal opposition to killing, theft and adultery) which need not be attributed to any single source. Other features of the Ten Commandments (such as the sabbath and the prohibition of idolatry) lack significant ancient parallels, and most of the Negative Confessions (the author drawing the parallels listed 42; 147 appear in all)[20] do not appear in the Ten Commandments (for example, "I have not carried away food . . . uttered evil words . . . laid waste plowed land"). Given the shared cultural continuum that shaped many features of Israel's culture, the parallels are not close.[21]

Much closer would be the shared continuum of northeast African and Near Eastern culture in which Israel could understand the symbol of circumcision.[22] Likewise one finds clear parallels for Israel's civil laws in earlier Mesopotamian legal collections, which indicate that most ancient Near Eastern societies, including Israel, functioned within a common legal milieu.[23] But such derivation no more invalidates the insights in Israelite texts than some conceptions of justice we affirm today are invalidated by their roots in Western philosophy or common law. One culture may set the agenda for discussion without forcing us to uncritically embrace all its suggested answers (thus, for instance, Israelite law commands harboring escaped slaves, whereas some other ancient Near Eastern legal collections forbade it on the pain of death).[24]

Israelite proverbs are closest in form to Egyptian proverbs, and sages of various regional cultures learned from one another (compare 1 Kings 4:30-31; 10:24).[25] A small section of Proverbs closely parallels an earlier Egyptian work, but the respected Afrocentric writer Yosef Ben-Jochannan characteristically overstates the case, charging that "most . . . if not all" Israelite proverbs derived from that source.[26] One may also compare the figures of speech shared by Israelite and Egyptian prophets,[27] as well as some other cultures.[28] By contrast, however, so far the legal collections most similar to those in the Bible are Mesopotamian.[29]

Ben-Jochannan claims that the sacrifices in Leviticus "are in every sense the same as in most Voodoo, Ju Ju, and Shango or Obyah feasts."[30] Yet sacrifice is a near-universal in traditional religions, and Canaanite, Hittite and other geographically nearer cultures provide closer parallels, often down to nearly identical titles for the kinds of sacrifices offered.[31] Is it not more likely that God gave the Israelites institutions they would understand most readily in light of immediately surrounding cultures, than in light of cultures more geographically distant? One distinctive characteristic of Israelite religion is its lack of sacrificial methods to secure divine cooperation (such as rain); fertility came not by sacrifice but by obedience to the covenant, particularly justice for the poor (Deut 15:10-11).

Of course, traditional African cultures are much closer to the biblical cultures, and much more prepared to understand them, than are Western industrial and postindustrial societies. But this does not always make them identical with the cultures in which the Bible originated.

Egyptian Resurrections?

Some have contended that doctrines like Jesus' resurrection derive from the Egyptian *Book of the Dead*.[32] But the *Book of the Dead* is mainly a collection of spells to ensure safety in the afterlife. Preparations included ritual washing along with some spells[33]—spells "for not letting a man's breast be kept away from him in the god's domain,"[34] and other spells to drive away "a crocodile that comes to take" the deceased's magic,[35] to prevent the person from "being eaten by a snake" in the afterlife,[36] to keep from having to eat dung or drink urine in the afterlife[37] or to become "greatest" in the afterlife realm.[38] Among moral issues people need to address before facing the afterlife, a primary one in the *Book of the Dead* is not to eat one's dung—not much of a moral emphasis in the Bible![39]

This *Book of the Dead* does not teach the doctrine of resurrection affirmed in Christianity. The soul is said to be "revivified" in the afterlife,[40] but the thorough University of Chicago index lists no reference to bodily resurrection (the Christian teaching); the soul rises and is free while the corpse remains in the coffin.[41] Likewise, judgment generally takes place after an individual's death rather than at a specified future time for all humanity.[42] Similarly, identifying with the deity takes the form of deification (becoming divine), a concept later prevalent also in Hellenism but historically rejected by Judaism and Christianity (compare Gen 3:5).[43] Aside from concern with the afterlife—a concern preeminent in *most* cultures—the overall parallels with Christianity seem a bit remote!

Fish, Mysteries and Gnosticism

Even so thorough a scholar as Martin Bernal succumbs to finding fanciful parallels to Christianity at least once, suggesting that Jesus called fishermen in the gospel tradition because the fish symbol was used in the Egyptian cult of Osiris.[44] Bernal mentions Jesus, Osiris and Tammuz as "deities of vegetation who are killed, mourned for and triumphantly resurrected," indicating survivals of Egyptian and Mesopotamian religion in Christianity.[45] Parallels he cites include some from Hermetic and Gnostic texts.[46] Such "parallels" may have some value: focus on the afterlife in Egyptian and other religions led some of their later adherents to be receptive to Christianity.[47] (Contrast modern secular thought, which frequently rejects beliefs in deities or afterlife altogether.) Yet arguments suggesting that early Christian understandings of Jesus, the resurrection and so forth derive from (or are nearly identical to) Egyptian religion are historically incorrect, as modern scholars have increasingly realized. Because a response to all possible objections to the historical accuracy of the Bible would take more than an entire book, we will merely respond to the objections above to provide the reader with a sample of the sorts of responses that can be offered.

First of all, fish was a primary staple of Galilean diets, and fishing was a respectable and common enough occupation around the Sea of Galilee.[48] By contrast, associations with a particular religious sect (worship of Osiris) that did not exist in Palestine (where the Gospel tradition originated) are historically implausible. Second, Osiris is magically revivified, not transformed into a new creation; his corpse is awakened through the same potencies that exist in procreation. In the myth he remains in the Netherworld, still needing protection by vigilant gods and replacement on earth by his heir.[49] Like most other ancient resuscitation stories, that of Osiris is cyclical, linked to the seasons and the rejuvenation of vegetation in the spring.[50] By contrast, the resurrection of Jesus is not related to the symbolic annual dying-and-rising of vegetation deities; it is rooted in the Jewish hope of the bodily resurrection of the righteous, a hope based on Old Testament promises and the Jewish belief that the body as well as the soul was important (Is 26:19; Ezek 37:12-14; Dan 12:2).[51]

Finally, the Hermetica and Gnostic literature do not predate the New Testament, and are at many places clearly dependent on it. One of the authors of this book has spent years researching primary sources from the first century (the time of Jesus and the first disciples), and although he has found much evidence for Greek and Jewish traditions that were antecedents to Gnosticism, he has found no explicit evidence of developed Gnosticism before the second century. Whereas many Gnostic sources are explicitly dependent on the New Testament, the New Testament is not dependent on Gnostic sources.[52]

Many of the alleged parallels are drawn from Greek and Roman evidence for Mystery cults into which many people sought to be initiated. Yet much of our evidence for rites in the Mysteries (as opposed to the early myths themselves) actually comes from second-, third- and fourth-century Christian authors, who tended to read the Mysteries through the grid of their own Christian experience.[53] In contrast to scholars early in the twentieth century, more recent scholars have thus become more cautious about reading earliest Christianity in light of these later Christian interpretations of the Mysteries. Further, many of the "parallels" the Mysteries exhibit with Christianity derive from a later period when Christianity was becoming increasingly popular, suggesting that the Mysteries borrowed features of Christian teaching rather than the reverse.[54] This may be why most characteristic Mystery vocabulary is lacking in the earliest Christian sources.[55]

The Mysteries are not, in fact, solely an Egyptian idea.[56] Some writers, such as George G. M. James[57] and Ben-Jochannan,[58] go considerably beyond the evidence in suggesting that they are. For instance, James's evidence for Egyptian Mystery systems is largely based on Greek-language texts by writers half a millennium after Greeks had begun to control Alexandria, after writers might not know the difference between legends and history. By contrast, archaeological evidence supports the practice of Mysteries in Greece three centuries before the conquest of Egypt.[59] The Greek sanctuary at Eleusis[60] was in continuous use from the sixth century B.C.E. or earlier,[61] and its propaganda reached Russia, Italy and Egypt by the fourth century B.C.E.—before the conquest of Egypt.[62] Dionysiac festivals, a religious import from the East, seem to be portrayed in sixth-century B.C.E. Attic vase paintings,[63] and most of the myth's components appear as early as the *Iliad*.[64] The Asiatic Cybele cult has origins in the Neolithic or Bronze Age[65] and appears in the Greek world by the third century B.C.E.66 Suggesting that such features derive from Alexander's conquest of Egypt in the fourth century B.C.E. ignores too much evidence.

Egyptian myths used in the Mysteries (such as Osiris and Isis) plainly originate before that conquest, of course, but Greek and Mesopotamian sources have parallels to these Egyptian stories, suggesting a shared continuum of ideas throughout Egypt and the ancient Near East. Arguments such as the idea that Aristotle stole Egyptian books from Alexandria's library and claimed authorship[67] will not persuade any classicist conversant with Aristotle and his literary style; for that matter, Alexandria was not built before Aristotle's pupil Alexander arrived there, and its library was constructed only after both of them had died—a detail that would make Aristotle's theft of its treasures somewhat difficult![68]

Parallels and Pseudoparallels

One of the authors of this book has spent years in detailed comparative analysis of ancient Mediterranean cultures and has published serious books on the subject.[69] He and other contemporary scholars have examined countless "parallels" earlier scholars tended to draw, often due to lack of experience or to knowledge of only a small selection of ancient Mediterranean cultures.

Before asserting that one culture's expression is dependent on another culture's expression, one must ask questions such as (1) which culture's expression came first, (2) whether the two were geographically close enough to suggest that one actually drew from the other, (3) whether the "parallel" may be coincidence (especially likely if more contrasts than parallels exist), (4) whether the parallel may simply reflect a similar adaptation to similar cultural circumstances or similar issues (for example, most cultures address the question of life after death, but their answers need not all depend on a common source), and (5) when influence is clearly present, whether the borrowing culture adopted the idea wholesale or simply packaged a preexisting idea of its own in another culture's form.[70]

In light of such questions, some Afrocentric writers have been mistaken to follow earlier Eurocentric writers' "backgrounds" for the Trinity.[71] For example, polytheistic pantheons that had three main deities cannot provide helpful parallels to the Christian Trinity.[72] Some of these pantheons had two, and some had more than three primary deities, and none had only three deities altogether. The Trinity doctrine, officially titled by the North African theologian Tertullian,[73] instead rests on evidence in the Bible for the deity and distinctiveness of the Father, the Son and the Spirit.[74] In other words, the evidence that led to the development of the Trinity doctrine is earlier than the doctrine itself. No one was trying to come up with exactly three members of the Godhead; they simply discovered three members (Father, Son and Spirit) in the biblical text (such as Mt 28:19). Yet from the start of African Christianity, the Trinity was an African Christian doctrine. The Ethiopian church accepted the same doctrines as the North African, Greek and Roman churches, doctrines formally recognized at Nicaea (A.D. 325), Constantinople (381) and Ephesus (431).[75] East African Christians maintained close relations with Egyptian and Syrian Christianity and functioned as part of the Eastern church.[76]

Even farther afield are those who simply label all demigods or mortal gods (which in some religions could encompass whole pantheons) as "Christ figures," then imply that Christianity's view of Jesus depends on such Christ figures.[77] Even if all demigods were "Christ figures"—and they were not— why would thoroughly Palestinian Jewish disciples of Jesus, having synthesized their experience of Jesus with Old Testament teachings and initially explained him in terminology and categories already established in Judaism, learn and then subversively include meanings from such religions?[78] Now that the excesses of early-twentieth-century Mystery comparisons have abated, such a hypothesis strains our sense of historiographic plausibility.

Another example is the assertion that the Bible "stole" the idea of the virgin birth from pre-Christian cultures.[79] First, many of the "parallels" cited for this notion (with inadequate documentation) are quite remote; one can produce a "parallel" for any concept if one casts the net widely enough. (For instance, some would count spontaneous generation, divine adoption, divine impregnation of a mortal producing a demigod and the like—none of which resembles the early Christian picture of the virgin birth.[80])

Second, the story of a virgin birth in Matthew and Luke is older than the Gospels of Matthew and Luke themselves. The differences in the two accounts suggest that their sources are independent of one another and that the common elements in the stories (such as the virgin birth) must predate them. This observation does not tell us how early the tradition of the virgin birth is, but clearly the tradition had been circulating a long time before the Gospels were written—and probably when the church was largely Jewish and uninterested in pagan birth stories.

Third, Luke, who knew James (independently attested as Jesus' brother in Gal 1:19), had ample opportunity to interview him fully,[81] thus confirming Luke's claim to have checked his sources with eyewitnesses (Lk 1:2-3); James would provide a direct link to the account of Mary herself, his mother. We treat Luke's accuracy in greater detail in our final chapter.

Inaccurate Attacks on the Bible

Some writers depart from their central Afrocentric theme solely for the purpose of attacking the Bible or Christian faith (although it is a faith held by some other Afrocentric writers); this suggests other agendas than simply Afrocentrism. In responding to their charges, we are not passing judgment on their knowledge of other matters, but responding solely to their arguments against Christianity.

One such writer, Yosef Ben-Jochannan, alleges that the Bible is full of errors; in support of this assertion he charges that passages calling Christ the first to rise from the dead (Acts 26:23; Rev 1:5) contradict narratives in which other dead people were raised (2 Kings 4:32, 35; Lk 7:12-15; Jn 11:43-44). "It should be obvious to anyone that the chroniclers, if at all acting from God's 'inspiration,' were not checking their own, or each other [sic], manuscript for errors and contradictions."[82]

Ben-Jochannan's example—representative of his arguments against the Bible—unfortunately suggests nothing except his lack of genuine acquaintance with ancient historical sources from the biblical period. No Jewish or Christian writers in the first century questioned that a few Old Testament prophets had resuscitated dead people; the New Testament writers did not simply "forget" this when speaking of Jesus as the "first" to rise from the dead. By "resurrection from the dead" Christians and most Jews meant a special future event when the dead will be raised never to die again (Ezek 37:12-14; Dan 12:2). Some people in the Bible were temporarily restored to life, but in mortal bodies doomed to die again someday; in contrast to this, the New Testament writers unanimously affirm that Jesus was permanently transformed in a resurrection body (for example, Jn 20:19; 1 Cor 15:35-54; Phil 3:21). The ideas are barely comparable, and no Jewish or Christian reader in antiquity would have confused them.

Ben-Jochannan elsewhere charges that some Jews, disenchanted with Mosaic religion, in 1 C.E. (= A.D.) "created a new God in the person of one 'Jesus Christ.' "[83] This unsubstantiated assertion sidesteps some critical questions: Why would Jews make up a new God, then elaborately associate him with the historic God of Israel in their writings? Why is there no evidence of *any* Jewish people creating *any* gods out of dissatisfaction with their people's God? Who would invent a crucified supreme God, when the cross was a universal symbol of shame and Jews found in it a curse (Deut 21:23)? What group of Palestinian Jews would invent a new god and then unanimously risk their very lives to support the belief? What makes the writer who proposes this idea a more trustworthy authority than eyewitnesses two thousand years closer to the time, many of whom sealed their witness with their martyrdom?

The writer does not substantially improve his credibility as an authority on the matter by suggesting all this happened in 1 C.E. Nearly all scholars recognize that Jesus was born before 4 B.C.E.—that is, before Herod the Great's death. The Romans crucified Jesus somewhere around 27-33 C.E., probably in 30. Are we to believe that the first witnesses invented the person of Jesus, then circulated stories in which Jesus was known throughout Galilee and Jerusalem, and yet Galileans and Jerusalemites believed their stories? Ben-Jochannan's presuppositions seem more essential to him here than historical data.

The same writer claims that books were accepted into the Bible only because they were "selected by the Council of Bishops at Nicene."[84] In his haste, the writer indulged some miscalculations. First, the council was called the Council of Nicaea (only the creed formulated there was called Nicene; the ancient African church in Ethiopia, by the way, accepted the views of the intercultural Council of Nicaea).[85] Second, that council addressed primarily Arianism, not the canon of the Bible.[86] Third, the councils that did formalize the canon of the Bible merely recognized which works were already accepted in common use by the church in their day. Although some books had been disputed until a later period, most of our current New Testament books were in universal use by the close of the second century (quite early, considering how long it took for these documents to circulate and be collected); the entire Old Testament was already widely accepted by the time of Jesus.

To take but one further example from the same writer, he charges that "most Jewish scholars" hold the teachings of 4 Ezra and the Cabala to be "at least old [sic] or older than Moses."[87] This assertion would immediately ruin his credibility for readers familiar with contemporary Jewish scholarship— 4 Ezra probably derives from the late first century, whereas the Cabala is medieval, and *no* mainstream Jewish scholars hold the view that he attributes to "most" Jewish scholars.

Although such poorly grounded assertions and attacks on Christianity may convince those without much knowledge of the period in question, they can only serve to alienate readers with a more accurate knowledge of the subject from firsthand sources.[88] Such sloppy scholarship sadly can endanger the credibility of the rest of such writers' work. It would be better for these to revise their scholarship on such matters or remain silent on areas in which their firsthand knowledge is limited.[89]

Conclusion
Africa has continued to play an important part in the drama of the God of the Bible, and will do so until the Lord Jesus returns. In the meantime, Jesus has called all who claim to follow him to make disciples from among all the nations (Mt 28:19-20; Acts 1:8). Those of us who believe in Jesus therefore

cannot reject other cultures or peoples in the process of acknowledging our own.

Christians affirm that Christian faith did not simply *evolve* from African, Asian, Western or any other culture; we affirm that God revealed his truth as he willed it.[90] At the same time, we recognize that God communicated that truth in the language and history of the day, in a world of which northern and eastern Africa constituted a continuing and important part.[91] (On Africa's role, note suggestions in our earlier work, as well as many Afrocentric Christian works.[92]) Much of the Bible also addresses questions raised by the cultures in which it was written. For those who wish to explore an example of a more balanced approach, drawing on *all* the evidence from the cultures around Israel, we seek to provide one in appendix A.

Yet some contemporary writers who reject Christianity have replaced it not with traditional African religions but with some form of Islam, claiming that Islam is the "true religion of the Blackman." Many of these teachings in the Black community stem from the writings of Elijah Muhammad, the first public leader of the Nation of Islam. In the following chapter, therefore, we will examine some of the claims in one of his most influential books.

5

How Do We Answer the Nation of Islam?

Many of the hypocrites who go out from me will still say to you that they believe in Allah but do not believe that I am the Messenger of Allah. This is as if they said that they do not believe in either one of us. You cannot get to Allah unless you come through a Messenger, Apostle or Prophet of Allah.[1]

Jesus said to him, "I am the way and the truth and the life; no one comes to the Father except through me. If you had known me, you would have also known my Father." (Jn 14:6-7)

Whatever else the Nation of Islam may teach today, its original teaching stems from Elijah Muhammad, whose views have circulated widely even outside the Nation. In this chapter we therefore respond primarily to the teachings of Elijah Muhammad. Elijah Muhammad was one of the primary voices in the African-American community circulating claims that Christianity was a "white" religion; two of the opening quotes in our first two chapters belong to him. Yet despite his influence for Islam in the African-American community, Elijah Muhammad was not a representative for orthodox Islam, but for a new religion that is less than a century old. His influence remains in the in-house teachings of Nation of Islam under Louis Farrakhan, and still more prominently among some smaller sects that preserve his teachings without apology.

Elijah Muhammad's View of Himself
Elijah Muhammad felt that he was destined to be the true leader of American

Blacks. He believed that anyone who opposed his economic program, for instance, "cannot be considered a man or woman who wants to see his or her people out of the chains of want and suffering."[2] Why was this? Black people's problem was that they lacked a teacher, but now "I, Elijah Muhammad, am from God, Himself! Why not believe and follow me?"[3] Sample some of his other claims:

☐ "I am the first man since the death of Yakub commissioned by God directly."[4]

☐ "We have a Savior that is born. . . . We have a Savior today. He is with me. He is able to feed you. He is able to clothe you."[5]

☐ "He [Allah] has made me a door. . . . You will come by me, and if you reject me, you will not go. I have been given the keys to heaven."[6]

☐ "You have been taught for the past 34 years from the mouth of Almighty God, Allah, through His Messenger."[7]

☐ "[Allah] did not raise me as a Messenger like the Prophets of old, but he raised me as a Messenger, a Warner and a Reminder to the Nations of that which was prophesied to take place in these last days."[8]

☐ "My mission is to give life to the dead. What I teach brings them out of death and into life. . . . There will be no other Messenger. I am the last and after me will come God Himself."[9]

Elijah Muhammad also claimed that the final messenger of Allah must be Black[10] and come among North American Blacks;[11] thus it was to Elijah Muhammad that Allah had revealed the end-time truth.[12]

Elijah complains against apostates who preach against him, the Messenger, while claiming to still follow Islam.[13] He warns his followers to beware of false prophets,[14] any who would lead them not to respect Allah's Messenger;[15] such will perish in hell.[16] The only two unforgivable sins are failure to accept Allah as God and failure to accept his Messenger as his Messenger.[17] One cannot have Allah without his Messenger; if one rejects the Messenger, one becomes an enemy of Allah.[18]

Because Elijah's own son, along with Malcolm X, was moving toward orthodox Islam, Elijah warned that a Messenger's son may not believe him.[19] (Some of W. D. Fard's first followers from the beginning repudiated Elijah as Fard's Messenger as well.[20]) In response to the defection of Malcolm X and Elijah's son Wallace Muhammad, Elijah announced that those who claim to follow Allah but reject his Messenger are Allah's enemies.[21] Thus Elijah concluded that Malcolm X was a "hypocrite" like Korah,[22] who never "had really believed in Islam."[23] Malcolm's charges about Elijah Muhammad's sexual sins, he said, were groundless and motivated by evil.[24]

Elijah Muhammad was hardly subtle about claiming to be the final Messenger—a role that orthodox Islam has traditionally reserved for Muhammad, whom they regarded as the greatest because the last of the great prophets. Those familiar with the New Testament will recognize that Elijah took many of his lines from Jesus—some of which orthodox Muslims allow for Jesus, more of which they allow for the seventh-century Muhammad, and some of which they allow for no one but Allah himself. Yet Elijah Muhammad made the claims he did because he believed that he had met Allah in the flesh, Master Wallace D. Fard.

Islam Versus Nation of Islam on God and His Messenger

Elijah Muhammad sometimes spoke as if his Nation of Islam (N.O.I.) were the same as Islam elsewhere, and that Asia, Africa and the Islands all followed the basic message he taught.[25] Yet Nation of Islam is a new religion distinct from historic forms of Islam, and Elijah Muhammad came to understand the distinction quite well.

On more than one occasion he sought to correct the "misunderstandings" of "orthodox Muslims." Elijah Muhammad claimed that various prophecies traditionally applied to the first Muhammad really applied to himself instead.[26] "There are many Arabs throughout the world who cannot bear witness to anyone that another messenger would rise up after Muhammad, who was here nearly 1,400 years ago. This is due to their misunderstanding of the Holy Qur-an."[27] "Old Orthodox Muslims" are wrong in preaching "a return of Muhammad of 1,400 years ago, or that there will be no need of another prophet after him."[28] The prophecy of a final Messenger refers not "to the Muhammad of 1,400 years ago," as orthodox Muslims think;[29] likewise, the lives of Moses and Jesus are merely examples, or types, of the final Messenger to arrive at the time of the end.[30]

The new Muhammad is not simply dependent on the teachings of his ancient predecessor. The Final Messenger must be a Black American, but not one "trying to learn from what Muhammad said to the Arabs nearly 1,400 years ago." Thus the Qur'an and Bible both show *another* scripture to be given in the time of judgment, because the Qur'an "takes us up" only to that time.[31] Why do the rest of the Muslims in the world disagree with Elijah Muhammad? These "weak Orthodox Muslims . . . reject the plain truth and warning that Allah has revealed to me" because they love Allah's enemies (Whites).[32] In the end it will not matter, Elijah says, for Orthodox Muslims cannot stop him: "Neither Jeddah nor Mecca have sent me! I am sent from

Allah. . . . I am not taking orders from them, I am taking orders from Allah (God) Himself."[33]

Elijah Muhammad frequently contradicts central tenets of historic Islamic teaching—the most notable being his claim that his teacher was Allah in the flesh. Orthodox Islam rejected the Christian claim that Jesus was divine precisely because Islam denied that God could be flesh; but according to Elijah, it was White devils who propagated the lie that God is a spirit rather than a man.[34] Around 1930 Wallace Fard Muhammad allegedly told Elijah Muhammad, "My name is Mahdi; I am God."[35] Thereafter Elijah continued to preach the deity of Fard, one of the most repetitive refrains of Elijah's *Message to the Blackman in America;*[36] Allah's appearance as W. Fard Muhammad in July 1930 is his twelfth and final affirmation of faith.[37] In the future millennium, everyone will "obey One God: Fard Muhammad the Great Mahdi, or Allah in Person."[38] One must submit to Fard as Allah to be successful.[39]

Elijah Muhammad is aware that orthodox Islam disagrees with this central tenet of his faith, but responds that it is because he is the first to fully understand the Qur'an: "Many of the Orthodox Muslims do not want to believe that Allah has appeared in the Person of Master Fard Muhammad or that He has made manifest the truth that has been hidden from their religious scientists—the truth of God and of the devil as revealed to me. Though they do have the Holy Qur-an, many of them do not understand the meaning of it."[40]

Elijah Muhammad suggested that God the creator no longer personally exists, but continues instead in his people, the Black race.[41] Malcolm X openly reported that in Elijah Muhammad's teaching Fard also claimed that Black people were gods and that he himself was Messiah, God in person.[42] According to Malcolm X's report, N.O.I. teaches that all Blacks are God (Allah being the Supreme Black Man, but other Blacks also being divine).[43]

Again, historic Islam rejected Christianity precisely because it taught that Jesus was God's Son and God in flesh; Islam affirmed instead that God had no son and could not become flesh. Historic Islam is no closer to Nation of Islam on this central point than it is to Christianity.

Elijah Muhammad on the Resurrection

At times Elijah Muhammad mixes components of Christianity and Islam, but always in ways that exalt Master Fard. For instance, while Elijah ridicules the notion that Jesus' death could have atoning value,[44] he declares that Fard offered his life to restore Blacks to their proper role.[45]

But when it comes to the doctrine of the resurrection, which is central to both historic Christianity and Islam, Elijah goes his own way.[46] For him the final "resurrection" is simply the awakening of mentally dead Black Americans through his own teaching.[47] In summarizing the beliefs of Islam, he does not hesitate to redefine the end-time resurrection: "One God, His Prophets, His Scriptures, His Resurrection (of the mentally dead)."[48] "The New Testament and Holy Qur-an's teaching of a resurrection of the dead can't mean the people who have died physically and returned to the earth, but rather a mental resurrection of us, the black nation, who are mentally dead to the knowledge of truth."[49] Because Black Americans need the mental resurrection most, they will be resurrected before anyone else.[50] Elijah claims that he is resurrecting the dead and that an Arab with an Arabic Qur'an could not do it.[51]

He regards as impossible, even ridiculous, the idea that one can be restored after death.[52] "There is no such thing as dying and coming up out of the earth. . . . I say, get out of such slavery teachings. . . . When you are dead, you are DEAD."[53] Elijah in fact attributes any belief in an afterlife purely to slavery teaching,[54] ignoring the afterlife doctrines of both orthodox Islam and virtually all traditional African religions.

The only proof Elijah offers for this proposition is that the contrary position lacks proof, because no one has ever come back.[55] To this argument two Christian responses are in order. First, orthodox Islam and Christianity generally reserve the resurrection for the end of the age, making it difficult to provide specimens to show that it has already happened. Any of Elijah's own teaching about the end time, including the "mental resurrection," could be dismissed on the same grounds. But second, Christians claim that one resurrection, that of Jesus, has already occurred in history (1 Cor 15:20). Rather than allowing Elijah to simply assume what he claims to prove, we will deal with the question of Jesus' resurrection later in the book. Suffice it to note here that orthodox Christianity and Islam stand closer on the doctrine of resurrection than Elijah Muhammad stands to either of them.

Islam and Nation of Islam on Other Doctrines

For Elijah Muhammad, the Qur'an is no longer inerrant. Although "the Bible and the Holy Qur-an are filled with truth," only a percentage of them remains accurate; "the [White] enemy has tampered with the truth in both books: for he has been permitted to handle both books."[56] As we shall note again in the next chapter, one can employ this approach to explain away anything in a holy book, resorting merely to one's own claims without evidence.

Probably the most obvious distinction between Elijah Muhammad's Nation of Islam and orthodox Islam is their differing view of Whites. Whereas many Blacks were attracted to the Nation of Islam because of its consistent portrayal of Whites as "devils,"[57] this portrayal conflicts with historic Middle Eastern Islam, the ethnic foundation of which is *Arab*. Malcolm X repudiated such racism after his conversion to orthodox Islam.[58] Elijah acknowledged that "some" orthodox Muslims did not agree that the White race were devils; but, he claimed, they "are gradually coming over with me in the understanding for the first time in their history." Thus he said that White reporters must have misrepresented the words of the general secretary of Mecca which implied otherwise.[59] He claims that because Allah taught him that Whites are a race of devils,[60] his followers are not free to repudiate this doctrine.[61]

Whites are devils by nature; there is no way out for them.[62] People should stop preaching that God loves all people, Elijah warns. God certainly does not love Whites;[63] in fact, he hates them.[64] The Bible teaches that all Whites will go to hell,[65] "an appointed people for hell fire from the beginning of their creation."[66] Biblical promises for the "righteous" can apply only to Blacks.[67] Of course, not all Blacks are righteous; some 90 percent who still love Whites will have to go to hell with them![68] Whites constitute the Adamic race in the Bible, a race that Blacks formed.[69] The evil scientist Mr. Yakub created them as a devil race to avenge himself against the pure and upright Black world.[70]

Thus the only solution to the racial problem is separation from Whites,[71] if possible in a Black state;[72] such separation is a more important spiritual matter than prayer.[73] In this the Nation of Islam formed the mirror image of White supremacists, sometimes consciously.[74] For Elijah Muhammad, love of enemies is foolishness, for God himself hates his enemies.[75] Whites taught love of enemies to keep the Blacks from complaining against them.[76] Thus Martin Luther King Jr. was "making a fool of himself";[77] further, King wanted to "fool you" into loving devils.[78] Only if King and his followers accepted Islam and demanded a territory for Blacks would Elijah join forces with them.[79]

One problem this ideology creates is that Master Fard, whom Elijah Muhammad believed to be Allah, was a Turk—not Black or an African. But this White appearance, Elijah concludes, was merely a disguise. Master Fard explained to Elijah that his father was really Black but went "into the mountains [governments of the Caucasians] picking out a white woman to marry so that she would give birth to a son looking white."[80] Because Fard was half Black and half White physically, "he is able to go among both black and white without being discovered or recognized."[81] Likewise Elijah claims that Muhammad as an Arab was Black but Jesus and Moses as Jews were White.[82] He ignores the fact that Middle Eastern Jews and Arabs were probably of roughly similar complexion[83] and that, whereas Muhammad's companion Bilal was Black, Muhammad and most of his companions are not portrayed as Black in the earliest Arab artwork.[84]

For a much more detailed yet gracious differentiation of Nation of Islam from historic Islam, see Mustafa El-Amin's *The Religion of Islam and the Nation of Islam: What Is the Difference?* Having been a disciple of Elijah Muhammad, El-Amin followed his son Imam Warith D. Muhammad into historic Islam after Elijah Muhammad's death in 1975.[85] After Malcolm X renounced the Nation as a corruption of Islam,[86] the Nation reportedly plotted to kill him.[87] Elijah Muhammad's son Wallace moved N.O.I. in the direction of orthodox Islam, which Malcolm had espoused;[88] but Louis Farrakhan and other breakaway groups led as many as 100,000 followers back into the more sectarian varieties of Islam that preserve Elijah Muhammad's teachings.[89]

Challenges to Christian Teaching

Elijah's words might be more credible to Christians if he did not misrepresent Christianity and the Bible so severely. Protestant and Eastern Orthodox Christians, for example, may be surprised to learn that the head of all Christians (and of the White race) is the pope in Rome.[90] That the pope is Christians' "god" would surprise Catholic Christians as well.[91] Black preachers are said to be simply pawns of White people,[92] more an enemy to their people than the White devils themselves.[93] Black Christians, Elijah claimed, are doomed to hell.[94]

Elijah Muhammad's successor, Louis Farrakhan, rarely speaks negatively of Jesus in public, but one wonders how often he speaks of the "historical Jesus" and how often he really means the final Messenger of whom the historical Jesus was merely a "type." Elijah Muhammad taught that his Master Fard would be "the Christ, the second Jesus."[95] "Jesus' history refers more to a future Jesus than the past," Elijah announced; "this Jesus made His appearance July 4, 1930 and His work is now in effect."[96] Elsewhere Elijah Muhammad claims that the historical Jesus was merely an example pointing to the final Messenger at the end-time resurrection, namely Elijah Muhammad himself.[97]

Elijah Muhammad instructed his followers to "forget about ever seeing the return of Jesus, Who was here 2,000 years ago." Rather they should look for the one he prophesied, Allah in the flesh, the "Son of Man," "Christ," "Comforter,"[98] that is, Wallace D. Fard.[99] This figure would come "from the East" (Mt 24:27), which Elijah interprets as from the land of Islam.[100] In context that passage actually refers to a coming of Jesus so public and indisputable that it will light up the sky "from east to west," a good ancient way of saying the whole sky (Mt 24:23-27). The coming will also be of the biblical Jesus alone (Mt 24:3).

But if the second Jesus, W. D. Fard, is what matters, what then of Christianity? Allah and Islam will overthrow and destroy both Buddhism and Christianity.[101] Christians worship Jesus, falsely claiming that he is Son of Allah "born without the agency of man, thus accusing God of an act of adultery."[102] (By contrast, although orthodox Islam denies that Jesus is God's Son, it acknowledges the virgin birth; see the next chapter.)

Lest one think that Elijah would therefore tolerate the Black church in the meantime, we should remember that he warned Blacks to "get away from the old slavery teaching that Jesus, who was killed 2,000 years ago, is still alive somewhere waiting and listening to their prayers."[103] Jesus was merely a prophet and, like other dead prophets, cannot hear prayers.[104] Jesus is dead and cannot return because resurrection cannot happen.[105] (By contrast, orthodox Islam generally denies that Jesus has died yet.) "Infidel teachers" speak of Jesus' resurrection, but "this is the greatest falsehood ever told," and the only proof Christians offer is the "spirit" they feel.[106] We will provide a brief defense of Jesus' resurrection in a later chapter.

Elijah regards the Bible as only partly holy;[107] God himself calls it "the Poison Book," because Whites tampered with its contents.[108] The Bible has deceived people[109] and, because it has been misunderstood, is the "graveyard" of Black people from which they must be mentally resurrected.[110]

Why then would Elijah Muhammad bother quoting from the Bible? Only because, as he points out, many Blacks would not hear him otherwise.[111] Thus Elijah affirmed the Bible's "truth" while feeling free to reinterpret it because it had been "tampered" with.[112] Of course this is convenient: like White slaveholders and countless others in history, he could make the Bible say what he wanted it to say!

It is not surprising that Elijah comes up with some unusual interpretations. The twenty-four elders of Revelation, for example, are the "Islamic Scientists";[113] every twenty-five thousand years, the length of time necessary to realign the earth's poles, twenty-four Black scientists write a new history like the Bible or the Qur'an.[114] Like some errant Christian prophecy teachers, Elijah interprets the Bible as if it were all written for his generation and his mission; for example, the "lost nation" he says the Bible predicts, which must be "in the wilderness," can only be the Black community in North America.[115]

Presumably he refers to biblical promises of Israel's restoration, which many Christian interpreters also apply to the church; yet far from fitting only Black Americans, the prophecies must be taken out of context to fit only Black Americans. Where a biblical text does not suit Elijah's purpose, he ignores the contradiction: "lost sheep of the house of Israel" (Mt 10:6) becomes Black Americans,[116] even though Jesus was borrowing Old Testament language for the Jewish people (Is 53:6; Jer 50:6; Ezek 34:5). At different points he interprets the beast in Revelation as "the white man," the United States or Christianity;[117] but given that the beast persecutes Jesus' followers (Rev 17:6), Revelation's beast cannot refer to true Christians.[118]

Elijah uses some interpretations to assault the Bible's authority without mentioning other, more carefully researched interpretations. For instance, he feels that "Lead us not into temptation" must imply "a lack of confidence in God to lead us aright," and the prayer for bread "this day" may imply seeking physical before spiritual bread.[119] But the "temptation" line in the Lord's Prayer is simply a prayer for *protection* in testing,[120] similar to Jewish prayers with which Jesus' disciples may have already been familiar.[121] As to "this day," God is practical in recognizing our daily need for food,[122] but the context is clear that disciples should seek God's kingdom first (Mt 6:9-10, 33). Elijah should not blame his failure to read the Bible in context on the Bible itself.

Responses to Some of N.O.I.'s Claims

None of these interpretations are particularly surprising given Elijah's logical system: he fits the evidence to the conclusions he already believes. No one who has been reading Scripture in context is likely to find such interpretations persuasive. One example of his logic runs as follows: in the name Europe, "EU stands for hills and cavesides of that continent and ROPE means a place where that people were bound in."[123] This suggestion presupposes that the first Europeans spoke a language that did not then exist (English) and ignores the actual use of the term at least as early as Greek. Nevertheless, he opines, "the truth is plain enough for a fool to see and say that it is the truth."[124] Although not as glaring as his interpretive errors, historical and scientific errors also appear in his argument.[125]

Some of Elijah's speculations are more interesting. He notes a wheel-shaped plane, a "humanly built planet" that contains fifteen hundred bombers to destroy the world's cities, which people can see in the sky twice a week.[126] It seems remarkable that astronomers who have mapped distant galaxies invisible to most telescopes have never noticed it. His predictions of the times also failed to come to pass; he expected America to be destroyed in 1965, 1966 or very soon thereafter.[127]

Many people, of course, misinterpret the Bible or make factual errors; such errors need not discredit their central message. What is more disturbing is the apparent character of Elijah Muhammad's God—neither supremely loving nor supremely powerful. When this God could not get all the people to speak one language, "he decided to kill us by destroying our planet," but he failed to kill humanity, though the cataclysm formed the moon.[128]

Perhaps most disturbing of all for Christians, however, are Elijah Muhammad's words about Christ. By claiming (as noted above) that most of the Gospel records refer not to the historical Jesus but to the future Jesus, a later prophet, Elijah Muhammad and his successor Louis Farrakhan fall directly into a trap that Jesus warned about:

> Be on your guard so that no one leads you astray. Many are going to come with my name, claiming, "I'm the Christ," and will lead many people astray. . . . If someone says to you, "The Christ is over here," or, "He's over there," don't believe them. False Christs and false prophets will rise up and show great signs. . . . Thus if someone tells you, "He's there, out in the country," or, "Over here, inside this building," don't believe them. When the Son of Man really returns, it will be like a lightning flash that lights up the whole sky. (Mt 24:4-5, 23-27)

Many other leaders have fallen into this trap. For example, David Koresh, leader of the Branch Davidian sect in Waco, Texas, expected a final manifestation of the Christ figure. From 1983 until the U.S. government's fatal raid on his compound, in fact, he claimed that he was this final messenger.[129] Many other people, including Sun Myung Moon, have made the same claims. Unlike Jesus, however, few of them have been able to pull off a resurrection, especially with eyewitnesses prepared to die for the claim that they saw him. This is not to doubt that someone will ultimately attempt to imitate this feat, but to note that it is a little late for Elijah to try.

Where Elijah Muhammad Was Right

Many of Elijah Muhammad's social claims were correct. In a capitalistic society people need land or (more so today) other kinds of capital (like education) to advance.[130] He denounced White plans to sterilize Blacks, which were under way on a small scale in some hospitals in his day.[131] No one should dispute his demands for freedom, justice and equality[132] or his complaint that Whites often turn a deaf ear to cries for justice while making Blacks sound like troublemakers for complaining.[133] We should note, however, that the Black church and its Bible had voiced such concerns for justice long before Elijah did.[134] We should also note that though he ridiculed Christians for not being radical enough, he opposed King's marches in the face of police opposition. He also condemned Malcolm X as a poor fool for seeking the United Nations' help to address America's race problem; Elijah said that only God could help America, and he would not act until people turned to Islam.[135]

Elijah's moral convictions often agree with those of Christians. He complains that most sports, play, entertainment and gambling are White games that waste the Black community's resources;[136] some nineteenth-century Black Christians had likewise warned against gambling and other practices that undercut support for the whole community.[137] He condemns the great sexual sin of the United States[138] and warns that White America packages sexuality to seduce Blacks to hell with them.[139]

He was correct to denounce White Christians for their frequent failure to embrace Black Christians as equals,[140] although, as we have argued in earlier chapters, Islam's history is no less stained.[141] The Bible would also agree with Elijah Muhammad that Whites have an evil nature and nothing less radical than being "born again" can change them;[142] but unlike Elijah Muhammad, the Bible paints that same realistic portrait of all humanity.[143]

Elijah Muhammad was also likely correct to announce judgment on the United States for its racial sins, even if his pictures of absolute destruction may be overstated.[144] But then again, Christians like David Walker and John Wesley offered the same sorts of prophecies of judgment on the United States, in times when it was far less popular to do so. More recent Christian writers like David Wilkerson, founder of Teen Challenge and pastor of Times Square Church in New York, have also announced judgment on this nation.[145] So Christians can agree with Elijah Muhammad on various points while disputing his claims about God, Christ and his own identity.

Conclusion

African-American Christians share many social agendas as matters of concern with the Nation of Islam; our faith overlaps in more respects, however, with traditional Islam.[146] Yet even here Christians and Muslims, while able to work together in some respects, differ on some substantial issues of the faith. Some orthodox Muslim writers have also attacked Christianity, inviting a response like the one provided in our following chapter.

6

How Do We Answer Orthodox Muslim Attacks on Christianity?

In this chapter we respond to one popularly circulated, though not well documented, booklet attacking Christianity. Although we disagree with some central tenets of Islam, our response is not intended as an attack on Islam, nor can a single chapter respond to Islam's claims in general; here we address only the pamphlet in question, authored by Ahmed Deedat.[1]

Some Common Ground
Committed Christians and Muslims stand together as a minority voice on many issues in modern Western society. We emphasize this point for several reasons: (1) While Christianity does not teach the popular but demonstrably erroneous doctrine that "all religions are the same," Christianity *does* teach (even if many professed Christians have failed to demonstrate) love for one's neighbor—which must include our Muslim neighbors. (2) It would misrepresent Islam's diversity to imply that all Muslims attack Christianity, and both authors have Muslim friends who do not attack Christianity.[2] (3) We know from experience that cultural differences sometimes lead to persecution or ostracism, and we explicitly repudiate the attempt of anyone to use our research to attack Arab culture as a whole or to repress foreigners or those expressing ideas that differ from our own.[3]

Like siblings who wrestle with each other but join forces when attacked from the outside, Jews, Christians and Muslims who are faithful to their traditions share some common ground over against secular American society.[4] Probably partly because of substantial Christian influence on Muhammad in the early years[5]—including a cousin of his wife who confirmed for him his role as a prophet[6]—Islam even shares some Christian teachings about Jesus.

These teachings may have appeared even closer during Muhammad's lifetime than they later came to be.[7] Archaeology shows that for the first seventy years after Muhammad, Arab rulers used general monotheistic statements on their coins, not invoking "any specifically Islamic phrases." This might suggest a greater cooperation with other monotheists in the beginning than later traditions would indicate.[8] In contrast to later traditions and practices of conquest, a Syrian Christian writer by the end of the seventh century declares that aside from taxation the *earliest* Muslim rulers permitted Christians religious freedom.[9] Thus early Syrian Christians tended to view Islam favorably—as less than orthodox, but an improvement over previous paganism.[10]

Some common ground from that early period remains. Thus, for example, Islam acknowledges that Jesus did miracles and was born of a virgin.[11] While affirming the virgin birth, the Qur'an denies that God has a son[12] because it understands this as the language of "physical generation."[13] Part of the conflict with Christianity here is semantic, because the New Testament image of the Son borrows a traditional Jewish messianic title and does *not* connote that God impregnated Mary.[14]

The Qur'an denies that Jesus is Allah[15] but affirms that Jesus is Allah's "Word,"[16] which allows the same point of contact for discussion John had with Jewish interpreters in his day via his image of the "Word" in John 1:1-18.[17] Long after Muhammad, some Muslims moved temporarily closer to a position more open to that of Christianity. For instance, the medieval Ash'arite school "taught that God's attributes were additional to his essence and subsisted eternally in him, thus recognizing distinctions within the one Godhead."[18] Islam maintains a high respect for Jesus, a role that was even more significant "in certain phases of Sufism."[19] Some Sufi mystics echoed Jesus, although identifying more fully with him (in typical mystical fashion) than biblical sources would permit.[20]

For all the points the two faiths share, however, one cannot harmonize them as if they were identical. The doctrine of the Trinity against which Muhammad was reacting was probably actually a distortion of Christian teaching rather than the true Christian doctrine of the Trinity.[21] But even so, "the Qur'an does not adequately represent Christianity as they, who believe in it, desire for it to be known. Therefore, they can never accept Muhammad in the same way that Muslims do. If they did, then they would be Muslims, not Christians."[22]

Muhammad reportedly thought his Jewish and Christian contemporaries "were the degenerate representatives of original pure monotheisms established by Moses and Jesus."[23] Yet it does not take much genuine historical study of information Muhammad did not have available to see that the earliest possible claims about Jesus conflict with Muhammad's portrait of him. For instance, the Gospels occasionally preserve Jesus' original Aramaic expressions, one of which was *Abba,* meaning "Father" (Mk 14:36). In contrast to Muhammad's later revelation, the earliest historical evidence suggests that Jesus saw God as his Father.[24]

Dialogue does not always mean agreement, just as disagreement need not yield disrespect or animosity. But dialogue does clarify which differences are merely semantic and which elements of a faith are essential and irreducible. The issue for Christians is not merely a difference in culture; a person could follow most Islamic practices culturally, but if that person followed the Christ of the New Testament we would embrace him or her as a fellow believer in Christ. Likewise, a person could adopt the culture of Western or other churches but not be a genuine disciple of Christ (in the sense in which the apostolic church meant the phrase) unless he or she affirmed Christ's lordship and the saving power of his death and resurrection.

Responses to Some of Deedat's Claims

We now turn to the attacks in a popular pamphlet by Ahmed Deedat. Deedat himself seems to have been hurt by professed Christians earlier in his life, and the best truly Christian response to him is for us to show him love. His arguments, however, affect the way many others view Christianity, and it is his arguments rather than his person we address here.

Deedat's attacks are mostly ad hominem. For instance, he seizes on the Christian admission that the Bible is human as well as divine to argue that it must not be divine at all.[25] This argument either wrongly interprets the writers he quotes, as meaning that the Bible is full of errors, or requires the unspoken assumption that God cannot work through human vessels—prophets—to communicate his will (contrast, for example, 1 Thess 2:13). Many Muslims may view the Qur'an as divine without elements of Muhammad's or others' own style (for questions regarding this premise, see below), but this is not the biblical teaching of the Bible about itself or the Christian view about the Bible. Deedat cannot simply assume presuppositions from his own beliefs, note that the biblical evidence does not fit his presupposition about the way God should inspire a holy book, and then claim that he has proved a point. He has not even offered an argument.

Protestants and the Apocrypha. When Deedat argues that Protestants, including conservative Protestants, do not believe the Bible because they expunged the Apocrypha from the canon (in which he wrongly includes the book of Esther and mislabels Tobit "Tobias," the name of Tobit's son),[26] he shows his unfamiliarity with the history of the canon. Palestinian Judaism never accepted the Apocrypha as part of its Bible, but because the most popular Greek versions of the Old Testament included the Apocrypha, many early Christians read it. The earliest church accepted the Old Testament and began using a variety of books written by the first followers of Jesus and their immediate successors. Despite disputes about some books in the beginning, Christians had settled on the Old and New Testaments as part of their Bible long before the Roman Catholic Church officially declared that the Apocrypha was part of it. Early Protestants, following Jewish tradition by this period, rejected the Apocrypha as part of the Bible but did not mind its being read (practical considerations, principally the cost of printing, ultimately excluded it from Protestant Bibles).[27] Neither those who reject nor those who affirm the Apocrypha have done so out of disbelief in the Bible; the dispute is over which books constitute the Bible, with the Apocrypha comprising the only disputed books.

Anonymous books in the Bible. In the same way, Deedat argues that the unknown authorship of particular books or a biblical author's editing of earlier traditions argues against the Bible's authenticity.[28] But this conclusion does not follow from the argument. If some New Testament books are anonymous, they merely follow the tradition of some Old Testament historians, who regarded the content of their work (the veracity of which could be checked with sources that were then still extant) as more important than the attachment of their name. Whether or not one believes that Moses wrote any of the Pentateuch, Deedat's argument that Moses had no hand in it because it is written in the third person[29] is a logical fallacy; the conclusion need not follow from the premise. Because a response to Deedat's argument here requires more detail, in appendix B we will briefly take up the documentary hypothesis and the historical reliability of the Pentateuch.

Differences and similarities among the Gospels. Likewise, Deedat assumes that for some Gospels to omit what another includes constitutes a contradiction.[30] Yet if all four Gospels included all the same material, would they not all be the same Gospel rather than four different witnesses? Whereas Islam rests solely on Muhammad's claims, biblical Christianity rests on the claims of a variety of witnesses and eyewitness traditions; and witnesses may attest an event without reporting identical details. Deedat contends that what Jesus preached (the *Injeel*) was good, but the Christian Gospels are just the records of eyewitnesses.[31] Yet would not most of us trust the record of eyewitnesses about Jesus more than a purported revelation about him in a document written over five hundred years later (the Qur'an)? We should note that many of the eyewitnesses also claimed inspiration and confirmed their testimony with miracles,[32] a feat not claimed for Muhammad's witness.

Deedat's complaint that Matthew's use of Mark and Q represents "cribbing" rather than inspiration misses the same point, showing unfamiliarity with how ancient writers used their sources.[33] That the Gospel writers used sources makes them *more* reliable; they depended on earlier witnesses rather than simply making up stories[34] (a charge that a skeptic might more successfully level against the Qur'an if he or she wished). Further, variation in detail was standard literary procedure among ancient writers;[35] if the Gospels agree in substance, we must focus on the substance and ask what those many agreements may imply for the truth of the Christian faith. Deedat makes up his own rules for what is acceptable and what is not as he goes along, but in our final chapter we will present some of the evidence for Jesus' identity.

Biblical reports of immorality. Further, Deedat complains that the Bible is immoral because it includes reports of gross immorality. In saying this he misunderstands the nature of ancient writing, which included both positive and negative moral examples and expected readers to be intelligent enough to discern which was which.[36] Thus, for example, Deedat says that the account of how Lot's daughters decided to sleep with him in Genesis 19:30 (he means 19:31-36) is "pornography" rather than instruction in a moral lesson.[37] Yet the text makes clear that this is a negative moral model; it is explaining the origin of the Moabites and Ammonites (19:37-38), which in turn is meant to explain to the Israelites why these particular peoples are so immoral as to be Israel's enemies.

In the same way, Deedat labels the story of Tamar's revenge on Judah in Genesis 38 a "filthy, dirty story" that teaches immorality rather than a moral lesson.[38] Yet Deedat again illustrates only that he misunderstands the story.[39] Levirate marriage was a standard ancient custom of providing for widows and the continuation of a brother's name;[40] it is practiced in many traditional societies, including many African societies.[41] Because the secondborn Onan would have inherited the double portion of the firstborn Er if Er had no children, Onan tried to make it seem as if Tamar were simply barren, rather than producing an offspring for his brother. God protected Tamar's honor by striking down Onan (vv. 8-10). Nevertheless, Judah treated his daughter-in-law as if these disasters were her fault; by ancient Near Eastern custom, he was to give her his next son in marriage, but he feared to do so. The story recounts how Tamar outwitted him in a manner that Judah recognized was more moral than the way he had treated her (in some surrounding cultures, a deceased husband's father would do if no brothers were available for procreation).[42]

The moral of the story involves just treatment of women.[43] But the story's focus involves far more as well: it contrasts Judah's shame with Joseph's exaltation. Judah sold Joseph into slavery (Gen 37:26-27) but now is shamed for his immorality (38:25-26). By contrast, Joseph, who resists immorality (39:7-20), is ultimately exalted (compare 38:18 with 41:42). The moral lesson is: Do what is right, trust God's promises, and God will reward you in the end.

Whereas Deedat complains that such immoral stories in the Bible have produced the decadence of modern Western society,[44] history suggests that it is Western society's apostasy from the standards of the Bible it once accepted that has produced the modern crises of sexual unfaithfulness, violence and self-centered rage. In earlier centuries, too, Western cultures selectively misinterpreted the Bible in other respects (for example, to subordinate women or certain races) or ignored it (as in the Crusades, but the problem is disobedience to the Bible rather than faith in the Bible). Deedat cites the activity of those who do not believe in the Bible (including professing Christians) as a challenge against the Bible itself; yet one wonders if he would similarly allow that bad Muslims reflect badly on the Qur'an, or if atheists would allow that Joseph Stalin's bloody purges reflect the values of all atheists. One does not judge a religion or value system by its least faithful adherents!

Problems with the King James Version. Deedat shows not only the weakness of his logic but also his poor acquaintance with some of the sources he cites. Comparing 1 John 5:7 in the King James Version with its absence in the Revised Standard Version, he proclaims that honest scholars know the verse (which refers to the Trinity) is fraudulent; "this key-stone of the Christian faith . . . has been a pious fraud all along."[45] Actually the issue is not fraud, although it does speak to the ignorance of some less-informed fundamentalist preachers who suppose that the King James translation is perfect. This verse ("three that bear record in heaven, the Father, the Word and the Holy Ghost") was *never* part of the accepted biblical text; appearing in only a handful of medieval manuscripts, it found its way almost accidentally into the Greek text used to translate the King James.[46] With more than five thousand Greek manuscripts currently available, including a significant number of very early ones, such a mistake would not be possible today. (Classicists concur that the New Testament is by far the best textually attested work of classical antiquity.[47])

The mistake is not with the Bible but with later copyists and translators of the Bible, just as one could later miscopy, mistranslate or misinterpret the Qur'an. (One could if one wished miscopy the Qur'an right now, on the spot, to prove the point.) Neither is the verse essential to the Christian faith; the marginal comment, later accidentally added by a scribe into the Latin text, originated in the already *established* belief in the Trinity.[48] That belief was based on other texts, texts that are not in question (a matter that Deedat either does not know or chooses not to comment on). Although Islam affirms the authority of the Jewish and Christian Scriptures, it charges that Jews and Christians distorted these Scriptures.[49] This tactic conveniently allows a Muslim apologist to cite texts he finds useful while dismissing those that challenge his thesis (a practice unfortunately replicated by many nominal Christians as well).

By comparing the RSV, Deedat also argues that the new translators removed "begotten" from the KJV's John 3:16, recognizing it to be blasphemous or not part of the original.[50] In fact, the debate over the term is an entirely natural and secular one given the evidence from the Greek language.[51] Most likely the Greek term simply depicts the uniqueness of Jesus' sonship, rather than implying a specific point of "begetting"; but the confusion was natural, and the dispute among scholars continues. The sense of this term does not affect the New Testament doctrine of Jesus' sonship. Elsewhere in the New Testament, though, his "begetting" generally applies to his enthronement at the resurrection (as in Acts 13:33; Heb 1:5), given that the psalm from which it is derived used an ancient Near Eastern designation for enthronement (see the academic treatments of Ps 2:7).

Inconsistencies in the Bible. Deedat points to what he thinks are inconsistencies in the Bible.[52] But scholars have pointed out numerous inconsistencies in the Qur'an[53]—and unlike the Bible, the Qur'an claims to stem from a single author and century. If Muslims seek to explain apparent inconsistencies in the Qur'an, one would expect them to allow Christians an easier time doing so with the Bible. The Bible consists of many different books with different authors, mostly with different emphases because they address different questions and situations over a period of more than a thousand years. Behind the different emphases, however, lies an essential unity of message, a succession of prophetic figures with the same basic voice;[54] this diversity of prophets is a strength of the Bible which the Qur'an cannot claim.

Thus when Deedat glibly contrasts Satan's moving David in 1 Chronicles 21:1 with God's moving him in 2 Samuel 24:1, he misses the point.[55] The language of Chronicles here is similar to that of Samuel, suggesting that this writer knows either 2 Samuel or its source. Satan rarely appears in early Israelite literature, but when he does appear he does so first as "ha-satan," literally, "the adversary," a sort of prosecuting attorney (Job 1—2). The Chronicler, writing after the exile, when Israel had contemplated evil more deeply, provides a theological explanation for how God moved David: Satan acted as an agent of a sovereign God, in the same way that God could later use the Babylonians or Assyrians to accomplish judgment.[56]

Deedat also details at length conflicts among numbers in the Old Testament.[57] What he does not mention is that transcriptional difficulties for copyists account for most of these changes—again reflecting a problem with later scribes rather than with the original biblical text.[58] By itself this suggests that later Hebrew scribes generally avoided *intentional* changes on such matters: these scribes were too meticulous not to have noticed the differences, but they chose not to harmonize them. A more relevant response to Deedat's objection, however, is simply, What do these differences affect? Christians do not view the Bible the way Muslims view the Qur'an; we emphasize the *meaning* of the text. Unlike Muslims, we are not concerned with reciting the words in the original language. We are not Muslims, and the Muslim objection would be persuasive only if the Bible were meant to be read the ways Muslims read the Qur'an (though, as we shall see below, similar charges have been leveled against the Qur'an as well).[59] These numerical differences do not affect what the Bible has to teach us for our lives and thus do not bear on the validity of the Christian faith as a whole.

Misrepresentations of the evidence. Deedat's arguments sometimes descend to the absurd. Thus he finds the name "Allah" in C. I. Scofield's notes to the Bible (never part of the Bible itself, and in our opinion sometimes contradictory to the Bible!) and, conveniently ignoring that Scofield is simply relating the verb *alah,* "to swear," to the divine name, seizes on this as an admission that Allah is God's name.[60] Having noted that Deedat's argument reflects poor logic, we have no problem adding that the Arabic term *Allah* is related to Hebrew terms like *El* and *Elohim;* the latter were also Canaanite terms for the chief deity and for deities, respectively. Arabic and Hebrew, like Phoenician, Akkadian and a number of other languages, are related Semitic languages and naturally share many roots. If a degree of influence existed either way, ancient Hebrew certainly preceded the forms of Arabic developing by the time of the Qur'an. But even had it been the other way, it would make no difference; *Elohim* is not God's personal name, but simply borrows the standard term for a god in that culture (the way we use the term *God* though the *term* can be applied to any god that is worshiped).[61]

Deedat regularly cites cultic or sectarian sources as representative of Christianity to make his case; this is somewhat akin to using Louis Farrakhan as a representative of Sunni Islam. Thus, for example, he cites *The Plain Truth* as a "Christian Journal,"[62] though all mainstream churches regard Herbert W. Armstrong's movement as sectarian in the period in which Deedat cites its magazine (only in recent years has that movement become orthodox).[63] Deedat cites Jehovah's Witnesses and their New World Translation as reflecting Christian ideas,[64] but all churches consider Jehovah's Witnesses cultic, while Jehovah's Witnesses officially reject the religion of all other churches. Unwittingly demonstrating the logical fallacy of guilt by association, he associates all Christians with Jim Jones's suicide cult. Aside from the fact that Jones's theology was not Christian,[65] one may question whether the analogy is valid on other grounds either; after all, practicing Christians do not believe in suicide or gratuitous violence, regardless of the values of Western culture.[66] This practice of guilt by association would be roughly comparable to taking Islamic terrorists as representatives of more peace-loving followers of Islam. Many Western observers make that mistake, and Deedat stoops to their level with this argument.

Common cause with skeptical scholars. Deedat quotes with delight Western scholars who dispute most of the Bible as if these quotations were the concessions of orthodox Christians or as if these scholars had no agendas or presuppositions of their own.[67] That Deedat could find some Western scholars who question the Bible is not surprising; far more scholars do so than he could possibly quote. What Deedat either does not recognize or does not acknowledge is that most Western scholars since the Enlightenment have been skeptical of supernatural phenomena, and hence of any document purporting to attest such phenomena (including the Qur'an).[68] Islam acknowledges that Jesus did miracles and was born of a virgin;[69] against the standard teaching of Islam, Western skeptics deny this. Nevertheless, modern skepticism is generally less thoroughgoing than it was in the nineteenth century, first of all because discovery after discovery has challenged earlier skeptical assertions (such as doubts concerning the Babylonian exile), and second, because more tolerant postmodern paradigms are quickly replacing Enlightenment presuppositions.[70] Conservative and moderate scholars who accept the Bible's reliability either wholly or substantially have considerable historical material to work with.

But had the skepticism of Western academia arisen in the Islamic world rather than here, it would have been the Qur'an and the Hadith, rather than the Bible, that would have been under attack.[71] To this issue we briefly turn.

Turning the Tables: Skeptics About the Qur'an
Non-Islamic and moderate Islamic approaches to Islam are much more critical of the Qur'an and Islam than are traditional Muslim scholars.[72] We pause to note here and at a few other points that our dispute is not with the Qur'an or with all Muslims. We merely intend to illustrate that Deedat's argument against the Bible would, if he were consistent, work even more against the Qur'an.

With little external corroboration for its events, the Qur'an would be more difficult to defend than the Bible. Further, one need attack only one witness's credibility to bring down the Qur'an (in contrast to the hundreds of witnesses that Jesus rose, or the multigenerational succession of prophets bearing God's message in the Bible). Western skeptics who deny the Bible would be no more merciful toward the Qur'an. Christianity is not Western rationalism any more than it is Western imperialism; however much some Westerners once identified the two, Christianity is not even Western in its origins, but Afroasiatic. (For one thing, Western Christendom has often been anti-Jewish, which is about as faithful to genuine Christianity as an anti-Arab Islam would be.)

Deedat and others might object that the Qur'an itself is a miracle, its own attestation, for Muhammad was not trained as a scribe. Yet the principles Deedat is ready to apply to the Bible would discredit the Qur'an far more quickly. Following the very sort of questioning he applies, one may suggest that the Qur'an has undergone substantial revision after its initial composition. The evidence for early Muslim history, including the life of Muhammad, is dependent on the Hadith (traditions) rather than the Qur'an, which tells us little about Muhammad's life.[73] Further, one cannot claim any definite interpretation of many narratives in the Qur'an, like some in the Bible, without understanding the historical situation they address; but understanding these traditions depends on the Hadith.[74]

Early Muslim traditions. Non-Muslim and some Muslim Islamicists suspect the reliability of many of the traditions, many of which may have arisen long after Muhammad's death.[75] Early traditions of interpretation often varied considerably from one another.[76] Many scholars argue that external history, based on documents known to date from Muhammad's time, contradict Islamic tradition—for example, regarding the date of Muhammad's death.[77] Some even suggest that Islamic tradition reflects invented stories. Thus, for example, some argue that later writers knew little of Mecca in Muhammad's lifetime.[78] Likewise, Muslim accounts of the conquest fail to match non-Muslim reports stemming from the very period they describe;[79] archaeology also shows that most Byzantine fortresses in Arabia were peacefully abandoned a century before the battles Muslim traditions report.[80] Some think that nearly a century after Muhammad, the Qur'an had not yet been "canonized."[81]

Editing of the Qur'an? Nevertheless, Islamic tradition is all we have to go on regarding the composition of the Qur'an, which is not attested in non-Muslim sources; so the best we can do is examine the earliest traditions.[82] According to one recent scholar, Caliph 'Uthman (ruled 644-656), Muhammad's third successor over Muslims,

> appointed a committee to assemble all the available versions, most partial, some recollected and some written, and collect them into a single normative text [this is the standard account of early Muslim tradition]. That was in the late 640s or early 650s—Muhammad died in 632 A.D.—but the search for significant variants in the partial versions extant before Uthman's standard edition, what can be called the *sources* behind our text, has not yielded any differences of great significance. Those pre-Uthmanic clues are fragmentary, however, and large "invented" portions might well have been added to our Quran or authentic material deleted.[83]

Some Muslims, failing to find the Prophet's successor mentioned, have suggested that texts were tampered with; but this charge is unlikely. More reasonably, while the Qur'an reflects Muhammad's teaching, it seems to have been arranged later.[84] The earliest Islamic traditions agree that others rather than Muhammad collected and edited his revelations. Yet even the early traditions diverge considerably among themselves. "We learn that some of

Muhammad's followers already knew the whole Koran by heart in his lifetime—yet subsequently it had to be pieced together out of fragments collected from here and there." He dictated it to a scribe; yet later, when those who had memorized it died, it was nearly lost. In one version, the first caliph collected it into a book; another version has the second caliph; another 'Uthman, the third. "Alternatively, it had already been collected before the time of 'Uthman, and he merely had the text standardised and other versions destroyed." The last view prevails today, but historically the choice is arbitrary.[85] Scholars generally concur that the fifty-third *sura* includes two interpolations (additions); also variant versions of the same passage appear in different places in the Qur'an, suggesting some changes.[86]

A Qur'an after Muhammad? Indeed, others suggest that the text of the Qur'an was not in its present form even some time later, though all the current copies have been standardized. They contend that we have no clear evidence for the existence of the Qur'an before the end of the seventh century;[87] further,

> when the first Koranic quotations appear on coins and inscriptions towards the end of the seventh century, they show divergences from the canonical text. These are trivial from the point of view of content, but the fact that they appear in such formal contexts as these goes badly with the notion that the text had already been frozen.[88]

Other evidence suggests that the current language of the Qur'an cannot be the language in which Muhammad delivered it. For one thing, its style may reflect an expectation that its first readers would be familiar with the Bible.[89]

Far more important and clear, the "classical" Arabic in which the Qur'an was written probably did not yet exist in Muhammad's lifetime. "No inscriptions in Classical Arabic have been found in the Hijaz from before the first years of Mu'awiyah's reign. The earliest date from the 40s [years after Muhammad] /660s [by the Western calendar], and come from the Ta'if area, which Mu'awiyah seems to have been interested to colonize around that time."[90] Further, "classical" Arabic does not appear to be the Arabic of inscriptions dating from Muhammad's time, but a particular form of Arabic including loan words from peoples later subdued by Islam.

> Classical Arabic occurs in the Hijaz in a developed form—there are, in that area, no traces of development from an earlier form of either the language or the script. To find such traces one must turn to Syria, where inscriptions in a close variety of Classical Arabic and early Kufic script appear (e.g. on church lintels) in the sixth century A.D. All these points together suggest, to a "revisionist," that Classical Arabic in fact arose in

Syria rather than the [Arabian] Peninsula, and penetrated to the Hijaz only as part of Mu'awiyah's colonization efforts in the 40s AH.[91]
Classical Arabic first appears after Islam began to spread: "there are no pagan inscriptions in Classical Arabic, nor do any Classical Arabic inscriptions make any mention of paganism, or include pagan names, such as are usually found among first-generation converts. This suggests that Classical Arabic arose in a non-pagan milieu."[92]

This is not to deny that the Qur'an reflects Muhammad's teachings. The Christian view of the Bible is that the *message* rather than the precise *wording* is what matters (hence we use Bible translations), and Christians would not object to reading another book by the same principles.[93] But the above data does appear to call into question the claim sometimes made today that the Qur'an's wording came by Allah's direct dictation to Muhammad, constituting in itself a sufficient validating miracle for the Qur'an.[94]

A divine revelation? Further, even if Muhammad received the revelation directly from an angel (a possibility we do not rule out), how does one verify that the angel was a good one? Did not pre-Islamic Arab seers receive revelations from the *jinn?* Muhammad thus had good reason to wonder whether it was truly Gabriel who had appeared to him:

> Muhammad found the experience disturbing, and concluded that he must be either a poet or possessed—in either case [by Arab tradition] the victim of a malign spirit. But a local Christian perceived that Muhammad's experience was comparable to that of Moses, and inferred him to be "the prophet of his people"; while a careful experiment devised by Muhammad's wife Khadija established that his supernatural visitor was indeed an angel and not a devil.[95]

The question that arises is whether this one test would be a sufficient basis to sustain the faith of hundreds of millions of people over centuries, when many other people (including some we have met) regularly claim to have revelations which they have "tested" yet which contradict Muhammad (and sometimes the Bible as well). Biblical tradition recognizes that some receive revelations from other kinds of spirits (as in 1 Kings 22:22; Gal 1:8; cf. 2 Cor 11:4, 13-14; Col 2:18); one must compare any new revelations (which people claim every day) with the standard of what has already been revealed through the succession of prophets whom history has proved right.[96] One may also compare them with God's own acts in history (for example, consider the hundreds of eyewitnesses to the risen Jesus; see chapter eight).

The Qur'an and other religions. How does the Qur'an measure against

these standards? Although parts of the Qur'an itself can be read as acknowledging that Jesus died, hence also acknowledging his resurrection,[97] the standard
traditional interpretation of the Qur'an is that it denies that Jesus actually died;
Allah took him alive into heaven.[98] This one revelation, received five centuries
after Jesus, contradicts hundreds of eyewitnesses who claimed to talk with Jesus
after his resurrection as well as revelations from the prophets and apostles of the
New Testament; by contrast, it accords with a later Gnostic tradition influenced
by Greek thought.[99] This is not the only occasion on which Muhammad seems
to have derived views from traditions that originated later than the Bible, rather
than from the Bible itself. The Qur'an includes many postbiblical Jewish and
Christian traditions,[100] although both internal and external evidence suggests that
more of Muhammad's views derive from the Judaism of his region than from
the Christianity there.[101]

Some Qur'anic rules even endorse pre-Islamic "religious customs of
pagan Arabia," such as the customs of a holy month and pilgrimage to a
sanctuary.[102] Of course, God is able to address specific cultural eras and
situations in culturally relevant terms, hence to adapt existing customs; but
Muslims who recognize this principle will not be the fundamentalists. They
will be those who interpret the Qur'an closer to the way Christian scholars
interpret the Bible, taking into account the situations the authors addressed
rather than assuming that every word applies to all situations in all eras.

Conclusion

We could say more, and certainly could cite more skeptical positions than
these, but our purpose here is merely to show that Deedat's attacks on the
Bible rest on principles he would never allow to be applied to the Qur'an.
Researchers may provide counterarguments against the arguments above, but
Deedat should know that we can also provide counterarguments to objections
he raises against the Bible.

Although much historical data no longer remains either for biblical times
or for the time of Muhammad, we believe that existing data supports enough
of the tradition about Jesus to provide strong arguments for Christianity's
most central historical claims on purely historical grounds. Addressing even
details of such an argument might require entire books, however (many of
which have already been written), so in this book we merely refer the reader
to chapter eight for a sample. Next we turn briefly to one more popular
polemicist against Christianity.

7

How Do We Answer Other Challenges to Christianity?

Because challenges to orthodox Christianity come from so many specific quarters (Jehovah's Witnesses, agnostics, relativists and so on), we provide here just one more sample response to the sorts of challenges often raised. In this chapter we briefly comment on one more book attacking Christian faith. This work has had a significant hearing in some African-American circles with which we are acquainted and represents a more "New Age" orientation than most of the other assaults. This work, however, like some of the other popular works we have examined, was authored by a person who quickly shows that he is writing outside his area of expertise. So weak is the "scholarship" on which the book is based that no self-respecting New Testament scholar or historian of Greco-Roman antiquity, whether Christian or atheist, would even deign to respond to his arguments under normal circumstances; but these are not normal circumstances.

As is the custom when scholars address popular works that claim to speak for yet actually misrepresent the scholarly consensus, we have to begin by explaining why we are even taking notice.[1] We supply a brief response here only because works such as these are sometimes more available on a popular level than works written by genuine scholars (Black or White, conservative or liberal), and those without firsthand acquaintance with ancient sources may have more difficulty evaluating which positions are most accurate.

Lloyd Graham, the author of the book in question, repeatedly asserts his antisupernaturalistic presuppositions without offering a shred of proof for them. (Antisupernaturalistic presuppositions stem from the Enlightenment assumption, never proved and now increasingly questioned, that miracles cannot happen.) On John the Baptist's miraculous birth, he mocks, "Is this the normal process in reproduction? No, it is either rank superstition and ignorance of nature or mythic symbolism."[2] On Jesus' walking on the water, he rages, "It takes a lot of ignorance to believe this literally. Yet, literally, millions do. And then we wonder what's wrong with our world."[3]

Assertions without proof invite neither acceptance nor response; they amount to no more than one person's opinion, in this case reflecting a naive Enlightenment rationalism now under increasing challenge in our postmodern culture. The only reason to presuppose that God cannot do miracles is to a priori presuppose that a God more powerful than we are cannot exist. If we do not share the premise, we are not obligated to accept the conclusion.

Misunderstandings of the Trinity

Graham's book abounds with logical fallacies. He charges that Christ must have incestuously impregnated his own mother, since the Bible says the Holy Spirit overshadowed her, and "if He didn't, He is no part of the Godhead."[4] Then he simply declares that this is the Hebrew version of the same incest story as Oedipus and Jocasta! Yet trinitarians do not identify Jesus with the *whole* of the Godhead and never have; further, even if the conception of Jesus were an incest story (though there is not the slightest hint in the text that it is), automatically assuming that all incest stories in all cultures (whether of gods or mortals, legendary or recent persons) represent the same story reflects no understanding of cultural comparisons. This is hardly an isolated example: nearly all Graham's parallels are false, whether or not they relate to the main thrust of his case.[5]

Did Jesus Plagiarize Heracles?

Early Christianity had to contend with both Jewish and Greco-Roman environments, but Graham writes as if Christianity simply plagiarized Greek myths. To address just one page of Graham's more apparently helpful parallels: like Jesus, Heracles had a god as a father[6]—but this claim for Heracles was hardly surprising in a Greek context where there were many gods, where such gods regularly raped and seduced women, and where the conceptions of both God and "son of God" had little in common with Jewish and Christian monotheism.[7] Trying to compare Heracles as the "only-begotten" of his father[8] Zeus with Jesus in John's Gospel ignores Zeus's other children like Apollo, Artemis and Dionysus—and that John's application of "only begotten" language to Christ evokes, if anything, the pathos of Abraham's sacrifice of Isaac in Jewish tradition.[9]

Heracles was indeed called "savior," or deliverer,[10] but so were most Greek deities.[11] The Greek term translated "salvation" applied to anything from good health and physical deliverance to immortality and national deliverance;[12] in any case, the Old Testament already spoke of God saving his people long before the Greek period (for example, 1 Sam 7:8; 14:6; Is 43:3, 11-12; 45:15, 17, 21; Hos 13:4). Graham cites a title for Heracles *(neulos emelos)* that supposedly parallels Jesus[13] but is nowhere close to the Greek expression the New Testament uses—which merely suggests that Graham does not know Greek or did not bother to check the alleged parallel in the New Testament. He notes that Heracles died as Jesus did (never mind that most people do) and then ascended to heaven (never mind that Heracles did so by being burned on a funeral pyre).[14] Then he cites a writer from the second century A.D. to associate Heracles with "peace" and prove that Jesus swiped the title "prince of peace"—never mind that this title, which Christians apply to Jesus, derives from the book of Isaiah (Is 9:6-7), written eight and a half centuries before the source the writer cites![15]

To prove that Jesus stole "new birth" language, Graham cites a *modern* writer applying his own new birth language to Heracles[16]—never mind all sorts of genuinely early cases of the use of this terminology, including in Judaism, that Jesus could have better used to make his point to the Jewish teacher Nicodemus.[17]

Weaknesses in Historical Understanding
Graham's historiography is uniformly questionable.[18] "Had there actually lived a man who could raise the dead, heal the sick and walk on water," he asserts confidently, "history would have recorded it," but didn't. He is mistaken, however; wonder-workers were common in Jesus' day, and historians paid them no attention until they attracted messianic movements that might cause problems for the state. Once Jesus' movement began to spread, Roman historians did take note of him from earlier records—and they tell us more about him than about the Roman governor under whom he was crucified![19]

When Graham provides arguments that Paul never existed,[20] he is bound to lose credibility with classicists (Greco-Roman historians); one is hard-pressed to see why the early church would have invented a Paul. To argue that Paul did not believe in a literal Christ but rather a Gnostic, spiritual one, that he "preached neither Jesus nor Christ but Christhood, that deified consciousness developed within the individual," does violence to nearly every letter Paul wrote.[21] At the same time Graham claims that Paul was otherwise ignorant and so wretched that he missed the "Creative Principle" and led Christianity into error, bringing about Origen's castration and much suffering through his statement about mortifying the flesh in Romans 8. Unfortunately this misses the whole point of Romans 8 in its historical context. Paul is hardly to be faulted if some writers ancient or modern misread him (in both cases because they lack firm knowledge of his own Jewish background as well as of his audiences' multicultural background).[22]

Allegorizing the Bible

Graham says the Gospel texts about Jesus were quickly misunderstood by literalists; he maintains that it was really the evolutionary Christ.[23] Yet one wonders how he knows better than the eyewitnesses in whose lifetimes the earliest Gospel traditions circulated. "Semienlightened Gnostic Jews created the Christ of the Gospels," he opines, "but they did not intend their Christ to be taken literally. . . . They did not reckon with the ignorant Gentile literalists who were to follow them."[24] Graham unfortunately fails to reckon with some facts him-self—for instance, that the original Palestinian Jewish followers of Jesus, given their culture, would be far more apt to take things literally than later Greek followers would be. Gnostic interpretations of Jesus also appear only in texts much later than the Gospels of the Bible; the Bible's Gospels fit Greco-Roman biographical forms, are written in historiographic rather than allegorical lan-guage, and are often punctuated with Palestinian Jewish customs and figures of speech.[25] Jewish interpreters who emphasized allegory were borrowing the practice of *Greek* thinkers embarrassed by literal readings of myths.[26]

Graham also fails to reckon with a spiritual warning in the New Testament. In John's day, spirits claiming to give a better interpretation of Christ contradicted the eyewitness accounts, and John responded that those who truly spoke from Christ were those who agreed with what Jesus really did and said on earth, not latecomers who made up their own version of Christi-anity or Jesus (1 Jn 4:1-6). This principle makes more sense than accepting later Gnostic myths far removed from the Palestinian Jewish Jesus of the Gospels (see chapter eight).

Graham's lack of historical perspective becomes clearest when one realizes— as one must realize shortly after picking up the book—that he is not actually interested in history but in his own mystical philosophy. For instance, he writes,

"The kingdom of heaven is the postsolid, evolutionary planes, and from the postsolid planes can be reached only by and through the violent sun period."[27] No one at all familiar with the common Jewish expression "kingdom of heaven" in Jesus' day would find anything in common with Graham's distortion of the term.

Graham claims that "Nicodemus" stands for "Neco-demon—matter and the devil"[28]—never mind that Nicodemus is elsewhere attested as a real name in Jerusalem in New Testament times.[29] (Further, the actual etymology has nothing to do with "matter" and the "devil," but with "victory" and "people"; had the writer simply consulted the Greek text on which he pontificates, he would have seen that the Greek word for "demon"—*daimonion*—is spelled quite differently from *dēmos,* "people.")

For Graham, Christ is just "a personification of the Planetary Logos,"[30] and everyone will be saved with planetary salvation.[31] Such wanton allegorizing of texts characterized not only pagan Greek philosophers but also some Alexandrian Christian writers—allowing them to justify slavery and other ideas prevalent in their culture, contrary to the more "literal" interpreters of Scripture like John Chrysostom. Allegorical interpretation permits one to read into any text what one already believes anyway, with no regard for the point of the text. Using this method, Graham reads an occult metaphysical system into the Bible—thereby totally wrenching the Bible from its historical context.

Conclusion

The fact that someone can write a book does not mean he or she has actually done solid research. Unfortunately, some readers may read only books like his and believe them without testing their claims. As our culture continues to drift in the direction of believing what is convenient rather than seeking what is true, such views may become increasingly common. But popularity is not a healthy test for truth.

We could examine other popular challenges to Christianity circulating today as well, but for now those we have covered here must remain sufficient as a sample. We could also pursue in some detail archaeological and literary sources that help to support the likely accuracy of many passages of the Bible. But because such an examination would extend this book beyond its appropriate length, we have provided only a brief sample of the kinds of responses we would give to common objections to Christian faith.

Now we turn to the two remaining issues this book must address: Is the Gospel portrait of Jesus reliable? And does it really matter? Or more specifically, is Jesus the only way to an eternally sufficient relationship with God?

8

Are the Gospels Really True?

Most of the challenges to Christianity surveyed in previous chapters question the authenticity of the Gospels. This skepticism is an important foundation for their attack on Christianity, because the most central claim of the Christian faith is the identity and mission of Jesus Christ.

Many people today like to make Jesus in their own image, as even the past century of scholarship makes clear. Yet modern reconstructions of Jesus that reject biblical evidence can at best be guesses, for they ignore the only solid evidence about Jesus we still have. The first generations of Christians preserved information about Jesus that would otherwise be inaccessible to us today.

Even if modern guesses that reject the Bible are doomed to be wrong, can we be sure that the biblical writers were right? How reliable was their witness?

In previous chapters we responded to objections to the claims of Christianity. Here we make an argument for the most central claims of the Christian message. Not everything associated with Christendom has much to do with Jesus, but true faith in Jesus must rise or fall on Jesus' identity and mission. Because Craig has documented some of the arguments in this chapter in greater detail in a forthcoming commentary on Matthew for Eerdmans,[1] we are including here the less academic (and more readable) version of his research, which he has often circulated among college students struggling with these issues and which may someday be available in booklet form. These final two chapters are especially Craig's work, hence written in the first person by him, but Glenn and Craig fully agree on their contents.[2]

When Scholars Fudge

Many professors at liberal elite universities today regard faith and reason as incompatible. Unaware of how thoroughly their own views have been shaped by certain philosophical fashions now prevalent in Western intellectualism, most have never given the evidence for the gospel a fair hearing. Indeed, in personal debates with professors at various institutions, I have found some of them unwilling to consider any reasoned arguments; instead they insist from the start that genuine evidence for any religious faith is impossible.

I can well understand the intellectual climate in which such professors move, for I myself was once an atheist, and I had little exposure to the content of the Bible before I became a Christian. Although the lack of commitment of most professing Christians kept me from taking the Christian faith very seriously, I wondered occasionally whether there was historical evidence for what Christians said about Jesus. After I became a Christian, my interest in such questions continued, and I pursued academic studies that eventually culminated in a Ph.D. in New Testament and Christian origins from Duke University. (I should note here that my views are my own, and not all my professors or colleagues shared them. This in no way diminishes my respect for their scholarship.)

I have found that there is in fact considerable genuine evidence for the most important Christian claims—too much evidence even to survey in a chapter like this one. The goal of this chapter is thus not to "prove" the whole Christian faith; our intention is much more modest. What I hope to accomplish here is to demonstrate convincingly the accuracy of the *central* claims of the Christian faith, focusing on Jesus' resurrection and the substantial reliability of most of the Gospel accounts. While I believe that a case can be made for much more, Jesus' resurrection and the basic reliability of the Gospel tradition are by themselves sufficient to call academic agnosticism into question and to call forth a decision for faith in the Lord Jesus Christ.

In the academy, all views on a subject must be seriously entertained and then critically evaluated. Unfortunately, all too often the historic Christian position has simply been rejected out of hand, usually by skeptics whose motives go deeper than philosophical presuppositions against Christianity. I suspect that many intellectuals' objections resemble the objection I once raised: most professing Christians do not appear to be intellectually honest or articulate about their faith, and most of them do not even believe it enough to live according to Jesus' teachings. I hope that true thinkers will, however, be willing to go beyond what is intellectually fashionable and consider whether Jesus himself might not be more real than the lives of some of his purported followers. I hope also that the lives and testimony of those of us who are *genuinely* his followers may count as a counterargument to those in the past and present who have abused or owned lightly his name.

The Gospels as Historical Documents

While working on my doctorate I heard a religion teacher tell his undergraduates, "The Gospels are clearly not biographies." He was both right and wrong. He was right that they were not written the way we write biographies today;[3] he was wrong in that they fit the general characteristics of ancient biography.

This teacher was not simply behind on his reading; he was a good scholar and must have known that the trend among scholars today is to see the Gospels as ancient biography.[4] Thus I have sometimes wondered if he told his students only one side of the issue because, as he plainly shared with others of us in private, the texts demand a style of living that he found offensive. Though very knowledgeable in his discipline, he had a personal reason to talk his undergraduates out of accepting the Gospel texts as very historically reliable.

Other professors have different ways of disputing the Bible's authority, although most of them are probably not driven by the same agenda as that professor. (Many have simply not been exposed to scholarly arguments contrary to the positions their graduate programs espoused, and many graduate programs and universities are still imbued with secular antisupernaturalism.)

How ancient people wrote biographies. In my first graduate course on Mark, the professor began his lecture by informing us that (1) Mark is ancient biography; (2) ancient biographies were fictional; (3) Mark is therefore fictional. Wishing to be polite, and afraid that the professor knew some information that I had not yet learned, I waited till after class to challenge his claim.

"I know some ancient biographers, like Livy and Plutarch, spiced up their biographies quite a bit and depended on legends when they wrote of characters from centuries before their time," I conceded at the outset. "But other biographers like Tacitus and Suetonius were far more dependable and wrote of events much closer to their time. Suetonius, in fact, follows his sources almost too slavishly and uncritically, rather than being very creative. So there seems to be a wide range between very accurate biographers like Tacitus and less accurate biographers like Livy. But even the least reliable biographers saw their task as mainly historical and often depended on sources that we can confirm independently. Biographies were not novels—that was a separate literary category in antiquity. It seems to me that even the most spicy biographers used sources they regarded as dependable and did not fabricate major events."

"I don't know," the teacher responded without batting an eye. "I don't know anything about ancient biography."

Apparently knowing little about the subject firsthand, this professor had taken his position from a book another New Testament critic had written. Simply borrowing someone else's view on a subject is always a dangerous method of determining truth, because given how often ideas are overturned in academic circles, material that one does not know firsthand may well later turn out to have been completely misinterpreted.

I quickly discovered that the New Testament scholars most acquainted with ancient biography, like David Aune, Richard Burridge, Graham Stanton and Charles Talbert, did not agree with my professor's conclusions. The general consensus among current scholars who have written on the subject confirms what I had discovered in my firsthand analysis of ancient documents: the Gospels are ancient biography, and ancient biography was at the least *basically* historical.[5]

But this by itself does not prove that the Gospels are historically true. Saying that ancient biographers intended to communicate history (though often in a lively way) is not the same thing as saying that they always accomplished their intention. Many ancient biographies, especially those concerning heroes of the distant past, are riddled with legends and rumors.[6] While some biographies were less than accurate, however, it is undisputed that others were based on contemporary sources and discuss recent history. The Roman historian Tacitus, for instance, often used the imperial annals in his histories, and he focused on relatively recent history, the century and a half before his time. Although his biography of his father-in-law Agricola is intended to praise the man, it is widely accepted as historically accurate. Such biographies of more recent figures are much more substantially reliable than biographies about characters of the distant past.

Where do the Gospels fit in this continuum between somewhat historically accurate and very historically accurate? To answer that question the way a neutral historian would (neither embracing nor hostile to Christian claims or the possibility of supernatural phenomena), one must ask what sources the Gospels used and *how* they used these sources. First, the Gospels depend on recent sources, just like Tacitus and Suetonius do. Second, we can evaluate how the Gospel writers used their sources. The sources used by most ancient writers are no longer available for our inspection, but two of the Gospels present us with a very different situation: one of the sources used by Luke and Matthew still exists, and we can reconstruct another of their sources from points at which they overlap. When we compare Luke and Matthew with their sources, we find that they used sources far more carefully than most ancient writers did.[7] By this measure, they were among the *most* historically accurate of ancient writers; Luke in particular appears to reflect a special interest in such accuracy.

The sources of the Gospels. When the Gospels were first written, their authors were not submitting them to be considered for inclusion in the Bible! Each writer composed his work separately, addressing the story of Jesus to a different audience with different concerns. Stories about Jesus had been told and retold in the early church, but some people had started writing them down. Other writers could check their own work against what those before them had written; some, though not all, of these Gospels were preserved by the church over the years and ended up in our New Testament.

Before continuing, I should add a warning: these early Jewish-Christian sources should not be confused with the apocryphal and Gnostic Gospels of the second century, which are based on later tradition, reflect a very different cultural environment, often (in the case of apocryphal Gospels) betray novelistic features in contrast to the style of the earlier extant Gospels, and are generally not historically reliable. The Gnostic Gospels betray Gnostic elements which identify them as second-century or later, in contrast to our canonical Gospels, whose sayings and actions of Jesus regularly reflect Aramaic figures of speech and Palestinian Jewish teaching methods and customs.[8] The Gnostic and most apocryphal Gospels are not even the same literary form as the Gospels we have in the Bible, so the use of the title *Gospels* for both is unfortunate.[9] That is why we cannot depend, as some do, on such "lost" works to reconstruct Jesus' life.

But the existence of some fairly accurate written stories about Jesus from the first generation or two after his ministry is clear from the introduction to Luke's Gospel. It was customary for an ancient historian to open his history with a historical prologue in the most stylish and educated Greek prose; Luke follows this practice in Luke 1:1-4. Historians often dedicated the work to their patron, or sponsor, who supported them in literary endeavors; Luke follows this practice when he dedicates the book to his sponsor Theophilus (a common name, especially among Jewish people living outside Judea) in

1:3-4. Most important for our purposes, Luke follows the common practice of beginning by explaining the reason for his writing, and establishes not only his historical purpose but also his historiographic methodology.

1. Written sources for the Gospels. Luke explains that others have written before him, and that they wrote concerning matters of public knowledge in the early Christian community: "since many have set about to put together an account about those matters which took place among us . . ." (Lk 1:1).[10] Most scholars are convinced that one of the earlier sources used by Matthew and Luke is our present Gospel of Mark, for the substance of all but about fifty verses of Mark occurs also either in Luke or in Matthew. Luke and Matthew freely adapt Mark's wording, but rarely his substance; Luke even follows Mark's sequence with only two exceptions, even though this was not expected in ancient biography. If Luke and Matthew use their other sources as carefully as they use Mark, they are clearly preserving, not creating, stories about Jesus. Can we check how carefully they used any of their other sources?

Even where they are not using Mark, Luke and Matthew often overlap, sometimes even in quotations and the sequence of events. For convenience's sake this source they share in common has been designated "Q." Though not all scholars agree that all of Q actually belongs to a single source, oral or written, the exact nature of Q is less important for our study than the fact that Luke and Matthew follow their common material closely by ancient standards.[11] Where it is clear that Luke and Matthew are both using Q, their substantial agreement with one another indicates again the credibility of their work as ancient historians.

So while the Gospel writers may not follow the conventions of modern historians, they certainly are among the more dependable of *ancient* historians. Ancient historical writers provide the primary sources for modern writers on ancient history; why should the Gospels be trusted any less?

2. Oral sources. But Luke was not solely dependent on written sources; he had oral sources as well. The events reported in the written documents were also "handed down by those who were eyewitnesses and ministers of the message from the very start of the matter" (Lk 1:2). In other words, he depended on oral reports that go back to the time of the events themselves.

Jesus was a Jewish teacher with Jewish disciples. Disciples, whatever their prior occupation, were disciples especially because they memorized the words of their teacher and imitated his actions, sometimes taking notes to aid in their memorization.[12] Memorization of famous teachers' sayings characterized education throughout the Greek and Roman world, and students of particular teachers were expected to circulate their sayings and pass them down to other disciples if they themselves became teachers.[13] Jewish disciples had perfected the art to its highest form, because of the great respect they had for their teachers and the central place teachers had in Jewish life in Palestine.[14]

In the ancient Mediterranean world, people collected sayings of famous teachers.[15] Over generations new sayings were sometimes added to these collections, but for the reasons mentioned above, the collections were quite dependable for the first two or three generations. Students could paraphrase the teacher in their own words, but were expected to accurately preserve and transmit their teacher's meanings.[16] Again, Jewish disciples became teachers in their own right by transmitting their own master's teachings; innovation occurred, but it was always secondary to preservation, and it tended to happen only long after the teacher's decease (usually in later generations).[17]

Luke uses a technical term here for the passing down of such tradition; eyewitnesses had "handed down" the narrative and sayings of Jesus to his own generation of Christians. Of course, it makes good sense that the early Christians would have transmitted Jesus' teachings carefully; it is difficult to imagine why the earliest church would be more likely to impose its own spontaneously composed views on one they called Lord than to seek to faithfully propagate his views. Why should we assume that Jesus' disciples radically departed from their Master's teachings yet retained him as a figure of honor, when we would not say that for other disciples in that period?[18]

We may compare this careful passing on of tradition with oral traditions in cultures that emphasize such concern. In some cultures, a storyteller can repeatedly relate a story several hours in length, without changing any details; or he or she can vary details, then return to the original form in the next telling. One may compare the activity of the African griot, who could relate hundreds of years of village history in great detail, entirely from memory.[19] Alex Haley in his book *Roots* notes how such details were often confirmable from written historical sources originating in Europe. Although oral memorization has become a lost art in our age of television, many other cultures are still quite familiar with it.

Some scholars doubt that the teachings and deeds of Jesus would have been transmitted accurately to the time of the Gospels. But Mark is usually dated before 70 C.E., and Q is probably earlier;[20] Luke was aware of a number of other written Gospels by his own time. This means that Gospels started being written down within three and a half decades of the events described— while most eyewitnesses were still alive to verify or reject the validity of their claims. The eyewitnesses could likewise serve as a check on one another's accuracy; for at least two decades after the events, in fact, an entire group of eyewitnesses remained in Jerusalem at the head of the Jerusalem church, along with James, who had grown up with Jesus (Gal 1:19; 2:9-12; compare Acts 21:18; 1 Cor 15:7).

Everything we know about the early church also suggests that the eyewitnesses remained in positions of prominence as repositories of the tradition, and could have therefore exercised a restraining influence on those who wished to change the tradition. Even churches the eyewitnesses had never visited knew of and respected them (as in 1 Cor 1:12). Further, despite all the early church's divisions over cultural and theological issues (like circumcision for Gentiles), it was united on the essentials of the life and teachings of Jesus; no detractors on this issue register themselves in the pages of indisputably first-century Christian literature.[21]

Consider a parallel today. Those of us in our twenties, late teens and early thirties would not remember much of the civil rights movement firsthand (I was born in 1960, so I should remember a little more than I do). Yet most of us have friends or relatives who participated in the marches and witnessed firsthand the events we now read about in history books. The memory of those events has not died in three and a half decades. There may be slightly different versions based on different perspectives, but the outlines of the story remain the same. Those who are older than we are may remember many of the details firsthand. Why would we think memory was any *shorter* in the first century, especially in a culture where oral traditions were memorized and passed on in the very kind of circle Jesus founded (disciples)?

By the time the eyewitnesses died, it would be too late for those in their shadows to make up radically different traditions about Jesus. By that time there were already too many people who knew the original stories about Jesus. Secular Roman history informs us that in the year 64, the Roman emperor Nero began burning Christians alive to light his imperial gardens at night;[22] he fed other Christians to wild beasts. To provide torches for large gardens night after night, all night long, and to be killing other Christians in various ways should have required thousands of Christians, and it is certain that Nero did not capture all the Christians of his day. Writings from Roman Christians over the next few decades make it clear that the Roman church remained strong despite the martyrdom of many of its members. This means that the Christian faith had spread so rapidly (under persecution and without force of arms) that three and a half decades after the events narrated in the Gospels, believers numbered in the several thousands even in the very heart of the Roman Empire.

The formative period of early Christianity occurred while the eyewitnesses were still alive and respected. By the time the eyewitnesses and the apostolic circle died, a large church throughout the cities of the Roman Empire already had an established tradition. Those who made up later stories that did not measure up well against what was already known would have to contend with the suspicion of most of the rest of the church (a situation that actually arose with the Gnostics in the second century).

Paul's greetings to Christians he knew in churches throughout the Empire also remind us of the cosmopolitan nature of early Christianity. Outside Palestine, it was especially an urban movement, and Christian travelers from city to city spread news quickly, networking the various churches.

3. Careful investigation. Luke does not stop at telling us that written and oral sources were widely circulated by his day; he adds that he has "checked it all out from start to finish" so he can write his account for Theophilus "accurately and systematically" (Lk 1:3). Luke could have consulted eyewitnesses still alive in his day and may have known some eyewitnesses well.[23]

There is in fact evidence that Luke did have direct access to eyewitness sources, even in Jerusalem itself. Luke wrote both the Gospel of Luke and the Acts of the Apostles, which served as volumes of a two-part history of earliest Christianity. Scholars call certain sections of Acts the "we-narrative," because Luke counts himself among the traveling companions of Paul with the word *we.*

Two attempts have been made to argue that this "we" in Acts does not mean "we" (that is, that Luke does not include himself in it). First, some scholars have pointed out that the term *we* appears in fictional narratives;[24] this use, however, should come as no surprise, since fiction usually employed the same vocabulary that history did, and hundreds of other words are shared by both. *We* appears in historical narratives no less, and only historical works, not novels, had historical prologues as Luke has.[25] The fiction view is thus usually rejected.

Another way of denying that the *we* includes Luke is more commonly accepted. On this view, Luke is simply using someone else's earlier travel journal.[26] The travel journal itself is extremely precise: the number of days he reports from one port to the next is exactly the number of days it would take for a boat in his time to make those ports under the weather conditions he describes, and the titles of local officials, which in his day varied from city to city and sometimes from decade to decade, are exactly correct. Clearly the travel narrative is reliable and reflects the experience of someone who traveled with Paul as he was planting churches. (No matter how skeptical a modern reader may be, it is impossible to deny that those churches got there somehow!)

Reliable though the travel journal seems, many scholars think the writer of Acts used someone else's travel journal rather than his own. This is very unlikely, however, when one considers Luke's typical style. Luke writes some of the most polished Greek in the New Testament, and he puts his sources in Acts into his own words so thoroughly that we normally cannot distinguish different sources there.[27] If this is the case in the rest of Acts, it would be remarkable if he left the *we* of someone else's travel journal in his narrative without changing it to *they*. Yet the *we* leaves off in one city as Paul moves on (Acts 16:12-18) and picks up there again after Paul returns (Acts 20:1-6; Philippi was in Macedonia).

While Luke probably did use a travel diary, it was probably not someone else's that had just fallen into his hands. The evidence instead points to the way most people would naturally read the text if no one had taught them to read it otherwise: Luke traveled with Paul, and the travel diary is his own.

If the author of Luke and Acts traveled with Paul in the "we" sections, he traveled with him to Jerusalem (Acts 21:15). On the way there he met a disciple who had been in the faith for many years (Acts 21:16), and, more important, he met with all the remaining leaders of the Jerusalem church (Acts 21:17-18). That the author is still with Paul when he sails for Italy two years later (Acts 27:1) may suggest that Luke had plenty of time to do his research in Palestine. His research undoubtedly includes some material that he could not have gotten from merely Mark or Q; although Matthew also reports the virgin birth, Luke emphasizes very different details and undoubtedly has a special source distinct from Matthew's. When we realize that he probably spent time with James in Jerusalem (Acts 21:18), this makes good sense; James was Jesus' younger brother and must have known the full story of Jesus' birth from their mother, Mary. Luke did significant firsthand research.

4. Luke's claims must be true. Luke finally tells Theophilus that he has simply been confirming the things Theophilus has already been taught (Lk 1:4). Luke had no way of knowing that we would still be reading his Gospel nineteen hundred years later; he did not write this line simply to fool twentieth- or twenty-first-century readers! Luke wrote to his patron, the sponsor who financially supported the publication of his writing project. Luke thus could not have told him that his account confirmed what Theophilus had learned if his account did not in fact conform to what was already being taught in the early church.

Suppose I wrote a letter to someone who had never been my student, saying,

"Hey, remember the first time you took my class?" The person would conclude that I was mistaken, demented or worse. Nor would I write a totally fabricated account of the civil rights movement to someone who knew much about that movement, and then say, "See, this confirms what you already knew." Luke is too brilliant a writer in other respects to be such a fool in this one!

One encounters similar claims to shared knowledge in Paul's letters. We may observe this in four letters of Paul that no modern scholar, conservative or liberal, disputes that he wrote: Romans, 1 and 2 Corinthians, and Galatians.[28] In two of these letters Paul mentions that healings and miracles occur regularly among his readers (1 Cor 12:10, 28, in a list fashioned for the situation in Corinth; Gal 3:5). Both of these letters address churches where he had worked and knew his readers. In another letter Paul speaks of miracles wrought through himself (Rom 15:19), and in yet another letter he appeals to his readers' eyewitness experience of plenty of miracles worked through him (2 Cor 12:12). It would make no sense to appeal to readers to confirm a claim that they would know to be false—namely, their knowledge of an event of which they know nothing!

Christians were not the only first-century people who claimed to work miracles, but they were the only people we know about, apart from attendants at special healing shrines, who believed they experienced them on such a massive scale. Although most ancient people believed in miracles and deities (they were more open-minded on such issues than are some contemporary intellectuals), the miracles were largely restricted to special temples or a few traveling wonder-workers. Such activities in local congregations thus set the early Christians apart, and among some of their opponents, including many rabbis and the pagan philosopher Celsus, Christians came to be known for such miracleworking.[29] (That non-Christian supernatural phenomena also occur and are reported in most societies is not objectionable on Christian presuppositions. Christian teaching makes mention of other spirits or supernatural forces in the world besides God. Reports of cures at pagan healing sanctuaries, some of which are credible, are more a problem for complete secularists than they are for Christians. Further, that some phenomena are humanly contrived does not bring all evidence for such phenomena into automatic disrepute.[30])

These insights invite us to treat Luke and other early Christian writers as useful sources about Jesus and early Christianity. Luke's meticulous travel journal very likely indicates that he went to the places he says. His appeal to Theophilus's prior knowledge indicates that he did not just make up his account. The excellent character of Luke's Greek also suggests that he was intelligent enough to know exactly what he was doing. His careful and meticulous dependence on sources where he can be checked confirms that this was Luke's normal way of writing. In short, the modern historians of Rome who have called Luke "a historian of the first rank" are quite right.

A Specific Case: The Resurrection

Those who presuppose that the Gospels are unreliable have constructed systems to explain the data—systems so complex that it is not possible to engage every one of their arguments in our brief treatment here; some issues must be debated passage by passage through the Gospels. But it is fair to point out that the Gospels themselves provide explanations that are simpler and no less reasonable than these suggestions of scholars who mistrust them—as long as one does not start with the premise that the miraculous is impossible.

Of all that the Gospels claim for Jesus, the most central and climactic claim is the resurrection. Because this was the central historical affirmation of the early Christians, the Christian faith stands or falls on this claim more than on any other particular claim in the Gospels. The proof or disproof of the resurrection constitutes the proof or disproof of the historical claim on which the apostolic faith was founded. Because it is also the most clearly miraculous of all miraculous claims in the Gospels, it is also the ideal test case for the possibility of other miracles.[31]

Some critics complain that even eyewitness testimonies to the risen Christ are unreliable, because the eyewitnesses had a vested interest; they were, after all, Christians. To this we must offer three responses. First, the eyewitnesses had quite a large stake in not being mistaken on this matter: their testimony to Christ ultimately cost most of them their lives. Many people in history have died for falsehoods they believed to be true, but we have no examples of a large number of people, with no detractors, dying for something they *believed* to be false. Even dying for something in which people believe requires more than average conviction. At Jonestown, where Jim Jones had often forced his followers to perform suicide drills, autopsies attested that most victims did not die voluntarily when they realized that this was not just a drill. Some of Joseph Smith's handful of "eyewitnesses" to his golden plates later renounced Mormonism. Chuck Colson, involved in the Watergate scandal, testifies that he and Richard Nixon's other handpicked henchmen were intensely loyal to their president, but the moment they faced prison they confessed everything they could think of, betraying one another to reduce their own sentences.

If Jesus' disciples' preparedness to die for their testimony merely established that they *believed* that Jesus had risen, however, it would not be saying
much except that they were sincere. Plenty of people have believed claims
that are demonstrably wrong (for instance, followers of Jim Jones, or those
who inadvertently drink mislabeled poison). But Jesus' disciples believed
and testified more than just that Jesus was alive; they believed and testified
that they had *seen* him alive. To sincerely claim the former requires no
evidence; for so many witnesses to sincerely claim the latter summons us to
consider that they in fact saw something that convinced them beyond any
shadow of a doubt that Jesus was alive. The Gospels, Acts and Paul concur
in calling people to faith not based on a mere claim of someone else's faith,
but based on the claim of eyewitnesses.

The Gospels and Acts suggest that there were a considerable number of
eyewitnesses; Paul lists among the eyewitnesses over five hundred on a single
occasion, "of whom most are still alive, though some have passed away" (1
Cor 15:6). Such a statement virtually constitutes an invitation to his readers
to check him out; the witnesses were still available in his day, and the
accounts of witnesses remain today.[32]

I was present when a prominent historian who specializes in first-century
history, to whom I listened often and whom I have never heard claim a
particular religious commitment, admitted to a class that, as little as he liked
to say it, the resurrection was the only reasonable historical explanation he
knew for the faith of the first disciples.

What may be more remarkable is the absence of detractors as the first
disciples testified to the resurrection. Large numbers of disciples maintained
their intense conviction that they had seen Jesus alive from the dead, and they
were prepared to die for it. Given the cost involved, surely some should have
recanted their testimony, even if they believed it only partly true. Had any of
the witnesses retracted their testimony, we can be certain that Jewish and later
Roman sources would have exploited the recantation as evidence against the
Christian claim, forcing the Christians to respond. But for all their attacks on
Christianity, and for all the defense against such attacks in the New Testament, no evidence remains of even a single such detractor. This is strong
evidence of the early disciples' conviction of what they had seen.

But the objection that witnesses to the resurrection were biased because
they were Christians invites two other, briefer responses as well. First, it is
difficult to conceive of anyone seeing the risen Christ and not *becoming* a
Christian. But second, while all witnesses to the risen Christ were Christians

after the event, not all of them were Christians *before* the event. The most notable witness to the resurrection who was not a disciple at the time (James may be another example) is Paul.

Because Paul was persecuting Christians at the time, he knew exactly what he would suffer if he confessed Christ. Not only the book of Acts but Paul himself tells of his former persecution of Christians (1 Cor 15:9; Gal 1:13; Phil 3:6)—hardly something for a Christian to boast in if untrue, especially when he cites potential witnesses (as in Gal 1:23). Paul also appeals to his readers' knowledge of what he suffered for the sake of his testimony for Christ (for example, 1 Thess 2:2). Paul was advancing in status among his contemporaries before his conversion (Gal 1:14); he had everything to lose and nothing to gain by becoming a follower of Jesus—unless he genuinely believed that Jesus appeared to him.

In a letter that no one today disputes Paul wrote, Paul says that he was converted by an encounter with the risen Jesus Christ (Gal 1:12); he compares this encounter with the experiences earlier witnesses had (1 Cor 15:5-8). There are no parallel accounts in history in which entire groups of people on successive occasions experienced the same encounter, certainly not with one they believed to be a living person still in his body (albeit a "resurrection body"). Explanations based on mass hysteria are inadequate; there are simply no other cases in history of group visions supplemented by successive encounters by different people.[33]

But what does Jesus' "resurrection" mean? Although most first-century Jews, like other peoples, believed in some form of life immediately after death, they did not describe such afterlife as "resurrection." To Palestinian Jews, including Paul's predecessors (1 Cor 15:5-7), "resurrection" meant nothing other than bodily resurrection, the belief that God would provide new bodies for the righteous at the end of the age.[34] "Bodily" does not mean simple reanimation of a corpse, of course; but it does mean transformation and a continuation of corporal existence. (In both the Gospels and Paul, the resurrection body is different from the present body—which makes sense, if it is to be immortal. In 1 Corinthians 15 Paul compares the relation between the design of the future body and that of the present body to the relation of a fruit to the seed from which it came.) Plenty of other terms were available for claiming merely immortality, reincarnation and other concepts, but all our diverse sources from first-century Christians are unanimous in their affirmation that the Jesus they saw had been resurrected bodily.

Not everyone likes the idea that the disciples encountered a bodily resurrected Jesus. Some have suggested that the disciples just had a spiritual experience; but lots of people back then had spiritual experiences, and no one would have persecuted them for saying that they had one. Some would suggest that they saw a ghost; but belief in ghosts was widespread,[35] and no one would have persecuted the disciples for claiming that they saw a ghost either. Nor would at least some of the many eyewitnesses have been content to stake their lives on the certainty that Jesus was bodily alive from the dead without confirming that this was true, both in their encounters with him and by checking the grave.[36]

The Gospels mention the empty tomb, and it is incredible that early Christians would not have checked the site. Given the veneration for holy sites in antiquity, the first witnesses would not have been the only pilgrims to the site. Further, the moment Jesus' followers began claiming his resurrection, their opponents would have checked the tomb too, and silenced their objections by producing the body if they found one.

Those who complain that our extant Gospels are written over three decades after the event do not have to look far to find evidence closer to the date. The New Testament witness is unanimous in affirming the bodily resurrection of Jesus, beginning with our earliest New Testament document, 1 Thessalonians. Here Paul connects Jesus' resurrection with the future hope of believers, a hope rooted in the Old Testament and Judaism. His case is even more explicit in 1 Corinthians 15, where he argues at length for Christians' future resurrection on the basis of Jesus' resurrection as a foretaste of that event.[37] Like Jesus, Paul shared Judaism's expectation of a judgment day in the future, not just an immortality of the soul.[38]

The Reliability of the Texts

Some have argued that later writers may have tampered with the New Testament and adjusted it, but this is hardly a credible position. The New Testament is textually the best-attested work of Mediterranean antiquity, and it frequently differs from the position of the later Christians who transmitted it. Here we will briefly review the state of the manuscript evidence before turning to our next point.

Classical historians often depend heavily on sources that are attested in only a single manuscript or a handful of manuscripts, manuscripts that are often nine centuries older than the original on which they are ultimately based. The second-best documented work of antiquity was Homer's *Iliad,* with, at a recent count, 643 manuscripts. But for the New Testament documents we have *five thousand* Greek manuscripts, plus ten thousand manuscripts in early versions! In other words, the New Testament is by far the most widely documented work of Greco-Roman antiquity. The number of documents attests the interest of the copyists, not the accuracy of the contents, of course; but we have far more evidence to work with than historians of the rest of ancient Mediterranean literature.[39]

Many of these fifteen thousand manuscripts, like most copies of other ancient works, are late; but some are quite early. A case in point is a fragment of the Gospel of John from the early second century. Although many critical scholars in the nineteenth century tried to date John a century after the traditional date for John (in the 90s of the first century), our earliest fragment of John predates their estimate of the date of composition by a considerable margin. This fragment is from early-second-century Egypt, a site far from the place where the Gospel of John was written. Allowing a few decades for the Gospel to circulate that far from the place of its original audience (especially since it was probably intended for more local circulation than the other Gospels), the manuscript suggests that the Gospel itself can be no later than the 90s of the first century. This is when most conservative biblical scholars have always dated it, based on the traditions of the early church; most scholars of all persuasions now agree that this is when it should be dated. Not only this fragment but also many other manuscripts date to the two centuries immediately following the composition of the New Testament. By any count, it is the best-attested work of the ancient world.

Muslims boast that their holy book has been copied for centuries without even minor changes, and they charge that the same cannot be said for the Christian Bible. In one sense this charge concerning the Bible is true: the different manuscripts of the New Testament are not identical with one another (though many of the differences are merely spelling mistakes). But this is because the books that make up the New Testament, unlike the Qur'an, were not usually copied in royal courts. Indeed, the first copyists often worked under conditions of secrecy due to persecution, because early Christianity was not a religion of royalty or conquest but of the oppressed. Even so, the variations are minor, and scholars who specialize in studying the ancient texts agree on most of the text of the New Testament; the 1 percent of significant variation does not affect any major teaching of the New Testament.

To make precision in copying the criterion of authority is hardly a sound method of judgment anyway; one would only need to recopy the other holy book very badly to prove that point. Christians never claimed that later scribes were inspired in perfectly preserving the text, only that Jesus appointed disciples who would preserve the tradition while it was being written down. The text evidence we have is far more than sufficient to attest the contents; we know which passages constitute the roughly 1 percent that is both significant and in doubt.

What makes the Gospels special is not the care with which later generations treated them; the textual evidence for 99 percent of their basic contents is secure, and far less than that is needed to establish the truth of the Christian faith. What makes them special is not their spelling or even the exact wording on every page; what makes them special is the truth they attest. Their evidence for the life, teachings, death and resurrection of Jesus is based on eyewitness sources,[40] which predate the statements about Jesus found in the Qur'an (which at some points reflects traditions from local fifth- and sixth-century versions of Christian teaching!) by half a millennium. (As we noted in chapter six, from a historical perspective one would think the firsthand testimony of many witnesses to how the risen Jesus revealed himself and talked with them would count for more than the other holy book's comments about Jesus purportedly revealed to one individual. But to each his or her own.)

Since the textual evidence is better than that on which most of our history of the ancient world is based, the New Testament records should not be doubted on textual grounds any more than any other historical records from antiquity are. Indeed, like many of those other documents, they are abundantly corroborated by how well their details normally fit the exact times and places they describe (such as in Luke's travel diary, above).

Objections to Viewing the Gospels as Historically Accurate

1. The Gospels take sides. Some argue that because the Gospels have an agenda they are not genuine history, but this objection presupposes a narrow view of history that did not exist in the ancient world. Undertaking the biography of his father-in-law Agricola, Tacitus wrote to praise a man he greatly admired. But does this mean that Tacitus fabricated events in the life of his father-in-law? To the contrary, he respected his father-in-law because he respected the man's life; had he found that life so wanting that it required serious revision, it is doubtful that he would have written the biography to begin with. (By the time he wrote, Agricola was already deceased.) Tacitus's interest in his character influenced which information he included in the biography; but historians are widely agreed that the biography itself is historically dependable.

Further, agendas can determine the questions we ask without prejudicing the reliability of our answers to those questions. Women scholars' questions about women in the ancient world have led to new insights and corrections to earlier works because of the evidence they probed; while some writers have distorted historical evidence (such as for universal prehistoric matriarchy), they usually remain the exception rather than the rule.[41] Similarly, while some extreme forms of Afrocentrism have sometimes distorted the historical record (such as the claim that Africa birthed *every* good aspect of history or religion), the questions raised by Afrocentric scholars have led to a deeper probing of Africa's involvement in world history and greater recognition of Africa's achievements and the European biases that have sometimes filtered them out.

Agendas can be used rightly or wrongly, but to insist that a Christian agenda or focus of discussion *necessarily* distorts history is simply to betray one's own bias against Christianity. To say that one cannot take sides is to take a side against taking sides—that is, to absolutize relativism. To put it a different way, to affirm that objective study cannot lead us to objective conclusions is to bring into question the whole reason for doing objective study to begin with. To be truly objective, are we required to presuppose that all conclusions (such as those that might support claims about Jesus' identity and mission) are invalid? Is it necessary to presuppose that evidence adduced in favor of Christian claims must be false simply because so many of our secular academic colleagues believe that to be the case?

2. The Gospels are Christian evidence. Some people today object, "But all the evidence for Jesus comes from Christians!" One would naturally expect that those who accepted the reality of Jesus' claims would *become* Christians, whatever their views may have been previously. Nevertheless, the claim that all our evidence comes only from Christians is not quite true; some early Roman historians do mention Jesus.[42] But the Romans by and large were not concerned with Jesus in the beginning, and this should not surprise us. Even when they do mention Jesus, it is only in connection with Jesus' followers, whose rapid multiplication and un-Roman ways seemed to pose a threat to the Roman social order.[43]

Roman historians' disinterest in Jesus in the beginning makes good sense when we understand what they wrote about. Tacitus and Suetonius were concerned about politics in Rome and foreign wars; Palestine comes up only rarely in their writings, and other Jews in Palestine who claimed to be messiahs are *never* mentioned (though we know a little about them from the first-century Jewish historian Josephus). Josephus provides more than enough information on Herod the Great to fashion a respectable soap-opera miniseries, but the Roman historian Dio Cassius treats Judea's most famous ruler only in passing.[44] The only time Roman literature bothers to mention Pontius Pilate is when a Roman historian points out that Jesus was crucified while Pilate was governor of Judea; if it weren't for Jesus, Josephus and an inscription, nobody after the first century would have heard of Pilate.

It is disputed whether Josephus, the Jewish historian, genuinely says much about Jesus, but he certainly mentions both John the Baptist and James the leader of the Jerusalem church, both in a positive light. Ever careful in his writings not to portray the Jewish people as eager to follow messiahs, Josephus played down plenty of other messianic elements besides Jesus. But second-century Jewish sources (and probably also archaeological evidence) indicate that the Christian faith had spread widely in Jewish Palestine, little as Josephus may have wished to emphasize it.[45]

Further, both Jewish and Greco-Roman sources tell us about Christians (in connection with whom they finally do mention Jesus) when the writers see it as an issue to be confronted. Tacitus's account of Nero's persecution makes it clear that the movement had spread throughout most of the Roman Empire in less than four decades after Jesus' death and resurrection.[46] Jewish and pagan sources (the rabbis and Celsus) in the second century both admit that Christians were working notable miracles in their day, although they attribute these miracles to sorcery rather than to God. (The charge of sorcery could best be refuted by examining the content of Jesus' teaching and its continuity with that of the Old Testament prophets.) But this claim of Christian miracles brings us to the next modern objection raised against the claims of early Christianity.

3. Miracles. A more popular argument against the reliability of the Gospel narratives has to do with their accounts of miracles. Many denials of the reliability of the Gospels, including a number of the claims briefly treated above, are rooted in the Enlightenment philosophical premise that miracles cannot happen, so that other explanations must be found for the accounts in the Gospels. Sometimes the many scholars who hold the Gospels to be reliable are accused of compromising their objectivity because of faith; but the charge could actually be reversed against the many scholars who simply dismiss the early Christian records out of hand. Much of the secular academy is dominated by unspoken presuppositions such as the following:

☐ Objectivity means ruling out the claims of religion, or at least those of any particular religion.

☐ Evidence presented in favor of such claims, including miracles, is therefore distorted.

☐ Scholars who present such evidence are therefore not objective.

Given such presuppositions at work in the academic subculture, the pressures that shape professors and graduate students are hardly those of religious faith. Many colleagues and I have found those who will not even grant us a hearing far less objective than they view themselves to be![47]

Although many historians of antiquity now seek to read all ancient accounts of miracles (both Christian and non-Christian) without prejudice as to whether they actually happened, other scholars are not so gracious. Many follow in the footsteps of Rudolf Bultmann, who claimed that no person in modern society believes in miracles and the New Testament miracles must thus be interpreted simply as existential encounters if they are to retain their relevance to modern people.

One of my graduate professors followed Bultmann fully on this point, arguing that God would not act visibly in history. Having volunteered to do the assigned class presentation on Bultmann, I first rehearsed many of the positive contributions Bultmann had made to New Testament scholarship. Then I turned to my main objection to his logic. "Bultmann says that modern people do not believe in miracles, but he apparently defines the modern world only by his brand of a twentieth-century Western academic elite. Not only orthodox Jews, Christians and Muslims but also traditional tribal religionists, spiritists and virtually all cultures not shaped by Western rationalism or one of its most prominent heirs, atheistic Marxism, accept the existence of supernatural phenomena. So do I and many of the other graduate students in this room. Bultmann holds his view because he is ethnocentric"—what we would call a cultural bigot.

Perhaps that was not the nicest way to put it, but it did get the discussion going. "Bultmann has presuppositions," the teacher conceded, his voice rising, "but you've got your presuppositions too."

"You are right; I do," I admitted. "When I was an atheist, I presupposed that miracles by definition could not happen. Now that I am a Christian, I presuppose that they can. Yet an agnostic starting point—the 'objective' starting point appropriate in a secular academic context—does not decide whether miracles can happen before examining the evidence. Bultmann never offers a shred of evidence that miracles do not happen. Indeed, to seek to argue inductively that miracles never happen, he would have to examine all claims to miracles and show them to be false; and even then he would not have demonstrated that miracles *cannot* happen. This is simply a philosophical axiom with him, a presupposition he never tries to prove."

I knew that what I was about to say violated an unspoken rule of the academy. Our classroom discussion was normally restricted to historical evidence, but our discussions in this course repeatedly had been turning to philosophy and epistemology (the question of how one determines truth), so I felt justified in proceeding with a different line of argument, in this instance eyewitness evidence, instead.

"To argue that miracles do happen, however, all I have to do is provide sufficient eyewitness testimony from credible persons who claim to have seen them. I have seen people instantly healed in answer to my own believing prayer, including a cyst, failed kidneys and what had been prediagnosed as possible lung cancer. I myself have been instantly healed a number of times in answer to believing prayer, including a twisted ankle, flu as I was preparing to disgorge, and just-acquired mosquito bites instantly vanishing from my arm."

Of course academic discourse deals only in the realm of probability; but most of these cases lacked other rational explanations, unless one preferred to think that the kidneys, ankle and so on recovered psychosomatically at the exact moment the prayers were offered. That explanation would demand unproved trust in dramatic human mental powers; this would require no less faith than Christian or spiritist explanations for supernatural phenomena. (Such an explanation would be especially hard-pressed to account for something like the resurrection of Jesus!) But there was one way for the professor to get out of the situation, and I was ready for him to take that escape.

"Eyewitness testimony is a valid form of evidence," I offered, "so if you wish to challenge the existence of miracles, your next logical step is to challenge my credibility as an eyewitness."

The professor changed the subject. One up for the Bible thumpers!

The method of determining truth in science is repeated observation and experimentation, but we clearly cannot use this method to determine truth in history. Historians, somewhat like lawyers in a courtroom, must depend on eyewitnesses, reports based on eyewitness testimony, and artifacts. Few events of ancient history are as well documented as the resurrection of Jesus, yet this event is questioned on the basis of an unproved assumption pervasive in much of modern academia—the assumption that smart people must discount miracles and any God who claims to work them.

This assumption can become quite coercive. I confronted one professor, after he had scoffed for several hours at different lines of evidence without offering any refutation of them. "If someone were raised from the dead in front of you, would you believe?" I demanded.

"No," he replied.

"And you have the audacity to call *me* closed-minded?" I retorted. Presuppositions die much harder than evidence does.[48]

4. The demands of the gospel. One objection that is not really intellectually quantifiable is the cost involved in consistently believing that Jesus is the authoritative representative of God as the resurrection and Gospel narratives affirm him to be. As one student objected to me during a campus lecture: "Sure, I'd accept this evidence if it were just evidence for some war that happened in history. But what you're asking from me is a commitment of my life!"

The stakes are higher, and the criteria for evidence become more demanding, when the historical claim we investigate can have so much bearing on our lives. Whether Julius Caesar lived or died affects history, but it does not affect us personally as directly as the claim that Jesus rose from the dead and that his teachings are therefore divinely authoritative.

Perhaps that is one reason Jesus provided a kind of evidence that is no more empirically quantifiable than the objection, but concludes the quest of the seeking heart that mere probabilities could not settle. His teachings speak of another witness, the Holy Spirit, who speaks through the record of the human witnesses. The heart that is open to truth cannot go wrong in asking his guidance.

For Further Reading on the Bible and History

The interested reader may consult Keener 1993b for samples of biblical scholarship offered on a popular level yet informed by real examinations of the Bible in its historical setting. Books by scholars specifically addressing the Bible's reliability include Bruce 1980; Yamauchi 1972; Robinson 1977 (dramatically reversing his earlier views); Witherington 1995; Blomberg 1987; Barnett 1986; France 1986; Kitchen 1978. On a more advanced level on the Old Testament, the reader must consult Kitchen 1966 (an Egyptologist putting the Old Testament in context); LaSor, Hubbard and Bush 1996; Harrison 1969; plus works by writers like J. Bright and G. E. Wright. For the New Testament, readers should especially consult the following with their questions: L. Johnson 1986; Carson, Moo and Morris 1992; Guthrie 1970; Ladd 1974b. On the nature of the Gospels as biography, see Aune 1987; for a more detailed treatment of many Gospel questions, see *Gospel Perspectives,* 6 vols. (Sheffield, U.K.: JSOT Press, 1980-1986); for an up-to-date survey of contemporary Jesus scholarship, see Witherington 1995.

9

Why Does It Matter?

After we have argued that Jesus is who the Gospels claim, some may respond, "So what?" In more precise terms, does recognizing Jesus as our rightful Lord necessarily demand that people abandon long-standing alternatives to Jesus? Even if Jesus is the rightful Lord, must one follow him to be accepted by him?

Because we live in an increasingly relativistic society where "anything goes," one of the biggest objections Christians face is the offensiveness of our "exclusivist" faith—that is, we affirm that Jesus is the only rightful Lord and Savior of humanity.[1] This affirmation of biblical Christianity is so offensive to modern society that this chapter may invite dismissal from some who affirm that all religions are equally true—all religions except, of course, the majority of religions which affirm that they are in some sense more true than other religions. Thus some may find value in other parts of the book yet dismiss this chapter out of hand because we argue—as do adherents of all historic monotheistic religions—that some truth claims are incompatible with others. Nevertheless, we hope to address the biblical Christian view for those who share our conviction that the apostolic message about Jesus is true. And we are so convinced that this affirmation remains central to the Christian faith that we are prepared to endure any opposition as we defend our right to maintain it. This is not to say that we expect those who are not Christians to share our view; it is to say that those who on other grounds affirm Christianity as true should likewise maintain this central premise of the Christian faith.

Relativism Challenges Many Faiths

Relativism—the belief that all views are equally valid—poses problems not only for Christians but for many other faith groups as well, and ultimately for relativists themselves (as we will suggest below).[2]

Talking with a Muslim friend, a physician from Egypt, I would never have guessed that his primary religious document teaches that one should slay polytheists who do not submit to Islamic conquest: "Then, when the sacred months have passed, slay the idolaters wherever ye find them."[3] I never would have guessed that his holy book teaches that even Christians and Jews must be fought until they offer tribute[4] and that Muslims should thus not be friends with Christians or Jews.[5] Our conversations did not remind me that under *Shari'a* (traditional Islamic law) a Muslim who recants (rejects Islam) and persists in apostasy is to be sentenced to death (following the *Hadith Al-Bukhari,* which cites Muhammad as commanding: "Kill him if he changes his religion").

In fact, I doubt that these random passages in the Qur'an or early Muslim traditions were prominent in my friend's mind when we talked. He considered himself a true Muslim, but also "progressive" and tolerant. My Muslim friend had undoubtedly grappled with the tension between the exclusive truth claims of his faith and the paradox of living in a society where many "good" people—religiously devoted people with hearts for compassion and justice— were non-Muslims. Perhaps he did believe, as some passages in the Qur'an could be understood, that non-Muslims go to hell;[6] perhaps he had more hope for me as one of the "people of the book," a God-fearing Christian. Whatever his theological view, our dialogue on Christianity and Islam remained cordial and intriguing. He was more eager to show the common ground between our two faiths (of which there was much) than the differences; I, in the same way, learned of his faith and tried to express my commitment to Christ in culturally relevant terms he could understand.

Tolerance Versus Relativism

The potential tension between our friendship and some teachings in my friend's holy book is the same sort of tension that Christians must face daily in secular America—the sort of tension that ancient Jews faced in Babylon and the early Christians faced in the Roman Empire.[7] We live in a world of conflicting, sometimes hostile, beliefs; we have no desire to compromise Christ's lordship or our faithfulness to his teachings, yet we do not wish to be offensive to people we care about.

The importance of tolerance. For the sake of avoiding offense, those who affirm and those who deny specific beliefs often avoid raising the subject in the others' presence. This means, of course, that we expect from others intolerance rather than dialogue; our experience has taught us that the public definition of "tolerance" too often means simply not expressing a view toward which others might prove intolerant. Thus most Blacks do not discuss their feelings about racism fully with Whites, Christians do not share much of their faith with non-Christians, and so forth.

Genuine tolerance is an important virtue, and those who practice the Christian ethic of love and accept the Christian doctrine of human moral responsibility must observe this virtue. Indeed, it often proves easier to talk with a friend of another faith who respects faith in general than with a Christian who defines the boundaries of orthodoxy so narrowly on secondary issues (like the mode of baptism, details about the end times or church order) that their overriding agenda is to convert us to their particular brand of Christianity.

Holding minority beliefs. But how does tolerance relate to "exclusive" beliefs that claim, "I believe I have something *true* to offer on this point," although most people disagree? Theoretically, it is easy enough for us to say, "I will tolerate and respect everyone, but also love them enough to tell them about Jesus." After all, the God who sent his Son to die for us but never forces us to accept him does not want us to coerce people into accepting Christ; at the same time, people are not genuinely exercising their right to accept or reject Christ until we have exercised our right to offer them the opportunity to hear about him.

But while Christians can distinguish between tolerance and evangelism easily enough, the outside world often cannot. Identifying tolerance with a relinquishment of convictions, outsiders often bristle when we claim to believe something that is true but unpopular.

"Truth" is not, however, determined by a majority vote; nor can one harmonize all conflicting claims about beliefs. Anyone who claims to have religious truth will hold some views offensive to others. Claiming that Muhammad is the greatest prophet offends non-Muslims; claiming that Jesus is the only true Savior and rightful Lord offends non-Christians; claiming that all religions are of equal value offends members of religions who affirm their faith to be unique;[8] claiming that no one can have religious truth (or have more of it than someone else) will offend adherents of most religions; and so forth. In other words, you cannot avoid offending someone without avoiding religion altogether—and that will offend some people too. But the very reason discussions about religion can become so heated is that religion addresses a universal human need for the transcendent, which means that religion is too important to simply ignore.

The issue of whether trust in Jesus is the only way to be made right with God is essential today for two reasons. First, it is important because if Jesus is the only way, there is nothing more important for us to do than to let all people know about him in the most constructive ways possible. Second, it is important because it is a natural issue of debate in a pluralistic society; to claim that any one view is "right" is to risk offending people who hold to other views.

Are All Religions the Same?
If "all religions are the same," as some people think, it would be arrogant of us to challenge the religiously sanctioned, racist caste system of a particular society, to argue against the practice of holy war and slavery apparently sanctioned by another religion's holy book, to warn people to avoid religious figures like Jim Jones or David Koresh, or, for that matter, to prefer one interpretation of any verse in the Bible to another interpretation. The moment any person claimed to believe any given view, that view would become correct. Such a position is absurd enough by itself; but even if it were not, anyone who actually compares the central beliefs of various religions will recognize that for all that many of them have in common, they are simply not all the same.[9] One claims that Jesus is God's Son; another claims that God has no Son. One claims that there is only one God, who made all things; another accepts many gods; still another says in effect that all things are God. Most religions oppose human sacrifice, but some religions in history have thought their deities demanded just this. Most religions claim matters like monotheism or the character of the deity or deities as part of their essence, so redefining such religions to make them alike actually disrespects the beliefs of those religions themselves. Religions *cannot* all be the same!

Once when I was discussing religion with a Taoist friend, he declared that he had no trouble believing that Christianity is true. "All religions are true," he explained.

"But if all religions are true, does that include those religions that claim to be the only true religion and reject all other gods as false?" I countered.

"Yes," he replied, undisturbed by the seeming discrepancy in his position. "Everything is true."

"If I say that something is false, is my statement that something is false a true statement?" I pressed, hoping to change his mind.

"Yes," he insisted; "everything is both true and false."

"That's not consistent," I laughed.

"I don't have to be consistent," he retorted. "Consistency is part of Western logic." In truth, consistency is not solely the domain of Western logic, as if *all* propositions were equally true and false. As Indian Christian philosopher Ravi Zacharias puts it, even in non-Western societies "people look both ways before crossing the street."

But Western logic is no longer as "consistent" as it once was, either; it has taken on an inconsistency of its own. In the name of "tolerance"—something good—we have abandoned any pursuit of "truth," regarding truth as unknowable and therefore irrelevant. We have absolutized relativism to the point that we accept anything as true unless it claims to be true—in which case, we reason, it is false.[10] Society often refuses to tolerate the "intolerant"—and *intolerant* has largely become a code word for those who hold minority convictions, no matter how graciously they may hold them.

On a deeper level, then, our culture's position is far more troubling than that of my Taoist friend. For us, everything in religious matters is equally "true" only because nothing in such matters is true in particular; religion, unlike science, is believed to make only statements that cannot be proved or falsified. If I tell you, "Don't drink that fluid; it's poisonous," you may be grateful; if I tell you, "Don't believe that cultic teaching; it's harmful," you may well be offended.

Of all people, Christians who follow Jesus' teachings should love those with whom they disagree. We should never ridicule others, and we should defend their right to hold and share their views (including the view of another religion that it is the only way), as we defend our own right to do the same. Yet loving people does not require us to relinquish our convictions or to affirm relativism.

Once I joined a friend of mine, a former Buddhist who had become Greek Orthodox, and we visited another friend's New Age group. My Orthodox friend and I politely disagreed with the others present, but our New Age friend, one of the gentlest and kindest people I knew, provided a telling illustration of relativism taken to its logical conclusion. After the New Age friend affirmed that evil does not exist, my Orthodox friend demanded whether the man thought that Hitler's murder of six million Jews was evil. "Maybe he had a reason for what he did," the New Age friend responded with chilling sincerity.

Most people would not take relativism as far as this friend did. Interestingly, relativism is rarely consistent; those who deny the existence of absolute truth are nevertheless often willing to call Christians "wrong" for affirming it. One man on Flatbush Avenue in Brooklyn threatened my life because I refused to back down from my conviction that Jesus is the only way of salvation!

What Does "Christianity" Teach?

The ancient Israelites were in a similar predicament when they declared that there is only one true God (Deut 6:4). Although they did not deny the existence of other spiritual beings in the universe, they denied that such beings are gods worthy of worship, arguing instead that all beings were created by the God they worshiped. Worshiping other gods, even if they continued to worship the true God as well, was not acceptable (2 Kings 1:3-4; 17:28-34). Once the Jewish people were scattered among the nations, they were often viewed as intolerant and were sometimes persecuted for their views by more "tolerant" majorities. When Christians began to announce Jesus as the one way to this one God, they merely compounded the offense; both people who believed in many gods and people who believed in other ways to the one true God were offended.

In our brief treatment of the issue, we hope first to survey some of the teachings of Jesus' earliest witnesses, on whose testimony the Christian faith is based. The witness of the New Testament is that, in a time when it was very dangerous to hold such views, Jesus' followers saw him as the only way of salvation and understood this position as basic to the gospel they preached. What was taught by those who knew Jesus' teachings firsthand is very relevant to the question, for if the very heart of their message about Jesus is to be abandoned today, the lordship of Jesus himself (hence the very basis of the Christian faith) must be equally in question. Second, we will examine some of the questions the early Christians' position can raise in our minds about God's justice and compassion. And finally, we will discuss the implications of this study for our lives as Christians today.

It should be noted that the subject of this chapter is *not* whether there is truth in different religions. Truth can be found in varying degrees in many places, including in documents used by various religions. The issue is not where some truth may be found, but by what means a person can be restored to full fellowship with God.

Nor is the issue whether we should cooperate on points of common concern with people who do not share our faith. Joseph honored the religious customs of Egypt, even though they were not the customs of his God (Gen 41:45; 47:21-22). Paul likewise had friends who were Asiarchs (Acts 19:31), officials who by virtue of their social status may have served the imperial cult, even though Christians were later persecuted for refusing to submit to the decrees of that cult.

Nor is the issue whether Christianity is true. Our question is, assuming that Christianity is true (as argued in the preceding chapter), What does Christianity teach? The issue here is whether the Christian faith truly claims that Jesus is the only way to be fully reconciled to God.

Many today claim to follow Jesus and the first witnesses who reported his teachings, yet reject those teachings. But if the core of Christian faith is the death and resurrection of Jesus as the basis for salvation, then those who reject that teaching should at least be clear about what they do or do not believe. They may accept some Christian teaching and even the title "Christian," but they should honestly admit that in their desire to tolerate (or to be tolerated), they reject one of the central beliefs of Jesus' earliest followers.

Conversely, if we accept Jesus as Lord, his lordship has every right to inconvenience us, even to challenge our prior belief system. If the unanimous witness of those who knew him best attests that he is the only way, this witness is decisive for those who acknowledge his rule over everything else in their lives. Faithfulness to Jesus' lordship requires accepting his teaching; if we choose to reject his teaching because we believe it is wrong, we may be sincere and hold some very religious convictions, but we should also be honest enough not to call Jesus the Lord of our faith.

Some may complain that we are drawing the boundaries of the Christian faith too narrowly, but we believe that these boundaries were from the beginning part of the apostolic faith and that we have no choice but to retain them if we are Christ's followers. For "Christian" to mean anything at all, Christ's lordship must be nonnegotiable. And if Christ himself demands that his followers acknowledge him as the only way to the Father, his lordship demands that we embrace this claim.

The New Testament Evidence

Entire books have been devoted to the early Christian reports of Jesus' teachings about himself; here we will attempt only to survey some of the relevant passages. (We responded briefly in the previous chapter to the objection of some people that we cannot really know what Jesus taught.) But if Jesus expected us to follow his teaching, and if the only remains of his teaching are those preserved by his first-century followers, all we have to go on is what we find in the New Testament. The teachings of Jesus' earliest followers therefore give us a better idea of what following him means than anything else could.

To avoid the charge that we are taking any of these passages out of context, we discuss them within their context, in the books of the Bible in which they occur. For the sake of space, we will sample three primary sets of data: Paul's letters, John's writings and the writings of Luke (together these three sets of data make up about two-thirds of the New Testament). Luke's writings reflect sources much earlier than Luke (Lk 1:1-4), as we argued in chapter eight and as the discerning reader may notice from the parallel references we have sometimes provided from Mark and Matthew.

Paul's Letters

Paul's surviving letters were all written between about two and three and a half decades after Jesus' resurrection and are our earliest witness to the views of many of Jesus' earliest followers. Despite his tenderness (1 Thess 2:7),[11] Paul was never embarrassed about his faith (2:5).[12] Confident that Jesus is the true Lord of humanity, he was more than ready to accept opposition for his view (2:2).[13] In Thessalonica, Paul had been persecuted for calling on his hearers to turn from idols to the true and living God (1 Thess 1:4-10), but he still limits the future hope to those who are "in Jesus" (4:14, 16).[14]

Two letters where Paul is particularly explicit about his convictions concerning the necessity of faith in Christ are Romans and Galatians, letters that concentrate on the issue of the right way to be reconciled to God. Romans was written to a racially and culturally divided church in Rome; Paul admonishes Jewish and Gentile (non-Jewish) Christians there that they have both come to God on the same terms and therefore must embrace one another as equal partners in the work of Christ. Galatians was written to churches that were being influenced by a form of Christianity that required something more than Christ for a person to be completely right with God. Although Paul states his case clearly elsewhere as well, his position is roughly the same in other passages, so we will examine only these two letters in detail.

Romans. Although the meaning of various isolated verses in Romans has been debated,[15] their sense in the flow of Paul's whole argument is difficult to dispute. Paul begins his argument like this: Gentiles worship false gods (generally true in his day), but they should have known better; God has provided enough evidence in the world for anyone to figure out what he is really like (Rom 1:18-23). Here Paul adapts an argument that had been used by many philosophers in his day (especially the Stoics)[16] and had already been taken over by many Jewish thinkers trying to explain Judaism to Gentiles.[17] Paul goes on to condemn sexual sin, which Jewish people regarded as a particularly Gentile vice (Rom 1:24-27), and then lists sins that were recognized as universal to humanity (1:28-32).

Very few readers in the Roman church would have disagreed with Paul's argument in Romans 1:19-32: the "pagans," unconverted Gentiles, are damned. While Jewish thinkers differed on whether all unconverted Gentiles were lost,[18] they all agreed that idol worshipers and sexually immoral persons—and they believed nearly all Gentiles fell into these categories— were lost.[19] Gentiles who converted to Judaism or Christianity similarly took a dim view of their preconversion lifestyle. Paul's argument in the first chapter of Romans would not have been particularly controversial.

But Romans 1 is a setup for Romans 2, where Paul argues that even the most religious Jewish people are damned as well (2:1-11).[20] Whether the sins are inward or outward, everyone sins (vv. 17-25); and whether people are condemned by the written law they have broken or only by the testimony of God's standards in their heart,[21] everyone has sinned (vv. 12-16; the latter also "perish," v. 12).[22] He allows that someone who does good without sinning will be saved (vv. 7, 10), but he ultimately believes this is possible only for those who have already received the Spirit (v. 29)—that is, believers in Jesus (8:9-10).

In case anyone fails to figure out Paul's point, he spells it out by quoting the Bible in Romans 3: everyone has sinned, and is therefore in need of God's forgiveness (vv. 10-23). If all this sounds unpleasant, we must remember that the point of Paul's argument is not to merely conclude that everyone is damned but to remind us that God provides salvation from sin for everyone on the same terms, since everyone was equally damned already.

Thus Paul's argument becomes more focused in following chapters. Jewish people usually believed that they were predestined, or chosen, in Abraham, and that this guaranteed their salvation.[23] They also celebrated the law as a special gift to Israel.[24] But Paul takes on each of these issues (Abraham, chapter 4; the law, chapters 7 and 10; and predestination, chapter 9) and argues that these points really proclaim salvation to those who trust in Jesus, not to anyone on the basis of his or her ethnic or religious status.[25] Whereas Jewish people celebrated their descent from Abraham, Paul reminds his readers of another Jewish teaching: everyone was descended from Adam, whether they were Jewish or Gentile.[26] But just as one person's sin introduced sin to all humanity, one person's righteousness—that of Jesus Christ—introduced salvation to all who are baptized into him (5:12—6:11).

Paul reminds the Gentiles to respect Judaism, including the Judaism of Jewish people who do not believe in Jesus (11:16-24; cf. 3:2; 9:1-5). But in the same passage he is emphatic that only those Jewish people who believe in Jesus are genuinely saved (11:5-10, 14, 20-23; cf. 8:29-30; 9:6—10:21), and only by turning to Jesus will his people as a whole be saved in the end time (11:11-16, 23-32).[27] Paul is not picking on Judaism here; indeed, he portrays faith in Jesus as the truest form of the Jewish faith rather than its antithesis, and observes that Gentiles who become believers in Jesus are spiritually grafted into the Jewish faith.[28] But he is reminding his readers that everyone comes to God on the same terms, through Jesus. This is part of the good news of Christ (11:30-32).

Galatians. If Paul's language is plain in Romans, it is much stronger in Galatians. Here Paul is addressing a group of Jewish Christians who believed that Gentiles must be circumcised to be full Christians.[29] Paul's opponents clearly believed that they were Christians who adhered to the part of the Bible God had already given; circumcision was the seal of the covenant, and Gentiles who wanted to be part of God's people had to join the covenant the way Gentiles always had joined it (Gen 17:9-14). True, Abraham had been justified by faith many years before his circumcision, while still considered a Gentile (Gen 15:6). But did not all Jewish people acknowledge that Abraham entered the covenant and became "a Jew" (in the later sense) only when he was physically circumcised? The position of Paul's opponents must have made perfect sense to them; undoubtedly it made equally good sense to most of the Christians in Galatia.

But Paul is not convinced; indeed, following the rhetorical style of his day for a corrective letter, he assumes an angry tone, alternately harsh and entreating.[30] He responds forcefully that if there had been any other way of salvation God would not have sent his Son Jesus to die for us (Gal 2:21). Paul regards certain aspects of the covenant as specifically intended for the Jewish people, cultural arrangements that should not be confused with the saving gospel. He argues his case in the best Jewish form of his day, laying Scripture against Scripture and one biblical principle against another.

Jewish people believed that they were saved by God's grace in the covenant, but participants in the covenant naturally kept the law.[31] Gentiles who wanted to enter the covenant, however, had not been raised with the law as a part of their culture, so that converting to Judaism could entail a long process of assimilating the details of Jewish culture. The problem was that the literal stipulations of the law were directed to a specific people and culture, whereas the covenant, as far as salvation was concerned, was kept by faith in the most recent saving act of God, as in the case of Abraham (chapter 3).

For Paul, the ultimate marker of God's work in a person's life is a seal far more significant than circumcision; it is the presence of the Spirit received through faith in Christ (3:2-5; 4:6, 29; 5:5, 16-25; 6:8). His opponents were afraid of the opposition they would receive if they relaxed the standards of their mission board and proclaimed Christ alone (4:29; 5:11; 6:12), the only One who can truly transform people to live a new way from the heart (2:15-20). But Paul will not tolerate any compromise of the spiritual equality of all believers in Christ; ethnic or cultural segregation is contrary to the gospel (2:11-14). Paul's opponents undoubtedly would have protested, "We too believe that people are saved through faith in Christ." But because they added requirements that did not flow naturally from faith in Christ,[32] they were misleading young Christians (3:1) and were to be cast out of the Christian community (4:30). So vehement is Paul in his opposition to Christians who add requirements to the gospel that he suggests they have rejected the truth of the gospel (5:4) and ought to mutilate themselves instead of other people (5:12).[33]

In Galatians, Paul is arguing specifically against claims of salvation based on the law of God—that is, on something that is true. How much more would he reject claims of salvation based on what he regarded as false, such as idolatry (1 Cor 10:20)? And Paul's insistence on the truth of the gospel is not directed only against "pagans" and non-Christian Jews. His opponents in Galatia clearly believed that they were Christians themselves. Elsewhere Paul warns Christians that they must not reject the teaching of the future resurrection of the righteous, since it is integrally connected with the resurrection of Jesus on which their faith was based. "And if Jesus was not raised," he warns, "your very faith is worthless" (see 1 Cor 15:14). From Paul's perspective, it is quite possible to accept a "false Jesus," a "false Spirit" (2 Cor 11:4) and a "false gospel" (Gal 1:6-11). For Paul, even a Christian label does not guarantee that someone is genuinely saved; a non-Christian label certainly guarantees that someone is not.

Examples from Paul's letters could be multiplied, but the point should be clear by now: Paul believed that a person must be committed to Jesus to be saved, and no substitutes—even professedly "Christian" substitutes—are adequate.

The Gospel and letters of John. Christians readers today often celebrate the portrait of the divine Christ they find in the Fourth Gospel. One of the most frequently memorized passages is John 3:16-17: "For in this way God loved the world: he gave his only Son, so whoever trusts him would not perish, but have the life of the coming world. For God did not send his Son into the world to condemn the world, but to save the world through him." Yet this implies what John also declares in the very next verse (3:18): "Whoever trusts him is not condemned, but whoever does not trust like this has already been condemned, for this person has not trusted the name of God's only Son." In other words, Jesus had to come to save us, precisely because all of us were lost. As Jesus tells a great religious teacher earlier in the passage, "Unless a person is born anew, that person will not see God's kingdom" (3:3).[34] Receiving Jesus is like beginning a new life; and beginning that new life is a necessary prerequisite to being with God forever.

Another favorite text in this Gospel is John 14:6: "Jesus replied, 'I am the way and the truth and the life. No one comes to the Father but through Me.' " The implications for our discussion, of course, are obvious: Jesus came to reveal the Father (14:7), and no one can personally know the Father any other way.

Yet not only these verses but the whole Gospel makes precisely this point: even all other truth, minus Jesus, is not enough to bring salvation. John was writing his Gospel for a specific purpose. According to most scholars specializing in the study of this Gospel today, John wanted to encourage Jewish Christians who had been thrown out of their local synagogues by leaders who claimed the right to define what all Jewish people should believe. These leaders wanted to exclude Jewish Christians from the Jewish community for their faith in Jesus.[35] According to what I consider the most likely understanding of John's Gospel, John responds by ironically conceding the title "Jews" to the opposing leaders of Jesus' day; yet his whole Gospel argues that it is not these leaders but rather Jesus' Jewish Christian followers who really follow the truth that biblical Judaism proclaims.[36]

Two thousand years later, when Christians outnumber Jewish people, John's words can easily strike us as harsh; Hitler and others exploited John's words out of their original context in an anti-Jewish way,[37] just as Aryan supremacists twisted later Jewish traditions against Judaism. But we need to remember that John was addressing his fellow Jewish Christians, a perse-cuted minority expelled from their own synagogues by a powerful faction within the Jewish community of his day. Had he written in our day he undoubtedly would have worded his Gospel differently (starting, for one thing, by not writing it in Koine Greek). But saying something gently (or saying it more clearly for a different group of readers) is hardly the same thing as not saying it at all.

John's language would be clear whether or not we knew the situation he addresses. He plainly divides humanity into two camps: followers of Jesus and "the world." Although the Jewish community was divided in its response to Jesus, and most of it was not nearly as hostile as its most negative representatives in the book (7:43; 9:16; 10:19), those who were not Jesus' disciples remained with "the world," on the "other" side (1:10-13; 3:1-5; 12:42-48; 15:18-25). The local synagogue officials who opposed the Jewish Christians were not at odds with John on everything. They agreed that Gentiles should not worship idols and that everyone should behave morally, and they believed in the authority of the law of Moses. But both John and his opponents regarded the issue on which they disagreed—the identity of Jesus—as a matter of spiritual life and death. In other words, the dividing line for both John and his opponents was not whether someone had some truth but where he or she stood in regard to Jesus, who is the truth (14:6).

But to reason as if John merely addressed the boundaries between Chris-tians and non-Christian Judaism misses his broader point: John calls the opposition "the world" precisely because it is much broader than the power-ful leaders troubling his own audience. For John and the Christian community that followed his teaching, even people who believe that they are *Christians* but do not believe in Jesus in the right way (1 Jn 4:2-3; 2 Jn 7-11; cf. Rev 2:14-16, 20-23) are in trouble. One has to believe in Jesus, and one has to believe in him in the right way, accepting him as both Christ and Lord. Salvation is available to everyone, but only those who truly embrace it in Christ will be saved (1 Jn 2:2, 19-25).

Luke-Acts. Luke and Acts were written by one author as two volumes of the same work. Luke's message is often described as "universalistic" be-cause, like many New Testament writers, he repeatedly emphasizes that God's purpose and plan is for all peoples (e.g., Acts 1:8).[38]

But Luke is also the author who reports that Peter claimed Christ as the only way of salvation. When a lame man was healed by Jesus' name, Peter quoted the Old Testament and announced, "Salvation is available by no one else, for there is no other name under heaven provided for human beings by which we must be saved" (Acts 4:12). Peter was proclaiming this message to the supreme religious authorities of his day, boldly telling them that they, as well as other people, were unsaved and needed to acknowledge Christ to be made right with God.

Like Matthew (as in Mt 4:17-22; 5:10-11; 8:19-22; 10:37-39; 16:21-27) and Mark (Mk 1:15-20; 8:31-38; 10:29), Luke reports Jesus' calls to followers to place him above all other commitments (Lk 6:22; 9:57-62; 10:39-42; 12:8-9; 14:26-35). As in the Old Testament prophets, mere religion is not enough (Lk 11:39-44; 16:15; Mt 23; Mk 12:38-40). Rejecting Jesus and his message is tantamount to rejecting the Father (Lk 9:48; 10:16; Mt 10:40; Mk 9:37; 12:6-9), and those who oppose the Spirit's miraculous testimony to Jesus' deeds are in grave spiritual danger (cf. Mt 12:22-45; Mk 3:22-30). Some hearers are, however, nearer or farther to the kingdom than others are (cf. Mk 12:34).

More to the point (since not everyone in the world has had the opportunity to reject Jesus), only those who understand and *accept* his teaching about the kingdom will persevere for salvation (Lk 8:10-15; Mt 13:17 23, 30, 37-43; Mk 4:11-20). Luke presumably shares with Matthew Jesus' view that the sheep of Israel are lost (Mt 10:6; cf. Is 53:6; Jer 50:6) since Jewish people who do not believe in Jesus, in contrast to even Gentiles who do, are in danger of damnation (Lk 13:28-30; Mt 8:10-12). Nor are professed Christians safe: one Christ to follow is not as good as another (Lk 21:8; Mt 24:4-5, 22-24; Mk 13:5-6, 20-22); it thus makes a difference in whom one believes. Jesus is judge (Lk 13:24-27; 19:12-27; 21:36; Mt 7:21-23; 25:31-46; cf. Lk 7:48-50; 12:36-48; Mk 2:10; 13:26-27, 35) and Lord (Lk 6:5, 46; 13:24-27; 17:5-10; Mt 1:23; 7:21; 18:20; 28:18-20; Mk 2:28; 11:3; 12:36-37); he is also the One who would die for all people (Mt 20:28; Mk 10:45) and the new Passover sacrifice of which all must partake to participate in the new covenant and receive forgiveness of sin (Lk 22:20; 24:47; Mt 26:27-28; Mk 14:24-25).

Luke further shares with Matthew Jesus' claim that cities will be judged strictly according to their response to him (Lk 9:5; 10:10-16; 19:40-44; Mt 10:11-15; 11:20-24; 23:36-39; Mk 6:10-11) and that people could know the Father only through Jesus (Lk 10:22; Mt 11:27). Most of all, Jesus' words are the only eternal foundation on which we can safely build (Lk 6:46-49; Mt 7:24-29); the gate to salvation is narrow, and few actually find it (Lk 13:23-24; Mt 7:13-14). Although Jesus' contemporaries offered many positive ideas concerning his identity, only one position was adequate, and following him accordingly was necessary for eternal salvation (Lk 9:18-26; Mt 16:13-27; Mk 8:27-38).

In the book of Acts, Luke reports Paul's impatience with Jewish hearers who rejected the gospel; he declared that they had rejected eternal life (Acts 13:46-47). He also reports that Paul demanded that Gentiles repent, whether they were farmers (14:15) or philosophers (17:30). After Paul had developed an argument in which he identified many points of contact with his Stoic hearers (17:18, 22-29),[39] he concluded that they must repent and acknowledge the truth of Jesus (17:30-31). Although Paul's method alienated some people (13:45, 50; 17:32), it was the only effective way to ensure that some people would be saved (13:48; 17:34).

Luke's Gospel stresses his concern for the socially oppressed classes of his day, and Acts shows his concern for all peoples. But the concern is not shown by denying the universal problem of humanity's need; it is shown instead by stressing Christ as the necessary solution to that universal need.

Summarizing the New Testament evidence. The New Testament writers often emphasize the absolute supremacy of Christ as God's supreme revelation, from Paul (1 Cor 1:30; 8:5-6; Col 1:15-18) to John (Jn 1:1-18) to Hebrews (Heb 1:1-4) to the early material scholars often call "Q" (Mt 11:25-27; Lk 10:21-22). The New Testament provides a wide variety of models of salvation. In various passages people can

☐ be justified by *faith* in Jesus

☐ be born again

☐ pass from death to life, or darkness to light

☐ be delivered from sin, the cosmic powers or punishment

Fully embracing Christ's salvation and lordship may involve a process, but unless one imagines the existence of a spiritual purgatory, these images all suggest a point of transition from a life away from Christ to a life submitted to him. Such turning to Christ was always central in the apostolic teaching of the gospel, as if God offers salvation in Christ and demands a human response (for example, Acts 4:11-12; 13:38-41; 17:30-31).

Although our survey of the evidence above was necessarily brief, it all points in a single direction: the earliest witnesses of Jesus believed that he was God's Son sent to reconcile the world to himself, and they did not believe that God had another plan if the Jesus method failed. (Most proposed objections to this view are based on isolated verses that, in context, say that God provides salvation for all—but not that all necessarily accept it—or that representatives from all peoples will be saved. But all these verses occur in books of the New Testament that plainly teach that only those who trust in Christ will be saved.)

According to the apostolic Christian view, humanity is in sin and can be reconciled to God only through faith in Jesus. To deny this is to contest the basis of the Christian faith—the absolute necessity of Jesus' coming, death and resurrection. While someone may choose to contest the Christian faith, it is important that they be quite clear that they are doing so; well-meaning *Christians* ought not to feel free to disregard the teachings of Jesus and those he appointed to spread his message.

What surprises me is not that my non-Christian friends would deny that Jesus is the only way of salvation; I would be surprised instead if they affirmed it yet remained non-Christians. But I marvel at how many Christians today are confused on the issue.

Christ, Not Culture

It may also be noted from the above evidence that most of the first Christians were Jewish. The New Testament writers did not require anyone to sacrifice his or her culture as a whole—least of all their fellow Jews, whose culture was permeated with biblical revelation. People were required only to surrender their sins. From the biblical Christian perspective, one can maintain most of one's cultural heritage, be it Jewish, Islamic or other, so long as one follows Jesus. I have friends of other faiths and enjoy the cultural experience of sharing with many of them in their places of worship (I especially feel at home in a synagogue reciting Hebrew with my Jewish friends). Yet for all the truth and sincerity of those practicing other religions, no religion can forgive people's sins and bring them into a personal relationship with God.

When I claim that no religion can forgive sin, I include "Christianity" itself in that category. Christian religion cannot save any more than any other religion can; millions of people claim to be Christians yet have no relationship with the risen Christ.

The issue is not merely a religious one, and it is certainly not a cultural one. The issue is whether someone by faith truly embraces Christ's forgiveness and his lordship. God did not provide a religion to save people; he did, however, provide his Son, because nothing other than his own Son's blood could bring us back to himself.

We emphasize that our claim is about Jesus, not about cultural Christianity, which quite often has little to do with Jesus. This distinction is significant, because sometimes when we talk about Jesus' being the only way to fully restored fellowship with God, people suppose we mean imposing a "Christian culture" on other people. Some values are part of the Christian faith—for example, love, sexual fidelity and devotion to justice for others. But particular styles of music, dress, architecture, language and so on merely reflect cultural traditions, few of which have anything to do with Scripture.

Following Jesus is, in fact, best done in culturally relevant ways. If an Arab follower of Jesus uses prayer rugs, if a Jewish follower of Jesus recites a Hebrew blessing over Shabbat candles, if a White American Christian attends a church with a steeple, if a Black American preacher perfects a traditional rhythm or cadence, all the better—so long as we do not identify our cultural form of following Jesus with following Jesus and impose it on Christians of other cultures.[40]

But appreciating and promoting cultural sensitivity does not mean that we cannot speak of Christ in relevant ways to those whose cultures currently predispose them not to appreciate him. Although we value cultural sensitivity, no one believes that any culture's values trumps all ethical norms. For example, some Hutus or Tutsis may have condoned genocide against the other people, but the world not directly involved regarded these acts as morally wrong. For the most part, people merely differ over which kinds of norms take precedence over others (consider the contemporary debate over whether a particular operation is a culturally relevant "female circumcision" or, as we Americans usually hold, an oppressive "genital mutilation").[41]

Many simply do not consider the claims of Christ true enough and/or important enough to warrant their taking precedence over a particular culture's traditional rejection of Christ's lordship. We urge those who might accuse us of cultural insensitivity because we maintain a particular view to be straightforward: they too maintain some particular views, and it is primarily our *view*, not our cultural sensitivity, to which they ultimately object. If they are straightforward, we can dialogue about our differences instead of being silenced by a stereotype. Because we affirm with apostolic Christianity that Jesus is the world's Savior, we affirm that the need for faith in Jesus matters more than the need to avoid offending a non-Christian by mentioning him.

Some people say that Christians (or members of other faiths) are arrogant to claim that we have "the truth." This charge against Christianity usually presupposes, against the evidence we presented in the last chapter, that Christians do not possess the most significant salvific truth. Nevertheless, Christians sometimes *can* have an arrogant attitude. Even while affirming that Jesus is true, we must remember that no human understands all the truth about God (1 Cor 13:9). Further, since truth about Jesus is given rather than earned, it cannot be a cause for boasting against others. The apostolic gospel teaches that God cares about and provided Jesus for all humanity. That is why it is next to impossible to genuinely believe that gospel and not be committed to making it available to all people in the world.

New Testament Evidence Reconsidered

If in all texts that are clear Jesus and his followers taught that he was the only way to a saving relationship with the Father, we can reject Jesus as the only way only by one of two responses. If Jesus is not the only way, then either (1) Jesus was wrong, and therefore we reject his teaching on this point (and so deny him as rightful Lord over some central details of our faith) or (2) his *true* teaching, for which the Bible gives us no clear evidence, coincidentally happens to agree with our view rather than that of those who reported his words (that is, we know we are right and Jesus would therefore agree with us).

But the proclamation of the apostles Jesus appointed focuses on Jesus' death and resurrection; would God have sent his Son to die if there were another way (Gal 2:21)? Is not Jesus' being the only rightful Lord and Savior at the very heart of the Christian gospel? Did not the apostles call all people to repentance, without assuming that some were already saved without Christ?

Essentially, Christ as the only way of salvation is at the heart of his witnesses' teaching. Someone who denies this belief may thus be sincere but should not confuse his or her own views with those of Jesus. The person who denies Jesus as the only way should be honest enough to admit that on a central point his or her religion is not the same as that which our only evidence suggests was proclaimed by Jesus and his first followers.

As noted above, such a denial is to be expected of those who are not Jesus' followers, and we are not offended when our Muslim or other non-Christian friends disagree. This denial should not, however, be expected among Christians.

Questions That This Discussion Raises

This chapter is not meant to address the issue of whether Christianity is true (the argument of the preceding chapter). Rather, this chapter is meant to address how we should respond *if* the Christianity of Jesus and his disciples is true.

Nor is the issue here how we would make up the rules for Christianity if we were allowed to invent them ourselves. Many people use religion to fortify what they already want to believe anyway; but if our goal is instead to find truth and shape our lives accordingly, we must acknowledge at the beginning of our quest that what we find will not always be pleasant. It would be more comfortable to believe that much of the world is not starving and we are therefore not called to do anything about starvation; unfortunately, that is not true. It is better to know what is true so we can do something about it, rather than just believing what we would like to believe. Politely warning someone of an uncomfortable but urgent divine truth is no different from warning someone that the temperature is rising if his or her building is on fire.

Below we offer a brief treatment of the logic of the case for Jesus' being the only way. But the question by its nature cannot be addressed merely on the level of cold logic; nearly all of us deeply care about many people who are not Christians, and many of us care deeply and pray for groups of people who have never heard the message of Jesus in an intelligible way. Despite the way we usually put it, it is more our sense of compassion than our sense of justice that is generally offended by the exclusiveness of Christ; we consequently hope to address both issues briefly below.

What About People Who Have Never Heard?

The urgency of a message that claims to be the only adequate way to God is that everyone must be properly informed as quickly as possible. If all people start off alienated from God and need to be reconciled to him in Christ—the whole reason that Christ came—then those who have never heard must hear, at whatever cost to us.

God's justice. One question the exclusiveness of Christ often raises has to do with God's fairness, since not everyone in the world has a chance to hear about Jesus. But the question actually risks missing the real point of this teaching, which is based on the whole notion of a just God who punishes sins according to an absolute standard of what is right. His justice is the last thing the exclusiveness of Christ could call into question!

First of all, the apostolic message was that all of us as sinners deserved to be punished; we had chosen our alienation from whatever God we had known. People who do not hear about Jesus are certainly not condemned for rejecting him; they are condemned, as we all were, for their own sins. By mere justice, God did not have to provide salvation for any who disobeyed him; it was his love that drove him to provide salvation for us.

Second, even though God, to be just, need not have provided salvation for anyone, he actually did provide it for everyone anyway. Nor did he simply decide to provide this salvation arbitrarily, by unjustly ignoring our sins; satisfying his justice, he executed the sentence rightly due us on Jesus instead. In other words, God provided salvation, and he did it at the price of his own Son's death. No one will be able to complain on the day of judgment that God did not go to the utmost lengths to restore us to himself, even though he was under no moral obligation to do so.

Third, God provided a way for everyone to *hear* about Jesus, too: he sent us to tell them. If God's people fail to tell them (whether because we love material or social advancement in our own land too much, or because it is too much sacrifice to go to people who have never heard, or simply because it never occurred to us, despite Jesus' command in the Bible), it is not God who is unfair to those people—it is we who are unfair.

Someone will object at this point, "But how could God allow anyone's hearing his gospel to hinge on the obedience of fallible human beings?" The answer lies in the curse side of the gift of choice. God does not force anyone to accept him; he gives us a choice when we are confronted with the gospel. His love is not coercive; if it were, we would not be thinking, volitional beings made in his image, but mere puppets on a string. But just as God does not force those who hear him to accept him, he does not force those who know him to proclaim him to others. The entire New Testament is clear that we must let everyone know about Jesus; various witnesses attest that this was his final command to his church (Mt 28:18-20; Lk 24:47-49; Jn 20:21-23; Acts 1:8). But the church does not always obey Jesus' commands.

Suffering for others' disobedience? One may object that it is unfair for some to suffer because of others' disobedience, and this objection has a great deal of merit. Clearly, it is *not* fair; but saying that it is unfair does not need to imply that it is untrue, nor does it necessarily lay the responsibility for the injustice at God's feet. (Blaming God for injustice is a difficult philosophical issue in any case, because that approach presupposes a standard of justice higher than God's character, though all human systems of justice are to some degree culturally defined.)

Whether we like it or not, the corporate effects of sin and guilt—some people's suffering because of other people's sin—is inescapably part of the reality of our world. Some people's sin keeps other people hungry, oppressed, segregated in ghettos and so on. Just as people starve to death through our disobedience as stewards of material resources, people die without the gospel because of our disobedience as stewards of spiritual resources.

Will God discipline his disobedient servants for such sins? If even half of the Bible is true, we'd better believe he will! Should we work to change this situation both socially and spiritually? If we claim to be on God's side, we clearly must!

And yet this situation does not call God's justice and compassion into question; for justice did not demand that God save anyone, and the cross declares the infinite nature of his compassion. The only complication is that, as persuasive as God can be, he refuses to coerce us against our will.

I often used to visit an agnostic friend named John, who has since given up his agnosticism. The conversation would always begin with John arguing that Christianity was not intellectually credible, and with me giving a reasoned defense of the Christian faith. The conversation would always end with John admitting that Christianity was not only reasonable but demonstrably true, that he just did not want to give up his sins and that he was being entirely inconsistent and illogical for acting this way.

But one day John hit me with an uncomfortable question. "If God provided Jesus as the way of salvation, then what about all those Hindus, Muslims and Buddhists in the world who never heard of Jesus?"

The question was not put entirely accurately; Muslims hear something about Jesus in the Qur'an, and a friend from a particular part of the Middle East tells me that folk Islam in some parts of the world calls on Jesus for healing because people learned that they are more likely to get healed that way than by calling on anyone else. (I suspect God is trying to tell them something, and probably in many cases is getting through.[42]) But John's point was still well taken; most Muslims, like many nominal Christians and most Hindus and Buddhists, have never heard and understood the Christian teaching about Christ's salvation. Yet the Holy Spirit quickly prompted me with the appropriate answer for John.

"John, you don't care about those Muslims, Hindus and Buddhists. You're just using them as an excuse to justify living the way you want to live. If you really cared about them, you'd get off your duff, commit your life to Christ and go tell them about Jesus, because you already know that Jesus is the truth."

John groaned, conceding my point. "You're right," he admitted. "I just don't want to give up my sin." That was how our discussions usually ended.

Degrees of judgment. But not everyone is like John. Some people have a legitimate struggle with the concept of people who have never heard being lost. Even if it is *fair* for God to allow all of us to be lost, many people would rather we all be robots than for God to allow us a choice that most of us will make wrongly. God gave us choice, however, for the sake of those who would choose rightly, even if many would choose against him. Everyone, whether they hear the good news or not, has something of an opportunity to reach out for God; it is only that some people get more of a choice to make than others.

Not all people are judged the same, although all people are judged. It is true that it is harder for some people to come to God than it is for others; that injustice is part of the world corrupted by human sin in which we live. It is also true that it is harder for some people not to murder or sell drugs because of the settings in which they are raised, and God will surely take such factors into account on the day of judgment. But the inequity of opportunity does not totally negate our moral responsibility for the choices we make. Two persons who choose to commit murder may not be *equally* responsible; but both are guilty.

The Bible does teach that those who know the most about the truth will be judged most strictly (as in Mt 11:21-24; 12:41-42; 24:45-51; Rom 2:12-16; 12:20; Jas 3:1). Someone who never heard of Christ will be judged less strictly than someone who grew up in a Christian home but rejected Jesus, even though both are still accountable for their sins against others and against whatever they knew of God. The Bible teaches that God provided enough knowledge about right and wrong in our consciences (Rom 2:14-15) that we could all choose to do what's right, but we chose to do what was wrong anyway. Because our offense is against an infinite being, an infinite punishment is an appropriate expression of divine justice; but not everyone will be punished to the same degree. The duration, but not the intensity, is infinite. Thus, in one sense someone who would not accept Christ anyway would be better off being born where they would not hear of him!

Nevertheless, this situation is clearly not what God wants, because he loved the world so much that he sent Jesus to die to restore people to right relationship with himself (Jn 3:16; Rom 8:6-9). How can God's love be reconciled with the reality that most people will eventually be alienated from his love if they do not hear and respond to the gospel?

The Great Divorce

Those who spend their lives rejecting God on earth are hardly declaring their desire to spend eternity with him in the future. If they do not want him now, why will they want him later? Perhaps, as C. S. Lewis suggests in his book *The Great Divorce,*[43] those who reject all the beautiful characteristics of God and his activity in this world become more and more self-seeking; Lewis suggests that they would choose alienation from God's character for themselves in the future just as they choose it now.

Those who have heard Christ's gospel are most responsible for their choice; but everyone makes choices for or against God, no matter how much or little they may know about him. By hating my neighbor, for instance, I am rejecting the God in whose image my neighbor is made.

One day a graduate student was talking with an undergraduate at Duke University after a Bible study in an African-American Christian group there. The undergraduate objected to the concept of Jesus' being the only way of salvation. "I believe in a God of love," she protested. "He wouldn't condemn anyone to hell." Although she was not limiting his mercy to those who had not heard the gospel, her objection certainly included them.

And the graduate student found himself having to explain, for the first time in his life, how the idea of some people's being eternally alienated from God's love is *required* by his infinite love rather than contradicted by it.

About two years before this, his wife had run off with her best friend's husband, never to return. Although the graduate student believed that the Bible does not condemn the innocent party in a divorce, that was not the issue for him at the time. He loved his wife, had been fighting the divorce and was therefore remaining faithful to her. Janina (not her real name) knew all this, and listened as the graduate student shared his heart with her. "On the days when I feel like she might return someday," he confessed, "I can bear the pain of her rejection. But on the days when I despair of her returning, I just want to get the pain over with, to get the divorce and put this agony behind me for good."

Since Janina was still listening, he proceeded. "A God of infinite love has infinite pain because we, the objects of his love, reject him. The pain of love was so great that he chose the cross as a pain less than that of our rejection of him. Yet if we continue to reject him day after day, despite the pain of the cross, we subject him to pain like the pain of the cross day after day—until finally God says it is enough. There must come an end to the pain of love, when the pain has become nothing more than an empty hope that will never be fulfilled."

I believe that both students gained a new appreciation for the depth of God's love that day. I know that I, the graduate student, did.

Many people treat God like an impersonal force that has no heart, but this is not the God of the Bible, the God whose heart was repeatedly broken by people's disobedience to him (as in Judg 10:10-16; Hos 11:8). In his mercy, he sent judgments to get people's attention, to turn them around (Deut 4:30; Amos 4:6-11; Hag 2:17; Rev 9:20-21)—to spare them from the greatest judgment of all, when God finally turns us over to the consequences of our choices. Being alienated from God is the greatest judgment of all, because we are finite beings dependent on our relationship with him to have absolute, eternal meaning and purpose in our lives. To oppose God is to oppose what is good for us, and God seeks our good by calling us to himself (Jer 2:13; Ezek 18:23; Hos 7:13; 13:9; 14:8).

This greatest judgment is also God's highest expression of respect to our right to choose: he lets us go our own way, even when our own way is away from him. Of course people attack Christianity for this doctrine of eternal alienation from God, just as they attack Christianity for saying that people should do what God wants. These opponents of Christianity are not, however, very consistent in their expectations of God. I hear some people complain, "I should be allowed to do what I want"; but when they find that God will let them be alienated from him forever, they protest, "He shouldn't let me go *that* far." God is not manipulated by our inconsistent protests; he requires us to live with the results of our choices.

But how has a person who has never heard of Jesus chosen to be alienated from God? When we let someone know about Jesus, we empower that person with the choice to either accept or reject him. But many people have never been granted that ultimate choice; what choices can they make?

Everyone has some knowledge of God, be it much or little; and everyone has failed to live according to the knowledge they have (see Rom 1:18-23; 2:12-16—discussed briefly above). Thus, for example, if I lived in a culture where it was considered right to be kind to people of my own tribe but acceptable to kill, maim or otherwise dehumanize members of an opposing tribe because of a blood feud with my relatives, I would know enough to be judged for at least two things. First, I would be judged for the times when I failed to live up to my own culture's good standards for how I should treat my tribespeople. Second, I would be judged for wanting to hurt members of another tribe, because I did not use the data at hand to evaluate my culture's ethics. Regardless of my culture's teachings, I should have enough data from comparing those other people with myself to realize that they are human persons just as I am. The same holds true for men in our own culture who respect other men but sexually harass or otherwise demean women; further examples could be multiplied.

When we fail to love other human beings as ourselves, we violate a standard of ethics that is innate in our very existence, and in so doing we defy God. If someone beats up my little brother, the aggressor has picked a fight with me; likewise, if I reject or mistreat other people, who reflect the image of God, I reject God himself.

By rejecting the knowledge we do have about God, we have made a choice. The more one knows about God, the more serious the choice becomes. Pure justice will be served on the day of judgment.

Only the message of Christ can free people from this practice of sin and the inevitable just punishment, to give them a new life and a new beginning on God's side. That is why we who claim to believe that Jesus is the only way of salvation must begin to live as if we really accept that claim.

Changing the Situation

Some people in the world will seek for God sincerely enough that he will see to it that they find him; many stories are reported of people around the world who began praying to God the Creator to reveal himself, and soon followers of Jesus came with his message. The Bible tells of a few individuals like Enoch and Balaam who seem to have come to know God without someone else telling them (although Balaam apparently trafficked with other spirits as well). A clearer example would be the Roman centurion Cornelius, who recognized the one true God and was being as pious as he knew how. Recognizing his prayers and gifts to the poor, God supernaturally arranged to get the good news of salvation to him as quickly as possible through a human messenger (Acts 10:1-6).

Crosscultural missions. But most people will not seek God that earnestly and will respond to him only if given the opportunity directly. Christians thus must devote their resources and lives to reaching the world with the truth of Jesus Christ. If we *really* believe that Jesus is Lord and Savior, then we need to put our money where our mouth is. We need to make sacrifices to make a difference in this world, to proclaim Christ both with our lips and with our lives.

This means that we must make it a priority to reach everyone in the world with the gospel. Some will accomplish that task best as "tentmakers" (physicians, nurses, development workers or other professionals) who share their faith one-on-one in "closed" countries. Others will go as full-time missionaries to "open" countries or as laborers for God in our inner cities or other places of great need. In lands where believers in Jesus are many, crosscultural ministers go to serve the local churches; but over a billion people in the world today need Jesus' witnesses to learn their culture and language and serve them with the gospel for the first time.[44]

Whether we go or God calls us to stay and support other crosscultural witnesses, our lives must be devoted to the spread of Christ's gospel. Nothing less than this devotion can satisfy the God whose heart weeps for a world alienated from him, that he sought to reconcile to himself through the death of his Son.

Some people today reject missions because missions has so often been done wrong, but Christians do not have this option. Without missions there would be no Christianity, for most of the first churches in Jerusalem, Antioch and elsewhere eventually perished, and had they not planted other churches none of us would know of Christianity today. (African-Americans can also take pride in historic African-American involvement in missions.[45])

The magnitude of the task. Jesus said that the end of the age would not come until the good news had been proclaimed among all the nations (Mt 24:14; cf. Acts 1:6-8; Rom 11:25-27; 2 Pet 3:4, 9, 15; Rev 5:9-10). Is the spread of our Lord's message among all peoples actually a reasonable goal? The early church, starting with a handful of witnesses who lacked our modern resources—finances, mass communication, mass transportation, literature to distribute—managed to evangelize nearly their whole generation, because they depended on the power of God's Spirit. Starting with that same flame in our hearts, we can trust God for another revival that will enable us to reach our generation for Christ.

Indeed, it is sometimes pointed out that if just one person began to disciple two people a year and each of them did the same, all other factors being equal, everyone in the world would be a disciple in twenty-two years. Of course not all other factors are equal; boundaries of language and culture must be crossed, hard hearts must be softened through prayer, and believers must persevere and grow mature in their faith to become active disciples. Yet we cannot afford anything less than revival, for the stakes have never been as high as they are in our generation. The world's population is now easily twice what it was in 1950, and five or six times what it was in 1830. This means that the stakes are higher than ever before, but it also means that the power God makes available to our generation to complete the task will be adequate to the task, if our faith is adequate to his power.

Personal discomfort with these beliefs. I do not *want* to believe that people who have not heard the gospel are eternally condemned for their sins. I confess that I do not even want to believe that those who have rejected Christ and have hurt other people will be separated from God forever; from my finite perspective, eternity sounds like far too long (though we offended an infinite God). I have struggled and struggled with the biblical texts, wishing that I could make them say other than what they say. But I remain bound by my integrity as a Christian and a scholar to submit to what the texts claim.

On the one hand, I can identify to some extent with those who do not want it to be true because it costs too much. We must be ready to pay any price to reach people for God if that is the mission of Jesus Christ, which he has shared with us. By contrast, if people who have not heard of Jesus are automatically saved, we should not proclaim Christ anymore, lest anyone become lost. Further, if there are other ways to God, if God's justice could decide between "saved" and "lost" on some other grounds besides Jesus, then Christ's death was unnecessary. This is not the gospel, which teaches that Jesus is the only way. Yet I cannot be faithful to the gospel and not stake my life on its claims.

On the other hand, I can identify far more with those who do not want this to be true because of its implications for the church's failure: millions of precious people have perished with far less chance to accept Christ than they should have had, and millions are perishing even now. This is uncomfortable, even agonizing, to believe, and everything within me revolts against it. If this teaching revolts you too, you should know that you are in good company. I believe that it breaks God's heart too, and that he wants it to break our hearts. If we were *not* revolted by it, something would be wrong; our hearts would be hard against the rest of the world whose humanity we share.

But pleasantness does not determine truth; if we are revolted by suffering in the world, then we must do something about it. If we are revolted by people's being alienated from God forever, then we must do something about it.

Conclusion

Suggesting that Jesus' teachings are true has rarely drawn as hostile a response as suggesting a certain corollary of that statement: his teaching that he is Lord is also true. In our culture it remains comfortable to believe that everyone might be right; our faith, however, demands more than mere tolerance as a response—it demands obedient decision. If Jesus is who he claims to be, if Jesus is our rightful Lord, then all people must submit to him or be declared wrong by him on the day of judgment. I have often presented historical evidence for the resurrection of Jesus to groups of students or to other scholars, and the discussion has rarely become heated; but once someone recognizes that the risen Christ demands obedience, the issue becomes far more personal and threatening.

Although I write now as one convinced that Jesus is the only way to a personal relationship with God, I know very well what it was like to be skeptical about Christianity's claims. I grew up in a nonreligious home and thought that I could explain the universe—with the exception of my own heart—without recourse to the hypothesis of a God. An atheist who flirted with many different philosophies and ideologies, I never actually heard the gospel until the day that I became a Christian. On that day my previous intellectual arguments crumbled before the Spirit's witness to God's truth, and I surrendered my life to him.

My biggest genuine objection to Christianity was Christians. I concluded that if there was one religion I could definitely never consider, it would have to be Christianity, because even the Christians didn't believe it. Eighty percent of people in the United States claimed to be Christians, yet most of them didn't live as if it made a difference. I knew that if I ever decided that I believed there was a God, I would give him everything I was and everything I had. On that day in 1975 I found out that the truth of the Christian faith doesn't rise or fall on the lives of professing Christians; it rises or falls on Jesus Christ.

But a surprise awaited me after I became a Christian. Once I announced this discovery to some of my closest friends, they declared happily, "Oh, we're followers of Jesus too." I was taken aback. How could they have been real followers of Jesus without ever telling me the truth that could have changed my life? True, I might have ridiculed them the first time; I didn't know the difference Jesus could make in my life until after he'd made it. But if it had been up to my Christian friends, I never would have had the chance to find out.

Christians who truly believe the gospel must believe that Jesus is the only way to be reconciled to God. Christians who believe that Jesus is the only way to be reconciled to God must dedicate their lives to bringing the message of Jesus to the world. Those who really love God must care about what he cares about, and he cares about people and the eternal hope for which he created us.

An apostle long ago shared the motivation for his ministry, a motivation that must become our motivation as well:

For we must all appear before Christ's judgment seat, so that each person may be rewarded for acts done while in the body, whether good or evil. This is why, since we know the fear of the Lord, we are persuading people. . . . For the love of Christ overwhelms us, since we have recognized this: that One died for everyone; thus all died. And he died for everyone so that they who live should no longer live for themselves, but for the One who died and rose for them. . . . If any person is in Christ, he or she is a new creation; the old things have passed away, and new things have come. All these things are from God, who reconciled us to himself through Christ and gave us the ministry of reconciliation. (Paul in 2 Cor 5:10-18)

Closing Words

This book provides suggestions for defending the Christian faith against some of its contemporary challengers. But winning intellectual arguments can never begin to be enough to win people to Christ or to truly counter their suspicions about Christianity.

The biggest case against Christianity is the hypocrisy of professed Christians, and the best case for Christianity is the transformation of life Jesus Christ can bring. Competing religions are not the main problem. We (the authors) have met more people on the street turned off to Christianity by professed ministers of the gospel who commit adultery or flaunt wealth at their congregation's expense than by anything said by those who follow other religions. For Christians to really commend Christianity, we must live holy lives and be prepared to confront and deal firmly with proved sin in our own ranks. We may not agree with all the views Afrocentric scholar Molefi Kete Asante holds about Christianity, but he is fully right to challenge the shallowness of many professing Christians and ministers: "Preachers who love to preach because they will be able to ride in Cadillacs and Chryslers must be prevented from assuming leadership roles in the community."[1]

Christians will also have to prove that we are as dedicated to solving the needs of our communities as some other groups claim they are. To be sure, we can name many pastors we know personally who are making a major impact on the social structures of their communities, such as Bishop Barbara

Amos in Norfolk, Charles Blake and Kenneth Ulmer in Los Angeles, Frank Reid in Baltimore, Jeremiah Wright in Chicago, Johnny Youngblood in Brooklyn and many others. But for every church that is deeply involved in the social needs of its community, probably ten churches are not. As the crises of crime, poverty, promiscuity and drugs increase in our society, Christians and non-Christians alike will rightly demand more and more from those who claim to be God's church. Are we prepared to meet their demand and God's?

Relevance to the rising generation's concerns will also prove essential. Glenn's church is actively committed to the youth of the community. It regularly sponsors Christian rap artists who preach biblical holiness in the language of a younger generation. On any given day one is more apt to find Glenn on a basketball court shooting hoops and talking with teenage men about Jesus than in his office. His congregation is building a church that during the week will double as a community center to provide recreation for youth. The members witness on the streets about Christ's love and transforming power, and they seek to support the positive social and educational programs in their community. But again, Glenn's church probably remains the exception today rather than the rule.

Many churches and ministers are also crossing racial and denominational boundaries, recognizing our common unity in Christ. Charismatic churches have frequently taken the lead on the congregational level, and branches of American Christianity from Pentecostals to Southern Baptists to United Methodists have taken dramatic steps toward reconciliation.[2] But for the moment reconciliation too often remains exceptional, once one gets past the lofty proposals. Too often Christians spew invective against fellow Christians with whom they disagree, and no less often we bring pain to our Lord by rending his body along racial lines.

Listen once more to Elijah Muhammad: "Christianity is not the true religion of God. It . . . makes it impossible to establish true love and unity of brotherhood."[3] "The powerless forces of Christianity [are] unable to bring about peace among those who profess it."[4]

> The Christians preach that which they do not do and cannot do. Such as "Love thy neighbor." I have as yet to meet one who loved his neighbor as he did himself. "Thou shalt not kill." I have as yet to meet such a Christian.
>
> They even fight against each other, rob and kill each other, but yet represent themselves as World peacemakers—with whom?[5]

Perhaps these exaggerated accusations reflect a broken heart; yet even if the charges are only partly accurate, they serve as a call to repentance. True repentance will prove the church's best self-defense of all:

> I am giving you a new commandment: love one another. Just as I have loved you, love one another. This is how everyone will know that you are my disciples: if you show love to one another. (Jn 13:34-35)

> I have shared with them the glory which you gave me, so they may be one, just as we are one: I in them, and you in me. This is so that they may be perfected in oneness, so that the world may know that you sent me, and that you loved them in the very same way you loved me. (Jn 17:22-23)

Appendix A

One Example of How the Bible Does Relate to Egyptian and Other Ancient Cultures

It is not enough to simply suggest, as one of our previous chapters did, that some parallels between the Bible and ancient culture may be legitimate but that other parallels are not. Because we argued negatively there (refuting inaccurate parallels), we pause here to provide an example of how ancient culture, including Egyptian culture, can illumine our understanding of the Hebrew Bible more accurately. Such information can highlight how even in God's dealings with Israel in the Old Testament, he made use of many insights and skills from surrounding cultures, including Egyptian culture.

Evidence regarding the Israelite tabernacle can reveal how cultural context is helpful and how it is not. The text of Exodus claims that at the time of the tabernacle's building the Israelites had just emerged from Egypt (Ex 19:1; 40:2, 17), so Egyptian background should be particularly helpful here.[1] If, as has often been held, the Hebrews were Egyptian slaves in the Delta region under Ramses II, they would have had ample opportunity to observe (and help construct) Egyptian temples.[2] At the same time, an unbiased approach also draws on information from other cultures and recognizes the contrasts as well as parallels between Egyptian and Israelite artifacts. We favor an earlier date for the tabernacle (hence more Egyptian provenance) than some scholars do;[3] still, a later date would affect the study of the parallels in only a few instances. We felt it necessary to provide at least one model of how to examine the Bible in light of its milieu, including its Egyptian milieu.[4]

The Tabernacle's Structure
The tabernacle was essentially a portable temple.[5] It was much smaller than Egyptian temples, but one would expect such dimensions for a wilderness shrine.[6] Apart from its size, however, its architecture matches Egyptian temples in significant ways; for example, Israelite builders followed the Egyptian practice of reckoning dimensions in multiples of ten.[7]

A portable tent-shrine. The tabernacle was not the only portable tent shrine of antiquity. Because such structures were perishable, archaeologists have discovered few complete remains,[8] but other evidences of such shrines exist. Although in some localities temples were constructed primarily for the use of travelers,[9] most nomadic peoples probably carried their gods and shrines with them and thus had portable sanctuaries of some sort.[10] Although we have no remains of purely Canaanite tent structures, the concept was certainly not foreign to them; later texts and artwork suggest an older Phoenician tradition at least as early as the seventh century B.C.E.[11] Archaeologists have uncovered possible evidence of a Midianite tent shrine, including red and yellow cloth.[12]

Ancient writers commonly used the term *tent* for the house of a god,[13] possibly recalling former nomadic customs.[14] Canaanites said that at the source of the Two Rivers, their god El lived in a tent shrine.[15] It was a place for the giving of oracles, and his assembly (the gathering of Canaanite gods) also lived in "tents" or "tabernacles."[16] That no shrines to El have been uncovered may suggest that his shrine was made only of perishable material.[17]

Scholars have also often drawn a parallel between Israel's portable red tabernacle and the pre-Islamic Arab *qubbah,* made of red leather and carried on a camel's back. Even after black hair became the norm for nomadic tents, the *qubbah* continued to be dyed red. It would be carried into battle and because of the betyls (holy objects) within, could impart oracles, lead a tribe in its migrations, determine when to camp and when to break camp, and so on. It also functioned as a place of worship.[18]

The evidence for Egyptian models is still clearer. During the Archaic and Old Kingdom periods of Egyptian history, prefabricated portable shrines were common. One example is the portable wooden bed-canopy of Queen Hetepheres I, overlaid with gold, with hooks for curtains, and constructed so as to be easily assembled and dismantled. The tent of purification for royal corpses before and after embalming provides an even stronger parallel. This tent resembled the tabernacle in a number of structural points, and its use was religious (although it pertained to the cult of the dead, which differed in content from Israel's faith considerably). Canopy poles have been found in tomb chapels from as far back as the twenty-ninth century B.C.E.—some sixteen centuries before Moses.[19]

The religious use of tents or light structures, which originated in the earliest period of Egyptian history,[20] continued into the Middle and New kingdoms as well. The stone structure of the great temple of Amun in Thebes was modeled after a large tent structure supported on wooden pillars. While it may be an enlarged copy of the kind of shelter used by Tuthmosis III (c. 1470 B.C.E.) in his campaigns,[21] it may have also been linked to the Sed festival, which sought to renew the king's powers. At the festival, from the First Dynasty through the end of the New Kingdom, special rituals apparently required light pillared pavilions on daises which could be conveniently assembled and taken down.[22]

In the New Kingdom tombs of the pharaohs, four wooden shrines overlaid with gold would be prefabricated and then assembled within the tombs. A complete set has survived from the tomb of Tutankhamun, c. 1340 B.C.E. Egyptologist Kenneth Kitchen notes:

> Each shrine is rectangular, roofed, and has double doors at one end; each was prefabricated in several sections which were then assembled in the King's tomb. These sections fitted together with tenon-and-mortise joints and dowels, and the

woodwork was overlaid with gold throughout. The largest shrine was about 16 ¹/₂ feet long by 11 feet wide by 9 feet high.[23]

At an Egyptian temple in Timna dedicated to Hathor, the Egyptian goddess of mining, the number of cloth pieces led the excavator to conjecture that the shrine was covered with a tent, possibly in keeping with nomadic religious customs.[24] A much smaller sacred shrine, kept within the holy of holies, was the portable bark shrine carried on the shoulders of the priests.[25] It is also noteworthy that Ramses II's royal tent, like the tabernacle, was strategically located in the center of a rectangular camp on military campaigns.[26]

The tabernacle's three-part structure. These parallels, however, are functional rather than religious: any structure less portable than the tabernacle would not have been suitable in the wilderness. Thus the Israelites could have changed the tent's religious meaning when they adapted its form.[27] (For that matter, its title as a "tent" could simply parallel the temporary wilderness dwellings of the Israelites themselves.)

More important is the tripartite division of the tabernacle complex (outer court, inner court and innermost shrine).[28] The temples of Baal and Dagon at Ugarit, possibly from the twenty-first century B.C.E., are the earliest known examples in the Levant following the tripartite format;[29] as early as the Middle Bronze Age IIC temple at Shechem, Canaanite temples were constructed in the same form.[30] Although William Dever traces this form's antecedents back to Hurrian and ultimately Mesopotamian influences,[31] these are hardly the most relevant parallels.[32]

Both Israel's tabernacle and tripartite Canaanite models have their roots in the structure of Egyptian temples; Egypt, after all, exercised a powerful political and social influence in Canaan, and Israelites had been employed as slaves in Egyptian building projects.[33] Egyptian temples followed a basic tripartite plan from a very early till a very late period.[34] Despite the addition of other rooms in the huge Egyptian temples, the basic plan consisted of three parts: the outer court, the inner court and the innermost shrine.[35] The general public apparently came to the outer courts; the inner court appears to have been reserved for the devotees, and the vestibule and shrine for the fully initiated and the priests.[36] The innermost shrine, or "great place," was shut off from the profane light of the world by hangings or wooden doors but was on the main axis of the temple opposite the entrance.[37] The farther one moved from the sanctuary, the broader and higher the rooms became and the more exposed to the light. These basic features are recognizable as far back as the Archaic Period (c. 3100-2686 B.C.E.), over fourteen centuries before Moses.[38]

Since temples symbolized the homes of deities and deities ruled like kings, it was only natural that these three divisions of Egyptian temples, presumably indicating the unapproachableness of the deity for those who were profane, would be adapted from the divisions of upper-class dwellings, particularly of the king.[39] That the high priest in the New Kingdom exercised the earthly power of the divine king of the Middle Kingdom heightens the significance of this architecture.[40]

The Religious Significance of the Tabernacle

Israel's faith sometimes agreed with points made by surrounding cultures (such as that the deity should be approached only with awe and reverence and that he reigned over his creation from a heavenly house). The similarities also show that God had the Israelites use architecturally relevant models for their temple; the Israelites needed to recognize that the tabernacle was a temple, a symbolic house for their deity.

At the same time, definite contrasts remain clear. For example, in Egypt the wooden (often gold-plated) statue of the god dwelled in the sacred bark;[41] in Yahweh's house, however, no image sat atop the climactic ark of the covenant. The conspicuous contrast served as a visual reminder to Israel to avoid any graven images of their God (Ex 20:4-6). If more than one deity was worshiped at an Egyptian temple, the cella would be flanked by two or more shrines;[42] yet Yahweh commanded his people to worship no other gods in his presence (Ex 20:3). The similarities of basic aspects of the tabernacle's architecture make the theologically significant differences all the more conspicuous.[43]

The tabernacle served some practical and theological functions of extreme importance. First, it served to unify the tribes;[44] second, its material gradations testified to the holiness of God and the reverence he demanded.[45] But the tent of Yahweh, like the later temple, would signify most of all the presence of God in the midst of his covenant people (Ex 25:8).[46] In the ancient world, a temple was mostly simply the house, or the dwelling place, of a god.[47] The magnificence of the deity's dwelling place also testified to the splendor of his reign, as the palace of a king would. In the Baal Epic, Baal needed a house to demonstrate his rulership.[48]

That Exodus devotes much space to the building of the tabernacle need not surprise us, since the building of a temple could draw great literary interest in that day.[49] As in the Bible, often the instructions for building a temple were attributed directly to a god.[50] At times even a temple's construction (at least that of the heavenly prototype) was attributed to a deity,[51] though the biblical account certainly differs from this view.[52] In Egypt a temple's founding was a religious act performed by Pharaoh with (most likely) the queen standing in for the goddess Seshat.[53]

The central focus of any deity's dwelling place was the image of the deity who lived there, often deep inside the shrine. Through this image the deity performed divine functions, such as the giving of oracles.[54] Daily rituals in Egyptian temples centered on caring for the images of the deities. The god would be awakened in the morning with a hymn of praise, given his morning toilet, perfumed, clothed and fed. He would then be brought out to conduct appropriate business transactions, deciding cases and acknowledging gifts, which he handled royally until it was time for his afternoon nap or entertainment. He would have his evening meal and then be put to bed for the night.[55]

We should not think that the Egyptians failed to feed their gods well. The daily offerings of the Theban temples of Ramses II or III included fifty-five hundred loaves of bread, making the tabernacle's offerings look like a fiscally conservative Congress's disbursement of food stamps.[56] Hittite culture also provided for the physical needs of its gods: washing, clothing, entertaining and feeding.[57] The Israelite tabernacle evidences a deliberate contrast in this regard.

Yet could Israel have misunderstood the point of the tabernacle? Could they have assumed that Yahweh's presence was confined to the tabernacle? Or did they recognize that he, as later prophets declared, filled heaven and earth (cf. 1 Kings 8:27; Is 66:1-2)? Egyptians, Canaanites and Mesopotamians alike would understand the answer to that question. Baal's temple represented his dominion over the whole world and was in essence a symbolic microcosm of that world.[58] In Mesopotamia and in Egypt the temple again appears to represent the cosmos.[59] In Egypt, the blue ceiling studded with golden stars represented the vault of heaven, across which the vulture goddess spread her wings.[60] A temple was a place where the god's image might be approached with reverence; but it could never be thought to imprison the god.[61]

An earthly temple merely reflected the glory of a heavenly prototype. That may be why constructing the earthly tabernacle according to a particular pattern would make it a suitable dwelling place for the deity and so bring his presence (cf. Ex 25:8-9; 29:45); the pattern might be derived from the heavenly temple (cf. Heb 8:5).[62] Baal's temples were constructed in the same form in which his heavenly house had appeared in ancient myth,[63] and the Babylonians believed that their glorious Esagila, the temple of Marduk, was situated facing the heavenly Esagila.[64]

The tabernacle was conceived as God's dwelling, yet he descended on it to meet the assembly (Ex 33:9). Ultimately it served only to symbolize a religious concept already embodied in Moses and later the Israelite prophetic movement: that Yahweh revealed himself to his people on a personal basis.[65] In the end, the tabernacle served as a symbol of God's holiness, his oneness and his presence among his people; but the reality to which that structure pointed was expressed by the writer of Exodus in this way:

> And it came about, whenever Moses entered the tent, the pillar of cloud would descend and stand at the entrance of the tent; and the LORD would speak with Moses. When all the people saw the pillar of cloud standing at the entrance of the tent, all the people would arise and worship, each at the entrance of his tent. Thus the LORD used to speak with Moses face to face, just as a man speaks to his friend. (Ex 33:9-11 NASB)

Materials and Skills Used in the Tabernacle

The Israelites naturally used many of the same architectural procedures and materials as their neighbors.[66] Practical considerations undoubtedly outweighed theological concerns in constructing the tent shrine; even after they had asked for items from the Egyptians before leaving (Ex 12:36), wilderness existence would impose certain material limitations on what they could build. Nonetheless, there was considerable wealth available in the East Delta region of Egypt in the thirteenth century B.C.E.,[67] and many of the materials would also have been available in the Sinai region after Israel had set out.[68]

The colors. Egyptians in this period already used the dyes mentioned in Exodus. Red dyes were fairly common;[69] blue dyes would have been available in Egypt (though limited, hence quite expensive, before their cultivation in Hellenistic times);[70] the very expensive purple dye was derived from a number of mollusks especially common in the coastal region of Phoenicia,[71] but was available in Egypt.[72] Dyeing was an ancient practice in Egypt reaching back to predynastic times.[73]

The dye colors used in the tabernacle appear to be graded, from most to least expensive. "Pure" blue was used only for the covering of the ark (Num 5:6); other vessels with blue do not bear the designation *pure.* "Purple" was used to cover copper utensils.[74] Red, the color of the tabernacle proper (if the extra skins were only special protection for bad weather), was less expensive still.[75] The material gradations place the most expensive materials nearest the ark. In the ancient world, this was a symbolic way of testifying to the holiness of God, inviting reverence and awe from worshipers.[76]

Wood, metals and skins. The wood may have resembled wooden palaces of the Egyptian Fourth and Fifth dynasties,[77] but the parallel is too early to carry much weight by itself. More significantly, acacia wood was the only available wood in the Sinai region,[78] and it would prove suitable for the purposes for which the tabernacle's builders employed it.[79] The mythical use of cedar wood for the building of Baal's famous temple would have made it the primary choice for theological value;[80] it was indeed later employed in Solomon's temple. But cedar was not available in the Sinai region.[81]

Egyptians had used bronze regularly after 1600 B.C.E.82 "Pure" gold, according to our best available evidence, was not refined gold but the natural gold used in Egypt, which was from 72.1 to 99.8 percent pure.[83] Only the mercy seat and the lamp stand were solid gold; other objects were overlaid with gold. This was due only to technical considerations commonly understood in the ancient world: their work was too delicate for overlay.[84] But the difference between "pure gold" for the furniture and simply "gold" for the planks again signifies the material gradation of holiness mentioned above.[85] Overlaying wooden implements with gold was an Egyptian practice, and Egyptian royal goldsmiths were renowned throughout the ancient world.[86] It was only natural that Israelite slaves employed in Pharaoh's construction projects would have learned their craftsmanship in Egypt.

Goats' hair is used even today as a protective cover for Bedouin tents;[87] traditionally prepared by women, it is dark brown in color. Because it shrinks and thickens when wet, it serves as good protection in hostile weather.[88] In ancient Egypt, skins were soaked, dried outside and then pulled back and forth over a wooden or metal blade set in a stake, since they would be quite stiff unless softened by this method.[89]

As slaves in Egypt, some of the Israelites would have learned many of the necessary skills required for the building of the tabernacle.[90] The techniques they used in construction had been used for up to fifteen centuries in Egypt.[91] The skills and implements for the task are all known to have been available in Egypt.[92]

The gradation of holiness. We must conclude with a final word about material gradations. Whereas the mercy seat was pure gold, the outer altar receiving the offerings was only bronze. The Hebrew text distinguishes among three different types of workmanship of varying levels of quality; fabrics are also listed in decreasing order of expense, as are dyes and metals.[93] As distance from the ark increased, value decreased proportionately.

Many ancient cultures share this symbolism as a way of signifying the sacredness of what was close to the deity: the more sacred the object, the greater its expense.[94] The same symbolism suggests a gradation of holiness in the tabernacle of Israel's God: the people could come as far as the court, the priests could enter the sanctuary, but only the high priest could enter the holy of holies, and that only once a year.

Most ancient Near Eastern and Northeast African temples, tripartite or not, show a progression of holiness increasing from the outer court to the innermost shrine.[95] The Israelites followed this architectural procedure, even adapting the language standard in their milieu. In the period of Moses (if Ramses II was the Pharaoh of the exodus) the most sacred part of Egyptian temples was called the "holy of holies."[96] Thus the materials, techniques and sometimes terms used for the tabernacle were those that were available to the Israelites at that time; but the varied use of those materials became a testimony to the holiness of Yahweh.

The Furniture of the Tabernacle

Since years of research could no doubt be spent on such items as incense altars, altars of sacrifice and tables of offering, we here provide only the briefest introduction to the tabernacle furniture.[97] Ancients would describe splendid utensils of a cult in order to glorify the cult.[98]

By far the most sacred item in the tabernacle was the ark. It was a sacred repository of the covenant of the Lord and always faced the way the camp would be marching.[99] Its precise significance, however, is debated. Some argue from its Hebrew title that it represents a casket, like those in Egypt.[100] The more common and probable view is that it communicated the concept of a throne.[101]

The cherubim, rather than being mere carvings,[102] were probably upright figures.[103] The Akkadian *karibu* from which the term may be derived referred to one who advised the great gods and whose role included especially intercession for the faithful,[104] which might be of particular significance here since the cherubim crown the propitiatory mercy seat. While cherubimlike creatures are pictured widely—for instance, at Mari,[105] on Tree of Life artistry in Mesopotamia, on a later Israelite bone handle from Hazor[106] and so on[107]—the most significant function in which they are pictured is support of the royal throne. It is in this way that they are pictured in the relief on the sarcophagus of King Ahiram of Byblos (c. 1000 B.C.E.), an ivory model of a throne from Megiddo and an ivory plaque from Megiddo (c. thirteenth century B.C.E.).[108] The point of the cherubim on the mercy seat seems to be that it is the throne of Yahweh and the ark is his footstool.[109]

The ark, like the sacred bark (portable boat shrine) of Egyptian temples, would thus be the focus of attention within the tabernacle. The presence of Yahweh was symbolically enthroned above it on the cherubim (as in 1 Sam 4:4; Ps 80:1; 99:1; 132:7-8). Tables of offering may be paralleled in many ancient Near Eastern cultures, including Assyrian,[110] Hittite[111] and Minoan.[112] But while the table in the tabernacle resembles these to an extent, in the tabernacle the bread was eaten every week by the priests (Lev 24:9), not by the god.[113] As one would expect, sacrificial altars were very common; a Late Bronze example from Hazor should suffice.[114] Lamps—necessary for the inner areas of temples secluded from profane light—were frequent; excavators have found examples from the Bronze and Iron ages which have seven wicks, though these do not branch out from the shaft.[115] Incense altars—undoubtedly needed to cover the stench of burning flesh from sacrificial altars—were very common and often had horns.[116]

But the limited differences are striking and significant. Thus, for example, the furniture of Baal's house included a throne, footstool, lamp, chest of drawers, table with utensils, and bed. The chest and the bed, which denote the god's bodily needs as if he were human, are deleted from Yahweh's tabernacle.[117] Again the cultural similarities render the differences all the more striking; Yahweh spoke through the religious culture of the day to show himself the only true and living God.

Conclusion

Ancient Israel adapted the architectural conventions of its time to build a shrine to their God. The Israelites also, however, modified some features of the tabernacle to reflect their own distinctive beliefs about God, beliefs that differed from those of nations around them. A balanced approach to any ancient culture, including ancient Israel, requires us to recognize both the influences of surrounding cultures and the distinctive contributions of the culture we are studying. This approach allows us also to appreciate Egypt's contributions to Israel's history without downplaying other contributions. We have offered these observations regarding the tabernacle as one example of how we can approach the Bible in a culturally sensitive way.

Appendix B

The Accuracy of Accounts in the Pentateuch

Many scholars debate the historical accuracy of the Pentateuch (the first five books of the Bible). The complexity of the issues meant that in chapter six we did not have space to respond adequately to Ahmed Deedat's statements about the Pentateuch. In this appendix, however, we survey some of the questions involved and present a brief defense of at least the historical plausibility of many of the biblical accounts.

We do believe that we know the discipline better than Deedat; thus though neither of us is a Hebrew Bible scholar by profession, it would be inappropriate for us to simply ignore Deedat's claims. Some Christians would respond to challenges like Deedat's by exhorting people to "just take the Bible on faith." That may be a legitimate approach for those who already accept the Bible on other grounds, but it does not help much in dialogue with non-Christians, who often seek historical arguments.

Specific historical information from the second millennium B.C.E. is for the most part no longer available, so history by itself can neither prove nor disprove most biblical accounts. Even purely historical evidence does, however, permit us to argue that the biblical accounts are much more plausible than Deedat allows.

The evidence available to support the historical picture in biblical stories about Israel's ancestors is not on the same level as that available for the Gospels (see chapter eight); much less is known about the earlier period. Still, not all scholars are as skeptical as Deedat implies, nor is there a permanent consensus on which matters warrant skepticism. In the brief space available here, we wish mainly to survey some views that dissent from Deedat's verdict on biblical scholarship, and to cite some limited evidence supporting the plausibility of historical narratives in the Pentateuch. Readers who are less interested in questions of the Pentateuch's date and editing should skip to the sections on the Abraham, Joseph and Moses stories.

How Much Do Authorship and Historical Verity Matter?
We believe that evidence supports the essential historical picture of Israel's ancestors in the Bible and that these stories, from Abraham to Moses, were collected around the time of Moses and the settlement of Israel in the Promised Land. Yet Deedat is not the only person to question whether these stories were collected in the time of Moses. On very different grounds, a number of reputable Christian scholars, including some prominent Afrocentric biblical scholars and some of our friends who are Hebrew

Bible scholars, accept in whole or in part the "documentary hypothesis," the view that editors much later than Moses wove together various strands of tradition in the Pentateuch.[1]

The primary issue is not who wrote down all the traditions in the Pentateuch, however, but to what degree those traditions provide moral instruction reliable for Christian faith.[2] Indeed, the early Christian scholar Jerome (c. 340-420) was unsure whether Moses or Ezra (after the exile) wrote the Pentateuch in its current form.[3] One can hold any of various views on how the Pentateuch was formed yet still regard it as God's message.[4] While we argue for the more traditional conservative position that the biblical stories were arranged near the time of Moses, we recognize that authorship is not the most crucial question.

The question of historical verity (accuracy) is more important but, like the matter of authorship, widely disputed. More liberal Christian scholars might answer Deedat by conceding that much of the material in the Pentateuch is not historical, but that it contains basic themes of theological truth that pave the way for later parts of the Bible which are far more demonstrable historically, especially Jesus' ministry and resurrection.

We prefer a more conservative historical approach, upholding the substantial historical accuracy of the biblical traditions and arguing that the Pentateuch's theology presupposes a God who can act in history the way its narratives depict. We believe this matter deserves attention because part of the narratives' theology is that God acts in history—a theological premise that would lose some important support if the narratives lacked historical foundation.

At the same time, we are seeking to state our position in a manner that is fair to thoughtful scholars who disagree. Genre, or the kind of writing involved in the Pentateuch narratives, is a legitimate question: methods of writing history vary from one culture to another, and ancients typically recounted narratives about the origins of their people in ways quite different from the way we write history today, or the way first-century biographers wrote about figures like Jesus.[5] On this issue, then, we respond to Deedat's objection somewhat more fully, though we cannot do so at the length the question deserves.

The Documentary Hypothesis

In its most common form, the documentary hypothesis proposes authors for the Pentateuch centuries later than Moses, and final editors who wove together these documents: J (narratives calling God Yahweh), E (narratives calling God Elohim), D (traditions related to Deuteronomy) and P (the late priestly and ritual traditions).

One should note that the reliability of the Pentateuch itself does not rise or fall on this claim; none of the books in the Pentateuch themselves *claim* to be written by Moses,[6] and some scholars think New Testament writers simply followed the convention of their day in attributing various passages in the Pentateuch to Moses. Thus many scholars who accept this hypothesis (especially those who find the arguments of

W. F. Albright, John Bright and other figures of the dominant mid-twentieth century school of American scholarship persuasive in an updated form) nevertheless believe that most of the traditions behind these sources go back to the period they depict.[7]

While an increasing number of scholars today reject the documentary hypothesis,[8] it probably remains the dominant position in scholarship concerning the Hebrew Bible. In fact, many who learned only this position in earlier years in seminary or elsewhere may not be aware that many scholars no longer hold the documentary hypothesis in its traditional form (though nearly all scholars, both liberal and conservative, concur that the writers and editors of the Pentateuch drew on earlier sources).[9]

Disagreements about the hypothesis. While the documentary hypothesis remains the most popular position, scholars disagree considerably on exactly how to apply it. There remains little consensus, including little agreement concerning which sources actually appear in which passages.[10] Thus A. F. Campbell and M. A. O'Brien, in a work on the Pentateuch's sources published by Fortress Press, warn that "a statement cannot just be about J; it has to be about Eissfeldt's or Hölscher's or Noth's J or the author's J, and so on."[11] Scholars who accept the hypothesis now join those who reject it in acknowledging its many problems.[12] "The elaborate, dogmatic structure erected by the proponents of this method in the nineteenth century cannot now carry conviction to the same extent as in the past," one scholar observes. "The naive belief that by dividing the Pentateuch into a few sources it is possible to arrive at texts marked by absolute uniformity has long been abandoned."[13] Some earlier assumptions about composition (such as Otto Eissfeldt's detailed source hypothesis) are now recognized as impossible.[14] Given that the theory's historical underpinnings have proved so weak, some of us wonder whether instead of revising the old theory we might not do better to start our search for sources from scratch, without the encumbrances of the original documentary hypothesis.

Some scholars trained in various aspects of ancient Near Eastern history have long challenged the traditional theory (for example, Umberto Cassuto and Cyrus Gordon from Ugaritic sources, Kenneth Kitchen from Egyptian, and P. J. Wiseman from Mesopotamian). The majority of biblically conservative scholars also reject the view (although some of the more extreme liberal scholars tend to dismiss the work of all conservative scholars as biased, ignoring the fact that their own critical tradition also has biases).[15] Israeli scholars have traditionally shown less commitment to the traditional form of the documentary hypothesis than European and North American scholars.[16] Even some scholars who date the Pentateuch's final editing as late as eight centuries after Moses[17] nevertheless affirm (in ways that the authors of this book might not) that the entire Pentateuch is a literary unity.[18]

The authors of this book are among those who question the traditional documentary hypothesis, particularly its dating of the sources, although we acknowledge that one can hold the hypothesis without abandoning the historical substance of events described in the biblical accounts. Various scholars have pointed out some weaknesses of the traditional hypothesis; we take the space to mention only a few. Newer, less speculative literary approaches have also argued that Genesis may be a cohesive literary unity not divisible by the traditional source methods.[19] Strong evidence suggests that Genesis 1—11, for example, functions as a literary unity in its current form, whatever its prior sources.[20]

Problems with the traditional hypothesis. The Pentateuch clearly does involve earlier sources, of course, and we believe stylistic criteria do allow some distinctions among sources. Even some conservative critics equate Moses with J who edited P or P who edited J;[21] conservatives can argue that one author employed a variety of sources (as is explicit in Num 21:14) and the language was updated later.[22]

But as is often acknowledged, J and E are stylistically similar,[23] and given the amount of data available, one might explain the divergences between them as coincidental (the range of difference would probably be about the same had we divided the sources randomly).[24] Many scholars therefore have begun to dispense with a distinct "E" source[25]—striking at the heart of the traditional hypothesis.

Claims for stylistic distinctions carry less weight than they once did. According to one statistical study, "Assigning the words of the storyteller, the utterances of the story's personages and those of the Deity each to a different writer is at least as justified as ascribing the text of the book to the three different sources *J, E,* and *P,* postulated by the Documentary Hypothesis"—an observation that at least raises suspicion about the objectivity of the traditional sources.[26] Some have identified as distinct units not the traditional sources J and E but an Abraham cycle, a Jacob cycle and the Joseph story.[27] Citing various lines of evidence, many scholars today also doubt that discrepancies[28] and "doublets"[29] indicate different written sources.[30]

Different proposed criteria for identifying separate sources often produce quite different sources. Certainly traditional distinctions on the basis of names of deities and patriarchs, based on nineteenth-century history-of-religions theories, fall apart when compared with analogous Egyptian models (such as three names for Osiris on the stele of Ikhernofret).[31] Further, whereas *Yahweh* seems to be God's name, *God (Elohim)* usually functions as a *title*—not as Yahweh's "other" name.[32]

D (Deuteronomy) clearly does reflect a different style from JE and P,[33] though by some proposed linguistic criteria, such as the differences between *ani* and *anochi,* it could appear *earlier* than JE (in contrast to the traditional theory).[34] P as a distinct source makes the most sense stylistically in the ritual portions of Exodus and Leviticus (perhaps collated by priests or scribes), but one would expect sections focusing on ritual material to share somewhat distinctive vocabulary, and later priestly writers (such as the Chronicler) to be steeped in it.[35] It probably represents a different source, but because conclusions about its date remain hypothetical, even the first editors of the Genesis-Exodus narratives (JE) could easily have incorporated it or an early form of it, if they actually contain it at all.[36]

Dating the sources. But the most problematic part of the hypothesis revolves not around the particular sources (although scholars frequently diverge on exactly which passages belong to those sources) but around the dates assigned to those sources.[37] First, the structure of Deuteronomy perfectly fits covenants written in the general period of Moses, but rarely or (some argue) never those written centuries later; this observation brings into question the hypothesis's traditional dating of D,[38] as may some other evidence.[39] Certainly the claim, for example, that Josiah would have already known of the Book of the Law unless it were a recent forgery is mistaken; business documents from the very eras of Mesopotamian law codes disregard those law codes, as did judges in legal decisions.[40] Perhaps few Mesopotamian kings after Hammurabi knew of his code; certainly few made public use of it.[41]

Critical tradition usually advocates a date for P after Israel's exile because of "late" Hebrew expressions paralleled in Ezekiel, but Ezekiel appears to depend on Leviticus considerably, and "P's vocabulary does not resemble that of late biblical Hebrew."[42] The nineteenth-century view that details of P are late because such priestly regimentation would not occur as early as Moses contradicts what we know of all other cultures in the ancient Near East; these features continued "from prehistory down to Graeco-Roman times."[43]

Even if the materials are early, however, one can still argue that they were combined with the narratives (which may serve as a prologue) only later, as may be true of the legal material in Exodus.[44] One can also argue that the laws developed or were incorporated into slightly different collections without doubting their essential antiquity,[45] and the same, again, could be true for the ritual materials. On the basis of Near Eastern parallels, Albright suggested that the collection predates the exile and that the laws themselves probably predate Moses.[46] Arguing that the material in the Pentateuch is early and/or authentic is not the same as arguing that all the material was collected into five books at an early date. The form of five books may have more to do with feasible scroll lengths than with the length of original collections; for example, the Joseph story of Genesis flows without much of a break into the Moses story of Exodus.

The final editing of the main structure of Genesis (which traditionally consists especially of J and E, with some P material)[47] remains a matter of dispute. Many argue for a postexilic editing, but some scholars have argued for a time from the Davidic empire.[48] With most conservative scholars, we would agree that some editing took place as late as the Davidic empire (as in Gen 36:31) but would argue for an earlier date for the main collection of Genesis than such traditional views favor. We note that the very structure of Genesis (including a curse on Canaan paralleling the curse of the serpent and of those who curse Abram), plus the focus of God's revelations and activity regarding the Promised Land (Gen 12:1, 7; 13:14-17; 15:18-21; 17:8; 26:2-3; 28:4, 13-15; 31:3, 13; 35:12; 48:4, 21; 50:24; Ex 6:4, 8),[49] make excellent sense for a people ready to go in and possess the Promised Land.[50] A primary theme of Genesis is the promise of the land; various literary cues may also suggest warnings not to return to Egypt (such as 11:31-32; 13:10).[51]

Some have also made an argument that the structure of Genesis 12—36 fits that of intergenerational family archives from the patriarchal period.[52] In this case Moses or those working under him could have later edited these earlier sources[53] (a view that would not need to rule out subsequent editing by later Israelite historians suggested by clues in the text, such as Gen 36:31). As we note elsewhere, social customs tended to prevail over a long period of time, so this final argument must be subjected to critical scrutiny by comparison with similar texts from other eras. But it should not be rejected simply on the basis that it offers a date for Genesis too early to fit the traditional critical position.

Philosophy behind the traditional hypothesis. In its earlier form, the documentary hypothesis assigns the various layers it finds to different historical periods based on a prior reconstruction of Israel's history. That reconstruction, however, depends on a nineteenth-century view of religious evolution[54] that violates what we now understand of the ancient world: ancient Egypt, for instance, experienced three kingdoms with rises and falls, not a unilinear evolution.[55]

Further, the original historical reconstruction assumed that "primitive" cultic religion as depicted in the priestly source was on its downward trend toward "late Judaism" and Pharisaism. But Eurocentric assumptions, not historical facts, dictated this approach.[56] For example, "In all other Near Eastern cultures, priestly material is early rather than late, so that if the appropriate sections of Exodus, Leviticus, and Numbers followed the contemporary priestly patterns, they too would have originated in the second millennium B.C."[57] In composing the standard form of the hypothesis, Julius Wellhausen drew on concepts proposed by others (J and E in Astruc and Eichhorn; a Josianic dating of D from W. de Wette; four documents from Graf).[58] The frame of reference that allowed Wellhausen to arrange these different materials into a coherent historical perspective, however, was G. W. F. Hegel's philosophy of dialectic in history—a philosophy that otherwise began to lose its credibility in the early twentieth century.[59]

As some Jewish scholars have shown, anti-Jewish views affected German Protestant scholars of that period. Martin Bernal has stated dramatically what others have also argued less dramatically, that most nineteenth-century European scholarship also held little respect for African civilizations.[60] Sacrificial cults naturally seemed further from German religion than the lofty ethics of the prophets, and though these were not necessarily incompatible (though the prophets complained against those who observed only the sacrifices), the former seemed unnecessary or even bad to liberated Europeans. And if they were bad, perhaps they were also late, products of the corruption of earlier, pristine faith (a view especially appealing in the Romantic era).

If that reconstruction of Israel's history rests on an ethnically biased perspective, Afrocentric and other biblical scholars perhaps should reexamine any dating of the sources that rests on such a reconstruction. One Hebrew Bible scholar complains thus about the nineteenth-century Eurocentric bias of the formulators of the hypothesis:

> Failing to allow for the vast cultural and psychological differences between the literate and scholarly society of western Europe in the nineteenth century AD in which they lived and that of a relatively obscure ancient Semitic people of the first millennium BC, they assumed that the authors and scribes of ancient Israel would have done their work along the same lines as those on which they themselves would have worked if they had been faced with the same task.[61]

Others have argued that Wellhausen could not have promoted his theory any later than he did, because the rise in comparative ancient Near Eastern studies would have discredited it.[62]

Concluding questions about the hypothesis. While we cannot hope to fully challenge pervasive critical theories in so brief a space, we hope that younger scholarship will continue to systematically probe them. Any developed system, including an academic paradigm, looks consistent from inside until adequately tested by external criteria. When allowance is made for the perspectives and emphases of particular traditions and authors, the biblical history of Israel makes no less sense than the scholarly critical reconstruction of Israel's history, and the former has the virtue of simplicity (Ockham's razor) and depending on sources closer to the hard evidence.

The observation that any system looks consistent from within has implications far beyond particular theories regarding the development of the Pentateuch. Dogmatic critical scholars have been known to chide less-educated committed Christians for trusting their Bible rather than critical scholarly perspectives. This chiding often has less to do with commitment to particular scholarly perspectives (the critical scholarly perspectives themselves require frequent revision) than with a belief that historic Christians' unwavering faith in Scripture is uncritical. Some scholars retain whatever views in which they were originally trained; some adjust their views to fit the rapidly changing consensus within the academy; more helpfully, others try to assimilate all relevant information and evaluate it.

For many critical scholars, believers who "uncritically" affirm the Bible's authority are offensive not so much for holding views that differ from those of a particular group of academicians, but for the believers' unwillingness to relinquish the Bible's truth claims. For some, any modern paradigm (even if some consider it outmoded) is better than a biblical paradigm, provided the former involves no appeal to a deity but remains wholly subject to scholars' human evaluation. In such circles, a scholar's "objectivity" and "critical" thinking are often measured more by his or her distrust of biblical accounts than by his or her suspicion of modern scholarly paradigms. In our discipline, we have sometimes seen the value of massively researched works dismissed because of their biblically committed "agenda" (rather than ranked with comparably well-researched works whose agendas are different), whereas some other works offering opinion with little documentation have been hailed as "thought-provoking." Scholarship is essential, but some philosophical presuppositions that inform secular scholarship are no less "agendas" than those that inform historic Christian faith.

The Accuracy of the Earliest Biblical Stories

Regardless of when the stories in the Pentateuch were written down, evidence that we will briefly survey below suggests that they contain much earlier traditions, at least many of which were passed on accurately until they were written down. Although later storytellers and writers adapted the way they recounted stories to their own day, just as most preachers do with biblical stories even today, many features of the stories fit the time of Abraham, and some cannot fit the setting of Israel in a later period.[63]

Ancient historians did not write precisely as modern ones do, nor does the theology of the biblical accounts focus on historical details. Neither of these observations should, however, lead us to despair of finding substantial historical tradition in the Pentateuch material. These are stories of faith intended to encourage Israel, but their potential to encourage must rest to at least some degree on their claim to be rooted in history.[64] We agree with the conservative Old Testament scholars who suggest that accurate traditions were put into oral form as entertaining and motivating origin stories, compiled into fuller oral or written cycles at the time of the exodus, and substantially edited around the time of David and the uniting of the monarchy to prepare for the larger cycle of traditions supporting the Davidic monarchy.[65] Lest anyone think such oral transmission in the early stages impossible, we should note that in Egypt and the ancient Near East, accurate information could be transmitted orally for up to a thousand years.[66]

We pause here to sample some of the evidence for the historical accuracy of some of these traditions in Genesis and Exodus. Although also citing other sources, we depend especially on some works by Nahum Sarna, W. S. LaSor, D. A. Hubbard, F. W. Bush and Edwin Yamauchi, citing them at various intervals. Among others, these scholars have nuanced and updated[67] some lines of argument especially developed by Albright and his followers in the mid-twentieth century.[68]

Shifting views. Many nineteenth-century critics, especially in Germany, had dismissed the biblical stories of Abraham, Isaac and Jacob as legends, along with most other ancient stories. Because in the nineteenth century much less was known about the ancient world, one could make assertions about what could or could not have happened without checking them against much hard evidence. When Heinrich Schliemann discovered the supposedly mythical city of Troy, however, interest in the historical basis of ancient legends increased. In time archaeology began to provide a new source of information about the ancient world, including what could or could not have happened there.

Earlier twentieth-century Old Testament critics like Albrecht Alt and Martin Noth had comparatively little archaeological data to work with and had to produce theories with less dependence on them; hostility between Germany and Britain kept Palestine inaccessible to German critics for part of this period. Yet since the 1890s Assyriologists, and from the 1920s archaeologists, began to conclude that archaeological data suited the Old Testament record better than the data fit the skeptical theories of biblical critics.[69] William Albright, originally trained in skeptical scholarship, began to respect the Bible increasingly as he worked with hard archaeological data. He went on to become a central figure in twentieth-century Old Testament scholarship, and his students remained a dominant force in such scholarship after him (G. Ernest Wright and Frank Moore Cross of Harvard, John Bright of Union in Virginia, and George Mendenhall of the University of Michigan).[70]

As discoveries about the era of the patriarchs increased, scholars reacted against many earlier assumptions that the patriarchal stories were late creations. Far more than expected, the stories did indeed fit the era they depicted.[71] Some assertions about archaeological proof also outstripped the evidence, however, inviting a more recent reaction in the other direction. Noting some flaws in the Albright school's approach, especially its overconfidence in archaeological verification, some have qualified or even abandoned the approach today.[72] Old Testament historical studies lack a consensus, and the future direction of the discipline is difficult to predict.

Methodology. Some arguments prove weaker than others. For instance, arguments against the narratives' reliability based on philosophic presuppositions, such as distrusting biblical narratives because they testify to "divine direction in human affairs,"[73] will not carry much weight with either believers or general postmodernists skeptical of Enlightenment antisupernaturalism.

Arguments against the narratives based on the silence of evidence are also weak. The burden of proof requiring concrete evidence must in any given case rest with an argument challenging rather than defending the narratives. Because no texts previously known indicated Greek speakers in Crete before 1300 B.C.E., most scholars doubted their presence—until the Linear B tablet proved otherwise. While new discoveries will not normally cause us to discard evidence already in hand, they will often shed fresh light by providing evidence where none before was known.[74] Because only a fraction of ancient evidence has survived, only a fraction of what has survived has been excavated,[75] and only a fraction of what has been excavated has been cataloged and interpreted, one historian estimates that only 0.006 percent of the evidence remains available to us.[76]

Thus we should not be surprised if specific evidences for individuals known to us from the Bible or other written sources do not turn up in excavations, especially when those individuals were seminomads wandering in the Judean wilderness as Abraham, Isaac and Jacob did.[77] We should be surprised more when historical records attest a particular person of the past than when they do not do so. How then can we test how accurate the stories may be?

We can check the stories on a number of points. Because later writers making up stories from scratch would not know enough about Abraham's time to make their stories fit that period (they did not have many archaeologists back then!), purely fictional stories would get most cultural details wrong (compare, for instance, the historical inaccuracies in the apocryphal story of Judith). In the same way, purely legendary stories would undoubtedly reflect the centuries during which they were passed along more than they would reflect the period of Abraham. But if the stories can be shown to usually reflect accurately the period of Abraham on many of the points where we can check them, this alignment will provide a good indication that the stories contain historically reliable information. Historical evidence is insufficient to prove or disprove the biblical accounts of the patriarchs, but we can at least note that elsewhere in the right period "Abrams and Jacobs were indeed doing much the same things . . . as Abraham and Jacob were doing" in Genesis.[78]

Abraham Fits His Period

At a variety of points, the Abraham stories fit the period they depict. One matter we can check is the names in this period.[79] Today if someone mentions a grandmother and her granddaughter, and one is named Mildred or Esther while the other is named Shamika or Shonda, you can probably guess which is the grandmother and which is the granddaughter. Some names are more popular in some generations and locations than in others.

This is not the strongest argument, because certain names can and do come back into vogue after falling into disuse.[80] But it is helpful to know that names like Abraham, Nahor, Serug, Terah and Jacob were prominent in the period in which the Bible indicates that Abraham lived.[81] "Amorite imperfective" names like Isaac, Ishmael, Jacob and Joseph appear roughly twice as often in the patriarchal period as in the time of Moses, and more than four times as often as in David's era.[82]

Considerably more important, Abraham's travels fit what we know of this period. In a later period, someone making up stories about Abraham coming from Mesopotamia might have claimed that he came from Babylon, the most prominent Mesopotamian city of their day. Yet the Bible locates him in the most prominent Mesopotamian cities of precisely his own period: Ur and Haran. These two sites were linked: both were thriving cities in this period, both were significant caravan stations, and both were devoted to the worship of the moon-deity Sin.[83] After the nineteenth century B.C.E., little is known of these centers until the early thirteenth century B.C.E.84

Also, a number of other people were migrating from Syria into Palestine in this general period (although it was not a mass migration), and caravans traveled from northwest Mesopotamia to Palestine.[85] Egyptian texts attest that some Mesopotamian deities even spread into Syria and northern Palestine in this period.[86] Archaeology attests that most cities mentioned in Genesis actually did exist in this period (Bethel, Dothan, Gerar, Shechem),[87] whereas many cities that became prominent only later are not named in Genesis.[88]

Archaeological evidence supports the biblical picture that this was largely a period of peace and prosperity in Palestine and that trade with Egypt was quite active.[89] The lifestyle of Abraham's family as pastoral nomads (herding livestock) fits the period;[90] indeed, seasonal occupation in the southern Judean wilderness, attested in the stories about Abraham and his children, appears primarily in this period and earlier, and not much again for another thousand years. Abraham has to deal mainly with tribal confederacies rather than with city kings, except on the Jordan plain, which also fits Egyptian evidence about Palestine in this period.

The most significant element of background that does not fit (which may simply represent updated language[91]) is the use of camels instead of asses,[92] and even in this case we have evidence suggesting that *some* families (which could include Abraham's clan) did have domesticated camels in this period.[93] But historians of other ancient Near Eastern societies continue to use texts as substantially historical despite occasional characteristic exaggerations or anachronisms, and historians should treat the biblical accounts in the same way.[94] Such "anachronisms," or "modernizations" (as ancient Near East scholars sometimes call them), appear in other ancient texts; for example, the Egyptian Story of Sinuhe, set around 1940 B.C.E. Manuscripts from the nineteenth- or eighteenth-century B.C.E. show that the story is early, but a thirteenth-century manuscript modifies the story slightly, introducing a recent loanword.[95]

Labels like "Philistines" and "Arameans" may also be later titles applied to earlier people,[96] but the peoples actually depicted in the text do not seem to be a later invention. Writers in a later period probably would not have portrayed most peoples the way Genesis does. From the time of David on, Arameans and especially Philistines were Israel's enemies, whereas Canaanites were usually a nonissue; but in Genesis the Arameans appear in a favorable light,[97] the Philistines appear as trading partners, and the Canaanites appear as a threat to Israel's spiritual security (a threat most relevant to the book's audience only from the time of Moses through the period of the judges). Although probably only a few Hittites lived in Palestine, Abraham's negotiations with them in Genesis 23 fit the sorts of legal procedures attested in their own documents (as well as those of other ancient Near Eastern peoples).[98]

It is not likely that the Israelites would have made up stories about their ancestors' following customs that differed dramatically from their own laws: Abraham planting a tamarisk tree as an act of worship, like some of his contemporaries (Gen 21:33 versus Deut 16:21); Abraham marrying his half-sister (Gen 20:12 versus Lev 18:9, 11; Deut 27:23); Jacob's sororal polygyny—that is, marrying two sisters (Gen 29:16-30 versus Lev 18:18); Jacob setting up pillars (Gen 28:22); or Jacob ignoring the right of the firstborn for the son of a more loved wife (Gen 49:3-4, 22-26 versus Deut 21:17).[99] If anything, these customs much more closely resemble old Mesopotamian practices than later Israelite ones.[100]

So disconcerting was the failure of Israel's ancestors to match up to Israel's laws that two centuries before Jesus some Jewish people wrote the book of *Jubilees,* telling the stories of Genesis differently and emphasizing the patriarchs' obedience to the law of Moses before it was given. Surely Israelites well past Moses' time would not have invented stories that violated their laws![101] Other accounts are simply embarrassing: for example, while the accounts of patriarchs endangering their marriage by passing a wife off as a sister emphasize the Genesis theme that God would preserve Abraham's line, they are hardly flattering to the patriarchs.[102]

The military customs in the Abraham story (Gen 14) also support the narratives' basic reliability.[103] In 1918 Albright wrote that Genesis 14 was a fabricated story dating to over one thousand years after the supposed period of Abraham, but his work as an archaeologist eventually forced him to change his position. The narrative fits the details of ancient warfare; the names of the kings all fit the period and place; further, one king was left unnamed, although a mere storyteller could have filled that detail in. More significantly, the invasion route described was the best invasion route, which excavations confirm was probably in use in this period (from the twenty-first to the nineteenth century B.C.E.). The cities described existed in this period, but apparently not after the nineteenth century B.C.E. The system of Mesopotamian alliances presupposed in the story only existed from around 2000 to 1700 B.C.E., between the collapse of Ur's Third Dynasty and the rise of the old Assyrian and Babylonian empires.[104] Thus when Albright wrote again on Genesis 14 in 1961, he concluded that the story was completely ancient and quite accurate.[105]

The Joseph Story

The Joseph story, like the Abraham story, fits much of what we know of the time of Joseph.[106] This is not to say that the writer was interested in providing a dry, annalistic account like most court reports of his day. The Joseph story is a first-class literary composition, and few ancient Egyptian or Near Eastern short stories rival its literary excellence.[107] But its literary brilliance hardly proves that we must read it as a novelistic short story or folk story without historical foundation;[108] one could employ graphic storytelling techniques to transmit orally or to write genuine historical information, as later Israelite historians in fact did.[109] In Egypt, even picturesque legendary narratives about much more ancient times often concerned demonstrably historical characters.[110]

The Joseph story corresponds to reality better than one would expect from a pure novel.[111] First of all, the story of Joseph's enslavement fits his time. We can check the locations where Joseph traveled while looking for his brothers. If later storytellers knew an earlier story about Joseph but not its details, they might have mentioned cities that existed in their own time but not Joseph's. Yet excavations indicate that each of the cities mentioned early in the narrative (Hebron, Shechem and Dothan) existed by Joseph's period. One can also check the price for which Joseph's brothers sold him, twenty shekels of silver. The average price of a slave rose steadily (along with inflation) in the ancient world, from twenty shekels in Joseph's day to about thirty by Moses' day to fifty by Menahem's day. Genesis *accurately records the exact price for which Joseph was sold* in his day.[112] Other elements of the story also fit well enough: Egyptians bought some slaves from Palestine;[113] male slaves often became warehouse managers; the *mer-per* (manager) might pass back and forth through his master's private quarters (where Potiphar's wife would be) because of responsibilities in both the storehouse and the front of the home. Potiphar is the good Egyptian name *Pa-di-pa-re*, "the one whom the sun-god has given,"[114] and the title for his office, literally "chief cook," was a good Egyptian phrase applied to any servants of Pharaoh.

The story of Joseph's imprisonment and exaltation also fits what we know of the period.[115] Bakers and cupbearers (KJV "butler") held important roles in Pharaoh's court. Royal bakers could be quite extravagant: the Egyptians had at least fifty-seven kinds of bread and thirty-eight kinds of cake. The chief cupbearer was a prominent official. Someone making up the story in Palestine might have used sheep (the most common livestock of Israel) in Pharaoh's dream, but Genesis mentions cows, which were more common in Egypt. The term for the reed-grass the cows were eating *(ahu)* is actually a term borrowed from the Egyptian language. Joseph's titles, duties and honor fit what we know of some high officials of Egyptian rulers, not simply Judean imagination. On was a center for the worship of the powerful sun-god Re. Further, evidence suggests that foreigners could rise to high offices in Egypt in various periods; if Joseph arrived during the reign of the Semitic Hyksos,[116] the Egyptians might especially have welcomed a fellow "Semite."[117] Joseph's adoption of an Egyptian name also fits common practice in his day,[118] although it was not a uniquely Egyptian custom. His shaving before being brought before Pharaoh fits Egyptian custom as well,[119] though this particular Egyptian practice was undoubtedly widely known.

The story of Joseph's brothers' arrival also fits what we know of the period, though not all details fit this period exclusively.[120] Herdsmen in Palestine frequently traveled to Egypt for food and pasture. Egyptians also seem to have disdained shepherds, as the narrative implies.[121] Because Goshen was near the palace, Joseph and his brothers probably came to Egypt during the reign of the Semitic Hyksos, who began to rule in northern Egypt by 1700 and apparently introduced the horse and chariot (Gen 41:43) to Egypt.[122] Before the Hyksos were expelled around 1500, evidence shows that the pharaohs had begun to control all the land, which fits Genesis 47:20. The practice of embalming also fits (50:2, 26),[123] although this Egyptian practice was widely known outside Egypt.[124] "One hundred ten years" (50:26) was a typical Egyptian round number for an ideal life span.[125] Some even suggest a parallel with an Egyptian story in which a prince teases a peasant, but this parallel appears weaker; in the context of the whole Joseph story, Joseph's motives for testing his brothers seem quite different. Concerned about the fate of his brother Benjamin and fearful that his brothers might not tell his father that he was alive, Joseph needed to be sure his brothers had changed before he revealed his identity to them.

One could argue that the Egyptian elements in the Joseph story, even including Egyptian loanwords, reflect what educated Israelites in Palestine would have known and been able to employ as part of a fictitious setting for the Joseph story.[126] But this proposal does not explain why they would have gone to so much more trouble than most other ancient novelists to embroider with accurate information the account of a character who lived in another era and culture.[127]

Stories About Moses

Like the Joseph story, the Moses story reflects many authentic Egyptian details.[128] In itself such realism does not prove the story true or provide it a certain date, but it does support the plausibility of the biblical picture. For instance, slaves in Egypt often took Egyptian names, and some Israelites in the story bear Egyptian names (for example, Moses, Phinehas, Merari and possibly Aaron), whereas some Semitic names in the story are attested among Egyptian slaves (such as Shiphrah, a name some earlier scholars wrongly thought storytellers had invented![129]).

Kings and slaves. After the Hyksos period, Egyptian kings ruled from the south; they restored their seat of rule to northern Egypt, to the Delta region, only shortly before the time of Moses (assuming a date for Moses in the thirteenth century B.C.E., which remains debatable but more likely than alternatives).[130] Seti I visited Avaris around 1330 B.C.E. and afterward built there, and his son made it his capital, naming it Pi-Ramses (a later name used in Gen 47:5-6, 11).[131] The information presupposed here does not likely derive from a substantially later era, for in the twelfth century Pi-Ramses fell into relative disuse, its great buildings becoming a mere stone quarry.[132] Ramses II was one of history's most powerful pharaohs,[133] and he had an ego to go with it; he used Semitic slave labor to dedicate huge monuments to himself and reportedly replaced others' names with his own on some earlier inscriptions to seize their glory.[134]

Ramses II used many foreign slaves for his massive building projects early in his reign.[135] His Semitic slaves were surely not all Israelites,[136] and many must have remained slaves in Egypt after Moses led the Israelites out (Ramses' successor, Merneptah, was still using Semitic slaves).[137] The exodus of a body of Israelites, however, is not unlikely: Egypt employed many Semitic slaves in the Delta region in this period,[138] and slaves escaping from such a region would most naturally head toward Canaan.[139] Further, captive peoples had escaped elsewhere, albeit not on such a large scale. Egyptians rarely recorded defeats.[140] More telling, Israelite tradition unanimously proclaimed its origin in the exodus, and who would have *invented* a history for themselves in slavery?[141] For that matter, they would not likely have invented the golden calf episode, which implies, as other sources suggest, that the Israelites had incorporated some Egyptian worship during their captivity there.[142] The exodus account is hardly the glorious propaganda piece that seekers of an honorable heritage normally invent—though many of us have found an honor in the heritage of slavery once we have experienced it.

Other details. It is not unlikely that Pharaoh's daughter could have adopted Moses;

Ramses II had fifty-nine daughters, and women of the royal court exercised considerable independence.[143] Trained in the court of Pharaoh, Moses would hardly have been illiterate; princes often learned scripts other than Egyptian, and Semitic princes in Egypt sometimes filled important posts.[144]

Moses' people, meanwhile, were struggling, as the stories in Exodus testify. Egyptian texts depict the suffering and low status of brickmakers and also illustrate the nature of their work. Workers formed alluvial mud from the Nile into bricks; some workers specialized in moving water, others in collecting stubble, others in other aspects of the process. Bricks would be hardened in the sun for about a week. Egypt's best brickmakers could turn out about three thousand bricks in a workday, but evidence from Ramses II's reign showed that most slaves failed to even make their quota of two thousand bricks a day, and supervisors sometimes threatened or beat those who fell short.[145] Workers sometimes requested leaves from work to worship their deity on special days, as in Exodus 5:1.[146] Even the accounts of Moses in the Sinai fit what we know of the time and location.[147]

The plagues. A pharaoh as proud as Ramses II would never have admitted in inscriptions his defeat at Yahweh's hands. Nevertheless, God's persuasive power in the plagues fits what we know of Egypt's ecology, not Israel's, and probably reflects specific judgments on Egypt's deities. To many scholars, these Egyptian elements suggest a historical core to the tradition about the plagues.[148] The plagues against the gods of Egypt (Ex 12:12; Num 33:4) showed such deities as the frog god, the life god that ruled the Nile, deities of moisture and other natural forces impotent against Israel's God; the penultimate plague of darkness declared God's triumph over Amon-Re, Egyptian god of the sun.

Aside from Pharaoh's faith in the superiority of his own deities, one reason he repeatedly questioned the absolute power of Israel's God may have been that most of the phenomena described sometimes occurred on a significantly smaller level with natural causes. Some scholars have pointed to reddish contamination of the Nile in times of heavy rains in Abyssinia, which would lead to the infection of frogs and their flight from the river and sudden death. Insects would breed quickly as the Nile retreated; cattle could acquire anthrax from the dead frogs; the storms in Abyssinia could also lead to destructive thunderstorms in Egypt and a massive locust invasion. Some scholars have overstated such natural parallels, but the parallels do illustrate the extent to which the plagues fit key elements in Egypt's ecosystem. Yet no natural explanation sufficed for the climactic final plague, the death of Egypt's firstborn.[149]

The conquest. An exodus also implies a conquest, or at least some conflict involved in the Hebrews' settlement in Canaan. Evaluating the archaeological data surrounding the conquest is very complicated,[150] and scholars debate the details concerning the period of Israel's settlement. The evidence fits the biblical account more often than it challenges it, but is still piecemeal and capable of being interpreted in a variety of ways.[151] Merneptah's stele, remains at Ebal and Shiloh, and the absence of pigs from the diet of the culture in Israel's hill country support the biblical account, but most other evidence is ambiguous, neither supporting nor challenging the narrative.[152] Below we provide an example of how it can be read in support of the biblical narrative, assuming a thirteenth-century B.C.E. exodus.

God may have destabilized Canaan through various means. Waves of invading "sea peoples" (some of whom probably were "Philistines") apparently caused some destruction in Palestine during this period (probably especially in the coastal region), weakening Egypt's hand in the region.[153] One therefore cannot prove that Israelites destroyed all the cities in this period.[154] Nevertheless, Israel was probably responsible for some of the destruction, especially inland (the areas of conquest cited in Scripture).[155] A stele of Pharaoh Merneptah, successor to Ramses II, indicates that the Israelites were in Palestine by the late thirteenth century B.C.E.,[156] although the pictograph designating them as a people rather than a settled nation probably indicates that they had not settled in yet.[157]

Exaggerated as they appear,[158] the large numbers for the Israelites cited in Numbers are not genetically impossible:[159] Israel's population would have to have doubled every sixteen years, a multiplication attested in the twentieth century for a Druse village carefully observed.[160] Complaints about the space occupied by the Israelite host walking single file miss the fact that the Israelites did not move single file; if one counts the number of people filling square rather than linear space, the camp's size quickly diminishes to workable proportions, calculations one can quickly verify.

Nevertheless, the numbers remain problematic for other reasons. Egypt's entire estimated population in this period was three to four and a half million, and one would have expected such a devastating trauma to the New Kingdom economy (assuming a thirteenth-century B.C.E. exodus) as the escape of over two million slaves (Num 1:46; compare 26:51) to show up somewhere in Egyptian sources.[161] Moreover, even though we have only random attestation of wilderness nomads, one might expect some attestation of such a large company. But our estimates for Israel's population may be too high; very natural scribal complications are possible with the numbers. Most significantly, the term translated "thousand" can also mean a "clan," a "village or other population unit that provides troops from among its able-bodied men."[162]

Many critical scholars today doubt that Israel, except perhaps for the tribe of Joseph under Joshua which was later joined by Canaanite elements,[163] left Egypt; they often propose instead a peasant revolt. But the peasant revolt theory remains "impossible to prove," as one historian notes,[164] and remains open to considerable dispute, including from those who also doubt the accuracy of the biblical accounts.[165] Others have suggested that the new settlements in the highlands merely reflect the movement of people already in Canaan.[166] Such scholars often cite the similarities with Canaanite architecture and pottery. But a generation of Israelites raised in the wilderness would have to adapt some of these features from the local culture,[167] and "the nature of the settlers' culture as a whole differed to a large extent from that of the Canaanites."[168]

No one doubts the "sharp increase in small unwalled settlements in the central Palestinian hills during the twelfth and eleventh centuries,"[169] a period that can closely match the biblical exodus and settlement. Hundreds of new sites were settled there, only to be deserted by the early tenth century B.C.E. as towns and cities grew and Israel's monarchy took shape.[170] Digs at these sites have revealed pottery and architecture that in some respects seem distinct from those of the surrounding Canaanite culture.[171]

Archaeology attests the destruction of many of the cities the Israelites destroyed in the book of Joshua (such as Hazor, Lachish, Bethel), also attesting the survival of cities not said to be destroyed (such as Megiddo, Taanach, Bethshean). Shechem seems to have been destroyed later—about the time Judges attests its destruction (Judg 9).[172] Sanctuaries reused from one culture to the next over many centuries were suddenly abandoned; idols, unlike most of the remains around them, were first purposely smashed and then buried—apparently by a generation of invaders who had no use for such gods.[173]

For some cities in the conquest narrative we lack archaeological evidence. Many of these cities appear in summary lists of conquests,[174] but this fits what we know of such lists in other ancient texts, which emphasize briefly the positive points, often without obligation to recount the temporary nature of the victory.[175] More critical are the major stories to which more space is devoted,[176] but even in these cases some of the evidence is missing.

Yet given the nature of the evidence, we would expect much of it to have been lost (for Gibeon, for instance, most remains have vanished, but a cemetery attests to habitation there).[177] Professor Kathleen Kenyon, excavator of Jericho, thinks that Jericho from this period eroded away, and she could well be correct. Because city walls prevented erosion and allowed mounds to form,[178] and because the remains of Jericho lay bare to the elements for four centuries from Joshua's to Ahab's time, one might expect fewer rather than more finds if the biblical account of the walls collapsing is true.[179] An interested Egyptologist remarks that "in barely half that length of time [during c. 1600-1400 B.C.], most of the Middle Bronze Age city had been eroded away, so that this is a real factor to be reckoned with and not just a harmonistic excuse."[180] Despite this erosion, some evidence does remain from the Jericho of Joshua's time, such as a house and tombs.[181] It also remained uninhabited in the early Iron Age, as the biblical record suggests.[182]

Rather than arguing from silence against the biblical narrative when the remains of antiquity tend to be sparse,[183] we should note how much attestation we have for what some today would like to view as mere legends or baseless fiction. When only a small fraction of ancient materials have survived, as we noted above, arguments from silence against a narrative are not very helpful.

Because ancient towns were not "labeled," archaeological opinion on the identity of particular sites shifts from time to time, but the general picture fits the biblical account. Nevertheless, the idea that Israel immediately subdued all Canaan is true neither to the Bible (Josh 13:1-7; 23:13; Judg 2:3; see especially the whole book of Judges) nor to archaeology.[184] Although Joshua's generation invaded the land quickly, the book of Judges is clear that the generations that followed could not retain power there. Archaeology attests the dissolution of city-states, the sometimes inferior architectural skills of what probably constituted the new culture, their settlement in the hill country, and the fact that a new wave of Philistine invaders possessed iron implements the Israelites lacked.[185] All these details fit the portrait painted in the book of Judges.[186]

Archaeological evidence for later periods, such as those covered in 1 and 2 Kings, is much more secure, attesting even the names, dates and activities of some rulers, Assyria's withdrawal from Hezekiah's Jerusalem, and so forth. Such evidence need not be treated here.

Can We Judge How Ancients *Should* Have Written?

We have argued that Genesis and Exodus reveal far more history than Deedat allows. Neither conservative nor liberal scholars, however, would claim that Genesis and Exodus are written exactly the way most historians seek to write history today. Although Christians find enough historical veracity in the narratives to take the rest of the material "on faith," most details necessarily remain beyond our ability to test on purely historical grounds, because the evidence that could be used to argue either way no longer exists. The historical evidence that remains is sometimes ambiguous and could be argued either way, depending on whether one starts with the assumption that the narrative is generally historically reliable or with the contrary assumption. The matter comes down to the burden of proof: if historical evidence suggests that the narratives preserve much history (and it does), should we not give them the benefit of the doubt where we lack secure evidence either way?

Yet a more critical question may be the nature of history the writer or writers intended, especially when it comes to matters of chronology. Some details in the Pentateuch, if pressed literally, hardly fit the usual modern perspectives on how to write accurate chronology. Would Hagar have carried Ishmael literally on her shoulder when he was sixteen (Gen 16:16; 21:5)? Would Zipporah have a young child by Moses (Ex 4:20, 25) perhaps nearly forty years after she met him (Ex 2:11, 21; 7:7)?[187] Descendants of Midian and Ishmael appear as traders in Joseph's boyhood (Gen 37:26-28), but Midian and Ishmael seem to have been Joseph's great-uncles (16:15; 25:2). Still more problematic, Amalekites appear in Abraham's day (14:7), but Amalek is Abraham's great-great-grandson (36:12).[188]

One could find various legitimate ways to explain such differences, but one explanation that comes naturally to some biblical scholars, both conservative and liberal, is that the earliest biblical writers, like many of their contemporaries, recorded some details differently from the way we would write history today, especially when they needed to fill in details about numbers and generations. One could even suggest that they may have written history somewhat differently from the way later Israelite and first-century Christian historians would write it.

Would such discrepancies of detail pose a problem to faith in the message and essential truth of these narratives? Ancient Israelites apparently did not think so. After all, the ancient Israelites recited these stories from generation to generation, yet seem not to have been troubled enough by such differences to have removed them; probably such minor differences were not problematic to hearers in the earliest period. They were simply part of the way the Israelites recounted their stories.

Those who would argue against the Christian faith because Christians hear God's message in those narratives are thus imposing their own ideas of how God *should* speak—usually based on their own religious or cultural tradition—on ancient narratives that cannot be forced to fit their preconceptions. Disagreeing with such narratives is an option, but merely assuming that one's own ways or genre preferences are better than theirs is ethnocentric cultural imperialism.

Christians do not read the Bible as if it were merely annalistic history. As one conservative Christian work puts it, "Biblical history is not an objective reporting of purely human events. It is an impassioned account of God's acts in history as he works to save his people. Accordingly, it is 'theological,' 'prophetic,' 'covenantal history.'"[189]

Nevertheless, as we have briefly argued, the Pentateuch narratives tell us much more about history than skeptics allow, despite these minor literary variations in details. It is difficult to imagine that a narrative would accurately preserve for centuries the price for which Joseph was sold into slavery or the cities he passed through before being sold, yet err concerning Joseph's existence, enslavement or exaltation. Sometimes evidence warrants that we become skeptical of the skeptics!

Deedat and others should not demand from ancient documents a modern kind of journalistic reporting in details that their ancient authors did not design them to give. If we wish to avoid ethnocentric bias, we must evaluate the historical character of such works according to the historiographic standards of their own times (in which case even these most historically disputed parts of the Bible make a strong showing). But we believe that many of the "Christian scholars" Deedat cites as conceding his point may have also erred in denying to these documents a degree of trustworthiness they seem to deserve. And far more evidence remains to substantiate many points in biblical history, even early biblical history, than Deedat could cite for the Qur'an were the tables turned (see chapter six).

The heart of the matter, however, goes beyond arguments about minor details in the traditions in Genesis or even most details of the Gospels. The Christian faith rises or falls on one central claim above all others: Jesus of Nazareth rose from the dead. If that claim is true, then God has furnished proof to all humanity and summons us to the obedience of faith (Acts 17:31).

Notes

Introduction

[1]Glenn J. Usry and Craig S. Keener, *Black Man's Religion: Can Christianity Be Afrocentric?* (Downers Grove, Ill.: InterVarsity Press, 1996). Compare Josephus's two-volume apologetic *Against Apion*, in which vol. 1 was largely (though not exclusively) devoted to defending the Jewish religion (see Josephus *Against Apion* 2.1).

[2]One book that was fairly popular for a while in some Afrocentric circles (F. Robinson 1993) primarily argues that one of the most popular *translations* of the Bible, the KJV, contains errors of detail; contrary to some readers' expectations from its title, the book is not itself anti-Christian. By contrast, Ahmed Deedat (n.d.) criticizes the KJV as if criticizing the Bible (apparently unaware that only the most ardent fundamentalists still regard it as the best translation) and wrongly says (ibid.:9) that it "is the only Bible available in some 1500 languages of the lesser developed nations of the world" (apparently unaware that the KJV exists only in English). We are not defending particular translations of the Bible or specific traditional ideas about Christianity, or even *details* in the Bible; instead we seek to provide a conceptual reply to broader challenges to Christianity itself.

[3]Reasons to Believe also provides a useful reading list in the sciences and Christianity. For philosophical apologetics, contact, for example, Ravi Zacharias International Ministries, 4725 Peachtree Corners Circle, Suite 250, Norcross, GA 30092, (404) 449-6766. Zacharias, a former visiting scholar at Cambridge, is a Christian philosopher from India.

[4]Here we refer to those who dismiss books without reading them, not simply to dialogue on details, on which we must always remain open to correction. Thus, for example, we might have worded differently the mention of "evidence" in Usry and Keener 1996:168 n. 67 had Lefkowitz 1996:34-52 already been available. At the same time, because we tried our best to remain close to the evidence, her critiques of some writers do not actually address any major point in our book.

[5]We also chose the title in consultation with women as well as men friends, all of whom favored it. Further, if the language were taken precisely rather than as a cultural allusion (that is, implying that Christianity is a religion only for Black males), it would have excluded one of the book's authors!

[6]One of us had already written a book defending women's ministry (Keener 1992). Many of the reviews of the book were kind (for example, *Journal for the Study of the New Testament* 54 [1994]: 122-23; 58 [1995]: 121), even when written by those opposed to women's ordination (for example, Yarbrough 1993; Pyne 1994). But some reviewers opposed to women's ordination proved quite hostile, and in some circles the author's Christian commitment has been dismissed merely on account of his position (in spite of his insistence that he has been beaten and threatened on the street for his witness—Keener 1992:11-12).

Chapter 1: A Black Religion

[1]Muhammad 1992:60; on the "white religion" see further pp. 47, 293. Elijah Muhammad also claimed that Christianity is the religion of the beast in Revelation (p. 263). He shares his claim that Christianity is a White religion with the Ku Klux Klan (pp. 330-32).

[2]This Nubian official was the first non-Jewish Christian; see further below.

[3]For example, Wace 1994:940; cf. A. C. Coxe in Roberts and Donaldson 1994, vol. 3, title page (the "founder" of Latin Christianity).

[4]Tertullian *Apology* 37.

[5]Mahjoubi 1981:497; also Holme 1969:2-3. On the strength of the North African church to 398 c.e., see Holme 1969:22-53. On the strength of North African Christians in the face of martyrdom, see Mahjoubi 1981:497; A. Jones 1970:330-35; cf., for example, the accounts of Felicitas and Perpetua (S. Donaldson 1909:128-37; cf. also Lefkowitz 1976).

[6]Du Bois 1965:144, quoting Mommsen 1886:2:345.

[7]Cf. Du Bois 1965:144. On the North African church, see also Sanneh 1983:6-13; Ezeigbo 1994, on the "Golden Age" of the North African church (especially Augustine), see Holme 1969:54-75. Many of the noted Christian "saints" in Egypt and further south were dark-skinned Africans (Snowden 1970:209-11); medieval saints in Egyptian art were also dark-skinned (Stewart 1971:93). Ben-Jochannan 1991:73-137 rightly emphasizes the African impact on early Christianity, including the persecutions Romans inflicted on African Christians.

[8]For some Black Africans in North Africa, see, for example, Ezekiel *Exagoge* 60 65; Desanges 1981:427. Not all North Africans were considered Black (Snowden 1970:112, 207-11). Catherine Clark Kroeger has shared with us photographs of paintings of many early North African Christians in Italy, of which many are plainly Black (such as Proclus, a deacon; see Kroeger n.d.).

[9]Isichei 1995:43. For early Coptic churches, see Kamil 1990:76-92; for monasteries, ibid.:116-39.

[10]Although the government officially recognizes a Christian population of only 6 percent, about 15.7 percent claim to be Coptic Orthodox Christians, and a smaller number claim to be Protestant.

[11]Mbiti 1970:300.

[12]On the weakening of North Africa, especially under the Vandals, see Salama 1981:500-501; cf. also Holme 1969:76-118. The Donatist Berbers of North Africa initially welcomed the Germanic invaders (Oliver and Fage 1989:45), but the Arian invaders often persecuted North Africa's more orthodox teachers (for examples, see Holme 1969:101-2, 119-242).

[13]Sanneh 1983:15; Isichei 1995:44; Kwapong 1961:20; cf. also Julien 1970:xvi. On the expansion of Islam and gradual conquest of North Africa, see El Fasi and Hrbek 1988a and 1988b; Monès 1988.

[14]Bianquis 1988:164; Kamil 1990:39; cf. Julien 1970:xvi.

[15]Kamil 1990:40.

[16]Ibid., p. 41.

[17]Ibid., p. 42, also noting evidence for the successive plunder and destruction, then rebuilding, of monasteries. Isichei suggests the Mamelukes acted partly in reprisal for Europe's Crusades and attributes the decline also to Arab immigration (Isichei 1995:43).

[18]Cf. Oliver and Fage 1989:59.

[19]See more detailed examples of repression in chapter 5 of Usry and Keener 1996.

[20]When the Turks took Tunis in 1583, they dethroned the more tolerant Muslim ruler; violently hostile toward Christianity, the new rulers reportedly forced the remaining Christians to choose Islam or die (Holme 1969:241-42).

[21]S. Donaldson 1909:8 suggests that most of North Africa today is Arab due to the Arab invasions.

[22]As a "eunuch," he probably reminded Acts's first readers of Ebedmelech in the book of Jeremiah (on whom see Adamo 1986:198-206).

[23]On Luke's point, see J. M. Scott 1994:533-38, who contends that part of Luke's "ends of the earth" (Acts 1:8) is the mission to "Ham," inaugurated in 8:27-40.

[24]On the Blackness of "Ethiopians," cf., for example, Petronius *Satyricon* 102; Seneca *Dialogues* 5.27.3; Sextus Empiricus *Against the Ethicists* 3.43; Philo *Allegorical Laws* 2.17, §67; *Apocalypse of Moses* 35:4-36:3; *Genesis Rabbah* 73:10; 86:3.

[25]Snowden 1970:110, 132-33, on an earlier period; cf. Hakem 1981:302-4. Bion of Soli in the *Aethiopica* noted that Candace was a dynastic title (like Pharaoh) rather than a personal name, applied to the ruling queen mother (Lake and Cadbury 1979:96); but it may be "a corruption of a Meroitic title" for all Nubia's "royal consorts or queen mothers" (W. Adams 1977:260); queen mother was a prominent office in Nubia (Oliver and Fage 1989:32).

[26]Bruce 1951:190-91. On Meroe's wealth and splendor, cf., for example, Diodorus Siculus 1.33.1-4; Oliver and Fage 1989:27-28; Crocker 1986:53-72; Taylor 1991:46-48; Leclant 1981; Hakem 1981.

[27]Oliver and Fage 1989:28-29.

[28]Snowden 1970:212-14; cf. Michalowski 1981. As Isichei 1995:30-31 suggests, the rapid conversion of Nobatia in northern Nubia (543 C.E.) may indicate a considerable prior Christian presence.

[29]W. Adams 1977:435; Isichei 1995:31.

[30]Williams 1987:145; cf. Hasan 1967:17-41.

[31]Taylor 1991:64. This was "the *only* treaty in which the Arabs recognized the independence of a non-Muslim state" (Isichei 1995:31).

[32]M. Gordon 1989:108.

[33]Sanneh 1983:16.

[34]Williams 1987:148.

[35]Cf., for example, the accusation against Christodulus (Hasan 1967:92-93).

[36]For such sources cf., for example, B. Lewis 1990:23, 50.

[37]Williams 1987:149. Archaeology revealed to the modern world Christian Nubia's brilliance, long obscured by its conquerors (Davidson 1968:102; see more fully W. Adams 1977). As long as possible, they also maintained contacts with Egypt's Copts, with Armenian, Syrian and Palestinian Christians and very likely with Ethiopian Christians (Jakobielski 1988:223).

[38]Hasan 1967:90-123, especially p. 90.

[39]Du Bois 1965:147; on the overthrow of Christian Nubia, see also Hasan 1967:124-27.

[40]W. Adams 1977:539-44; on Islam's role in Nubia's fall, see also Du Bois 1965:215.

[41]W. Adams 1978b:125.

[42]Hasan 1967:125.

[43]Ibid., p. 127.

[44]Hansberry 1981b:60, 66-67, 71; Isaac 1968:20; Reynolds 1994; cf. Sanneh 1983:5-6; Davidson 1968:99-100; on Ezana, Pankhurst 1967:1-7. The account is undoubtedly historical; both the Ethiopian account and the European account of Rufinus *Ecclesiastical History* book 1 (from Edesius himself) agree (see Jones and Monroe 1955:26-31).

[45]Hansberry 1981b:74; cf. also Williams 1987:135. Inscriptions support these fourth-century claims (Hansberry 1981b:80-82). On Ethiopia's emergence as a Christian state, see especially Hansberry 1981b:60-82; on its early development as a Christian state, see pp. 83-109 (the African church became the central cultural and unifying agent of Ethiopian society).

[46]W. Adams 1977:386, 388. On its power in general, including archaeological and literary data, cf. Jones and Monroe 1955:21-25; Anfray 1981:362-80; Kobishanov 1981. For Axum's subjection of Nubia in the early fourth century, see also Dunston 1974:41.

[47]Hansberry 1981b:131. For more on Amda Tseyon (1314-1344), see Pankhurst 1967:13-28.

[48]Hansberry 1981b:132; Sanneh 1983:16.

[49]See Du Bois 1965:203; Isaac 1968:26, on Prester John; in more detail, see Hansberry 1981b:110-50.

[50]On its distinctly Christian literature, see, for example, Mekouria 1988:568-69; in general, see Mekouria 1981.

[51]"African-American advocates of Islam seem to have forgotten that historically wherever Islam has spread beyond its original geo-ethnic cradle . . . to become the absolute religion, it has done so primarily by the sword. . . . Needless to say, this meant the rupture of the non-Arab culture and usually its replacement by the Arab Islamic culture" (Ellis 1996:122).

[52]Isichei 1995:47. In general, see Cerulli 1988.

[53]Isichei 1995:46-47.

[54]Sanneh 1983:16; cf. Isaac 1968:24.

[55]Isaac 1968:26-27; see further Pankhurst 1967:49-69 (including mention of a Muslim who became a Christian, p. 67). The three largest monotheistic religions dominate in that general region: Judaism in the Jewish tradition, Islam in Arab tradition, and Christianity in Ethiopian/East African tradition (Isaac 1968:18).

[56]Many European missionaries suffered for their commitment to bring Christianity to Africa: lacking immunity to local diseases, only one in four survived the first term of service in the Congo, and most survivors buried children or spouses there (R. Tucker 1983:155-56). Rowland Bingham's work in East Africa followed the death of his companions and nearly his own, but once the work was indigenous the church quickly expanded from forty-eight to ten thousand—only to face severe repression from Western colonial powers (in this case Italy; R. Tucker 1983:295-300). Although many Western missionaries accepted colonialism, they fought its evils, including the slave trade, and faced the ridicule of their intellectual contemporaries in Europe who thought race theories had a scientific basis (R. Tucker 1983:140).

[57]Cf., for example, Sanneh 1983:36, 167, and examples in R. Tucker 1983 and Neill 1964.

[58]Sanneh 1983:181-83. His church later (1917) sought entry into the World Evangelical Alliance (ibid.).

[59]Isichei 1995:54. The ungodly lifestyles of clergy in the Congo hindered the spread of Christianity there (Isichei 1995:66; cf. p. 68).

[60]Noll 1992:341.

[61]Isichei 1995:233.

[62]Ibid.

[63]Ibid., p. 75. While they too often remain "foreigners," "missionaries are often the most socially integrated of any foreigners living in a given society" (Smillie 1995:4).

[64]Even when they mistakenly supposed that Western commerce would raise the standard of living and undercut the slave trade, Western missionaries like David Livingstone were among the leading opponents of African slavery, and their reports of its horrors particularly stirred the conscience of the West against it (for examples, M. Gordon 1989:10, 199, 203, 209; cf. Pierard 1976:9, on Dr. John Philip).

[65]Isichei 1995:242-43.

[66]Egyptian rather than Axumite (Ethiopian) missionaries birthed the church in Nubia (Davidson 1968:100-101).

[67]Hasan 1967:131, including an eyewitness report where they virtually begged Ethiopia to send them more clergy, but Ethiopia had none to spare.

[68]See Britten 1996:23, 30.

Chapter 2: What Do You Say When a Muslim Says Christians Were Proslavery?

[1]Muhammad 1992:18. On Christianity as supportive of slavery, see pp. 70, 221, 285; Blacks must "drop slavery (Christianity)" and accept Islam (p. 99). Elijah Muhammad also claimed, "We cannot deny the fact that the Christian West is responsible for this universal corruption in the land and sea" (p. 284), and that the United States was part of Christendom (pp. 279, 281); freedom of religion in the United States had made the nation nonreligious and rebellious against Allah (p. 277). Those of us who have been beaten, ridiculed and threatened for Christ's gospel may be less inclined to agree with him that the "West" is very Christian.

[2]Muhammad 1992:76; see also pp. 68, 78, 233, 320-22. He truthfully declared that he did not advocate violence (pp. 215, 322), preferring to let Allah, who was angrier at Whites than he had been at Pharaoh, carry out the final battle (p. 181). Not only his followers (pp. 321-22), however, but also many groups of Christians were pacifist, including the early years of C. H. Mason's Church of God in Christ.

[3]Afrocentric scholar Molefi Kete Asante is among those who think Christianity a non-African religion, but he emphasizes that Islam is no more African than he thinks Christianity is. Historic Islam claimed that God's language was Arabic, required pilgrimage to and prayer toward Mecca, and expected Arab name, garb and customs. This "like Christianity makes us submit to a strange God" (1988:2-3). We trust that our first chapter responds adequately to the claim about Christianity, but on Islam see also Al-Hariri, p. 23, as cited in Houssney 1989:14: "anyone who becomes a Muslim becomes an Arab." Cf. also Ellis 1996:122, 182.

[4]Also pointed out by others, including Williams (1987:23), whose criticisms address imperialism in general and are not theological critiques of Islamic religion.

[5]Waines 1995:35-36.

[6]For example, Numidia, which survived Rome and (barely) the Vandals; Du Bois 1965:141-42.

[7]Asante 1990:61.

[8]Bianquis 1988:164.

[9]Kamil 1990:40.

[10]See, for example, Dramani-Issifou 1988:112-15; Hasan 1967:177. North Africa as a whole has now become culturally Arabized and Islamized (Eickelman 1989:9-10); Ben-Jochannan 1991:127 speaks of "the Asian population that presently occupy and control Egypt." Some repression of what remains of the indigenous culture has continued in more recent times (cf. W. Adams 1978a:22; "Cupolas and Culture" 1990; Brooklyn Museum 1978:10).

[11]Cook 1983:88. It has nevertheless become more diverse today than in the past (ibid.)

[12]M. Gordon 1989:28-29. Neighboring peoples were often accused of apostasy so they could be enslaved (ibid., p. 31). From around 1700 to 1900, Muslim reform movements seeking to Arabize West African Islam spread through the region, but West Africans continued to mix Islam with more traditional African beliefs (Sanneh 1983:212-13, 228-29; indeed, African Muslims in the 1600s and 1700s often combined their Islam with Christianity—Sanneh 1983:214).

[13]B. Lewis 1990:59. Cf. also the enslavement of captured or impoverished Christians unable to pay tribute and unwilling to convert (M. Gordon 1989:25).

[14]B. Lewis 1990:12.

[15]L. Bennett 1966:16; cf. Williams 1987:197. Extant evidence indicates that this Soninke empire existed at least by the fifth century C.E. (M. Gordon 1989:109-10).

[16]L. Bennett 1966:16-17; cf. Williams 1987:197.

[17]Weakened further by the Berber Abu Bakr, it suffered at the hands of the Muslim Fulani, once subject to it,

from the 1200s (see Davidson with Buah 1966:39-51; cf. Williams 1987:199).

[18]Du Bois 1965:211-12. The university used Arabic because it was the main language of trade and main written language available, not to invite conversion to Islam (Williams 1987:206).

[19]L. Bennett 1966:18. Its university (the University of Sankoré) trained scientists, physicians, lawyers, geographers, artists and members of other academic disciplines (Williams 1987:205).

[20]Williams 1987:204.

[21]Sanneh 1983:229.

[22]Ibid., p. 230.

[23]Dramani-Issifou 1988:115.

[24]Williams 1987:209.

[25]Ibid.

[26]Ibid., p. 207. Jackson 1970:301 gives the date of Babo's deportation as March 18, 1594.

[27]Williams 1987:208. For the enslavement of fellow Muslim Africans who had once abetted the slave trade, see M. Gordon 1989:112-13, following sources from the 1500s; cf. B. Lewis 1990:58-59.

[28]Williams 1987:209.

[29]Du Bois 1965:212.

[30]On this empire in general, see Oliver 1961 (including excavations, Arab reports and the like).

[31]Williams 1987:284-85.

[32]Ibid., pp. 285-86.

[33]B. Lewis 1990:79 (Yemen and then Saudi Arabia a few weeks later); Fogel and Engerman 1974:13.

[34]M. Gordon 1989:233, also citing the assessment of journalist Eric Rouleau.

[35]Domínguez 1979:91; M. Gordon 1989:233. Mannix 1962:257 complained that "the great powers are too much concerned with oil diplomacy to investigate the situation." Besides these traditional, hereditary slaves there, many migrant workers in that region continue to be *virtually* enslaved—bound to their masters, unable to leave or complain, and paid only about thirty dollars each month (MacShane 1991). In Roman and even many cases of U.S. slavery, slaves were paid small bonuses or wages (in the U.S., Fogel and Engerman 1974:148-49)—but it was slavery nonetheless.

[36]It provided some legal protection for the slave (B. Lewis 1990:6, 78, 99; M. Gordon 1989:14, 19, 39; Talib with Samir 1988:720; see also John Wesley's claim in Sunderland 1835:91). In this section we depend especially on research by Murray Gordon and (especially, citing mostly primary Arabic sources) Bernard Lewis, who both provide full documentation which we have not chosen to duplicate here.

[37]The enslavement of Africans is as early as the Pharaonic Egyptian enslavement of Nubians (Talib with Samir 1988:714); on nonethnic Roman slavery see, for example, Keener 1992:196-98.

[38]Bredero 1994:9.

[39]M. Gordon 1989:105.

[40]This was also the practice of "those of his companions who could afford it," some of whom "acquired more by conquest" (B. Lewis 1990:5).

[41]See, for example, M. Gordon 1989:xi.

[42]B. Lewis 1990:78, citing Qur'an 5.87 and Muslim comments on it. This principle contrasts with Jesus' way of interpreting some Old Testament laws as concessions to human sinfulness rather than the ideal standard (Mt 19:3-8; Mk 10:2-9; cf. discussions of this hermeneutic in Keener 1991a and 1992).

[43]N. Bennett 1971:16; Mannix 1962:257.

[44]This is commonly noted, for example, by L. Bennett 1966:34-35; B. Lewis 1990:12; and in many sources cited throughout this book. Because of Nation of Islam propaganda, William D. McKissic (1990:52) notes his astonishment to learn that "Arab Muslims" were the first "to target Blacks . . . for slavery" and that many Black Africans in earlier periods converted to Islam only to gain better treatment from their masters. Nevertheless, the Europeans certainly did their best to make up for lost time!

[45]Ogot 1993, in the *Daily Nation* of Nairobi, Kenya, responding to Ali Mazrui and citing substantial historical data. On the duration, see also B. Lewis 1990:59.

[46]M. Gordon 1989:ix, 147-49.

[47]Ibid., pp. 149-50.

[48]Ibid., pp. 57, 150; cf. ibid., p. 43; B. Lewis 1990:13. Talib with Samir 1988:720 points out that Islam borrowed its practice of slave concubines (recognized by the Qur'an) from pre-Islamic Arab custom.

[49]M. Gordon 1989:92-93. By the nineteenth century, the sultan had four hundred Black eunuchs, thirty to forty White ones, and a harem of fifteen hundred women.

[50]B. Lewis 1990:94, 97. Cf. the story of the husband slaying his wife and the African slave with whom she slept (M. Gordon 1989:86). For Arab artistic depictions associating Black slaves with sexual evil, cf. B. Lewis 1990:plates 21-23 (all plates are between pp. 22 and 23). The sexual use of slaves, regardless of race, has been a common historic practice (in precolonial Africa, see Henn 1984:5-6); in Mediterranean antiquity, see, for example, Keener 1992:197, 217; more fully, Keener 1991a:79, 185 n. 133.

[51]M. Gordon 1989:83; see all of chap. 4 ("Sex and Slavery in the Arab World," pp. 79-104).

[52]B. Lewis 1990:91; cf. M. Gordon 1989:43. The demographic growth of mulattos seems to have been lower than for the strictly Arab population, perhaps due to infanticide (though the report on which M. Gordon 1989:16-17 depends may be exaggerated). Ellis 1996:266 follows an Islamicist in reporting that Black male slaves were castrated.

[53]B. Lewis 1990:101-2. On racial prejudice in Islam, see also M. Gordon 1989:98-104.

[54]B. Lewis 1990:18-20.

[55]Cf. Snowden 1970 and 1983:46-59, 63-108. "The very striking similarities in the total picture that emerge from an examination of the basic sources—Egyptian, Greek, Roman, and early Christian—point to a highly favorable image of blacks and to white-black relationships differing markedly from those that have developed in more color-conscious societies" (1983:vii).

[56]Cf. B. Lewis 1990:17-20.

[57]Snowden 1983:99-108, especially pp. 99-101. The darkness/light symbolism of the church fathers reflects the symbolism of the day (common throughout history among both Black and White peoples—pp. 82-83), and while we would see it as somewhat less benign than Snowden does (pp. 107-8), in context its intention was surely as nonracial as its origin. It rarely (Snowden documents no instances, but unrecorded exceptions may have occurred) affected practical matters (such as slavery) as the more derogatory, anti-African language of some later Arab writers did.

[58]Cf. B. Lewis 1990:21-25, 44; M. Gordon 1989:100.

[59]M. Gordon 1989:102.

[60]For instance, the term *'abd,* originally applied to Black slaves (White ones were called *mameluks*), eventually applied to slaves in general (M. Gordon 1989:98; B. Lewis 1990:56). Because Arabs took so many Nubian slaves, *al-Nuba* in time became nearly synonyous with "black slaves" (Hasan 1967:8).

[61]M. Gordon 1989:104.

[62]White supremacists in Europe, following Islamic tradition (Copher 1993:110-13), then their successors in the United States (see, for example, Peterson 1978:141-58) and among the Boers in South Africa (Davidson 1968:228-29).

[63]By Wahb ibn Munabbih in Ibn Qutayba, *Kitab Al-Ma'arif,* p. 26, as translated in Bernard Lewis, ed., *Islam from the Prophet Mohammed to the Capture of Constantinople,* vol. 2, *Religion and Society* (Oxford: Oxford University Press, 1974), p. 210 (from Ellis 1993:109-10); cf. also Talib with Samir 1988:721, though they doubt that this was the majority view. See earlier Palestinian Talmud, *Ta'anit* 1:6, §8; Babylonian Talmud, *Sanhedrin* 108b; *Genesis Rabbah* 36:7; Copher 1993:103. Whereas Ahmad Babo insisted that the Ham myth did not justify the enslavement of Muslim Africans, many of his contemporaries disagreed (B. Lewis 1990:57-58).

[64]M. Gordon 1989:32. We say "even" because this action contravened Islamic law; see further chapter five, below.

[65]B. Lewis 1990:55; although some Arab writers rejected the idea, it was widespread.

[66]See, for example, objections by Rankin 1838:6-7 (though some of his responses are biblically and scientifically inaccurate).

[67]So, for example, Dunston 1974:53; among non-Afrocentric writers, for example, A. Walls 1982:18. Arthur Custance's speculation that the curse was explicitly applied only to Canaan lest Noah curse himself by cursing his own son (cf. 1975:25), while plausible on the level of the story itself, and Cheikh Anta Diop's suggestion that Noah meant to curse Ham and thereby not Canaan but Israel's oppressors in Egypt (1974:7) both neglect the book's intention of equipping the Israelites to seize the Promised Land from Canaan. This latter point also diminishes the force of Custance's suggestion that the curse was not severe (1975:149).

[68]So often Afrocentric Christian writers, such as J. Johnson 1993:222; P. Boyd 1991:114. On our reading, Genesis was written to encourage Israel in possessing the land, but even the curse on Canaan was clearly not permanent; in later times Jesus acted on behalf of a Canaanite (Mt 15:21-28).

[69]B. Lewis 1990:53.

[70]Ibid., pp. 82-83.

[71]M. Gordon 1989:81; B. Lewis 1990:56, 75.

[72]Ibid., pp. 72-73.

[73]Ibid., pp. 56, 77.

[74]Ibid., p. 59. One Black eunuch who did rise to power in Egypt thereby drew the satirical abuse of an Arab poet (ibid.).

[75]M. Gordon 1989:69. Mamelukes, White military slaves, became politically dominant under the Ayyubid dynasty, although Black military slaves became more prominent again in the late eighteenth century (ibid., pp. 72, 75).

[76]Ibid., pp. 102-3; B. Lewis 1990:92. See also Talib with Samir 1988:721-22, noting the data and its Greco-Roman origin.

[77]B. Lewis 1990:92.

[78]Further examples include writers from throughout the Arab world (see examples in ibid., pp. 45-48).

[79]Ibn Qutayba, *Al-Ma'arif,* ed. Tharwat 'Ukasha, 2nd ed. (Cairo, 1969), p. 26, as cited in B. Lewis 1990:46. Medieval Islamic physiology drew many of its ideas from Galen (cf. Good 1980, surveying also modern consequences), as medieval European writers also drew from Greek sources.

[80]B. Lewis 1990:89-90.

[81]For example, though proselytes were theoretically equal in ancient Judaism, their social status generally remained inferior; cf. *m. Horayot* 3:8; *Numbers Rabbah* 6:1; perhaps *Cairo Damascus Document* 14.4; cf. Jeremias 1975:272, 323; Baumgarten 1972; Blidstein 1974.

[82]B. Lewis 1990:37, B. Lewis, ibid., pp. 28-36, provides substantial evidence for insults and discrimination against Blacks and dark Arabs in Islamic sources by the eighth century.

[83]Ibid., p. 20, citing the 467th-468th nights (omitted in Lane's version) in *The Thousand and One Nights.*

[84]M. Gordon 1989:161-62. These popular sentiments sometimes contrasted with the pragmatism of the actual British officials in charge of pursuing the Empire's trade interests, but ultimately prevailed (see ibid., p. 8).

[85]B. Lewis 1990:79.

[86]M. Gordon 1989:162-63.

[87]B. Lewis 1990:78-79.

[88]Cf. ibid, p. 80. Cf. Theodore Weld (1839) on reports of Turkish slavery in Ruchames 1964:167.

[89]B. Lewis 1990:80.

[90]Libya and Arabia, free from foreign domination, remained centers of the slave trade long after it was shut down elsewhere (B. Lewis 1990:81). Fogel 1989:236-37 claims abolitionism as the one noble motive of colonialism.

[91]M. Gordon 1989:164-65. The sultan appealed to considerable historical precedent for continuing slavery (B. Lewis 1990:3). The nineteenth-century Moroccan writer Ahmad ibn Khalid al-Nasiri (1834-1897) noted the continued "unlimited enslavement of the blacks," complaining that "men traffic in them like beasts, or worse" (B. Lewis 1990:58).

[92]M. Gordon 1989:171.

[93]B. Lewis 1990:79.

[94]M. Gordon 1989:46-47.

[95]Ibid., pp. 177-82.

[96]Hallett 1974:111.

[97]M. Gordon 1989:51-52.

[98]Ibid., p. 51.

[99]Mannix 1962:259. For a fuller discussion of the East African trade, see chap. 11, "Slave Catching in the Indian Ocean," pp. 241-62.

[100]M. Gordon 1989:191-92.

[101]Ibid., pp. 192-207.

[102]Hallett 1974:580. On British force ending Zanzibar slavery, see also Oliver and Fage 1989:153.

[103]Williams 1987:23. Arabs may have been darkened through mulatto blood (ibid.), which rarely appeared in the White U.S. population because of the White American prohibition of interracial marriage and enslavement of all products of interracial unions.

[104]Ibid., p. 47. This is not to diminish European shame; for one serious reaction to recent European colonialism (in this case the bitter French colonialism in Algeria), see Fanon 1963.

[105]Williams 1987:56.

[106]Ibid., p. 208. Williams (ibid., p. 155) says his field studies in the Sudan have confirmed this practice in modern times as well.

[107]Ibid., p. 158.

[108]Ibid., p. 159.

[109]Ibid., p. 47.

[110]Sanneh 1983:74; see further Isichei 1995:219, 233, including discrimination against African Christians. Mbiti points out that Western colonial rulers actually helped finance the building of mosques and pilgrimage to Mecca, and generally "created conditions which facilitated the spread of Islam" (1970:330).

[111]Sanneh 1983:214-16; on collaboration in education (at Western initiative), see pp. 219-20; cf. Isichei 1995:233.

[112]Masland et al. 1992:37.

[113]"Child Laborers" 1992, following studies by journalists in the Philippines. One may also compare the child soldiers recruited for the rebel Mon Tai Army in eastern Myanmar, whose government opponents more forcibly exploit the labor of local populations (see Falise and Loviny 1994); on child labor, see recently especially Sutton 1995-1996 and the various stories subsumed under the cover story in *World Press Review* 1996:3, 8-13.

[114]"A School for Iqbal" 1995.

[115]Cf. many reports, such as in *Africa News* 1992; *Newsweek*, October 12, 1992, p. 49; *ESA Advocate* 1992; *World Press Review* 1989 and 1991; *Amnesty Action* 1993:2.

[116]*World Press Review* 1994, based on a report in the *Herald* of Harare, Zimbabwe. "Sudan" 1995 estimates instead one million deaths and three million displacements.

[117]Gregory 1996:39.

[118]See, for example, "Sudan—The Ravages of War: Political Killings and Humanitarian Disaster," 1993, pp. 6 9. This is available for three dollars from Amnesty International U.S.A., 322 Eighth Ave., New York, NY 10001. Cf. also "Civil War Brings Suffering" 1993.

[119]"Forgotten Slaves" 1991; Masland et al. 1992:32; Brander 1996.

[120]M. Gordon 1989:xi. A U.S. scholar visiting that region also told us that he personally was shown sales receipts for "Christian slaves."

[121]Gregory 1996:37.

[122]"Sudan" 1995:3. Amnesty International reports that the Sudanese government has ignored human rights to maintain its power: "virtually every kind of human rights violation known to Amnesty has been perpetrated by the political and security establishments, including arbitrary arrest and detention without charge or trial, torture and ill-treatment, extrajudicial executions" ("Sudan" 1995:1).

[123]Bhatia 1995. For releasing his findings Mahmoud was rewarded with two years in a Sudanese jail.

[124]Ibid.

[125]Masland et al. 1992:30. This is despite the *official* emancipation of slaves there on July 5, 1980 (M. Gordon 1989:x; cf. B. Lewis 1990:79).

[126]Masland et al. 1992:32. M. Gordon 1989:x places the estimate at 200,000 men, women and children.

[127]Gregory 1996:38.

[128]Masland et al. 1992:32. On Arab beatings and brandings of African slaves in the Sudan, see Bhatia 1995.

[129]Pierce 1993:80.

[130]*Amnesty Action* 1993:4; "Saudi Arabia—Religious Intolerance: The Arrest, Detention and Torture of Christian Worshippers and Shi'a Muslims" (New York: Amnesty International, September 14, 1993; available for three dollars from Amnesty International U.S.A., 322 Eighth Ave., New York, NY 10001).

[131]M. Gordon 1989:231; the quotation is excerpted from a letter by M. Morillon, French ambassador to Saudi Arabia, dated November 7, 1953.

[132]*Amnesty Action* 1991a.

[133]*Amnesty Action* 1991b. Cf. similarly the Sunni Muslim Iraqi repression of Sunni Muslim Kurds—for example, *Reach Out* 1993; for the torture (such as splitting open feet, wounding testicles, beating and starving) of Kurds in Turkey, see Zana 1995:13-15.

[134]Lalevée 1993, noting, for example, the guerrilla movement in Uganda. Idi Amin's earlier brutal regime in Uganda murdered thousands.

[135]Some predominantly Muslim nations like Jordan, Lebanon, Mali, Niger and Senegal are largely tolerant, but nations currently under or close to Shari'a, traditional Islamic law (such as Sudan, Saudi Arabia, Pakistan), are much stricter and restrict religious freedom of expression for non-Muslims with severe penalties.

[136]Cf., for example, the *fatwa* on apostasy enacted in Lebanon, November 13, 1989. See more fully, for example, Shahid 1992.

[137]Shapiro with Peterson and Mabry 1993.

[138]Gregory 1996:37-38.

Chapter 3: What Do You Say When Others Complain That Christians Did Not Oppose the Slave Trade?

[1]Noll 1992:199.

[2]Ibid., pp. 101-2, 226. For example, "when a small Baptist congregation tried to organize in Tidewater, Virginia," the local parson beat the Baptist minister, repeatedly slamming his head against the ground; the sheriff then gave him twenty lashes with the whip—after which the beaten man returned and preached. The wealthy planters viewed "Baptists and other dissenters" as undermining "order by refusing to defer to their social betters and by insisting on the rights of absolutely everyone to act on the gospel message" (pp. 101-2). In the early 1700s, church membership was as low as 5 percent in the South, much lower than in the North.

[3]Raboteau 1978:126. Following Aristotle's view that Greeks should not enslave Greeks, Europeans felt that Christians should not enslave Christians. Slaveholders thus came up with a simple solution: do not allow Black people to become Christians (Pelt and Smith 1960:22-23). Christians in the Roman Empire, however, had undercut Aristotle's ideological basis for slavery altogether (ibid., p. 22).

[4]See, for example, material on the A.M.E. and A.M.E. Zion churches in Sernett 1985:135-59; Payne 1969; D. Bradley 1956-1970; R. Allen 1960; Handy n.d.; W. Walls 1974; Dickerson 1995.

[5]Raboteau 1978:101-3; Haynes 1953:51. Raboteau's work is extremely well documented, so where we cite him the reader may find other sources (which we have not duplicated here) by consulting his work. Charles C. Jones (1842:44-45) complained how little religious instruction had initially targeted African slaves in the colonies.

[6]Raboteau 1978:103; Noll 1992:79.

[7]See Raboteau 1978:123-25; cf. also J. H. Clarke 1991:46: "Some slaves took the Christian version of the Bible literally and believed that God meant all men to be free."

[8]Isichei 1995:71.

[9]Raboteau 1978:132, cf. p. 148; J. B. Childs 1980:29-30; Washington 1986:ix. Cf. Phillis Wheatley's praise for George Whitefield for the hope his message inspired among her people (Noll 1992:109).

[10]L. Bennett 1966:63. Inspired Black preachers began to preach to White as well as Black audiences, at times even planting interracial churches (Raboteau 1978:133-41).

[11]Against the view of many nineteenth-century scientists and historians, the Reverend Thomas Smyth argued eloquently for the positive historical contributions of Africa and that the specific enslavement of Blacks as a race was of modern origin (E. Clarke 1979:111).

[12]Raboteau 1978:133-41.

[13]Noll 1992:138. On Liele and David George, see also Washington 1986:8-9; Pelt and Smith 1960:29-41; on Bryan, see Pelt and Smith 1960:41-45; Sernett 1985:48-50.

[14]Noll 1992:138-39.

[15]Washington 1986:11.

[16]Ibid., p. 12.

[17]Raboteau 1978:147; Pelt and Smith 1960:59-65 (though many Whites disagreed with these policies—p. 65-66); see Goodell 1853:326-27. Even in freer times, slaves were sometimes forbidden to attend church, depending on the slaveholders' views (C. Sanders 1987:85); but separate Black churches continued to exist in many parts of the South (Raboteau 1978:196-207; E. Smith 1988:75-100).

[18]On the African Methodist movement, see especially Wilmore 1983:80-89; Dickerson 1995; cf. Noll 1992:201-3. For Black congregations in the North from 1740 to 1800, see E. Smith 1988:29-40; for 1800-1860, see pp. 41-74 (Philadelphia, pp. 42-46; New York, pp. 47-48, 58; Boston, pp. 48-56; Providence and Newport, pp. 56-57; Wilmington, p. 57).

[19]Raboteau 1978:209-10.

[20]See Mukenge 1983:36-38. Thus the C.M.E. grew from 67,888 in 1873 to 120,000 in 1880; the Baptists from 25,000 (recorded) in 1850 to 500,000 in 1870; the A.M.E. from 20,000 in 1856 to 400,000 in 1880; and the A.M.E. Zion from 4,600 in 1856 to 120,000 in 1880 (ibid., p. 39); cf. comparable statistics in Dickerson 1995:70.

[21]E.g., Wilmore 1983:36-44.

[22]Grimké 1973:59-60.

[23]Wilmore 1983:40. He was soon followed by Henry Highland Garnet (1843).

[24]Wilmore 1983:42.

[25]See notes on A.M.E. and A.M.E. Zion history, above.

[26]Fordham 1975:111-37.

[27]Ibid., p. 111.

[28]Anglican bishop William Fleetwood in 1710 (Klein 1971:172-73), though he did not represent Anglicanism in general (Noll 1992:90); Quaker John Woolman (1754-1762; on other Friends in the early nineteenth century, see Mannix 1962:171-90); Samuel Hopkins in 1776 (in the later collection Hopkins 1854).

[29]Raboteau 1978:143; J. B. Childs 1980:27-28 (noting that Wesley also prophesied slavery's destruction). Abolitionists like William Jay (1835) charged that "men buyers" (slaveholders) were as sinful as "men-stealers" (slave raiders; Ruchames 1964:97), a line of argument probably stemming from Wesley (Angelina Grimké, 1838, in Ruchames 1964:154).

[30]A. Adams 1964:97. In the formative period, Methodist abolitionism prevailed even in the South (Wilmore 1983:34; A. Adams 1964:97), and slaveholders were ineligible for church office (A. Adams 1964:97).

[31]See A. Adams 1964:100-101; Haynes 1953:111-12; Washington 1986:27-38. Some, however, opposed slavery but felt that the Baptist doctrine of "individual liberty of conscience" prohibited them from interfering with slaveholders' choices (Washington 1986:16-17, 25). The few minutes of Baptist meetings and letters of Baptist missionaries from the 1700s reveal Baptist opposition to slavery; the minutes of Virginia Baptists in 1789 include a call for its abolition (Pelt and Smith 1960:27).

[32]A. Adams 1964:98-100.

[33]Ibid., p. 97; cf. Raboteau 1978:144-45. While churches in the earliest period did not promote slavery and some actively opposed it, most failed to address the issue (see Scherer 1975)—just as most people today, Christian and non-Christian, remain silent on contemporary injustices, including chattel slavery. Alice Dana Adams declares that Episcopalians and Catholics appeared to remain neutral (1964:101); Catholic work among U.S. Blacks mainly began in 1929 (C. Johnson et al. 1947:283). For Congregationalist antislavery, cf. C. M. Clark 1940.

[34]In addition to some accounts in Usry and Keener 1996:122-33, Tarrants 1992, and regularly in *The Reconciler* and elsewhere, see recently Clary 1995, recounting the conversion of a former imperial wizard of the Klan who now works with Black pastors.

[35]Most remained uncomfortable with the most radical abolitionists like John Brown, who would not stop short of violence. Other white abolitionists besides Brown died (such as Elijah P. Lovejoy—Ruchames 1964:139-41).

[36]Sernett 1975:37-41, noting that the compromises failed to stem the antislavery reputation. See more fully Haynes 1953:108-11; D. Matthews 1965:62-87, until abolitionism's rise in the North from 1832 on.

[37]Noll 1992:174.

[38]J. B. Childs 1980:29; cf. Dickerson 1995:15-16.

[39]Dickerson 1995:13-22.

[40]See especially H. S. Smith 1972, for example, pp. vii-viii, 73.

[41]A. Adams 1964:96; cf. ibid., pp. 58-62. Cf. the beating of Amos Dresser, a northern minister, for merely having antislavery papers in his possession (Savage 1938:34).

[42]For example, Stampp 1978:157-58; Sernett 1975:47-51; D. Matthews 1965:113-282; Pelt and Smith 1960:67 (1845).

[43]For example, Sawyer 1858; F. Ross 1857.

[44]For example, Sunderland 1837.

[45]Raboteau 1978:152-80; cf. Wilmore 1983:32-33; Stampp 1978:160; Davis 1975:523-56. For a fuller treatment of the repressive biblical hermeneutic practiced by Whites who favored slavery, see Cannon 1995:119-28; for a treatment of how oppressors have abused Jesus, see J. Grant 1995, especially pp. 133-36.

[46]Stampp 1978:159-60.

[47]Those who favored slavery took verses out of context or simply appealed to the institutions that existed in biblical times without taking into account whether the Bible supported or resisted such institutions. The abolitionists, by contrast, looked for broader principles in Scripture (see, for example, R. Groothuis 1994:35-37). Slaveholders' abuse of Scripture remains a textbook example of culturally insensitive hermeneutics even to this day (see, for example, Klein, Blomberg and Hubbard 1993:12).

[48]Those who thought that slavery was "against nature" believed that it was immoral (Aristotle *Politica* 1.2.3,

1253b; see Keener 1992:205); this reportedly included two other radical Jewish sects with wording similar to that of Paul, the Essenes (Josephus *Antiquities of the Jews* 18.21; Philo *Every Good Man Is Free* 79; cf. *Hypothetica* 11.4) and Therapeutae (Philo *Contemplative Life* 70). In the nineteenth century, slavery's defenders still insisted on the *natural* character of slavery, against those who decried it as unbiblical (as in Seabury 1861:iii); abolitionists contended, as Paul evidently believed, that it was against nature (as in Rankin 1838:60).

[49]On the context and cultural background of this passage, as well as Paul's request for one slave's freedom so he could join Paul in ministry, see especially Keener 1992:184-224 and 1995b; on Paul's particular mission strategy, cf. also Keener 1995c. We have summarized our response only briefly here because it is argued in detail in these other publications with extensive documentation.

[50]Besides Usry and Keener 1996:103-4 and Keener 1992:184-224, see here B. Dodd 1996:81-110, especially pp. 87-89 (although the differences may be overstated at some points, the general outline remains quite helpful). That whole book responds to modern aversions to Paul based on the cultural differences between his world and ours.

[51]Some have also recently complained that when civil rights activists were suffering untold brutalities in their marches in the 1960s, Nation of Islam condemned the marches. Now, with police protection rather than violent repression, it has suddenly become fashionable to support public marches. This may represent a genuine change of heart, but it remains ironic. Some have also charged that Nation of Islam's leader, "while preaching separation from Jews and white devils," lives "in the fashionable, partially Jewish Hyde Park" (Cross and Scott 1993:28).

[52]For the information in this paragraph, besides what appears in Usry and Keener 1996, see Keener 1992:184-224.

[53]See Lydia M. Child (1833) and African-American abolitionist Theodore S. Wright (1837) in Ruchames 1964:68, 137-38; cf. David L. Child (1854) in ibid., p. 106.

[54]Skinner 1970:20-21; see also Pobee 1979:35.

[55]That something can be used contrary to its original purpose may also be illustrated by an opposite sort of example to the one above: the "natural rights" philosophy of John Locke, which later proved helpful in combating slavery (Scherer 1975:107), did so even though Locke himself justified slavery "as a continuation of a state of war in which a captive was enslaved rather than killed" (ibid., p. 106).

[56]Noll 1992:79.

[57]Bebbington 1977:561; cf. "William Wilberforce" 1992:12:654.

[58]Bebbington 1977:556.

[59]Cf., for example, the debate in Brownlow and Pryne 1858 (both ministers).

[60]Sunderland 1835. Abolitionist preachers like Sunderland, the Reverend Willis and especially Theodore Weld argued that the Bible was against slavery (for example, Hardesty 1984:76; Rev. Willis 1854; cf. also A. Brown 1854; Marsh 1854; W. Brock 1854:158; Bacon 1846).

[61]Cheever 1857. For other abolitionists who contrasted true Christianity and slavery, see, for example, Ruchames 1964:33, 37, 101, 114-15; for the Bible's opposition to slavery, ibid., pp. 36, 59. One Christian, Stephen Foster (1844), harshly denounced Christendom for its sins of tolerating slavery (Ruchames 1964:187-90). A true Christian will want everyone subject to God rather than to himself or herself (Henry C. Wright, 1837, in Ruchames 1964:111).

[62]Tappan 1854:164. Tappan supported Garrison in the early period (1833; Ruchames 1964:75-78).

[63]Elizur Wright (1833) in Ruchames 1964:59. Slaves rather than slaveholders should be compensated (Garrison, 1833, in Ruchames 1964:81).

[64]The evangelical revivalists shifted the earlier emphasis on salvation as primarily an ultimate goal to salvation as primarily the beginning of a transformed life seeking to transform the social order (Barnes 1964:3-11; Hardesty 1984:49-51). Finney's revivals produced new leaders for the antislavery cause like Weld and influenced the wealthy Tappans (Barnes 1964:12, 19-21). This movement also planted the seeds of women's emancipation; see Barnes 1964:12-13 and especially Hardesty 1984.

[65]Barnes 1964:71-72; Filler 1960:68-69; cf. Hardesty 1984:46; Wendell Phillips in Ruchames 1964:20, 235.

[66]Barnes 1964:74-78. Radical for its time, it became the nation's first coeducational school and the first school where Black and White students enrolled together (Filler 1960:69-70; Hardesty 1984:46-47; T. Smith 1980:252). Some Oberlin abolitionists felt that this stance was too radical even for Oberlin, lest it precipitate undue opposition; but the Tappans were even more radical, preaching "amalgamation"—complete mixing of Blacks and Whites (cf. Hardesty 1984:118).

[67]Weld's work constituted the primary source for the events in Stowe's famous abolitionist work *Uncle Tom's Cabin* (Barnes 1964:73). The hero allows himself to suffer so that Cassy and Emmeline can flee to freedom; although in modern usage his name often symbolizes compromise, when Stowe wrote the work in 1852 Uncle Tom "was a Christ figure meant to encourage others in the spiritual struggle against human bondage" (Noll 1992:410).

[68]David Walker denounced slavery in God's name in terms that terrified most Whites; see Walker 1993.

[69]For example, Blockson 1981:13-14, 35-36, 41, 46, 60, 64, 87, 105.

[70]Ibid., p. 12.

[71]Noll 1992:318.

[72]C. Sanders 1987:231. Cf. similarly Wilmore 1983:4; Noll 1992:551.

[73]James Curry, whose holder's oldest son taught him how to read (Blassingame 1977:130-31).

[74]Quoting L. Bennett 1966:80. Frederick Douglass noted that many of the slave spirituals were coded with messages about escape to the North (Blockson 1981:180-84); they functioned as protest songs providing divinely sanctioned hope (Owens 1971; Hale 1995:198-201).

[75]L. Bennett 1966:111; Wilmore 1983:53-57. The Scriptures played a critical role in the revolt (Noll 1992:161).

[76]Joyner 1984:156-57.

[77]Ibid., p. 158.

[78]Ibid.; cf. Raboteau 1978:101-2. The preachers also could not avoid texts that speak of all Christians as spiritual priests and having similar roles (Sernett 1975:59-81).

[79]Sernett 1975:68.

[80]Despite objections to many aspects of Garvey's message in the Black church, many sermons from leading Baptist and Methodist churchmen appeared in his *Negro World,* opposing his imprisonment and reflecting favorably on his organization's work (see Burkett 1978).

[81]Garvey 1922:27. Similarly, Du Bois, hated by many Whites for his unflinching resistance to injustice, prayed, "Incarnate Word of God . . . we are not Christians because we profess Thy name and celebrate the ceremonies and idly reiterate the prayers of the church. . . . We must be . . . merciful and not oppressors. . . . The cause of our neighbor must be to us dearer than our own cause" (Du Bois 1980:63).

[82]Douglass 1968:120, as quoted in Ellis 1996:20. Douglass both appealed to Christian conviction (as in Quarles 1968:97) and professed growing alienation from the segregated White churches and the nonabolitionist Black churches influenced by them (cf. Quarles 1968:15, 47; Van Deburg 1975:7-8).

[83]See, e.g., Wilmore 1983:62-73.

[84]See, e.g., ibid., pp. 57-62; Dickerson 1995:19; Carroll 1938:86-87 (the latter also complaining because Vesey took the Bible as God's literal Word). One of his counselors was the Reverend Morris Brown; Brown later became a protégé of the founding A.M.E. bishop Richard Allen, who may have supported his role in the conspiracy, and ultimately an A.M.E. bishop himself (Wilmore 1983:60). Other religious elements (as in the case of Gullah Jack, an African conjurer) also played roles (cf. Wilmore 1983:59; L. Bennett 1966:115), but the exodus and conquest story of the Bible remained central (Wilmore 1983:58-59; L. Bennett 1966:113).

[85]See, e.g., Wilmore 1983:53-57.

[86]In Africa, compare, for example, John Chilembwe, who joined the National Baptist Convention and worked with African-American missionaries for schools, agriculture, health needs and the abolition of liquor in Nyasaland until he and some followers died in an aborted revolt against colonial authorities in 1915 (Isichei 1995:249-50).

[87]Sernett 1975:37-41, 47. From 1788 to 1831 Black Baptist churches grew quickly as White Americans in general began to emphasize freedom of worship, but after Nat Turner's revolt southern slaveholders began to repress Black Baptists (Washington 1986:23).

[88]Sernett 1975:101.

[89]For example, Noll 1992:205.

[90]See Bradford 1869—for example, p. 1: "Well has she been called 'Moses,' for she has been a leader and deliverer unto hundreds of her people."

[91]Cone 1984:123-25; C. Sanders 1995b:122-23. Wilmore 1983 thoroughly treats the religious roots of most historic Black resistance. With the exception of a few like Jupiter Hammon, most Black preachers were involved in the struggle against slavery, but their particular positions varied from that of Richard Allen (who "condemned slavery but counseled the slaves to love and obey their masters" till it was abolished—p. 68)

to that of Nat Turner; cf. Hamilton 1972:37-69.

[92]For examples of the Christian commitment of many Black leaders in this period, one may peruse the Charles N. Hunter Papers, 1818-1931 (Raleigh, N.C.; now in the Duke University manuscripts collection), including, for example, E. Hunter 1900. For the ways that Christians, especially southern Christians, adapted to work against Jim Crow, see R. White 1990. Although exceptions existed, more Black Christians were like "Francis J. Grimké, who was a theological conservative making liberal social pronouncements," than the reverse (R. White 1990:120).

[93]J. D. Roberts 1974:88, as cited in Sider 1993:116.

[94]L. Bennett 1966:313.

[95]Juster 1995:149.

Chapter 4: What Do You Say When Someone Claims That All Christian Doctrines Began in Africa?

[1]Besides Usry and Keener 1996:60-82 and many of the sources cited there, see, e.g., Dunston 1974; Adamo 1986; Felder 1989; McCray 1990; McKissic 1990; P. Boyd 1991; Copher 1993; McKissic and Evans 1994.

[2]By contrast, Molefi Kente Asante (1988:2-3) believes that Christianity, like Islam, is not African, and that all religions arise out of someone's nationalism (for Islam's ethnic-specific prophetology, see Wansbrough 1977:53). We would respond that historically part of the genius of the first Christians, especially in Paul's circle, was to *transcend* their Jewish allegiances to preach the gospel to the Gentiles without mandating circumcision. To be faithful to the vision of Jesus and Paul, Christianity must transcend any ethnic confines.

[3]J. H. Clarke 1991:358. He likewise denigrates Islam as "an unoriginal religion, the most unoriginal, unimaginative religion of them all . . . a bastard child of Christianity and Judaism" (ibid., p. 357). Cf. Ben-Jochannan 1991:xxii: "This work's ultimate goal is to show the definite links between Ju Ju, Voodoo, and other exclusively indigenous traditional African religions with Judaism, Christianity and Islam, among other religions."

[4]Cf., for example, Mbiti 1970.

[5]John Henrik Clarke (1991:358) is right to complain that Christianity, Judaism and Islam have been exploited as "political instruments," but his suggestion that African religions "were never intended to be" is more questionable. Traditional religions were inseparable from the social fabric of the local tribe. As John Mbiti (1970:5) notes, "Traditional religions are not universal: they are tribal or national. . . . There is no conversion from one traditional religion to another. . . . A person has to be born in a particular society in order to assimilate the religious system of the society to which he belongs."

[6]See, e.g., Richardson 1974.

[7]Olmstead 1959:479.

[8]Olmstead 1959 elsewhere refers to the Persian doctrine of immortality (e.g., p. 40) and images like the righteous crossing a bridge to eternal reward on the day of judgment while the foolish "go to the House of the Lie" for eternal torment and people in between end up in "an intermediate abode" (pp. 100-101). But these are not assertions of *bodily resurrection*, as we see in Daniel 12:1-2 and probably Isaiah 26:19 and Ezekiel 37:1-14. That doctrine probably appears in the Hebrew Bible earlier than it is attested in Persian texts (Yamauchi 1990:456-57, 461, cf. 409). It naturally came to the fore in early Judaism through a confluence of factors, such as the biblical doctrine of the goodness of creation (including bodily human life) and the concept of eschatological justice.

[9]For one recent critique of the overstatement of Persian influence on early Judaism, see Yamauchi 1990:458-66 and the sources he cites. The most important Zoroastrian sources may not have been written down till as late as the sixth century C.E. (Yamauchi 1990:405).

[10]On the cosmic conflict between Ahura-Mazda and the Evil Spirit who had struggled with him from the beginning, see Olmstead 1959:98.

[11]Compare the Greek report in ibid, p. 479, in which one god rules the other for three thousand years, then they fight for three thousand, and in the end Ahura-Mazda brings victory and rests. In time this scheme of six millennia followed by a sabbath age appeared in Jewish texts, but it remains an optional rather than central figure of early Jewish eschatology.

[12]Hood 1990:105-10; he is correct that the church councils borrowed thought categories that were largely Greek. But even here, they were interpreting earlier sources. For instance, in John 1:1-18, on which some councils depended heavily, Jesus as God's Word or wisdom is a Jewish image (see Epp 1975; cf. Hamerton-Kelly 1973), rooted in ancient Israelite personifications of wisdom related to analogous ancient

Near Eastern and especially Egyptian personifications of wisdom before Israel had as much contact with Greece (see Ringgren 1947:9-52: Kitchen 1960:4-6; Bright 1981:448; Vos 1913:388-89).

[13]See, e.g., Lieberman 1962; Hengel 1974; Avi-Yonah 1978.

[14]Hood 1990:110-20 provides samples of how far he goes; whether one agrees with how far, however, the issue of recontextualization he raises is a valid one.

[15]For instance, we regard Robert E. Hood's discussion of the Spirit in ibid., pp. 185-89, showing a limited familiarity with Jewish pneumatology, as inadequate for the sweeping conclusions he draws from it (see Keener 1997c; Fee 1994).

[16]Thus the fact that a view is attested in history, say among the Mandeans (Hood 1990:65; they were anti-Christian, and our earliest written evidence for their views stems from perhaps half a millennium later than Hood suggests—see Yamauchi 1966b:89; cf. Burkitt 1932:102; Drower 1962.21-22), does not make it compatible with the earliest Christian message.

[17]The New Testament does contain many literary allusions to earlier Jewish literature such as the Old Testament, the Apocrypha and *1 Enoch*, and it is not such data that we dispute (one of the authors has focused most of his scholarly research on such background). But when subordinating historical objectivity to ethnocentric expediency, rather than simply asking specific historical questions arising from one's perspective, one is inclined to disseminate ideas that are convenient instead of historically accurate data. Thus for instance when some contend that because the Ethiopian church alone preserved *Jubilees* and *1 Enoch*, these documents derive from Africa, we believe that they betray incomplete knowledge of the evidence. Our late medieval Ethiopic manuscripts of *1 Enoch* depend on earlier originals, but archaeologists have found Aramaic portions of the document from the second century B.C.E.—among the Dead Sea Scrolls in Palestine. The theology is plainly Jewish and reflects the perspectives of second-century B.C.E. Essenes (including their calendar), the style of language from that period and so forth; likewise with *Jubilees*, a rewriting of much earlier biblical accounts. The historical accuracy of the earlier biblical accounts can (in contrast with *Jubilees*) sometimes be confirmed by archaeological evidence and ancient Near Eastern parallels from the early periods in question (see appendix B).

[18]Repeated more than once in the Pentateuch, the Ten Commandments appear central to Israel, perhaps as a condition for community membership (see Weinfeld 1991).

[19]Ben-Jochannan 1991:69-70; cf. Sarna 1986:139.

[20]P. Boyd 1991:190 compares the keeping of the 147 Negative Commandments with the Mosaic law, which he believes teaches justification by works, contrasting them with the "dispensation" of grace that he believes Christ brought.

[21]See more fully Sarna 1986:137-39 for parallels with other ancient Near Eastern texts and pp. 140-48 for contrasts with other texts.

[22]Egyptians (as in Pritchard 1955:326), Syrians and Phoenicians practiced circumcision (de Vaux 1961:28); Palestinian peoples reportedly adopted it from the Egyptians and Ethiopians (Herod. *Hist.* 2.104; Diod. Sic. 1.28.3). The Israelites may have already had an Egyptian form of circumcision and taken the new form in Joshua 5:2 (Sasson 1966:474). It appears, perhaps independently, in some other traditional societies (see Nadal 1950:348; Beidelman 1971:185, 196).

[23]See the collections of Hammurabi, Lipit-Ishtar and Eshnunna in Pritchard 1955. Even regulations concerning mildew (Lev 14) may have Mesopotamian parallels, though the Bible's regulations are more practical (Crocker 1990a). Sarna 1986:172-82 compares Israelite with other legal collections, emphasizing points of distinctiveness. So far we lack such collections from Egypt, probably because the ruler's word was law (Bright 1981:39, on the Old Kingdom; but cf. the views of Diodorus Siculus 1.70.1; 1.71.1; 1.77-80 for a later period). Polemicizing against Israel, Manetho thought Israel's laws a deliberate *contrast* with Egypt's (Josephus *Against Apion* 1.240).

[24]See, e.g., Keener 1992:190 on Deuteronomy 23:15-16 and Hammurabi §§15-19.

[25]Sages' sayings were collected in a variety of cultures (cf., e.g., Albright 1968:256 and 1960), but Egyptian parallels are much closer than Akkadian models. Collections of wise sayings of almost identical genre also carried over into later Roman culture (e.g., the first-century B.C.E. collection of Publilius Syrus). Egyptian love songs also closely match the Song of Solomon.

[26]Ben-Jochannan 1991:164.

[27]Although Hebrew prophetism exhibits distinctive traits (see especially Buber 1949:70-75; Heschel 1962:465-66) and many scholars date Egyptian social justice oracles after the reigns they critique, the closest ancient parallels to Hebrew oracles concerning justice would be moralistic Egyptian oracles (e.g., the

Admonitions of Ipuwer; Prophecy of Neferohu) on the same theme (*maat,* truth and justice); cf. McCown 1929:213-16; R. Scott 1954:57-58; Kitchen 1960:6-7; Lindblom 1962:31. Despite some claims for divination's influence in Israelite prophetism (e.g., Long 1973), it was never central (Lev 19:26, 31; Is 2:6; Jer 14:14; Heschel 1962:457-58), quite in contrast with its prominence in Mesopotamian models (see R. Wilson 1978:10; Lawrence 1980); for divination among the Hittites and others see Gurney 1954:158-59; Lindblom 1962:31; Rainey 1965a:123.

[28]Some oracle forms (victory oracles and oracles against nations) are widespread in the ancient Near East (van der Toorn 1987; Hayes 1968:84-86; Moran 1969:17; Nilsson 1951:124-27; Craigie 1983:35; cf. Pritchard 1955:274-75, 320, 354-55, 416, 449-50, 482-85). For the image of prophets as envoys of the divine suzerain, see J. Holladay 1970:31-34; this image fits the suzerain's covenant lawsuit (Rabe 1976:127; Weinfeld 1977:187-88; Blenkinsopp 1971; cf. Ramsey 1977). Prophetesses appear in both Hebrew (Ex 15:20; Judg 4:4; 2 Kings 22:12-20; Is 8:3; Joel 2:28-29) and Mari (Moran 1969:29-31; J. F. Ross 1970:14-15; Paul 1971:1159-60) tradition, but are absent in many places. Mari and Ebla may provide the closest parallels in *form* for many types of Israelite prophetism (see Bright 1981:88-89; J. F. Ross 1970:11-12; Pettinato 1981:319 n. 12; Kitchen 1978:47, 117); but significant differences in content remain (see especially Paul 1971:1160; cf. Buss 1969:338)—most of all regarding the character of the deity (Heschel 1962:471-73; Craghan 1975:52).

[29]E.g., the collections of Hammurabi, Lipit-Ishtar, Eshnunna and Nuzi, mostly from the biblical period of the patriarchs, before the era of Moses. Subsequent discoveries or study may reveal corresponding collections in Egypt as well, but we do not know of them.

[30]Ben-Jochannan 1991:35.

[31]Cf., e.g., Pfeiffer 1962:37-39, 57; Gurney 1977:48; Moyer 1969:49, 58, 69. The avoidance of honey (Lev 2:11) may be early and polemical (cf. Pritchard 1955:336, 337, 341, 346, 351; Diodorus Siculus 5.62.5; Pausanias 1.18, 7; 6.20.2; Gurney 1977:51; C. H. Gordon 1965b:136). For holy fire (Lev 10:1), cf. Pritchard 1955:209; for the use of turtledoves (e.g., Lev 1:14) in sacrifices cf. *Ugaritic Text* 611.5, 13 in Kaiser 1973:187; for the use of blood for consecration, cf. Moyer 1969:69. Choosing animals of a particular color or gender (e.g., Lev 1:3; Num 19:2) conveys important symbolism in many traditional cultures (e.g., Mbiti 1970:49, 269; Gurney 1977:48; F. Grant 1953:27); that a sacrifice should be without blemish (Lev 1:3) is likewise not unexpected (Moyer 1969:58).

[32]Yosef Ben-Jochannan (1971:568) is even more confident, tracing all monotheistic religions (Judaism, Christianity and Islam) to this source (never mind that the *Book of the Dead* is polytheistic; his dating is also off). He merely demonstrates his own lack of acquaintance with seminaries when he goes on to revile seminary professors by claiming that documents such as Josephus, the Mishnah and the Tenach (the last-named is the Hebrew Bible, which many of us teach!) are unknown to most of them. Some texts he cites are from the medieval or modern period and shed no light on ancient thought, as any academic historian who has studied them will testify. Unfortunately, many readers will follow Ben-Jochannan simply because they prefer his assertions, being themselves unfamiliar with the sources he cites.

[33]*Book of the Dead* 1974:36 (spell 20, parts T-1-2, 3). Cf. the similar traditions carried into late antiquity in magical papyri, e.g., in Betz 1992). Examining such texts makes it understandable why some Jewish teachers thought Egypt was a primary center for magic (e.g., *'Abot de Rabbi Nathan* 28A; 48, §32B; *b. Qiddušin* 49b; *Exodus Rabbah* 9:6; 20:19).

[34]*Book of the Dead* 1974:39 (spell 30, part P-1).

[35]Ibid., p. 41 (spell 31a, part P-1).

[36]Ibid., p. 44 (spell 35a, part P-1).

[37]Ibid., p. 52 (spell 53, part P-1).

[38]Ibid., p. 69 (spell 79, part P-1).

[39]Ibid., p. 96 (spell 124b, part S). On African societies in general (in contrast to ancient Egypt), note Mbiti 1970:274: "With a few exceptions, there is no belief that a person is punished in the hereafter for what he does wrong in this life. When punishment comes, it comes in the present life."

[40]*Book of the Dead* 1974:185 (spell 177, part P-1).

[41]Ibid., p. 191 (spell 180, part S-5, 9).

[42]Ibid., p. 101 (spell 125d); cf. similarly Greek and other Near Eastern conceptions. Messianic concepts and Christian beliefs about the end time fit only uncomfortably into traditional African worldviews; "since the future dimension of time in African societies was so short, there could have been no messianic hope, and our traditional rulers are rooted only in the Sasa and Zamani periods" (Mbiti 1970:244). Though many

elements of Christian teaching make more sense in traditional African culture than in traditional European culture, members of most cultures have to learn to think differently to grasp the Jewish-Christian-Muslim view of the end time.

[43]Although the existence and nature of deification in Greek Mysteries of the New Testament period are debated, Greek philosophy emphasized participation in the divine (e.g., Seneca *Dialogues* 1.1.5 and *Epistles to Lucilius* 48.11; Epictetus *Discourses* 2.19.26-28; Philostratus *Vita Apollonii* 3.18; Plotinus *On Virtues* 1.2.7), and some regarded deceased (e.g., Cicero *De Optimo Genere Oratorum* 6.17, *De legibus* 3.1.1 and *De Natura Deorum* 2.12.32; Plutarch *Profit by Enemies* 8, *Moralia* 90C, and *A Letter of Condolence to Apollonius* 36, *Moralia* 120D) or living (Diogenes Laertius 2.100; 8.1.11) philosophers as divine. This influenced to some degree the language of Hellenistic Jewish and later Hellenistic Christian writers (e.g., Philo *De Vita Mosis* 1.279; Pseudo-Phocylides 104; *Sentences of Sextus* 7; *Testament of Adam* 3:2), but they qualified their sense (Philo *De Virtutibus* 172; *Epistle of Aristeas* 211, 263; *Sibylline Oracles* fr. 1.1-2; C. Holladay 1977:236). Palestinian Judaism and earliest Christianity never lost sight of the distinction between God and his people (Gen 3:5; 11:4; Is 14:14; *Jubilees* 3:19; 10:20; *Apocalypse of Moses* 18:3; *Exodus Rabbah* 8:2; 1 Cor 3:4; Urbach 1979:1:252).

[44]Bernal 1987:128. Lloyd Graham (1991:326) sees in the five loaves and two fish a symbol of the seven elements (one wonders then about the different numbers in Jesus' other feeding miracle!) and cites fish symbols from other religions (some inaccurate, e.g., his Talmudic reference)—though one could cite any number of symbols in any religion without demonstrating that they are related. The application of "ICHTHUS" to Christ is a post-New Testament development.

[45]Bernal 1987:130.

[46]Cf. ibid., pp. 131, 145.

[47]Cf. N. Lewis 1983:100, both noting the Egyptian view of annual resurrection of vegetation, symbolized in a dying-and-rising god myth, and how widespread it was and is in many unrelated societies.

[48]Freyne 1988:172, 241; Neusner 1984:23; Applebaum 1974-1976:685; Safrai 1974-1976b:747.

[49]Wagner 1967:119. The more skeptical version includes merely the apotheosis typical of mortals achieving immortality among a pantheon of finite deities (Diodorus Siculus 1.20-22; cf. 1.25.2).

[50]Most current writers stress this aspect of ancient deities' rescusitations—e.g., Gasparro 1985:29, 43-49; W. K. C. Guthrie 1966:55-56.

[51]Cf. Metzger 1955:15, 20; Nock 1933:136. Frazer's whole scheme of "dying-and-rising gods" has been open to much criticism in recent times; see the documentation in Gasparro 1985:30 n. 16.

[52]Although this could be argued at length due to the debate on either side, we cite here in passing Yamauchi 1973 as a thorough treatment. A less complete survey may be found in Keener 1991b:6-16.

[53]E.g., Tertullian *Apology* 47.14, see Eliade 1958:120. Paul C. Boyd (1991:30) is also correct that some features of later (postbiblical) Christian tradition derive from the Mysteries, although his sources for this matter are not all accurate and some reflect an anti-Catholic bias. Ideas like baptismal regeneration (p. 33), a scale of merits versus demerits (p. 36) and the use of December 25 (pp. 70-71) may represent borrowings from paganism.

[54]Metzger 1955:10-11; Eliade 1958:115. In contrast to the story of Adonis's death, for instance, the rising of Adonis is not documented before the second century, and that of Attis not before the third century at the earliest—that is, long after the resurrection of Jesus (Wagner 1967:171-207, 219, 229). Cf. the typical story, in which Attis's corpse remains uncorrupted, so one of his fingers remains alive and continues to move (Vermaseren 1977:91).

[55]Metzger 1955:11; cf. Nock 1964:31.

[56]One admittedly could get this idea from Greek texts (e.g., Diodorus Siculus 1.29.3).

[57]James 1954.

[58]Ben-Jochannan 1971:375-452.

[59]We noted this same information in Usry and Keener 1996:163, but it has been argued still more forcefully by a classicist, Mary Lefkowitz (1996:91-154, especially 134-53), who complains that George James ignores demonstrably African elements in ancient Egypt in favor of Greek legends reinterpreted in light of Masonic myths from the Eurocentric French Enlightenment (p. 156). It is unfortunate that some radical Afrocentrists will probably dismiss all of Lefkowitz's careful analysis here. This is not to deny that Afrocentrists will have some reasons to complain; Lefkowitz does admit a pro-Greek bias (p. 161). One might find a Eurocentric bias in some of what she claims for Greece and Rome (cf. p. 6). For example, she does not point out that Athenian democracy (which she praises) applied only to free male citizens, a relatively small percentage

of people living in Athens; "freedom of speech" even in Athens was relative (cf. Socrates' bout with hemlock); despite the Renaissance bias, ancient Israelite literature also affirmed history's value for the present (and for that matter, Plato proposed the creation of the sort of edifying myths that Lefkowitz rejects). But such oversights probably stem mainly from her specialization and do not reflect the entire work (see, for example, her agreement that the Egyptians were Africans, people of color, and spoke an Afroasiatic language—pp. 13, 58, 160).

[60]Cf. Epictetus *Discourses* 3.21.14: *palaiois* rites.

[61]Burkert 1987:2.

[62]Ibid., p. 37.

[63]Burkert 1985:166.

[64]Otto 1965:54-55.

[65]Burkert 1987:5-6 and 1985:177.

[66]Gasparro 1985:49.

[67]E.g., Ben-Jochannan 1971:379 and 1991:111; P. Boyd 1991:28.

[68]The library dates to c. 297 B.C.E.; Alexander died in 323 B.C.E., over two decades earlier. This is not to discount all that James says. Even if we disagree with James's reason (Greek philosophy is "stolen") and if some will think he goes too far in calling for the abolition of all Greek fraternities and sororities on Black campuses ("because they have been a source of the promotion of inferiority complex and of educating the Black people against themselves"; James 1954:160-61), many will agree that Black intellectuals can find other models besides Greek philosophers (see ibid., p. 160).

[69]His detailed methodology may be examined, e.g., in Keener 1992, whose index of primary ancient references alone is twenty pages long, with three columns on each page; or the more recent Keener 1997c or his forthcoming commentary on Matthew with Eerdmans. On a more popular level, cf. Keener 1993b, which applies this methodology in more summary fashion to the whole New Testament.

[70]In some cases, the genetic relationship is genuine, such as Israel's borrowing of many Egyptian architectural devices in the tabernacle, below; but the contrasts (such as the absence of an image on the ark and the absence of shrines for tutelary deities) indicate some divergence of perspective. For a more extensive list of qualifications regarding proposed parallels, see Boring, Berger and Colpe 1995:24-32.

[71]Against Diop 1974:194; cf. P. Boyd 1991:57, 163. Hood (1990:124) objects to making the Trinity central to Christian doctrine; but while some of his other observations are important (some statements of doctrine were simply Greek concerns and ways of putting matters), the Trinity follows naturally from New Testament teachings as early as Paul, whose extant writings begin only two decades after Jesus' resurrection (see, e.g., Fee 1994:841-42). As Keener's forthcoming Matthew and John commentaries should illustrate, the doctrine is *most* heavily emphasized in the streams of early Christianity embedded in Palestinian Judaism.

[72]Ancient Egyptian literature emphasized a number of gods, not just a triad, and writers select three in particular to make the parallel, not because Egyptians typically thought only of three; cf., e.g., *Book of the Dead* 1974:5 (spell 1), 119 (spell 142, part S-4). Persians had also modified Zoroaster's one Ahuramazda by adding the goddess Anahita and the popular god Mithra (Olmstead 1959:423), but this temptation to add a mother-goddess is not part of the early Christian Trinity (though one was added in some later sectarian movements). The Persian addition of Anahita eventually accommodated other Persian views still more fully, making Ahuramazda "again an oriental monarch with a harem full of mother-goddesses" (Olmstead 1959:475); even during the stage where three main deities were prominent, many other deities remained alongside them (Olmstead 1959:444). And in contrast to Egyptian formulas in which deities blended into one another (e.g., *Papyri Demoticae Magicae* 14.349, where one is both Ra and son of Ra), the New Testament never confuses or mingles Father and Son.

[73]See, e.g., Richard 1967:297. North African theologians like Tertullian and Athanasius were among the foremost defenders of the orthodox faith in early Christianity (though many Gnostics and Arians also taught in that region). Ethiopian Christians continued to praise Father, Son and Holy Spirit (e.g., Emperor Amda Tseyon, in Pankhurst 1967:20, 25).

[74]See, e.g., Fee 1994:839-42.

[75]Isaac 1968:28. The rejection of Chalcedon (451), shared with many other Eastern churches, is no longer held to be a major issue (most historians today regard the Monophysite-two natures controversy as largely semantic); and despite Rome's opposition to its own Monophysites, it maintained strong alliances with Ethiopia (Isaac 1968:22).

[76]Isichei 1995:18, 31. Greek thought often defined the questions Christians in the eastern Roman Empire

asked, but most of the early answers came from the Bible.

[77]E.g., Jackson 1939:28-29; Ben-Jochannan 1971:572-73.

[78]One may compare, e.g., most current commentators on the *Marana tha* prayer of 1 Corinthians 16:22 (e.g., Fee 1987:839; J. Robinson 1962:154-57; Gerhardsson 1979:54; Cullmann 1963:201-9; A. Hunter 1966:65), which reflects the earliest stratum of Christian belief (the earliest Palestinian Christians prayed in Aramaic). We leave aside a more detailed defense, though it has often been undertaken elsewhere. A more thoroughly documented case for the Jewishness and earliness of early Christian beliefs about Jesus will be found in some subsequent works, especially in the introduction to Keener's detailed academic commentary on the Fourth Gospel.

[79]Ben-Jochannan 1971:575. Graham 1991:287 cites Heracles as a Greek parallel to a virgin birth—conveniently ignoring the fact that Heracles' mother was hardly a virgin after Zeus had sex with her (the biblical account, by contrast, lacks sexual associations). Graham also parallels divine mothers in other cultures with Mary (Graham 1991:302). But Mary wasn't divine—she was just the human mother of Jesus in his human incarnation; while "divine mother" imagery affected the portrayal of Mary in some later traditions, one searches in vain for traces of parallels to this idea in the New Testament!

[80]This note derives primarily from the current working draft of Craig Keener's forthcoming academic commentary (Eerdmans) on Matthew. Most proposed parallels to the virgin birth (surveyed in W. Allen 1977:19; Soares Prabhu 1976:5-6; cf. R. Grant 1986:64) are distant, at best representing supernatural births of some kind—a not unnatural expectation in any society that experiences births and believes in deities (cf. Barrett 1966:6-10). Even most proposed Jewish parallels (Daube 1956:6-9; cf. also *2 Enoch* 71; *Genesis Rabbah* 53:6) are too late to provide a source for the Gospels or on closer examination have little merit for other reasons. When, for example, Philo affirms that God supernaturally opened wombs (Schweizer 1975:33; cf. Vermes 1973:220), he adds little to the earlier biblical picture (cf. Gen 30:2). Although no direct Old Testament precedent existed for virgin births, *supernatural* births (e.g., Gen 21:2; 25:21; 30:6, 17; Judg 13:3; cf. Maillot 1978) and prenatal annunciations (e.g., Gen 16:11; Judg 13:3-14; cf. *1 Enoch* 107:3) abounded, and the language in such Old Testament texts is considerably closer to Matthew 1:21 (modeled on Is 7:14 in Mt 1:23) than most other ancient accounts are.

[81]Acts 21—27 presupposes that he not only met him in Acts 21 but also remained in Palestine two years until Paul's departure for Rome. This particular argument depends on our reading of "we" as including the author—the more natural interpretation, which we defend in more detail below; Luke and Acts are currently virtually universally attributed to the same author. On the "we" see, e.g., Dupont 1964:167-68; Munck 1967a:xliii; Fusco 1983:73-86; Maddox 1982:7; see also Keener 1993a:17, 22-23.

[82]Ben-Jochannan 1971:574. For a Christian response to Ben-Jochannan that also recognizes his valuable points, see C. Sanders 1995a:169-74; for her responses to Asante (who is more ecumenical and less hostile than Ben-Jochannan), see pp. 166-69.

[83]Ben-Jochannan 1991:49.

[84]Ben-Jochannan 1971:572-73.

[85]Hansberry 1981b:91 note; Isaac 1968:28. Although the language of the theological issues was especially Greek (the primary language of the eastern Mediterranean of that period), the competing Greek views the council was evaluating were being especially fought out in the Egyptian church, and Athanasius, the leading defender of what is now recognized as the orthodox position, was called by his enemies a "Black dwarf."

[86]See, e.g., Chadwick 1967:130-32.

[87]Ben-Jochannan 1971:363-64.

[88]The repetitive grammatical and typographical errors on nearly every page of this work, combined with consistent historical errors and reliance on outdated or refuted sources, also will put off many scholars. While typists, assistants or editors can introduce some errors, and while grammatical and typographical errors need not imply errors of substance, few academic works boast so many.

[89]For example, sources of tradition like later legends composed by the Masons are clearly unreliable (cf., e.g., the speculations of Ben-Jochannan 1971:417).

[90]Cheikh Anta Diop (1974:6) thinks Moses got monotheism from Akhenaton (also J. H. Clarke 1991:34-35) and dates Moses about 1400. Some conservative scholars date Moses before this period (for a neat survey of arguments pro and con, see Walton 1978:29-30). More often today, relatively conservative scholars (those who believe in a historical Moses and Exodus) who are familiar with the details of the biblical accounts, and synchronizing with Egyptian and Canaanite data, date Moses to the time of Ramses II, the early 1200s (cf., e.g., Albright 1946:194-95; Kitchen 1978:144 n. 46; C. H. Gordon 1965a:145; Bruce 1951:167; J. A.

Thompson 1962:56-58; for a more detailed discussion, see LaSor, Hubbard and Bush 1996:59-60; Sarna 1986; G. E. Wright 1962:53-85). In the 1400s, Egypt strongly controlled Canaan (cf. texts of Thutmose III and IV in Pritchard 1955:234-49; contrast less substantial achievements by Seti I and Ramses II in ibid., pp. 253-57). (By contrast, Ben-Jochannan 1991:49 probably dates Moses' flight too late, c. 1232; Pharaoh Merneptah's stele has Israel as a people in Canaan by 1220.) Yet Akhenaton also followed 1400, reigning about 1364-1347 B.C.E.

A half-century later, however, by the time of Ramses II, Akhenaton's *direct* influence in Egypt was largely obliterated (beginning with his successor Seti I; Groenewegen-Frankfort and Ashmole 1967:65). Not only Moses but also the Hebrew patriarchs, centuries before Akhenaton, seem to have regarded their God as the supreme one, but seem to have allowed that the spirits of other deities existed, though subordinate to their God—as they continued to hold subsequently (e.g., Ex 12:12; cf. 1 Cor 10:20; cf. LaSor, Hubbard and Bush 1996:45-46). Meanwhile, Egyptologists debate the nature of Akhenaton's "monotheism" and the extent to which it influenced the elite (cf. Blumenthal 1992). The king seems to have consolidated Egypt's pantheon primarily as a political move to resist the priests of Amon—who probably eventually did him in (see more fully Sarna 1986:151-57). It may be that the educated in the New Kingdom generally accepted a unity of the godhead while worshiping many gods, making Akhenaton "heretical" only in his rejection of other gods (Yoyotte 1981:126).

At the same time, despite differences, the similarities between the biblical and Egyptian creation stories (cf. Currid 1991) may well prove more substantial than between the biblical and oft-cited Mesopotamian ones. To whatever degree Moses adapted and to whatever degree he reacted against contemporary models (the Israelite perspective of Yahwism's triumph over Egyptian deities suggests more of an emphasis on the latter), Egyptian culture provided the general cultural matrix in which the statement was made (Ex 12:12; Num 33:4). African peoples nearly all affirm one supreme God (Mbiti 1970:37-38). For henotheistic tendencies in Egypt and various other cultures, see, e.g., C. H. Gordon 1953:129; Albright 1968:231; among some Greco-Roman intellectuals, Seneca *On Benefits* 4.8.1-3; Ferguson 1987:252; Nilsson 1948:115-24.

[91]That Israelites actually lived in Egypt is likely; who, after all, would *make up* a history in slavery (Bright 1981:121)? Evidence for Semitic slaves in Egypt, which presumably included Israelites, includes proto-Sinaitic inscriptions (c. 1500 B.C.E.); as the inscriptions might suggest, many Israelites abandoned monotheism in Egypt, which explains the golden calf in the wilderness (also the view of later rabbis, *Mekilta Pisḥa* 5.39-40). Such syncretism also occurred in Egypt proper and in Asia; cf. Pritchard 1955:249-50; C. H. Gordon 1965b:127; cf. Albright 1963:12-13; Aharoni 1982:146.

[92]Usry and Keener 1996:60-82.

Chapter 5: How Do We Answer the Nation of Islam?

[1]Muhammad 1992:253. African-American Christians have already offered many responses to N.O.I. on a useful popular level (e.g., Akridge 1995; see also his fact sheets available from West Angeles Church of God in Christ, Christian Education Department, 3045 South Crenshaw Blvd., Los Angeles, CA 90016). For further relevant information, lectures and apologetics training, contact especially Project Joseph, P.O. Box 1661, Chattanooga, TN 37416-0616, (423) 490-0605, which specializes in African-American Islamic apologetics.

[2]Muhammad 1992:202.

[3]Ibid., p. 232.

[4]Ibid., p. 171. If he means here the scientist Mr. Yakub, he means he is the first in about six thousand years—which would rule out Jesus and orthodox Islam's prophet Muhammad.

[5]Ibid., p. 234. Cf. p. 246: "Come follow me, your brother Elijah Muhammad." Technically the "savior" is Master Fard: "In 1877 a Savior was born" (p. 237), whereas Elijah was born in Sandersville, Georgia, on October 7, 1897 (Lincoln 1994:180).

[6]Muhammad 1992:235.

[7]Ibid., p. 244. W. D. Fard left in the early thirties, and Elijah Muhammad's quote is from 1965.

[8]Ibid., p. 247; now "we have come to the end of the Prophets" and the end of the world.

[9]Ibid., p. 306.

[10]Ibid., p. 251.

[11]Ibid., p. 264.

[12]Ibid., p. 295.

[13]Ibid., pp. 253, 256.

[14]Ibid., pp. 252-54.

[15]Ibid., pp. 255-64.

[16]Ibid., p. 263.

[17]Ibid., p. 306.

[18]Ibid., p. 307.

[19]Ibid., p. 254; cf. his brother, who rejected his mission in 1935 (p. 257). Elijah promises judgment on apostates, including family members, in *Muhammad Speaks* (April 24, 1964) in Majied 1994:320-29.

[20]See Lincoln 1994:180-81.

[21]Muhammad 1992:307-8.

[22]*Muhammad Speaks* (September 11, 1964), in Majied 1994:330-37 (quote from p. 333, referring to Qur'an chap. 9). Majied's son Ija Ali Majied ("From a Teenager's Point of View," Majied 1994:11-14) notes that his mother's book shows how Malcolm "became a hypocrite to the Most Honorable Elijah Muhammad. The hypocritical Malcolm X is the one white society projects out and holds up as a hero" (p. 14).

[23]*Muhammad Speaks* (September 11, 1964), in Majied 1994:334.

[24]Ibid., p. 335.

[25]Muhammad 1992:100, perhaps dating from the earlier period.

[26]E.g., ibid., pp. 158, 248-49.

[27]Ibid., p. 250.

[28]Ibid., p. 287.

[29]Ibid., p. 187. Elijah claims that orthodox Muslims are "absolutely wrong" here (p. 188).

[30]Ibid., pp. 187-88.

[31]Ibid., p. 251. He felt that the new Muhammad must come to Black Americans because they alone had not yet received a prophet (p. 249); but if this is true, how can Islam have been the original religion of Blacks? Sister Muriel X Duncan ("Foreword" to Majied 1994:7-9) believes that the Bible and Qur'an agree and both support Elijah Muhammad. Elijah followed the traditions of early Islam (Waines 1995:56) and Christianity in finding teachers in prior scripture. For the ethnic-specific nature of Muslim prophetology, see Wansbrough 1977:53.

[32]Muhammad 1992:295.

[33]Ibid., p. 329.

[34]Ibid., pp. 6-10, 19, especially 9, 19; cf. HEM 7, 65 in Majied 1994:25, 181.

[35]Muhammad 1992:17.

[36]Ibid., pp. 16-17, 42, 156, 172, 179, 233, 242, 246, 259, 267, 281, 294, 325, 340, for worship to Fard, see pp. 147, 156. Muhammad is also a divine name (p. 47).

[37]Ibid., p. 164.

[38]Ibid., p. 142. Mixing in some language from Christian tradition, he adds that Fard is "our Lord and Saviour" (p. 142); Master W. F. Muhammad accepted names like "Son of Man, Jesus Christ, Messiah, God, Lord, Jehovah," and especially Mahdi (p. 294), "God and Judge" (HEM 183 in Majied 1994:209), "your God and my Saviour" (Muhammad 1992:298).

[39]Muhammad 1992:146-47.

[40]Ibid., p. 187.

[41]Ibid., p. 9. "The black man is the first and last, maker and owner of the universe" (p. 53; cf. p. 244); the plural of Genesis 1:26 refers to the Black race who created whites (pp. 53-54).

[42]Malcolm X 1965:207-8.

[43]Lincoln 1994:69.

[44]Muhammad 1992:54, 91. He claims that no father would kill his son to atone for others' sins; but Jesus' first followers claimed this as the amazing measure of God's love toward us (Jn 3:16-17; 17:23; Rom 5:6-10).

[45]Muhammad 1992:137.

[46]On the importance of the final judgment and bodily resurrection in Islam, see, e.g., Qur'an 41.39-40, 50; Bell 1958:155-61; Esposito 1991:31-32; on resurrection "as a second creation" in Islam, see Wansbrough 1977:31-33; on the seriousness with which some medieval Muslims took deviations from standard views of the resurrection, cf., e.g., Cook 1981:87. Islam may in fact have corrected a pre-Islamic Arab doubt of the afterlife (on that pre-Islamic belief, cf. Denny 1987:22).

[47]Muhammad 1992:19, 249, 264, 289. "Hell" refers to mental death (p. 269), heaven to the Islamic brotherhood in the present life on earth (pp. 70, 304).

[48]Ibid., p. 82.

[49]Ibid., p. 97.

[50]Ibid., p. 163.

[51]Ibid., p. 189.

[52]Ibid., p. 32.

[53]Ibid., p. 168.

[54]Ibid., p. 304. On Elijah's doctrine of the resurrection and afterlife, see also, e.g., Malcolm X 1965:207; Rashad 1991:88.

[55]Muhammad 1992:168.

[56]Ibid., p. 90.

[57]Ibid., pp. 23-24; HEM 77 in Majied 1994:190 calls Jews and other Whites devils, based on John 8:44, but John's point is spiritual (referring to those who oppose Christ), not ethnic.

[58]Malcolm X 1965:169. Elijah Muhammad complains about this public repudiation in *Muhammad Speaks* (September 11, 1964), in Majied 1994:335.

[59]Muhammad 1992:328. Elsewhere he claims that the Qur'an itself declares Whites to be the enemies of God's people.

[60]Ibid., pp. 208, 313.

[61]Ibid., p. 313.

[62]Ibid., pp. 320-21. Contrast the more balanced perspective in Asante 1988:15.

[63]Muhammad 1992:228.

[64]Ibid., p. 270.

[65]Muhammad 1992:323. Fard would set the Blacks in heaven and the Whites in hell, and kill the Whites (pp. 20-21).

[66]Ibid., p. 323. The allusion to Matthew 25:41 certainly ignores the context: there the righteous are those who receive Christ's servants (25:42-45; cf. 10:40-42). Most scholars in history and today regard the "sheep" here as disciples (see, e.g., Michaels 1965; Grassi 1965:46; Cope 1969; Ladd 1974a:191-99; Harrington 1982:101; Gundry 1982:511-14; France 1985:355; Blomberg 1992:377-78; Hagner 1995:745; most fully, S. Gray 1989; cf. love for fellow Christians in Akano 1992). The popular view that this text refers to treatment of the poor or those in need (e.g., Gross 1964; Hare 1967:124; Feuillet 1980; Lapoorta 1989) would fit Jesus' other teachings, but not the context; and even in this case it would refer to all the poor, not simply those of one race. For further information, see Keener 1997b and also Keener's forthcoming Matthew commentary with Eerdmans.

[67]Muhammad 1992:90, 128. In the latter instance he cites Revelation 16:6, but the "saints" this verse cites are those who follow Jesus (14:12; 17:6; cf. 12:17), as are its "prophets" (19:10). This passage also refers to martyrs, Jesus' followers (12:11, 17; 17:6; 19:2, 10; 20:4).

[68]Muhammad 1992:231.

[69]Ibid., pp. 133, 233; cf. pp. 317, 320-21, 325.

[70]Ibid., pp. 110-19, 244; Malcolm X 1965:165-68. This was apparently a case of evil genius; even in his childhood Yakub was noted for his unusually large head (Muhammad 1992:112).

[71]Muhammad 1992:36.

[72]Ibid., pp. 56, 162.

[73]Ibid., pp. 203-4.

[74]West 1993:99-100. Despite the disagreements, see the many agreements between the Ku Klux Klan and N.O.I. doctrine in Muhammad 1992:330-41, especially on Christianity being a White religion (pp. 330-32).

[75]Muhammad 1992:96. This false Christian teaching has corrupted the Bible (HEM 33 in Majied 1994:41).

[76]Muhammad 1992:231.

[77]Ibid., p. 318; also James Meredith was foolish for trying to get into a White school that did not want him.

[78]Ibid., p. 236. For other criticisms of King, see pp. 240-42.

[79]Ibid., pp. 217-18.

[80]HEM 183 in Majied 1994:209.

[81]Muhammad 1992:20.

[82]Ibid., p. 94.

[83]See, e.g., Usry and Keener 1996:60-82.

[84]Cf., e.g., ibid., p. 63.

[85]El-Amin 1991. Cf. also Rashad 1991. Historic Islam itself is very diverse; see, e.g., Eickelman 1989:256-73.

[86]Malcolm X 1965:318-82, and especially Alex Haley's epilogue, pp. 383-456.

[87]E.g., Malcolm X 1965:308-9. Suspicious circumstances seem to imply that some White officials who could have stopped the assassination failed to intervene, spreading the guilt (cf. his warning about his impending death to C. Eric Lincoln, noted in Lincoln's third-edition postscript: "The police already know it" [1994:263]). One would not have expected much protection from the FBI, given their files on and general lack of protection for Black Americans during the civil rights movement (see O'Reilly 1989, starting with its opening story of Fanny Lou Hamer).

[88]Lincoln 1994:263-66.

[89]Ibid., pp. 267-71. The "million-man" agenda began not with Farrakhan but with his mentor: *Mr. Muhammad Speaks* 1, no. 1 (May 1960), front cover (reproduced in Majied 1994:309): "If one million of you will get behind me, I'll lead you to freedom, justice and equality overnight."

[90]Muhammad 1992:80, 126, 132, 286-87. It was for denouncing this sin that Whites hated Judge Rutherford (an early leader of Jehovah's Witnesses; p. 323).

[91]HEM 204 in Majied 1994:219. According to Elijah, the pope worships idols (pp. 286-87).

[92]Muhammad 1992:18, 21, 47.

[93]Ibid., p. 282. The "scribes and Pharisees" Jesus denounced were not ancient Jewish leaders but Black American preachers (p. 213).

[94]HEM 162 in Majied 1994:204.

[95]Muhammad 1992:111.

[96]HEM 152-53 in Majied 1994:208.

[97]Muhammad 1992:188-90. Elijah's assumed name may also be significant for his followers; the Messenger who will prepare God's way (Mal 3:1) is called Muhammad (e.g., Qur'an 48.29) and Elijah (Mal 4.5; cf. Majied 1994:3).

[98]Muhammad 1992:10-11. Because Jesus did not know the time (Mt 24:36), Elijah concludes that Jesus could not refer to himself (pp. 10-11), but historic Christianity affirms that Jesus laid aside absolute omniscience in becoming fully human (see Phil 2:6-11).

[99]Muhammad 1992:16-17, 20.

[100]Ibid., pp. 12-13; Majied 1994:31.

[101]Muhammad 1992:76.

[102]Ibid., p. 151; cf. HEM 152-53 in Majied 1994:200.

[103]Muhammad 1992:26.

[104]Ibid., p. 32.

[105]Ibid., p. 168; cf. HEM 194-95 in Majied 1994:214.

[106]Muhammad 1992:140. By contrast, some other Afrocentric writers appreciate ecstatic worship in the Spirit, including traditional expressions in Black Pentecostalism, as positive links with traditional African religion (Asante 1988:74-75; Hood 1990:205-7). We have treated pneumatology elsewhere in more detail (Keener 1996 and 1997c).

[107]Muhammad 1992:89.

[108]Ibid., pp. 94, 98.

[109]Ibid., p. 97.

[110]Ibid., pp. 82, 98-99.

[111]Ibid., p. 82.

[112]Ibid., p. 163.

[113]Ibid., pp. 158-59. For more accurate studies on these passages, see the concise summaries from the standpoint of ancient culture in Keener 1993b. The twenty-four elders may recall the twenty-four courses of priests (1 Chron 24—25; Josephus *Life* 1.2; *t. Ta'anit* 2:1; 3:1; *Sukka* 4:26-27), hence the worshiping saints (see Rev 1:6).

[114]Muhammad 1992:108.

[115]Ibid., p. 250.

[116]Ibid., pp. 251-52.

[117]Ibid., p. 267; HEM 204 in Majied 1994:219; also *Muhammad Speaks* (January 15, 1965), in Majied 1994:340. The link may be that he interprets the beast of Revelation as by definition a "devil" (Muhammad 1992:125), though the image actually stands for evil kingdoms, derived from Daniel.

[118]Likewise he reapplies language of a final war (Joel 3:14) to the coming of Master Fard, as if this were self-evident (Muhammad 1992:267-68); a locust invasion against Judah (Joel 2:2) becomes America's fall (p. 270).

[119]Muhammad 1992:154-55.

[120]Cf. the very same construction in Matthew 26:41 and Psalm 141:3-4. The underlying Aramaic construction might also tend in this direction (see Jeremias 1971:202; cf. G. Willis 1975; though contrast Moule 1974:72-73).

[121]Such a prayer later became part of the daily liturgy; see Jeremias 1964:105 and 1971:202.

[122]This was also a common prayer in antiquity, when poor people could not afford the luxury of being impractical (cf. Yamauchi 1966a:148-53).

[123]Muhammad 1992:267.

[124]Ibid., p. 269.

[125]The temple was not destroyed seventy years after Jesus' death (Muhammad 1992:286) but about forty years after, in 70 C.E.; Moses did not live around 2000 B.C.E. (Muhammad 1992:28; HEM 13-14 in Majied 1994:173), important as this appears to Elijah's schema for history, but somewhere between 1220 and 1600 B.C.E., most likely between 1300 and 1220. Elijah's claim that the tribe of Shabazz came to earth sixty-six trillion years ago (Muhammad 1992:31, 110) is impossible in light of modern knowledge of physics, in which the universe is at most roughly twenty billion years old and life could not yet exist during most of that period.

[126]Muhammad 1992:18, 290-93. At times he cites unchecked or inaccessible authorities, e.g., that the world of evil expired in 1914, "as all the religious scientists agree" (p. 142).

[127]Ibid., pp. 270, 272, 276, 280.

[128]Ibid., p. 31.

[129]Tabor and Gallagher 1995:55-56, also citing Ebionite adoptionism for a similar position in the second century.

[130]Muhammad 1992:37, 56.

[131]Ibid., pp. 64-65. A White friend who completed his Ph.D. in a lab connected with a southern hospital has told us of records of needless hysterectomies performed deliberately on Black women in the fifties. It has also been argued that Margaret Sanger, founder of Planned Parenthood, sought to promote her birth-control program especially in the Black community, sometimes even using Black clergy (see G. Grant 1996; Marshall and Donovan 1991:1-54).

[132]Muhammad 1992:161. To his credit, Elijah Muhammad insisted on justice for all, Muslim or not (p. 163).

[133]Ibid., p. 165.

[134]See, e.g., Usry and Keener 1996:99-117.

[135]Muhammad Speaks (September 11, 1964), in Majied 1994:336, 338.

[136]Muhammad 1992:246-47.

[137]E.g., Maria Stewart in 1833 (Sterling 1984:157); on nineteenth-century Black women's clubs and urban renewal, see C. Sanders 1995c:chap. 3; Riggs 1994.

[138]Muhammad 1992:277, 285.

[139]Ibid., pp. 274-75. From a Christian writer, cf. West 1993:17.

[140]Muhammad 1992:71.

[141]The problem here may be not so much one of religious conviction but of culture: African culture is far more hospitable toward foreigners than European culture is, and in this respect is closer to biblical teaching.

[142]Muhammad 1992:245. The Bible is also much more optimistic than Elijah Muhammad that Whites *can* be born again.

[143]See chapters one through three above for some historical confirmations of that problematic condition.

[144]Muhammad 1992:17, 46-49. Although his *interpretation* of the biblical texts consistently misrepresents their original sense, one can understand his *comparison* of the United States with Babylon (pp. 273, 277). For overstatement, one may sample his claim that the United States (and only the United States) will soon become the lake of fire (HEM 162 in Majied 1994:204).

[145]First in Wilkerson 1974. One need not agree with every detail to concur with the emphasis on coming judgment.

[146]On Islam in the African-American community, see *Reach Out* 7, nos. 3-4 (1994), including Haney 1994; Porter 1994; Edgerly and Ellis 1994. The back issue is available from Reach Out, P.O. Box 18478, Boulder, CO 80308-1478.

Chapter 6: How Do We Answer Orthodox Muslim Attacks on Christianity?

[1]Deedat n.d.; this work circulated previously in South Africa and was brought to our attention by William Johnson, an A.M.E. Zion minister, when he was a student at Hood Seminary in Salisbury, North Carolina.

We respond to Deedat because of the circles in which his booklet is being used. For a sound, thorough and remarkably accurate point-by-point response to Maurice Bucaille's Islamic polemic against Christianity, see W. Campbell n.d.; its place of publication may be unnamed to protect the author from violent attacks, but the book may be ordered via an organization specializing in science apologetics: Reasons to Believe, P.O. Box 5978, Pasadena, CA 91117-0978.

[2]On different major forms of Islam, cf., e.g., Nasr 1994:147-78; also note various adaptations of Islamic principles by various political regimes, e.g., Anderson 1983; Fischer 1983.

[3]For some U.S. perspectives on Islam, see von der Mehden 1983. Thus although forty-four of forty-five member states of the Islamic Conference in March 1989 rejected Ayatollah Khomeini's *fatwa* against Salman Rushdie, as had religious leaders in Saudi Arabia and Cairo, the Western media focused primarily on the *fatwa* (so Armstrong 1992.12).

[4]On common ground and differences, cf. also Imam Mohamad Jawad Chirri in Chirri 1965:57-66.

[5]For a summary of likely borrowing from Judaism and Christianity, see, e.g., Bell 1958:140-72. For Jews, Christians and other pre-Islamic monotheists in Arabia, see, e.g., Esposito 1991:6-7.

[6]Waraqa ibn Qusayy, e.g., in Esposito 1991:9. Even Muhammad's superiority *(sayyid al-mursalin)* over all previous messengers is a "later doctrinal development" that may actually contradict some Qur'anic teachings (Wansbrough 1977:55-56, citing 2.136, 285; 3.83-84; 41.43; 46.9, and noting that various passages grant special distinction to various prophets, including Adam in 2.31, 37; Abraham in 2.124-30; Moses in 4.164; 7.143-44; 26.10; 27.8-12; 28.30-35; and Jesus in 4.171-72; 19.19, 21).

[7]The first Christians reporting on the growing Muslim movement in its first generation saw little difference between Islam and Christianity; see Koren and Nevo 1991:100. Muhammad apparently assumed that his own revelation for the Arabs essentially reproduced the Jewish revelation until he encountered the hostility of the Jewish community in Mecca (Bell 1958:148).

[8]Koren and Nevo 1991:103-4. Jews and Christians probably had introduced monotheism to Arabia (Lapidus 1982:63); some argue that Judaic rather than genuinely remembered pagan Arab sources stand behind the Meccan sanctuary's later representations (Hawting 1982).

[9]S. P. Brock 1982:16-17, citing John of Phenek.

[10]S. P. Brock 1982:13. Dionysios of Tellmahre (d. 845) probably understood it "as a new religion" (ibid.).

[11]E.g., Qur'an *surah* 19.20-22; cf. 3.47, 59 (cf. 3.59 with 15.29); 4.171; 21.91, 66.12.

[12]E.g., 4.171; 19.35; 21.26.

[13]Guillaume 1956:195.

[14]See Longenecker 1970:93-99; Ladd 1974b:159-72.

[15]3.64; 4.48, 171.

[16]4.171.

[17]See Craig Keener's forthcoming commentary on John; for now, note Keener 1991b:234-54; Epp 1975.

[18]Guillaume 1956:199.

[19]Nasr 1994:34.

[20]Cf. Guillaume 1956:145-47; Hallaj clearly overstepped the boundaries of monotheism toward Eastern mysticism.

[21]E.g., Bell 1958:141; Speight 1989:108.

[22]Speight 1989:108.

[23]Bell 1958:12.

[24]This fits what we know of Jesus' era. The form of synagogue Judaism we know from later rabbinic literature commonly calls God "our Father in heaven" (*m. Soṭa* 9:15; *t. Baba Qamma* 7:6; *Ḥagiga* 2:1; *Pe'a* 4:21; *Sipra Qiddušin* pq. 9.207.2.13; *Behuqotai* pq. 8.269.2.15; *Sipre Deuteronomy* 352.1.2); other Jewish circles also maintained the view of God as father (Wisdom of Solomon 2:16; 3 Maccabees 5:7; 6:8; 7:6). Yet individuals apparently only rarely called God "my Father" (Sirach 23:1, 4; cf. Jeremias 1964:26, overstating the case), whereas Jesus nearly always did (Jeremias 1965:17; cf. Jeremias 1964:29-31). Because the Greek-speaking church must have gotten *Abba* (Rom 8:15; Gal 4:6) from the Aramaic-speaking church, which would not have learned it from Jewish culture in general (examples for God there are few; see Witherington 1990:217-18) and probably would not have dared use it regularly without the authority of Jesus, most scholars concur that Jesus sometimes used the informal and intimate title *Abba* (e.g., R. Martin 1982:34-35).

[25]Deedat n.d.:1-2.

[26]Ibid., p. 9.

[27]For details on the Apocrypha, see Bruce 1963:163-75 (especially Jerome's clear distinction between

canonical and apocryphal works—p. 172); on the canon, ibid., pp. 95-13; for English versions, see Bruce 1978.

[28]Deedat n.d.:58-59. That the Gospels circulated early and universally with the same titles may favor Matthew's authorship, but Matthew's dependence on Mark leaves this an open question with many scholars (and closed against Matthew's authorship with many others). If Deedat is correct that Jesus' disciple Matthew did not write Matthew, however (ibid., p. 26), the authority of the text is not changed; the writer depends heavily on eyewitness traditions already accepted by mainstream first-century Christianity; see chapter eight, below.

[29]Ibid., p. 25.

[30]Ibid., pp. 17-19.

[31]Ibid., p. 8.

[32]E.g., Romans 15:19; 1 Corinthians 2:4; 12:10, 28; 2 Corinthians 12:12; Galatians 3:5; 1 Thess 1:5; 2:13; Hebrews 2:4; James 5:14-15; see the discussion of miracles in our final chapter.

[33]Deedat n.d.:28-29. See chapter eight, below, for a brief survey of some of the data.

[34]See here and elsewhere chapter eight in this book, or in more detail Keener's forthcoming commentary on Matthew (Eerdmans) or its more popular version in the IVP New Testament Commentary series (Keener 1997b).

[35]On the range of permissible rhetorical liberties, see, e.g., Diodorus Siculus 20.1.1-2.2. Even Martin Luther apparently considered concern over divergences among the sources on matters of detail a pedantic exercise (Stanton 1995:8).

[36]On moral examples in ancient Mediterranean texts, see, e.g., Aune 1987:36.

[37]Deedat n.d.:50.

[38]Ibid., p. 47.

[39]The "sacred prostitution" (Albright 1946:178), security (De Vaux 1961:171), seal (G. E. Wright 1962:160), Judah's authority over Tamar (C. H. Gordon 1965a:136; cf. C. H. Gordon 1965b:96) and other details all fit known ancient Near Eastern social patterns. Most of the mythical motifs purported by Astour 1966 (such as Tamar's possibly becoming a tree), however, are excessively speculative.

[40]See Nadal 1950:350, on Nuba mountain people. We include under this general rubric both the true levirate (Hebrews, Nuer and Zulu) and widow inheritance, which can be distinct customs; see Radcliffe-Brown 1950:26, 64; Gluckman 1950:183. The Ashanti practice the latter custom (Fortes 1950:271; Farber 1968:91).

[41]Lowie 1968:58; R. Abrahams 1973; Stephens 1963:194-96. This includes the Nuer (Evans-Pritchard 1951:112-15), the Swazi (Kuper 1950:97), and elsewhere the Mappilla (as well as Islamic law—Gough 1973a:432). Some impose some limitations on the practice (e.g., the Tswana—Schapera 1950:140, 153); some formerly practiced it but no longer do so (Kgatla in Schapera 1966:67), and others lack the custom (e.g., Anlo [Nukunya 1969:96-97, 116], Nayars and Tiyyars [Gough 1973a:432]). Cf. also the sororate (e.g., Kuper 1950:97; Radcliffe-Brown 1950:26), which occurs where sororal polygyny (cf. Gen 29—30) is permitted, and sometimes also where it is not allowed (cf. Lev 18:18); see Gough 1973b:624.

[42]E.g., Hittite laws, 2.193 (Pritchard 1955:196; C. H. Gordon 1965b:95). In some cultures one may inherit one's father's wives, but until that time the incest taboo prohibits this (Farber 1968:74), though permissive sex is more likely where eventual marriage is permitted (Stephens 1963:250); Reuben's going into his father's concubine (Gen 35:22) thus violates the expectation in any case.

[43]Incidentally, the status (and sometimes progress) of women in Islamic cultures has been the subject of much discussion in recent books (e.g., Delaney 1987:39; Mernissi 1987; Haeri 1989; Shaaban 1991; al-Shaykh 1992; Ahmed 1992; Keddie and Baron 1992; J. Tucker 1993; Brooks 1996; Stowasser 1994), and has long been the subject of journal studies (e.g., Papanek 1973; Chaudhury 1977; Heer and Youssef 1977; Fischer 1978; El Sadaawi 1981; El-Guindi 1981; Haim 1981; Ahmed 1982; Andezian 1983; Benkheira 1983; El-Guindi 1983; Vandewiele 1983; Afshar 1984; Danforth 1984; Eastman 1984; Larson 1984; Afshar 1985; Molyneux 1985; more popularly and focused on problems, cf. MacShane 1991; "Islam's Veiled Threat" 1995; Nasrin 1995). One should note, however, that women probably exercised more freedom in the beginning of Islam (Parrinder 1980:172-77), that European and American stereotypes have often proved insensitive to the way women in these cultures view their roles (Pastner 1978; cf. Dorman 1979) and that women's roles tend to be more progressive in African-American Islam (McCloud 1995:135-59, 172). For some studies on early Christian commitment to women's advancement, see, e.g., Keener 1992; Witherington 1984 and 1988.

[44]Deedat n.d.:47.

[45]Ibid., p. 16.

[46]For the story, see, e.g., Metzger 1968:100-102; Carson 1979:34-36.

[47]See, e.g., Bruce 1963:180-81 and 1980:14-19. For the principles of textual criticism in general, see Metzger 1968.

[48]On early African Christians' defense of the Trinity, see comments in Usry and Keener 1996:38, 154. Cf. also the Trinity's defense by the Egyptian Christian Athanasius, called by his enemies the "Black dwarf." African-American Christians taught the Trinity from the start as well (e.g., Richard Allen in Washington 1994:8).

[49]Interpreting, e.g., Qur'an 5.15; Esposito 1991:20. According to the earliest Syriac sources regarding Islam, Muhammad "accepted the Torah and the Gospels, apart from the crucifixion narrative" (S. P. Brock 1982:12).

[50]Deedat n.d.:15.

[51]See, e.g., Du Plessis 1968; R. L. Roberts 1973.

[52]E.g., Deedat n.d.:35-36. Those who claim contradictions must provide concrete examples, if they are to be fair enough to give those of us who have analyzed the texts in detail in their different historical contexts the opportunity to respond specifically. Unfortunately, Deedat's generalizations sound weightier than his examples.

[53]Cf., e.g., Cook 1983:67.

[54]See more fully Heschel 1962:472; R. Scott 1954:57 (cf. pp. 59-62).

[55]Deedat n.d.:35-36.

[56]Cf. similarly but in more detail, e.g., Williamson 1982:143-44. Williamson is lecturer in Hebrew and Aramaic at Cambridge University.

[57]Deedat n.d.:37-44.

[58]On Old Testament textual criticism, see, e.g., Waltke 1978.

[59]He contrasts the accurate transmission of the Qur'an, which—as we note below—is not above question from an historical standpoint, with the many versions of the (English) Bible (Deedat n.d.:7), as if translations were the same thing as transmission of the original Greek text.

[60]Deedat n.d.:22.

[61]*Allah* was also a pre-Islamic Arabic term for the supreme God above other gods; see Waines 1995:8.

[62]Deedat n.d.:35; cf. also pp. 50, 55. The Worldwide Church of God has thankfully moved into orthodox Christianity in more recent years, but most Christians previously regarded Herbert W. Armstrong and especially his son Garner Ted Armstrong as sectarian (among older evangelical works, cf., e.g., W. Martin 1977:295-324, critiquing the former's British Israelitism, view of the Trinity and so on).

[63]We qualify this statement with "in the period" cited because the Worldwide Church of God has more recently moved into what we and most other Christians would regard as orthodoxy.

[64]Deedat n.d.:12-13, 24, 48. Numerous Christian writers have exposed the misrepresentations of Jehovah's Witnesses (an example is W. Martin 1977:34-110, who critiques not only the doctrine of the movement but such embarrassments as the documented perjury of the cult's founder when claiming to know Greek when in fact he knew none).

[65]E.g., at its most advanced stage the cult reportedly considered Jim Jones himself to be God (Sparks 1979:288). Although Jones had been affiliated with the Disciples of Christ, his doctrine was far from that of that group in particular or Christianity in general. For some popular Christian critiques of the cult from the late 1970s, cf., e.g., Sparks 1979:257-305; Kerns with Wead 1979; M. White 1979.

[66]For a specific example, cf. research psychologist Larsen 1992:21; see Keener's comments on Matthew 27:5 in his forthcoming commentary (Eerdmans; also Keener 1997b).

[67]E.g., Deedat n.d.:1-2. More recently, the Jesus Seminar has received much popular attention by billing itself in public as the voice of scholarship, but its totally noneschatological Jesus reflects the views of the group rather than a consensus of New Testament scholarship as a whole. Views concerning the Jesus tradition are very diverse, as one may note by examining works by John P. Meier (1991, 1994), Raymond Brown (1994), Luke T. Johnson (1996), E. P. Sanders (1993) and Ben Witherington (1994); all of these rank among the leading scholars on the subject from varying perspectives, yet none of whom fall close to the views of the Jesus Seminar. See especially Ben Witherington 1997; G. Boyd 1995; cf. Keener 1995a. For responses to less scholarly, more popular approaches (such as those of John Spong, Barbara Thiering and A. N. Wilson) see N. T. Wright 1992. On the earliest New Testament Christologies, cf. Witherington 1990; Marshall 1990.

[68]For critiques of the Western rationalistic bias against miracles, see Craig 1986; Bockmuehl 1988:9-76, especially pp. 70-74; Davies and Allison 1991:2:62-65; Meier 1994:2:11, 519-21; cf. also Kee 1983:3-41; Borg 1987:33-34; Pilch 1991:183; R. Brown 1994:143-44. Antisupernaturalistic presuppositions do not

fare well in an African context; cf., e.g., Abogunrin 1980; Mbiti 1970:253-57; Arowele 1981:17-28; Hollenweger 1988:129; Nanan 1994.

[69]E.g., Qur'an *surah* 19.20-22; cf. 3.47, 59 (cf. 3.59 with 15.29); 4.171; 21.91; 66.12.

[70]Establishing the uniqueness of specific truth claims may be more difficult in a postmodern context, but at the moment gaining a hearing is becoming easier.

[71]Indeed, although it is less often addressed than the Bible, it does come under Western scholars' scrutiny as well; cf., e.g., Cook 1983:75 (which contrasts early Muslim history with externally attested events that dispute it). "Probably we shall never know with any comfortable degree of certainty the details of 'what really happened' during, say, the first Islamic century" (Waines 1995:34). Judith Koren and Yehuda Nevo (1991:99-100) find no external documentation before the conquests, or indeed before Caliph Mu'awiyah. In citing these sources we do not ally ourselves with particular reconstructions of Muslim origins, but point out that Deedat's blade of Western skepticism cuts in his own direction too.

[72]E.g., Koren and Nevo 1991, especially pp. 87-88.

[73]Cook 1983:69-70.

[74]Wansbrough 1977:1.

[75]E.g., Juynboll 1982b:174-75; Crone 1987:203-30; Peters 1994:265. Those skeptical of such written traditions suspect that they derive from speculations of Islamic scholars two centuries after Muhammad (see, e.g., Koren and Nevo 1991:93-94). Even more orthodox scholars may acknowledge that not all traditions are "equally valid" (cf. Armstrong 1992:48).

[76]Wansbrough 1977:25. See especially Kister 1982:107, which notes both the diversity of early views and that second-century compilations impose "no obligatory conclusions . . . and no prescriptions."

[77]Cook 1983:75; cf. Crone 1987:230; more generally, Crone and Cook 1977. Juynboll 1982a:3 notes that Crone and Cook may rely "too heavily and too exclusively on non-Arabic sources," but contends that historians could not rely solely on the Arabic Islamic sources. Some allegedly early Islamic religious epistles could also challenge Patricia Crone and Michael Cook's reconstruction of Islam's evolution, though Cook 1981 (see especially p. 154) provides reasons to doubt the authenticity of those most damaging to his thesis.

[78]Crone 1987.

[79]Koren and Nevo 1991:100.

[80]Ibid., p. 101.

[81]Ibid., p. 100, citing evidence in John of Damascus *De Haeresibus* (743 C.E.). John Wansbrough (1977:52) finds evidence for the Qur'an's use as a *canonical* document no earlier than the third Muslim century, with the formulation of the Sunna.

[82]Koren and Nevo 1991:92 mentions among modern critical objections to the Qur'an the acceptance by some of an argument from silence. We, however, reject arguments from silence unless the document in question can be demonstrated on other grounds to be basically unreliable (i.e., an argument from silence is not valid without proper assignment of the burden of proof).

[83]Peters 1994:257.

[84]Ibid.

[85]Cook 1983:67-68; cf. Wansbrough 1977:43-44.

[86]Cook 1983:69. Richard Bell (1958:82-88) finds revisions and alterations (which he believes occurred in Muhammad's lifetime). Variant accounts in the Qur'an may also reflect oral transmission or the development of various regional traditions taken whole into the Qur'an (Koren and Nevo 1991:95, summarizing the position of Wansbrough).

[87]Wansbrough 1977:44; Cook 1983:74. If one accepts this argument on the basis that so central an institution should have shown up (i.e., that its centrality here adequately shifts the burden of proof so that an argument from silence becomes acceptable), it does not challenge the Qur'an's importance, but only the claim that it stems in its entirety and as canon from Muhammad's time.

[88]Cook 1983:74.

[89]Wansbrough 1977:16, 20, 118.

[90]Koren and Nevo 1991:104.

[91]Ibid., p. 105. Note also that a suitable South Arabian script was available for the Islamic Arabs, but they instead adopted an Aramaic script from the north (ibid.). Appeals to classical Arabic pre-Islamic poetry will not help, since this was collected and revised by ninth-century classical philologists (Islam's third century); Wansbrough 1977:97-98.

[92]Koren and Nevo 1991:104-5. Koren and Nevo even think that some of the eighth-century traditions about

pre-Islamic paganism in Arabia were based on what was known of pagan sanctuaries in the Negev in their own day (Nevo and Koren 1990).

[93]Seizing on one writer's admission that the Bible has been inaccurately translated, Deedat says that he has refuted the idea that the Bible is God's Word (Deedat n.d.:23, citing Ellen G. White of the Seventh-day Adventist Church). But Christians emphasize the meaning, not the wording; we would regard a focus on the wording as a magical fetish. Muslims and Christians differ in their understandings of Scripture and God's Word (Nasr 1994:43-44; in Islam the latter is the Qur'an, whereas for Christians it is first and foremost Jesus).

[94]Indeed, that God appears in both "first and third persons in one and the same sentence" (Cook 1983:68) may also weaken the idea of direct dictation in the Qur'an. Deedat accepts only the dictated parts of the Bible as God's Word, not the history or other portions (Deedat n.d.:5-6). Again he simply presupposes the way God must work, rather than examining the evidence to see if God really could have inspired prophets and apostles yet worked through their styles and a variety of literary genres.

[95]Cook 1983:15.

[96]See the argument on hearing God's voice in Keener 1996, chaps. 2 and (especially) 3. Even pagan prophets in antiquity generally required verification for prophets (Weinfeld 1977:179-80); in other cases a lock of hair or fringe from the prophet's garment was taken to identify the prophet, perhaps to hold him legally accountable (Hayes 1967:407-8; Malamat 1966:225-27; Craghan 1975:542-43). Unlike biblical prophecy, however, prophecy at Mari was tested by divination (Moran 1969:22-24; cf. Huffmon 1968:109).

[97]Surah 19.33-34; cf. 4.159. Guillaume 1956:196 cites also 3.48 (3.55 in our version) as a possibility (though the wording there may refer to sleep, as in 6.60, its usual Arabic meaning could support the idea of death; for discussion, cf. Guillaume 1956:196).

[98]This is especially likely in surah 4.157, in which Jesus' opponents did not kill him; the next line might be translated that they killed one who resembled him, or they thought they killed him. According to the traditional understanding, Judas was crucified in Jesus' place; but if we read "thought they killed him" (cf. Pickthall n.d.:93) the point could be simply that Jesus had authority to lay down his own life and no one took it from him, as in John 10:18. The Docetic idea of a wraith substituted for Jesus on the cross ultimately derives from Hellenistic mythology, e.g., in Euripedes Helen (following Recantation of Stesichorus).

[99]E.g., R. Brown 1994:1094. Cook (1983:79) recognizes the influence of Docetism here, even though the Qur'an elsewhere presents Jesus as human, in contrast to traditional Docetism.

[100]Cook 1983:78-79.

[101]Ibid., p. 82; Crone 1987:248; cf. S. P. Brock 1982:12.

[102]Cook 1983:80; see further, e.g., Peters 1994:131-32. Cf. the later Buddhist and Hindu influences in Persian Islam argued by Morony 1982.

Chapter 7: How Do We Answer Other Challenges to Christianity?

[1]Cf., e.g., Stanton 1995:vii; L. Johnson 1996:v-vii. This is not to suggest that scholars simply dismiss minority positions or positions with which they disagree; we refer here not to disagreements of perspective defended by sound rules of evidence, but to exposing academic charlatans.

[2]Graham 1991:297.

[3]Ibid., p. 329.

[4]Ibid., p. 299.

[5]Why would one cite the Argo as a parallel to Noah's ark (ibid., p. 90) in view of the many actual parallels to the flood story in ancient Near Eastern legend (e.g., the Atrakhasis epic; the nearer Greek story of Deucalion and Pyrrha also renders the Argo parallel virtually useless). Graham says that Jesus is "just another Odin" because both were on a tree (p. 351)—never mind that crucifixion was a common Roman punishment and is described in Jewish texts as being hanged on a tree. Graham claims that the cross is just pagan mythology (p. 353), but far from it—it was the standard Roman method of execution for lower-class persons in the provinces (and who would make up a story that the founder of their faith died as a condemned criminal by crucifixion?).

[6]Ibid., p. 287.

[7]E.g., "Son of God" appears as a messianic category in the Old Testament and the Dead Sea Scrolls (4Q Florilegium).

[8]Graham 1991:287.

[9]Cf., e.g., the discussions and various views in R. L. Roberts 1973; De Kruijf 1970; I. J. Du Plessis 1968.

[10]Graham 1991:287.

[11]E.g., Pausanias 1.40.3; 2.20.6; 4.34.6; 8.31.2; 9.26.8; Athenaeus 7.288-89; *Orphic Hymns* 14.8; 27.12; 74.4; Plutarch *On Borrowing* 7, *Moralia* 830B. For Israel's God, see, e.g., 1 Maccabees 4:30; *Sibylline Oracles* 1.73, 152, 165; 2.28; 3.35.

[12]E.g., Demosthenes *On the Crown* 324, *Oration* 60, *Funeral Speech* 10, 23; *Letter* 1.2; Diodorus Siculus 11.24.2; Dionysus of Halicarnassus 12.1.8; Apuleius *Metamorphoses* 6.28; in Jewish circles, e.g., Exodus 14:13, 30 LXX; Sirach 46:11; Judith 8:17; 9:1; 11:3; *Psalms of Solomon* 16:5; Josephus *Antiquities of the Jews* 2.339; 3.1; 11.282; 4 Maccabees 15:8.

[13]Graham 1991:287.

[14]Ibid. Language for ascension is widespread—how else would one get to "heaven"?—and Jewish texts even apply it to divine Wisdom.

[15]Ibid.

[16]Ibid.

[17]Cf. Keener 1991b:155-84.

[18]Graham even cites medieval Cabala to confirm his eccentric interpretations of Genesis (Graham 1991:82)—though Genesis consists of texts perhaps two millennia older than the interpreters on which he confidently depends for his point.

[19]See further Bruce 1974; cf. also Bruce 1980; Barnett 1986; France 1986. F. F. Bruce, by the way, was a Greco-Roman classicist before he became a New Testament scholar, and he argues his case from the standpoint of a Greco-Roman historian. Compare Greek and Roman historians' usual neglect of even major events in Judea (e.g., Dio Cassius *Roman History* 49.22.6; 54.9.3; Josephus *Against Apion* 1.60-65).

[20]Graham 1991:409-11. Paul's letters in the New Testament argue against Graham's position, even if one regarded some of them as inauthentic; unless a real and authoritative Paul had existed, no one would have been tempted to add later forgeries in his name! Claiming that Justin Martyr never mentions Paul or his letters (ibid., p. 409) ignores Pauline allusions and the lack of a universal canon at that point (and ignorance is not always opposition). The King James Version notes that say Stephanas and others wrote 1 Corinthians (ibid.) refer to the use of amanuenses—from well-educated to peasants, most ancient writers used scribes, as is well known. Graham claims that Tertullian and Origen doubted the Pauline authorship of Hebrews—yet this is hardly relevant to the case, for few contemporary scholars, even the most conservative, would claim Pauline authorship for Hebrews anyway.

[21]Ibid., pp. 411-12. He thinks the same view existed in the Mysteries—perhaps he is behind on his reading of scholarly views on the Mysteries—but that "literalists" destroyed Paul's meaning. His interpretation of Paul is similar to the Gnostic counterreading, but historically has nothing in its favor.

[22]See Keener 1993b on this passage and others.

[23]Graham 1991:359.

[24]Ibid., p. 286.

[25]This is often argued, but the reader may consult Aune 1988 or Keener 1993a for a sample study of the background here, and especially Meier 1991:112-66. Graham (1991:279-80) is simply wrong when he calls them four mythic sources and simply an allegorical "rewrite" of earlier myths (p. 281)—as if all New Testament writers shared the same perspectives and conspired to use the same language. No contemporary scholar—whether Christian or atheist—would suggest such a thing; the diverse Greek styles of the different New Testament writers simply do not allow it.

[26]E.g., Josephus *Against Apion* 2.255; Ferguson 1987:98; Mickelsen 1963:27; Sandmel 1978:113. In later Gnosticism, see, e.g., Irenaeus *Adversus Haereses* 1.18.

[27]Graham 1991:330. The Creator is just a "morally unqualified principle," a "substance" (p. 28); Jesus mythically represents the Principle of Involution, and Christ as Savior that of Evolution (p. 279).

[28]Ibid., p. 350.

[29]The prominent, pious and wealthy Nakdimon (Greek Nicodemus) ben Gorion, e.g., *'Abot de Rabbi Nathan* 6 A; 13, §31 B; *Sipre Deuteronomy* 305.2.1; *b. 'Aboda Zara* 25a, bar.; *Ketubot* 66b; *Ta'anit* 19b-20a; *Lamentations Rabbah* 1:5, §31; Josephus *Jewish War* 2.451; one may also compare the name of another "ruler of the Jews" named Nicodemus in a Roman funerary inscription (*Corpus Inscriptionum Judaicarum* 1:295, §380). It is not clear if the former is the same Nicodemus; this was a common Greek name used by many Jews (Barrett 1978:204; cf. R. Brown 1966-1970:1:129-30; Bowman 1975:32).

[30]Graham 1991:283.

[31]Ibid., p. 387.

Chapter 8: Are the Gospels Really True?

[1]Craig has also written a briefer commentary on Matthew for the IVP New Testament Commentary series. It includes some of the documentation, but in considerably less detail than the fuller commentary for Eerdmans will.

[2]Craig copyrighted most of this chapter under the name "Gospel Truth" in 1994. To save space we have kept documentation minimal here, because fuller documentation appears in Craig's forthcoming Matthew commentary with Eerdmans.

[3]Thus, for example, they were free to arrange their account topically instead of chronologically (cf., e.g., 4 Maccabees 12:7; Aune 1987:31-32; Stanton 1974:119-21); they could also expand or abridge their account (as in 2 Maccabees 2:24-25; Theon *Progymnasmata* 3.224 40; 4.37 42, 80 82).

[4]See, e.g., Aune 1987:46 76; Stanton 1974:117-36; Talbert 1977; Burridge 1992. Aune is the most widely available.

[5]When ancient historians addressed events lost in centuries past (in contrast to nearer events as in the Gospels), they would make their account as reasonable as they could (e.g., Plutarch *Theseus* 1.3; Aune 1987:83) or would cite varying sources (e.g., Diodorus Siculus 5.70.1; Dionysius of Halicarnassus 1.84.4; 1.87.4; Diogenes Laertius *Lives* 1.23; 6.113; 8.2.67-72; Arrian *Alexander* 1 preface 1; Plutarch *Lycurgus* 1.1). Nevertheless, even under such circumstances historians sought to write history as best as their resources allowed (Josephus *Antiquities* 20.156-57; cf. Mosley 1965). Historical accuracy varied from one biographer to another and according to the historical distance of their sources, but biographies were always intended as essentially historical works (see Aune 1988:125; Witherington 1994:339; cf. Polybius 8.8).

[6]The more distant the past, the more difficult to be accurate (cf., e.g., Diodorus Siculus 1.6.2; 1.9.2; 4.1.1; Dionysius of Halicarnassus 1.12.3).

[7]A synopsis of the Gospels is especially important here; e.g., Aland 1980-1982.

[8]See here especially the sound case of Meier 1991:112-66, as noted above.

[9]Burridge 1992:249-50.

[10]All translations from the Greek are my own unless otherwise specified.

[11]Most scholars are not as certain of themselves as the "Q Seminar," which, like the "Jesus Seminar," tends to make pronouncements concerning the scholarly consensus (or to state that their views have been "established" in such-and-such a work) that hardly reflect the consensus of the rest of the scholarly community. Many scholars are skeptical of the value of the quest for finding specific layers of redaction (e.g., Theissen 1991:204; Meier 1994:180; see further G. Boyd 1995:136-39 and Witherington 1994:215, following R. A. Horsley). F. G. Downing compared Q to Cynic *Lives* (1988; 1991), but this comparison is too narrow (Tuckett 1988; cf. ancient biographies in general).

[12]Greek moral teachers expected disciples to take notes on what they said (Stowers 1988:74); disciples sometimes later published the notes (Kennedy 1980:19). These notes could reflect even the teacher's style (Epictetus *Discourses* 1.preface); some teachers later attested the accuracy of such notes (Quintilian *Institutes of Oratory* 1.preface 7-8). More confident of their oral transmission skills, Jewish students played down notes, but did use them at times (see Gerhardsson 1961:160-62, despite scholarly disputes on some of his other points; cf. Safrai 1974-1976a:966).

[13]Greco-Roman education focused on memorization (Quintilian *Institutes of Oratory* 1.3.1; 2.4.15; Isocrates *Demonicus* 18, *Oration* 1; Koester 1982:1:93; Ferguson 1987:84). Ancient Mediterranean memory was highly developed; Roman orators could memorize speeches several hours long (Quintilian *Institutes of Oratory* 11.2.1-51); members of Greek schools also transmitted sayings of their founders from generation to generation (Culpepper 1975:193; cf. Diogenes Laertius 10.1.12).

[14]Cf., e.g., Josephus *Life* 8; Safrai 1974-1976a; Gerhardsson 1961:124-25; Riesner 1982. This is true even though scholars have rightly noted that Birger Gerhardsson originally took matters too far, especially with his emphasis on *verbatim* transmission.

[15]E.g., Proverbs; *'Abot;* cf. Diogenes Laertius 2.18-47; Plutarch *Sayings of Kings, Moralia* 172B-194E.

[16]Greco-Roman education included paraphrase as a standard school exercise (Theon *Progymnasmata* 1.93-171; cf. Gerhardsson 1961:136-48). Despite theological differences among them, most scholars recognize that Jewish and Christian writers preserved as well as edited earlier tradition (W. D. Davies 1967:156; Draper 1984:269-87).

[17]No later than the second century (from which the bulk of our earliest recorded material derives), Jewish teachers already expected disciples to memorize their teachings through repeated practice (e.g., *Sipre Deuteronomy* 48.1.1-4; Goodman 1983:79). Although after a number of generations disciples could confuse

some sayings, these early teachers reiterated the importance of transmitting sayings carefully (e.g., *t. Yebamot* 3:1; *Mekilta Pisha* 1.135-36; *'Abot de Rabbi Nathan* 24 A).

[18]The view that ancient peoples had a weaker concept of fidelity to a teacher's meaning than today is historically false (see *Gospel Perspectives*, ed. R. T. France and David Wenham, vols. 1-2 [Sheffield, U.K.: JSOT Press, 1980-1981]); the view that sayings of Jesus were invented by Christian prophets is rendered unlikely by how carefully early Christian writers distinguished their own teachings from those of their Lord (e.g., 1 Cor 7:10-16; cf. Mk 10:11-12); cf. Hill 1979; Aune 1983.

[19]Cf. also B. Lewis 1975:43.

[20]Places where Matthew and Luke follow Mark's context but diverge together at the same point (Mt 12:28; Lk 11:20; against Mk 3:23-29) suggest that Q may have even been one of Mark's sources, though he does not draw on it much. Minor variations were to be expected in the written sayings accounts because paraphrase was a standard rhetorical exercise along with memorization. I have treated these details more thoroughly and with much more documentation in my academic commentaries on Matthew and John, currently in progress.

[21]An argument circumventing the lack of evidence for such divisions, on the basis of compounded speculations based on much later evidence read back into this period, popular in some scholarly circles, is simultaneously a tacit admission that the evidence for such divisions on this issue is weak or nonexistent. For a recent pointed critique of arguments from silence, see R. Brown 1994:7-8.

[22]See Tacitus *Annals* 15.44.

[23]Early-second-century Christians said that Mark, for instance, got the material in his Gospel directly from Simon Peter, with whom he worked for years. That the second-century church was unanimous on the authorship of the Gospels as reflected in the Gospels' titles may not prove Mark's authorship but certainly favors that possibility, given that (in contrast to some second-century traditions) there is no substantial contrary evidence against it. Normally if people found a matter they could dispute, they disputed it. See Hengel 1985.

[24]See Dibelius 1956:202-3.

[25]Cf. Aune 1987:124. On the genre of Acts, see especially Palmer 1993.

[26]Cf. Foakes Jackson and Lake 1979:158-59; Morton and MacGregor 1964:41; Cadbury 1968:60-61.

[27]Earlier in the century some thought they determined an Aramaic source for the first half of Acts (Torrey 1916); but Luke may simply adopt a Semitizing style where appropriate, as also in Luke 1—2.

[28]The Tübingen School in the nineteenth century accepted only these four; today nearly all scholars accept also Philippians, 1 Thessalonians and Philemon; many accept 2 Thessalonians, Colossians and Ephesians, and most conservative scholars accept the rest but most liberal scholars reject them. Some of Paul's writings are so bound to the local situation he was addressing (e.g., 1 Cor) that they would have been valueless as forgeries after Paul's death; thus almost no New Testament scholars today reject the seven mentioned above, which by themselves are more than sufficient to establish our case.

[29]On their acknowledgment of Jesus' and his followers' miracles and consequent attribution of such miracles to sorcery, see, e.g., Justin Martyr *Dialogue with Trypho* 69:7; *b. Sanhedrin* 43a; 107b; Dalman 1893:45-50; Herford 1903:50-62; Gero 1978; Yamauchi 1986:90-91.

[30]For more on the charismatic character of early Christianity, see on the popular level Keener 1996, as well as Keener 1997c, his more technical and heavily documented volume on the Spirit in early Christian narratives; see also Fee 1994, Aune 1983 and other works cited in these books.

[31]The differences in the Gospel accounts of the resurrection are not irreconcilable, but they do point to the fact that the accounts are distinct—and hence independent witnesses to the basic facts on which they do agree, such as women as the first witnesses (something too scandalous in ancient Jewish culture to have been fabricated by the early Christians, though this undoubtedly explains why Paul omitted mention of them in 1 Cor 15:5-8!). See especially Craig 1980, 1981 and 1985. On miracles in general, see the section on "signs" in the introduction to my forthcoming John commentary.

[32]Compare to a lesser degree Bernal 1987:1:75, on Herodotus *Histories* 6.55: even those who doubt Herodotus in general cannot suggest that he "was lying about the existence of such chronicles. His was not an unverifiable statement about some remote peoples, but one which readers could easily check, if they did not know about it already."

[33]On a fairly popular level, see the arguments in Habermas and Flew 1987, a debate between a Christian and a non-Christian on the resurrection. I thank my former Duke student Scott Lasater for bringing this work to my attention.

[34]See Craig 1980:47-74; on the empty-tomb traditions, see Craig 1981, 1985 and 1995:146-52; Ladd 1963.

[35]E.g., Plutarch *Brutus* 36; Dio Cassius *Roman History* 42.11.2-3; Achilles Tatius 5.16.1-2.

[36]Conditions in first-century Judea and Galilee were quite different from those that produced the seventeenth-century messiah Sabbetai Zevi, many of whose followers failed to be deterred by his apostasy (Grayzel 1961:516; Bamberger 1962:240), and some even by his death (Scholem 1973:920; Greenstone 1906:225-30). Aside from different social conditions, knowledge of the Christian belief in Jesus' resurrection and redefinition of messiahship could provide later messianic movements a model for redefining the messianic mission in a manner that did not exist prior to Jesus.

[37]Those who believe that Paul later abandoned this hope, in 2 Corinthians 5, need to reckon with Philippians, which includes both the kind of immortality portrayed in 2 Corinthians 5 (Phil 1:23) and the future resurrection as in 1 Corinthians 15 (Phil 3:19-21); like most of his Jewish contemporaries (cf., e.g., Gundry 1976), Paul could hold both perspectives simultaneously. Some scholars have divided Philippians and could thus argue that Paul changed his views between parts of that letter; but ancient rhetorical conventions and the hazards involved in transporting even one letter (Phil 2:25-30) argue against the partitioning of Philippians, the unity of which is accepted by most scholars today.

[38]Some scholars, perpetuating the nineteenth-century liberal lives of Jesus, have tried to explain away references to the future kingdom in Jesus' teachings (e.g., Crossan and Mack), while other scholars (e.g., E. P. Sanders) regard all Jesus' authentic teachings on the subject as oriented to the future. To be brief, we simply note here that 1 Thessalonians 4—5 and 2 Thessalonians 2 document that Jesus' future teaching was flourishing in the early church before the Gospels were written (see chap. 24 in Keener's Eerdmans commentary on Matthew for more detail; also Waterman 1975; D. Wenham 1984). For critiques of Crossan and Mack, see, e.g., L. Johnson 1996; Keener 1995a; Witherington 1997; G. Boyd 1995.

[39]For more complete information, see especially Bruce 1980:14-20. Bruce was a scholar of Greco-Roman classics before entering the field of New Testament.

[40]Testimony to the most important kinds of data (e.g., the future kingdom, Jesus' lordship, Jesus as God's Son) occurs in varying degrees in every stratum of Gospel tradition (Mark, Q, special sources of Matthew and Luke, John). Some of Jesus' teachings are also attested in Paul's writings (1 Cor 7, 11; 1 Thess 4—5; 2 Thess 2; possibly Rom 12—13). Those who reject some of this data thus do so partly on theological rather than evidential grounds.

[41]Of the seven hundred or so sources cited in the bibliography of my second book (Keener 1992), many are by skilled classical scholars accurately addressing women's issues in antiquity (e.g., Pomeroy 1975; MacMullen 1980; Gardner 1986).

[42]See Bruce 1974:19-41.

[43]Bruce 1974:17-18 compares the death of Hajji Mirza Ali Khan in 1960, a major event to his followers in India but only briefly mentioned by the British media, and unlikely to figure in twentieth-century histories by Western writers. This "Fakir of Ipi" was known to oppose British control in his region, but was not significant to the British. If, however, his followers had arrived in London and begun stirring dissent in the Indian community there, matters would immediately become different. One could multiply examples of the principle.

[44]Dio Cassius *Roman History* 49.22.6; 54.9.3. Josephus likewise compares Herodotus's neglect of Judea (*Against Apion* 1.60-65) with his (and Thucydides') neglect of Rome (*Against Apion* 1.66).

[45]For second-century and later rabbinic reports, see, e.g., Herford 1903; Dalman 1893; for possible archaeological evidence, see Meyers and Strange 1981:125-39.

[46]Tacitus *Annals* 15.44.

[47]A Kantian segregation of faith (which is held to be entirely "subjective") from "reason" (held to be "objective," socialization notwithstanding!) cannot hold much longer; history has likewise proved disastrous Kant's desire to rest ethics on reason without faith. The modern prejudice against miracles (gradually being supplanted by postmodern agnosticism and relativism) reveals more concerning Enlightenment presuppositions than it does concerning historical reality (see Craig 1986:43; Benoit 1973:1:39; France 1976:105-7; cf. Kee 1983:3-12; Goppelt 1981:1:145).

[48]See especially Wenham and Blomberg 1986. For the miraculous today, see further Keener 1996 (although this work was kept on a popular level, more documentation appears in Keener 1997c); Deere 1993; Wimber with Springer 1986.

Chapter 9: Why Does It Matter?

[1]Craig is the author of this chapter, an earlier form of which was copyrighted as "Jesus Only Way" in 1994; but both authors fully share the views represented here.

The approach of Asante 1988:109 is much more appealing to our culture (and perhaps especially to our people, who have learned to appreciate tolerance because we have been oppressed so often): "The Way is not contradictory to Hinduism, Judaism, Christianity, Islam, Yoruba, or any other way of peace and power; it is complementary" (quarter 1, point 8 in "Njia: The Way").

[2]For some of relativism's logical problems, its own historical context and other responses to it, see, e.g., Juster 1995:17-19.

[3]Qur'an *Sûrah* 9.5 (from Pickthall's explanatory translation, pp. 145-46); cf. 5.33, 36; 9.14; cf. also 8.15-17: when you must kill them, Allah accepts responsibility. Because Muslims believe that the true Qur'an cannot be translated, we are here citing an "explanatory translation," not claiming to render the Qur'an verbatim. We owe most of these citations to articles in Horizons' publication *Reach Out.*

[4]Qur'an *Sûrah* 9.29-30; pp. 147-48.

[5]Qur'an *Sûrah* 5.51; p. 101; cited also by Muhammad 1992:160.

[6]Cf. Qur'an *Sûrah* 9.63, 73, although one might apply these texts only to those specifically hostile toward Islam.

[7]Although he disagrees with the premise, Ben-Jochannan finds it understandable that North African church fathers affirmed Christian orthodoxy such as Jesus being the only way (1991:119-20).

[8]Denver Seminary professor Douglas Groothuis rightly pointed out (in a tape he sent me of a debate in which he participated on April 11, 1996) that the attempt to reduce all religions to some universal commonality of experience strips all of them of beliefs important to each, in essence redefining them in ways their own adherents would reject. Thus an approach like that of John Hick, claiming respect toward all religions, is actually disrespectful and offensive to most religions. For brief and readable surveys of some irreducible differences among various world religions, see D. Groothuis 1994 and 1996; cf. Nash 1994; Netland 1991.

[9]This is true even if one arbitrarily narrows one's claims to the "major world religions," thus avoiding unpopular religious groups without much cultural power (popularly classified as cults). Narrowing the claim to "major world religions," however, is an arbitrary move to begin with. If what began as a deception gained widespread adherents by conquest or further deception, it might by virtue of its numbers or social power become a "world religion," but how would this new power increase the transcultural validity of its truth claim?

[10]This is endemic in our culture; cf. even Asante 1988:116 (quarter 7, point 3): "Refuse to be dogmatic in all things except The Way."

[11]Moralists commonly emphasized that they were "gentle as a nurse" (see Malherbe 1970:211-13; cf. Plutarch *How to Tell a Flatterer from a Friend* 28, *Moralia* 69BC). Paul could appeal to the image of a nursing *mother* (as in Plutarch *Education of Children* 5, *Moralia* 3CD; 4 Maccabees 15:4; Safrai 1974-1976b:768), but more likely he appeals to the image of a hired wetnurse (on wetnurses, cf., e.g., *Corpus Papyrorum Iudaicarum* 2:15-20, §§146-47; *BGU* 4.1058, 1106-9, 1153; *Papyrus Oxyrhynchus* 91; *P. Tebt.* 399; *P. Rein.* 2, 103-4; *PSI* 9.1065; *CILS* 8536; N. Lewis 1983:146-47; Marcus Aurelius 5.4; Epictetus *Discourses* 1.11.22; 2.16.28; Carcopino 1940:104). Aristocrats preferred educated nursemaids to uneducated ones (Plutarch *Education of Children* 5, *Moralia* 3DE; Quintilian *Institutes of Oratory* 1.1.4-5; Lefkowitz and Fant 1982:110-11, 164-66). Although free nurses may well have differed (cf. Dixon 1988:146-48; Plutarch *Table-Talk* 5 intr., *Moralia* 672F-73A), S. R. Joshel (1986:3-22) rightly warns against overestimating slave nurses' appreciation for their job (cf. also K. Bradley 1986:220-21; Chariton *Chaereas and Callirhoe* 1.12.9).

[12]E.g., Paul did not engage in "flattery," telling the Thessalonians what might have best pleased them. This denial of flattery reflects a common practice of moralists (Malherbe 1970:212-13, 216-17); they considered sound rebuke far better (e.g., Publilius Syrus 10). Flattery was widely condemned (e.g., Isocrates *Demonicus* 30; Cicero *De Amicitia* 25.94-26.99; *De Officiis* 1.26.91; Horace *Epistle* 1.16.25-39; Epictetus *Discourses* 1.12; 1.9.20, 26; 3.24.45; 4.6.33; 4.7.24; Plutarch *Education of Children* 17, *Moralia* 13B; *How to Tell a Flatterer from a Friend* 1-37, *Moralia* 48E-74E; Juvenal *Satirae* 3.86-87; 4.65-72; Marcus Aurelius 1.16.4; Diogenes Laertius *Lives* 6.1.4; 6.2.51; 6.5.92; Pseudo-Phocylides 91), but "demagogues" were accused of often practicing it (e.g., Athenaeus *Deipnosophists* 6.236E).

[13]For a comparison with the boldness of some philosophers of his day, see Malherbe 1970:208. On the public humiliation to which this passage alludes, see differing comments of Milligan 1908:16; Bruce 1982:25; Best 1977:90.

[14]On the gods worshiped in Thessalonica, see, e.g., Rossano 1958; Donfried 1985; Gill 1994:408-9.

[15]Because Romans, especially Romans 1—2, lies at the crux of most contemporary debate, we have chosen to document this section most heavily.

[16]Cicero *Tusculanae Disputationes* 1.13.30; 5.25.70; *De Natura Deorum* 2.54-58.133-46; Seneca *On Benefits* 6.23.6-7; Epictetus *Discourses* 1.6.7, 10; 1.16.8; cf. Plutarch *Isis* 76, *Moralia* 382A. The revelation in nature, however, does not produce salvation; it merely makes humanity accountable for their idolatry (see O'Rourke 1961:306). Most of the earliest interpreters regarded the natural revelation here as inseparable from Christ (Vandermarck 1973:36-52); the text itself implies only that God revealed himself, not that people found him (see Ott 1959:50, Hooker 1960:299; Coffey 1970:676; S. L. Johnson 1972:73).

[17]*Epistle of Aristeas* 131-32, 156-57; cf. *Sibylline Oracles* 3.757; *Testament of Naphtali* 3:3; W. D. Davies 1980:28-29; Longenecker 1976:54-58. For Philo, see Wolfson 1968:1:332-47, 2:73-93. Paul's early Christian missionary tradition probably drew from both Palestinian and Diaspora Judaism, the latter applying Stoic language; see Schulz 1958:173; cf. Jeremias 1954:119-21.

[18]For their eschatological damnation, cf., e.g., 1QM 11.12-13; 14.7; 15.1-2; 17.1-2; *t. Sanhedrin* 13:2; for surveys of diverse opinions on the eschatological lostness of the Gentiles in ancient Jewish texts, see E. P. Sanders 1977:206-12; Bonsirven 1964:66-70. Probably most of Judaism allowed for the salvation of "righteous Gentiles" (*Epistle of Aristeas* 279; *t. Sanhedrin* 13:2; *Sipre Deuteronomy* 307.4.2)—those who kept the laws of God's covenant with Noah (on which see, e.g., *Mekilta Baḥodeš* 6.90ff.; *Sipre Deuteronomy* 343.4.1; *b. 'Aboda Zara* 64b, bar.; *Sanhedrin* 56ab, bar., 59a; cf. Schulz 1975:48-49).

[19]For denunciations of idolatry, which was largely (though not exclusively) a Gentile sin, see, e.g., *Bel and the Dragon; Epistle of Jeremiah; Epistle of Aristeas* 134-38; *Sibylline Oracles* 3.8-35; 4.4-23; *Testament of Solomon* 26; *t. Bekorot* 3:12; *Pe'a* 1:2; *Sanhedrin* 13:8; *Sipra Vayyiqra Dibura Dehobah* par. 1.34.1.3; *Sipre Numbers* 112.2.2; *Sipre Deuteronomy* 43.4.1; 54.3.2; *'Abot de Rabbi Nathan* 40A. Jews regarded homosexual behavior much more exclusively as a Gentile vice, virtually inconceivable among themselves in this period (e.g., *Epistle of Aristeas* 152; *Sibylline Oracles* 3.185-86, 596-600, 764; 4.34; 5.166, 387, 430; *t. Horayot* 2:5-6). Many texts associate Gentiles with oppressing God's people and breaking God's laws (e.g., 1 Maccabees 5; *Jubilees* 1:9; 15:34; 22:16-18, 20-22; 23:24; 24:25-33; Pseudo-Philo *Biblical Antiquities* 7:3; 12:4; 4QpNah. 1.1; *m. 'Aboda Zara* 2:1; *Terumot* 8:12; *Sipre Deuteronomy* 213.1.1).

[20]Paul already moves the argument in this direction with his vice list in Romans 1:28-32. Sins such as envy (e.g., Wisdom of Solomon 6:23; *Epistle of Aristeas* 224; Josephus *Antiquities of the Jews* 2.13; *Jewish Wars* 1.77; Philo *Quod Omnis Probus Liber Sit* 13; *Sibylline Oracles* 3.660-64; *Testament of Gad* 7:2; *Testament of Simeon* 3, *Testament of Solomon* 6:4), pride (e.g., 1QS 4.9; Sirach 3:28; 10:7, 12-13; 13:1, 20; 22:22; 25:1; Philo *De Posteritate Caini* 52; *Testament of Reuben* 3:5; *Testament of Judah* 13:2; *Testament of Job* 15:8-10; *m. 'Abot* 1:13) and slander (e.g., 1QS 7.15-16; Philo *De Specialibus Legibus* 4.59-60; *Sipre Deuteronomy* 1.8.2-3; 275.1.1; *'Abot de Rabbi Nathan* 9; 40A; 16, §36; 41, §116B) also appear in condemnations of Jewish vices or warnings to Jewish hearers. Vice lists were a standard rhetorical form (e.g., Plato *Leges* 1.649D; Aristotle *Eudemian Ethics* 2.3.4, 1220b-21a; *On Virtues and Vices* 1249a-51b; Epictetus *Discourses* 2.8.23; Diogenes *Epistle* 36, to Timomachus; Maximus of Tyre *Discourses* 36.4; 1QS 4.9-11; Wisdom of Solomon 14:25-26; Philo *De Sacrificiis Abelis et Caini* 32 and *De Posteritate Caini* 52; *Sibylline Oracles* 2.255-82; *Testament of Levi* 17:11; *Didache* 5).

[21]Paul may appeal to the philosophers' idea of the innate law (Plato *Phaedo* 75CD; Aristotle *Politica* 3.8.2, 1284a; Cicero *Topica* 7.31 and *De Legibus* 1.22.58-59; Plutarch *Uneducated Ruler* 3, *Moralia* 780C; Apuleius *Metamorphoses* 3.8; Diogenes Laertius *Lives* 2.68; 3.86), which in some thinking corresponded to the law of nature (on which see Aristotle *Art of Rhetoric* 1.15.6, 1375ab; Cicero *De Inventione* 2.22.65-66; 2.53.161, *De Legibus* 1.10.28; 1.12.33; 2.4.10; 3.1.3 and *De Officiis* 1.16.50; 1.28.100; 3.17.72; 3.28.101; Seneca *On Benefits* 4.17.4; cf. Remus 1984). For the Greco-Roman notion of the "conscience," see, e.g., Isocrates *Demonicus* 16, *Oration* 1; Publilius Syrus 194; Seneca *Epistle to Lucilius* 42.2; 43.5 and *On Benefits* 4.14.1; 4.21.5; Quintilian *Institutes of Oratory* 5.11.41; Juvenal *Satirae* 13. For Diaspora Jews, cf. *Testament of Reuben* 4:3; *Testament of Judah* 20:2; Wallis 1974-1975 and 1975; in Paul, cf., e.g., Sevenster 1961:84-102; Harris 1962; Thrall 1967.

[22]Paul borrows a frequent philosophical argument against "the pretentious philosopher" (Stowers 1981:112; Epictetus *Discourses* 2.19), though his argument may also have roots in the Jesus tradition (e.g., C. H. Dodd 1967:63-64).

[23]On the Jewish doctrine of election regarding the righteous of Israel, see, e.g., *1 Enoch* 1:1, 3, 8; 5:7-8; 25:5; 38:4; 48:1, 9; 50:1; 58:1; 61:4, 12; 93:2; *Jubilees* 1:29; 22:9-10; 2 Maccabees 1:25; *Testament of Job* 4:11; *Mekilta Širata* 9.118ff.; E. P. Sanders 1977:84-107, 147-80; Bonsirven 1964:47. Specifically in Essene texts or concerning Essene practice, see, e.g., Josephus *Antiquities of the Jews* 18.18; 1QS 1.3-4, 10; 2.5; 4.24-25; 8.6; 9.14; 11.7, 16; 1QM 10.9-10; 12.1; 15.1-2; 17.7; 1QpHab 5.3; 9.12; 10.13; 4QpPs 37 fr. 1; for comments

on Essene election and grace, see E. P. Sanders 1977:257-66; Flusser 1988:28-35; Marx 1967. The Essenes narrowed the scope of election much more severely than the Pharisees and other traditions (e.g., Sirach 46:1), who seem to have extended it to all Israel.

[24]Israel alone was suitable to receive Torah (*Sipre Deuteronomy* 311.2.1; school of Rabbi Ishmael in *b. Beṣa* 25b; *Pesiqta Rabbati* 50:2, bar.). Compare the tradition that God offered Torah to all seventy nations but Israel alone accepted it (e.g., *Mekilta Bahodesh* 5; *Sipre Deuteronomy* 343.4.1; *b. 'Aboda Zara* 2b; *Pesiqta de Rab Kahana* 2:1; 12:10; *Pesiqta de Rab Kahana Supplement* 1:15).

[25]Most of Paul's contemporaries would have agreed that God called Abraham while he was still a "Gentile" (Rom 4:10-12); see, e.g., Montefiore 1979:43.

[26]Paul again appeals to a common Jewish understanding of his day; cf., e.g., Sirach 25:24; *1 Enoch* 98:4; *Life of Adam and Eve* 44.3-4; *Sipre Deuteronomy* 323.5.1; 339.1.2; and especially 4 Ezra 3:7, 20-22, 30; 7:118-26; *2 Apocalypse of Baruch* 17:2-3; 23:4; 48:42-45; 54:15, 19; 56:5-6.

[27]This is one of the most controversial passages in Romans, but it seems unlikely to me that Paul means something by "Israel" here different from what he meant in the preceding context. Cf. Munck 1967b:136; Ladd 1964. As most commentators note, comparing *m. Sanhedrin* 10:1, "all Israel's" salvation refers to Israel as a whole, not every Jewish individual.

[28]See T. Donaldson 1993:98.

[29]Committed Jews preferred death to inability to circumcise their children (e.g., 2 Maccabees 6:10; 4 Maccabees 4:25; Josephus *Antiquities of the Jews* 12.256) and regarded circumcision as a standard element in conversion (e.g., Judith 14:10; Josephus *Antiquities of the Jews* 20.44; *t. 'Aboda Zara* 3:12; *Berakot* 6:13). Interestingly, the practice may have been borrowed originally from some Egyptians or Ethiopians (Artapanus in Eusebius *Praeparatio Evangelica* 9.27.10; Josephus *Against Apion* 1.169-71; Herodotus *Histories* 2.104; Diodorus Siculus 1.28.3).

[30]On letters of rebuke and reproach see especially Stowers 1986:22, 133-34, 139. Some view Galatians as an apologetic or judicial letter (Betz 1976 and 1979; Brinsmead 1982:37-55), but it is probably deliberative (Kennedy 1984:144-52; Aune 1987:206-7; Lyons 1985:112-19; Hall 1987).

[31]See especially E. P. Sanders 1977:141, 362.

[32]For a discussion of some Jewish perspectives that may have grown into the later doctrine of merits, including the merits of the ancestors (e.g., *3 Enoch* 18:17; *m. 'Abot* 6:11; *Makkot* 3:16; *t. Pe'a* 1:2; 3:8; *Mekilta Pisha* 16.165-70; *Beshallah* 4.52ff; *Širata* 9.24ff; *Sipra Behuqotai* pq. 8.269.2.5; pq. 13.277.1.14; *Sipra Qiddušin* pq. 8.205.2.6; *Emor* pq. 7.227.1.6; *Behar* 5.255.1.10; *Sipre Deuteronomy* 2.1.1-4; 8.1.1; 57.1.1; 176.1.1; 176.2.2; 229.4.1; 252.1.2; 283.7.1; 329.3.1; *'Abot de Rabbi Nathan* 12, §30B), see a survey of data in Keener's forthcoming Matthew commentary with Eerdmans. For the denial that merits are supererogatory in rabbinic texts, see also E. P. Sanders 1977:183-98; Carson 1981:87-88. Despite some attempts to qualify still more distorted works of predecessors, Rudolf Bultmann's portrayal of "legalistic" rabbinic Judaism thus remains a serious misrepresentation of Jewish piety (Bultmann 1958:67-73).

[33]Bligh 1970:433; Kcck 1979:6. Ancient writers regularly mocked self-mutilation, particularly associated with Cybele's Asiatic priests (e.g., *Rhetorica ad Herennium* 4.49.62; Lucretius *De Rerum Natura* 2.614-15; Horace *Satire* 1.2.120-21; Juvenal *Satirae* 2.110-16; Epictetus *Discourses* 2.20.17, 19; Lucian *Syrian Goddess* 51; Heraclitus *Epistle* 9, to Hermodorus; Sextus Empiricus *Outlines of Pyrrhonism* 3.217), and the summons to self-mutilation was a particularly insulting blow (Epictetus *Discourses* 3.1.31; Betz 1979:270). In view of Deuteronomy 23:1, the insult was particularly degrading to Jewish hearers (*Sipre Deuteronomy* 247.1.1-2; *p. Yebamot* 8:1, §11).

[34]For fuller exposition of John's teaching on regeneration in its first-century context, see Keener 1997c:143-51.

[35]This is the prevailing view in contemporary Johannine scholarship; I have surveyed the views more fully in my Duke dissertation, Keener 1991b:1-51, and in my forthcoming commentary on the Fourth Gospel (Hendrickson).

[36]See appendix A, " 'The Jews' and Johannine Irony," in Keener 1991b:330-49.

[37]E.g., Sikes 1941:23; S. Wilson 1979:28.

[38]See, e.g., S. G. Wilson 1973; Dupont 1979. For early Christianity's ethnic universalism but christocentric exclusivism, see also Boccaccini 1991:265.

[39]Unable to find many points of contact with the Epicureans, Paul emphasized contacts with Stoics and other groups, e.g., in his affirmation that Deity transcended temples (e.g., Heraclitus *Epistle* 4, to Hermodorus) or dependence on human worship (e.g., Plutarch *Isis* 1, 75, *Moralia* 351D, 381B, and *Stoics and Poets* 4, *Moralia* 1058C; Seneca *Dialogues* 7.8.4; Marcus Aurelius 7.16 and *Pythagorean Sentences* 25), ideas

repeated in relevant Hellenistic Jewish texts (e.g., *Epistle of Aristeas* 211; 3 Maccabees 2:9; Josephus *Antiquities of the Jews* 8.111; Marcus 1931-1932:55).

[40]Most missions literature today (we could cite many sources), heavily informed by cultural anthropology and related disciplines, has become very sensitive to cultural concerns and indigenous church leadership. Although nineteenth- and early-twentieth-century missionaries, like nineteenth-century anthropologists and others, were often insensitive to other cultures, in many cases missionaries identified even more fully with culture than is today usually considered appropriate; e.g., Hudson Taylor's China Inland Mission and, earlier, Matteo Ricci (on whom see, e.g., Spence 1985); cf., e.g., Wolcott 1976.

[41]See, e.g., in Kaplan et al. 1993. Assaad 1980 argues that the custom (which appears in many traditional African religions) came into Islam from ancient Egypt.

[42]Green 1989:58 (following John Taylor's *Go-Between God*) recounts that one Malam Ibrahim discovered enough about Jesus in the Qur'an to be converted. He thereupon gathered others who began to pray in the name of Isa Masih, Jesus the Messiah; "when the Islamic authorities discovered this, he was charged with heresy, refused to recant, and was crucified in Kano market place thirty years before a Christian preacher arrived in the country." Similar reports abound.

[43]C. S. Lewis 1946.

[44]African-American overseas ministries include denominational agencies (such as with A.M.E. Zion missions, whose supervisors kindly allowed Craig to write a column for *The Missionary Seer* for a number of years), the Lott Carey Convention, Carver Foreign Mission (Atlanta), Ambassadors Fellowship, the Destiny Movement and numerous others. Interracial ministries (e.g., Campus Crusade, World Vision, YWAM) are still more numerous (for a listing with addresses, see Johnstone 1993:631-40, although unfortunately it lacks most of the majority African American ministries).

[45]See, e.g., information in Usry and Keener 1996:76-77; Dickerson 1995:121-30.

Closing Words
[1]Asante 1988:78. (On the biblical demand for ministerial marital fidelity, see, e.g., Keener 1997a.)
[2]Besides resources cited in Usry and Keener 1996:111-39, see on reconciliation Perkins and Rice 1993; Dawson 1994; Washington and Kehrein 1993. For a challenge to white supremacists, see also Abanes 1996.
[3]Muhammad 1992:198.
[4]Ibid., p. 222.
[5]Ibid., p. 284. He overstates his case unfairly when he claims that Christians are responsible for the world's evils (p. 285).

Appendix A: One Example of How the Bible Does Relate to Ancient Culture
[1]A. S. Yahuda (1947) finds Egyptian coloring even in the depiction of Aaron's priestly garment. Some writers in the past have overstated the case for Egyptian background (e.g., possibly Yahuda 1933; more recently perhaps Rendsburg 1988), but a more common error of the early twentieth century was a pan-Babylonian approach that neglected Egyptian sources.
[2]Badawy 1968:189: "Pi-Ra'messe, the Delta Residence of Ramses II at Tanis, was extraordinarily rich in temples."
[3]For the tabernacle's antiquity, see also J. Scott 1978, a Ph.D. dissertation for the University of Pennsylvania; cf. Cross 1947:51 (also Cross 1961, adopting a largely Davidic date with earlier traditions); Andrews 1886:68 (admittedly with a poor argument); Friedman 1980 (arguing from the literary evidence that the tabernacle existed within the temple and must thus predate it; but we suspect that the tabernacle perished at Shiloh—1 Sam 4; Jer 7).
[4]In our desire to provide more complete bibliographic information in these appendices, especially the second, we have depended at points on *Old Testament Abstracts*.
[5]So also Josephus *Antiquities of the Jews* 3.103.
[6]It falls in the same range as the three Middle Bronze I temples at Megiddo (Schofield 1967:315) but is generally smaller than Canaanite temples and much smaller than Egyptian, Mesopotamian, Hittite (Kitchen 1978:85) or Persian (Houtman 1994) temples. The relatively small Arad temple (see Aharoni 1967:395; cf. Aharoni 1982:232) probably was modeled after the tabernacle and thus cannot be involved in our discussion.
[7]J. Scott 1978:109, 315. Scott uses the seven-palm cubit (20.6 inches) (ibid., pp. 327-28). Evidence indicates also Solomon's use of the "royal" Egyptian cubit in building projects (Milson 1986).
[8]Albright 1968:193.

[9]One has been uncovered at Tell Mevorakh (Stern 1977:89-91).

[10]Thus a bas-relief from the first century C.E. at Palmyra in Syria also depicts such a portable shrine (Cross 1947:49; also in de Vaux 1961:296-97).

[11]Diodorus Siculus; according to Philo of Byblos, the god El had a sacred image drawn in a portable shrine by two oxen. Apparently in earlier times also it was on a portable throne that could be carried forth to battle (Albright 1943:42-43; J. A. Thompson 1962:72; cf. Num 14:44-45; 1 Sam 4:3-4 and especially 1 Sam 6:7). Wen-Amon's idol in his "tent" is probably not an adequate parallel.

[12]Singer 1978:20; Bright 1981:127. Cf. also on the Egyptian shrine at Timna, below.

[13]Koch 1977:122. See, e.g., *Aqhat* A.5 (though the tent here *could* be Danel's rather than Kothar's—Pritchard 1955:151 n. 19).

[14]Letter for letter the Ugaritic designations of the dwelling place of El are *mskn* and *'hl,* exactly the Hebrew designations for the tabernacle (Cassuto 1967:322-23). The tabernacle of El in the Ugaritic material, like the tabernacle of Israel's God, was made of boards, which were erected on pedestals (also noted by Cross 1947:62). Albright 1943:40 is in basic agreement with Cassuto.

[15]Clifford 1971:222; cf. translation by H. L. Ginzberg in Pritchard 1955. A Hittite fragment noted by Clifford concurs here. Cf. perhaps Psalm 46:4. His tent is also located on his "holy mountain" (Clifford 1971:223). For one study understanding Israel's divine language by comparison with Ugarit's El, see Pope 1987.

[16]Clifford 1971:223. "Tents" might, however, simply reflect an archaic usage, as is frequent enough in the Hebrew Bible (e.g., 2 Sam 20:1; 1 Kings 12:16). Against John Van Seters's emphasis exclusively on the first millennium B.C.E., tent dwellers may be attested in the third millennium B.C.E. and appear most frequently in second-millennium texts; see Kitchen 1978:58-59; D. J. Wiseman 1978:195-200 and 1980:142; cf. the third-millennium-old Assyrian use of "tent-dwellers" in Bright 1981:50.

[17]Clifford 1971:225. Baal, in contrast, had a house (perhaps this adds significance to 2 Sam 7:2-7, 13).

[18]I. Abrahams 1972:684-85; Morgenstern 1942-1943:208-9, 216; Cross 1947:60; noted briefly in G. E. Wright 1962:65; de Vaux 1961:296-97; and C. H. Gordon 1965a:145 n. 2.

[19]Kitchen 1960:8-9. Hetepheres I lived before 2600 B.C.E. There were also "booths" for funerary equipment and food offerings, and both fragments and a number of representations of these portable structures (assembled within the tombs) have been found. The earliest Egyptian temples, like the early houses, were made mainly of lattice and clay, with timber for the lintels.

[20]Shrines dating to the fifth millennium B.C.E. are portrayed as light structures of latticework; the outer court would be enclosed by a latticework fence. The structure of the chambers, with the holy of holies in the back, seems to have begun to develop by this point (Murray 1963:226-27 and n.d.:2, 5; Nelson 1961:147). In that period at least, worship could be conducted in such structures (reed sanctuaries, used in fourth-millennium Mesopotamia, were displaced when sun-dried bricks came into use; cf. Oppenheim 1961:158).

[21]Murray n.d.:87-88.

[22]Kitchen 1960:10.

[23]Ibid., pp. 10-11.

[24]Aharoni 1982:136-37.

[25]Nelson 1961:148-49. By the time of Seti II and Ramses III, the temple of Amun accommodated three such bark shrines. Also Lurker 1980:120 and J. Scott 1978:314.

[26]Kitchen 1960:11 and Cross 1947:55 both stress this parallel from Moses' probable contemporary. For an example of the importance of the royal tent in warfare, see Breasted 1906:3:143.

[27]The worship of a New Kingdom temple in the Sinai region, partly modified by Ramses II, appears to show strong Semitic influence (Badawy 1968:321). This should indicate to us that Israel could have been innovative as well as imitative.

[28]On the basis of the temple at Arad, Aharoni argues that the tabernacle was not tripartite (1982:232; but cf. p. 227). This is, however, true of the tent shrine proper (the fully enclosed building as opposed to the outer fencing) only because a tripartite tabernacle proper would be too unwieldy for a wandering people who needed a portable shrine.

[29]J. Gray 1967:146-47.

[30]Dever 1974:43, referring to Temple 7300 (Hazor, Tell Mardikh and Alalakh still had two rooms in Middle Bronze II). Tripartite buildings for various uses became common in Palestine by the Iron Age (Herr 1988).

[31]Dever 1974. Megiddo's and other Canaanite Early Bronze temples follow primarily Anatolian and North Syrian models (Thalmann 1989; Milson 1988), but Egypt exercised considerable influence on Megiddo from the nineteenth century B.C.E. on (Briend 1989).

[32]Hittite temples are not closely related (cf. Gurney 1954:145, 210). Apart from the rectangular shape, Mesopotamian temples were also quite dissimilar; cf. Lloyd 1978.120, Delaporte 1970:144-49; Oppenheim 1961:158-69, a brief perusal of which should suffice to demonstrate the point. The temple at Beth-shan, with a few parallels (cf. Aharoni 1982:122), was built by Egyptians during the Amarna Age. Although the temple at Tell Qasile is tripartite, it is very dissimilar to the tabernacle (A. Mazar 1973b:45). The Iron Age fortress temple at Shechem does not even have an inner sanctum (Schofield 1967:319). Ebla is too early if taken alone, but cf. Kitchen 1978:47.

[33]As one would thus expect, a temple in the Sinai reflects the straight-axis Egyptian design (Ventura 1988).

[34]Nelson 1961:147.

[35]Murray 1963:235 and n.d.:2; J. Scott 1978:314; Badawy 1968:176-77. Some reckon four parts by counting a separate vestibule; Israel's tabernacle was, however, too small to warrant such a vestibule.

[36]Murray 1963:235.

[37]Ibid.; Nelson 1961:147.

[38]Lurker 1980:120.

[39]Badawy 1968:176-77; cf. also ibid., pp. 38, 113, 115, 117; for kings, pp. 42, 91; Michalowski n.d.:287.

[40]Michalowski n.d.:287.

[41]Badawy 1968:177. Cf. also the sacred animals in nearby enclosures, "Apis the bull at Memphis, Sobk the crocodile at Arsinoë, Anubis the dog at Kynopolis . . . and so on" (N. Lewis 1983:94).

[42]Badawy 1968:180.

[43]Given literary parallels between the tabernacle and golden calf narratives, as well as the pattern including both temple building and rebellion in Akkadian texts, the golden calf episode is probably part of the extended narrative, reinforcing the warning against idolatry, which distorts the true pattern of worship God ordained (see Hurowitz 1983-1984).

[44]Andrews 1886:61. J. A. Wainwright (1980:137-38) tries to make such a case for Solomon's temple (perhaps with an inadequate argument, though the conclusion may be correct). Canaan and the Israelite period of the Judges illustrates the principle in reverse: see G. E. Wright 1961:173.

[45]More expensive materials were used nearer the sacred ark, a symbol that would communicate in many cultures. G. H. Davies 1962:4:498-506; cf. also Haran 1965:200-206.

[46]See also Kaiser 1978:120.

[47]G. E. Wright 1961:169-70 and 1944:42. The palace of Baal was called a "house," a "dwelling," a "shelter" and a "mansion" (for English translation, see Gibson 1977:46-67).

[48]The Hebrew word for the house of the king and the house of the god, from a Sumerian root meaning "big house," distinguished between the dwellings of gods and kings on the one hand and lesser beings on the other (Pfeiffer 1962:56). We may well remember the parallels we have seen between Egyptian god temples and the palaces of pharaohs.

[49]For Canaan, note the Palace of Baal epic; for Egypt, see (for example) Badawy 1968:161, 172-73. Compare also elaborate descriptions of palace building in ancient literature (C. H. Gordon 1965b:275).

[50]Cylinder A of Gudea portrays Ningirsu delivering the likeness and sketch of the sanctuary Gudea is to build, as noted by Cassuto 1967:322; de Vaux 1961:277. The regulations given by Egyptian priests for temple construction were attributed to Thoth, as noted in Lurker 1980:120. De Vaux 1961:277 also compares instructions of Marduk to Nabopolassar and Sin to Nabonidus.

[51]Kathir-wa-Hasis built Baal's palace of cedar trees, as noted by Clifford 1971:226 and Cassuto 1942:55. In the *Iliad* 21.446-47 and the Gilgamesh Epic (tablets 1 and 2), deities constructed city walls (C. H. Gordon 1965b:236-37).

[52]For the possibility of polemic, cf. Cogan 1985.

[53]Murray 1963:232.

[54]Nelson 1961:154-55.

[55]Murray 1963:183-84.

[56]See Kitchen 1978:86. Hittites by this period also were far more elaborate in their consecration of shrines than the Israelites here.

[57]Gurney 1954:149-50. Ritual purity among Hittite priests at some points parallels that of the Levites, but at other points it is in contrast. Cf. 1 Kings 18:27; Psalm 50:5, 7-15.

[58]G. E. Wright 1961:172. By contrast, Spieckermann 1992 contrasts the universality of Israel's God with the Ugaritic localization of El.

[59]G. E. Wright 1961:180; cf. also later sources (Reitzenstein 1978:196). The "seas" of 1 Kings 7:23-25, 39,

44 also point to this usage.

[60]Lurker 1980:120. Tuthmosis III founded his temple to be founded like the heavens (Badawy 1968:161). Although this was probably not the case in earlier temples, it came to be in these later ones (Nelson 1961:150-52). Some writers contend that the tabernacle replaced the vulture goddess with cherubim (cf. J. Scott 1978:165-66), though apart from wings these share little in common.

[61]G. E. Wright 1961:170-71. Cf. Psalm 104:2. Some have also suggested that "P" links the tabernacle to the creation narrative (Kearney 1977; Weimar 1988).

[62]See, e.g., Wilcox 1988. The Talmud and the early Christian epistle "to the Hebrews" are not far off base at this point (despite their ready adaptation of Platonic categories, as in Philo), although the same cannot be said for later allegorizations isolated from an ancient Near Eastern perspective.

[63]Clifford 1971:226.

[64]Cassuto 1967:322. Cf. Harrelson 1969:4-5, which notes the commonness of this concept even in the Babylonian theology of creation.

[65]I. Abrahams 1972:687.

[66]E.g., the earthen altars of Israelite regulations (Ex 20:24) are paralleled by most of the altars at Mari (Parrot 1967:138). Against Julius Wellhausen's view that the tabernacle story grew from a shorter account, the biblical account fits Ugaritic and Mesopotamian sources (see Hurowitz 1985, citing Samsuiluna B; Gordon *Ugaritic Text* 51 v 74-vi 21).

[67]Kitchen 1960:12.

[68]Flax and goat hair were readily available to people in the Sinai area at about this time (J. Scott 1978:25-30, 310). Necessary dye stuffs were native to the Mediterranean coast and the Sinai peninsula (ibid., pp. 38-39). Rams' skins and dolphins' skins would have been the most accessible types of leather in the Sinai in this period, as were the materials necessary for preserving and tanning them (ibid., pp. 39-45, 310).

[69]Forbes 1966:4:102-10. Judging from later artwork, red was also apparently used on a Phoenician portable shrine (de Vaux 1961:297).

[70]Forbes 1966:110. A poor-quality blue dye was derived from the seed pods of the "suntberry" *(Acacia nilotica).* Haran 1978:159 notes that blue was more expensive and finer than purple, and both were better than crimson (Haran 1978:160).

[71]For Tyrian purple, see, e.g., Pliny *Naturalis Historia* 5.17.76; Athenaeus *Deipnosophists* 3.88; Achilles Tatius *Clitophon and Leucippe* 2.11; Horace *Satires* 2.4.84 and *Epistle* 1.10.26; Martial *Epigrams* 2.29.3, 4.28.2, 8.48.1; Juvenal *Satirae* 1.27, 10.334; Apuleius *Metamorphoses* 10.20; Petronius *Satyricon* 30; Chariton *Chaereas and Callirhoe* 6.4.2, 8.1.14, 6.7; 1 Maccabees 4:29; Jensen 1963. Archaeological evidence indicates the use of purple dye in Phoenicia as early as 1700 B.C.E. (Ziderman 1990). For its association with wealth, see, e.g., Lucretius *De Rerum Natura* 5.1423; Horace *Ode* 1.35.12, 2.18.7-8; Cicero *De Senecute* 17.59; Athenaeus *Deipnosophists* 4.159d; Diogenes Laertius *Lives* 8.2.73; 1 Maccabees 10:20, 62, 64, 14:43-44; *Genesis Apocryphon* 20.31; *Sibylline Oracles* 3.389, 658-59 and 8.74; Petronius *Satyricon* 38, 54; Epictetus Fragment 11; Martial *Epigrams* 5.8.5; 8.10; Juvenal *Satirae* 1.106; 4.31; Apuleius *Metamorphoses* 10.20; Chariton *Chaereas and Callirhoe* 3.2.17; *Pesiqta de Rab Kahana* 2:7, 15:3; *Testament of Abraham* 4 A; *Joseph and Asenath* 2:2/3, 8/14-15, 5:5/6. Some writers complained about its extravagance (Seneca *Dialogues* 12.11.2; Plutarch *Table-Talk* 3.1.2, *Moralia* 646B; *1 Enoch* 98:2 MSS [Knibb, p. 231]).

[72]Haran 1978:114-22. One also finds a purple dye industry on the coast below Mt. Carmel starting in the ninth century B.C.E. (Karmon and Spanier 1988) and elsewhere (Horace *Ode* 2.18.7-8; Charlesworth 1970:125; Meeks 1983:46).

[73]Forbes 1966:4:139.

[74]Haran 1978:158-60.

[75]It parallels the dyed red leather of the pre-Islamic *qubbah;* see G. H. Davies 1962:4:499. He also notes, "There is no need to seek symbolic meaning in the colors. They simply represent what was available, though violet is prominent."

[76]Haran 1965:202.

[77]J. Scott 1978:313.

[78]B. Mazar et al. 1959:1:161; also noted by Cassuto 1967:328. Ziony Zevit (1992) finds the acacia beams in the Sinai region inadequate and prefers north Israel; but further study would be necessary to determine how long this has been the case.

[79]J. Scott 1978:215-16. Acacia would not ignite below 900 degrees C or higher, while a wood campfire

generates only about 600 degrees C, so it would have been suitable for the altar of burnt offering. Of course it is possible that wood was only a mold for the bronze over it; in durable molds it could be discarded once the bronze had been completed. Lucas 1962:442 notes its use in boat building. Acacia was often used for construction in Egypt.

[80]Some pieces of burnt wood on the floor of an Iron Age temple at Tell Qasile were identified as cedar of Lebanon by Nili Lipschitz of Tel Aviv University (A. Mazar 1973a:67); Lipschitz later identified more cedar of Lebanon at what may have been a temple at Tell Lachish (Ussishkin 1977:49). Further on cedar of Lebanon, see Liphshitz and Biger 1991. Pfeiffer 1966:88-89 notes that Solomon's temple, designed by a Phoenician architect, is comparable with north Syrian sanctuaries of the same period (but cf. also 2 Sam 7:2); for other Phoenician elements, see Fritz 1987. In the first millennium B.C.E. Phoenicians were copying (but adapting) Egyptian iconography (Hölbl 1989).

[81]Note B. Mazar et al. 1959:1:161. Cedar wood was imported even to Egypt (fifteenth-century B.C.E. inscription in Pritchard 1955:243; cf. twenty-seventh-century B.C.E. record in Pritchard 1955:227). The frames are often paralleled with those in the Tent of El (Cross 1947:62).

[82]Petrie 1910:100.

[83]B. Mazar et al. 1959:1:175. "Pure" gold (in the sense of fully refined gold) is not found in Egypt until the Persian Period, according to R. J. Forbes; although refining went back to the Ur III period (Middle Bronze IA), Egyptian gold in this period was often up to 75 percent copper (Forbes 1966:8:174, but accepting only epigraphic evidence); Lucas 1962:229 concurs.

[84]Haran 1965:201. The work on these two objects was too delicate for overlay.

[85]Haran 1978:158.

[86]B. Mazar et al. 1959.1.175.

[87]Schedl 1973:2:153.

[88]J. Scott 1978:25. *Tahash* is probably worked leather, the term being derived from the old Egyptian word *tj-h-s* (Kitchen 1960:8).

[89]Forbes 1966:5:24-25.

[90]I. Abrahams 1972:684; Kitchen 1960:12. Kitchen notes that there is evidence from the New Kingdom for the use of foreign slaves as workers in stores and workshops attached to temples and government institutions.

[91]Kitchen 1978:85-86.

[92]B. Mazar et al. 1959:1:172, 174 portrays many of these. Egyptian carpenters were master woodworkers. Saws, chisels, drills and hammers were all used in the thirteenth century B.C.E., appearing on artistry from the tomb of one Apy. Cf. also J. Scott 1978:311-12.

[93]G. H. Davies 1962:4:501; Haran 1965:202; cf. also Haran 1978:160-61.

[94]Haran 1965:206.

[95]The temple to Ishtar at Ashur, c. 3000 B.C.E., rebuilt c. 1200 B.C.E., had a statue of a goddess in an alcove above a flight of stairs (Pfeiffer 1966:86). At Beth-shan in Canaan the holy of holies from this period was on an elevated platform (G. E. Wright 1962:115). De Vaux 1961:314 notes the commonness of an elevated cella in the ancient Near East. Cf. the holy place in the interior, away from the outer court, at Ugarit (Callot 1987).

[96]Cf. Breasted 1906:3:100 (no. 246); Bowling 1975:616 notes that this was often the case.

[97]Despite the architectural differences between the temple at Arad and certain features of Solomon's temple, the cultic artifacts are essentially the same, indicating their importance and continuity in Israelite religion and possibly a source for Arad's models of these (cf. Aharoni 1982:230).

[98]For the principle, cf., e.g., descriptions of Ptolemy Philadelphus's (noncultic) wealth in Athenaeus *Deipnosophists* 5.196-203.

[99]G. H. Davies 1962:4:499. Schedl 1973:1:157 notes that in Egypt, Babylonia and the Hittite Empire, important documents would be deposited in the sanctuary "at the feet of the divinity," as a guarantee of fidelity to the covenant.

[100]Von Rad 1962:1:237 n. 110.

[101]Schedl 1973:2:157. The chest (same word) among Bedouins was offered to a guest as a seat. On the throne, see Psalm 80:1; 99:1; 132:7-8; 1 Sam 4:4; 2 Sam 6:2; 2 Kings 19:14; 1 Chron 13:6. Pfeiffer 1966:89 thus rightly calls the holy of holies in the temple "the throne room of Israel's God."

[102]Claus Schedl's view, 1973:156-57.

[103]Cf. J. Scott 1978:173.

[104]Ibid.; de Vaux 1961:319.

[105]B. Mazar et al. 1959:1:162.

[106]Ibid., p. 22.

[107]Cf. the eighth-century artwork in "Treasures from the Lands of the Bible," *Biblical Archaeology Review* 11, no. 2 (March 1985): 36-37. Late attestation from some other sources about Phoenician images: see Kaiser 1973:22. Albright 1938 also parallels Egyptian winged sphinxes (or griffins) and winged lions.

[108]Edwards et al. 1975:2/2:600-601; B. Mazar et al. 1959:1:162; Cross 1947:63.

[109]G. E. Wright 1962:142; Cassuto 1967:323; Haran 1978:254-55; Albright 1938 and 1961b:95-97; for a polemic against Canaanite divine kings imagery here, cf. Hendel 1988.

[110]Schedl 1973:154 n. 10.

[111]Gurney 1954:188.

[112]Edwards et al. 1975:2/2:859. G. H. Davies 1962:4:507 mentions Isaiah 65:11 as implying other nations' use of the table in an idolatrous manner; cf. Josephus *Antiquities of the Jews* 3.139. For curtains, see Pausanias 5.12.4.

[113]I. Abrahams 1972:682.

[114]Aharoni 1982:125 and 1967:395-96 also notes the altar of burnt offering at Arad. Sacrificial altars could also have horns.

[115]B. Mazar et al. 1959:1:163.

[116]May 1935:12-13; Pfeiffer 1966:34; Schofield 1967:322; Edwards 1975:3/2:858-60; Biran 1986. J. A. Thompson 1975:274 notes their commonness and their use in Canaan while Egypt was attacking at the walls. Some unhorned incense altars have been proposed (e.g., Herzog 1987, though the identification remains uncertain). Incense burners were probably not limited to cultic settings (Fowler 1985).

[117]Cassuto 1967:322-23.

Appendix B: The Accuracy of Accounts in the Pentateuch

[1]Christians also held pentateuchal source theories even before Wellhausen; e.g., Bishop John William Colenso of Natal (1814-1883; Le Roux 1990) and French Catholic priest Richard Simon (1712; Ceresko 1992:53-54).

[2]Conservatives today often hold that Moses' message stands behind the Pentateuch though the words may have changed (cf. Livingston 1974:262; Christensen and Narucki 1989).

[3]Livingston 1974:220. The later Jewish scholar Ibn Ezra in the twelfth century may have questioned Mosaic authorship of some parts of the Pentateuch, though not on literary grounds (Jacobs 1973:20).

[4]As has long been the case: see, e.g., Driver 1957:viii-xiii (reprinted from his 1897 introduction). For a survey of views in history till the nineteenth century, see E. M. Gray 1923. On the importance of hearing the Old Testament as a word from God, see, e.g., W. Holladay 1995:5-8.

[5]Garbini 1988:82-84 compares Rome's origin myth and Greek use of eponymous figures. The comparison may have some value at points, but only a further comparison of the Pentateuch stories with contemporary historical data can help us ascertain to what degree these stories' genre compares with classical counterparts on the matter of historical reliability.

[6]Naturally later interpreters applied *ha-Torah* in Deuteronomy 31:24 to the whole Pentateuch (from an Amoraic perspective one might even apply it to oral rabbinic tradition!), but one could as easily apply these words simply to the legal material (though modern scholars often date that later than the narratives).

[7]Thus "even if the sources could be pinpointed with some accuracy in time and place, one would still have to press back behind the sources to find the origin of their contents" (Craigie 1986:118-19). In view of new evidence from twenty-five thousand Mari texts, thousands of Cappadocian texts and other discoveries, John Bright (1981:69-71) argues that "a new and more sympathetic evaluation of the traditions is called for" (p. 69). Although T. L. Thompson and John Van Seters (e.g., Thompson 1974; Van Seters 1975) exercised a more lasting impact than Bright anticipated in 1981, Bright was undoubtedly correct that in 1981 most scholars held that the traditions derived from the patriarchal era (1981:73 and his citations from Luke 1977; earlier, see Albright 1963:2; C. H. Gordon 1965a:115). For one fair early review of Thompson and Van Seters, see Selman 1977.

[8]Cf., e.g., views surveyed in Nicholson 1989 (though he accepts the hypothesis); Gibert 1992; Blenkinsopp 1985. Fretheim 1996:26 notes that source-critical approaches are currently in disarray, though it is widely agreed that earlier traditions were later edited.

[9]In past decades some scholars could write as if "no competent scholars" denied that the Pentateuch emerged at the end of Israel's ancient history (W. Smith 1955:229) or, earlier still, that despite variations, nearly all

scholars concurred essentially with Wellhausen's basic view and dates for the sources (Brightman 1918:14). Most current Old Testament introductions provide a broader survey of views (e.g., Hayes 1979:156-97, especially 194-97; cf. B. Childs 1979:112-35).

[10]Rendtorff 1990:102-36; Blenkinsopp 1992:25; Campbell and O'Brien 1993:ix. "There is today scarcely anything more than a general, ill-defined consensus about [J], a consensus, however, to which there is no agreement among the exegetes in any single important, concrete detail" (Rendtorff 1990:178).

[11]Campbell and O'Brien 1993:xii, also noting that Noth's own views on particular sources shifted over time (pp. xii-xiii).

[12]Cf., e.g., Levinson 1994b:9; for surveys of current problems (of varying weight), see, e.g., Pury and Römer 1989; Briend 1992; Blenkinsopp 1992:19-25; Campbell and O'Brien 1993:10-19. Earlier, Lloyd Bailey (1981:54), after surveying the hypothesis (which he held—pp. 35-54), noted questions and warned that it remains only a hypothesis.

[13]Loewenstamm 1992:15-16.

[14]Campbell and O'Brien 1993:7.

[15]One of us came up with a point-by-point critique of the main arguments for the documentary hypothesis when grappling with it during his graduate work. Because the documentary hypothesis is not the focus of most attacks to which we respond here, however, and because one may hold the basic theory without rejecting the substantial message of the text, we retain only the briefest discussion in this appendix. For a brief summary of the hypothesis (now substantially modified), see Barton 1992:162-63; for a discussion of both final unity and signs of prior traditions, see, e.g., P. J. Wiseman 1985; LaSor, Hubbard and Bush 1996:3-14

[16]Cf. Cornfeld and Freedman 1976:19.

[17]For this proposed date, see Clines 1978:11; Whybray 1987:221; Houtman 1989:200. This late dating must, however, assume an argument from silence (that what we cannot prove early must be late); see Blenkinsopp 1992:26.

[18]E.g., Clines 1978; Whybray 1987; Houtman 1989:200; for unity but with an earlier dating, see Hill and Walton 1991:71; Sailhamer 1992. David Clines can work with the documentary hypothesis (pp. 89-96), but also notes that "I am no devotee of the Graf-Wellhausen theory, and I suspect that many who stick with it do so only on the ground that they would rather have a theory, however bad, than no theory at all" (p. 14). R. N. Whybray (1987:9) concedes that a satisfactory alternative to the hypothesis is difficult because insufficient evidence may exist to demonstrate any position; but he remains convinced that the documentary hypothesis and its cousins are "false trails" (p. 10). Against literary unity, see McCarter 1988.

[19]E.g., Clines 1978; Garrett 1991; Nicol 1992; Alexander 1993; on its theological unity, Mann 1991. From such analysis D. W. Baker (1980) argues forcefully against discernible sources in Genesis; Donald Slager (1992) argues that one should translate divine names from the perspective of the book's literary unity, not source criticism. The hypothesis also becomes increasingly irrelevant in view of current "postcritical" trends toward an emphasis on "the final form of the biblical texts" (e.g., D. Gordon 1985:64). All this differs from an older form of "literary criticism" (e.g., Habel 1971).

[20]See, e.g., Clines 1978:61-77. Clines concedes that the Pentateuch may have been compiled in the fifth century B.C.E., but argues that it was arranged as a literary unity (p. 11); the promise to the patriarchs provides movement for the Pentateuch (pp. 25-27; for examples, see pp. 32-43; for theme of the promise, see pp. 45-60). We see *partial* unity in the Pentateuch. Literary clues clearly indicate a unified editing for the history of Adam through Moses in Genesis and Exodus, perhaps for an introduction for Deuteronomy or for the legal collections in Exodus and Leviticus; editors collected priestly and legal material with that history, but not as a unified part of it.

[21]Dillard and Longman 1994:47.

[22]E.g., Hill and Walton 1991:76-77.

[23]Already Bright (1981:71), while affirming the documentary hypothesis, confesses to the "remarkable homogeneity" of J and E. Antony Campbell and Mark O'Brien (1993:7) note that the earliest source critics failed to find distinctive theological language characteristic of J and E (unlike P and D). Differences of style or word usage in the sources often depend on circular reasoning (Houtman 1989:191-92; cf. Cassuto 1961:42-54). If the statistical results of Radday and Shore et al. 1985 are correct (cf. also Radday et al. 1982), J and E are 82 percent similar stylistically (G. Wenham 1988; for dispute of the data, see Portnoy and Petersen 1984 and 1991).

[24]One may sample the vocabulary of these sources in Carpenter 1902:379-523. This work assumes the

traditional hypothesis and arranged the sources to demonstrate the opposite of the inference we have drawn from it. Whybray 1987:56-58 shows how the word-choice criterion for differentiating J and E fails; stylistic evidence opposes the view of different styles for these "sources" (pp. 58-62). For a defense of J and E in Genesis, however, see L. Schmidt 1988.

[25]"E has long been problematic, and there is no longer much enthusiasm for retaining it" (Blenkinsopp 1992:26; cf. Rendtorff 1990:103); "the existence of E has come to be widely doubted" (Barton 1992:162-63).

[26]Radday and Shore et al. 1985:214.

[27]E.g., Rendsburg 1986:106 (who notes they might share a common editor). For larger blocks of stories as the sources (e.g., the patriarchal story, primeval story, etc.), see, e.g., Rendtorff 1990:181-89; one can also point to large literary units, such as Genesis, Exodus through Numbers, and Deuteronomy (Houtman 1989:198, though we see more connection between Genesis and the narratives in Exodus). Ze'ev Weisman (1985) thinks the Jacob stories reflect a different and older milieu than the Abraham and Isaac stories.

[28]Cf. Whybray 1987:84-91; cf. Cassuto 1961:55-68. No one disputes that the author has failed to harmonize various prior traditions, but discrepancies need not arise from the conflation of written sources (Whybray 1987:85).

[29]E.g., Loewenstamm 1992:16; Houtman 1989:192-94; cf. Cassuto 1961:69-83. Whybray 1987:74 argues that the two creation accounts are not doublets. First, the author does not intend his audience to press them literally in all details and hence find contradictions; rather, they are complementary. Second, the two accounts diverge in focus; Genesis 2 is part of Genesis 2—3, not mainly about the world's creation. Most genuine doublets are, Whybray thinks, intentional literary devices, sometimes both appearing in the same traditional "source" (pp. 75-78; Alexander 1992). Repetition is characteristic of the author's style (e.g., Joseph's and Pharaoh's double dreams—Whybray 1987:78) and ancient Near Eastern literary custom (pp. 80-84; P. J. Wiseman 1985:117-18; Heidel 1963:7 n. 1; C. H. Gordon 1965a:134, 139). Many others contend (cf. Sandmel's view in Whybray 1987:76; contrast Alexander 1989), however, that many doublets stem from different versions developed by oral tradition, both of which the editor regarded as too valuable to discard; this is a reasonable position.

[30]In Acts, for instance, parallels among various figures seem to represent intentional architectonic patterns (cf., e.g., Talbert 1974 and Goulder 1964).

[31]Kitchen 1966:121-25. Whybray 1987:68, 71-72 cites "Baal" and "Hadad" in Ras Shamra texts and (with Segal) suggests the importance of stylistic variation; cf. Houtman 1989:190-91. Compare also the list of Marduk's names in Enuma Elish tablet 7 (see in Heidel 1963:57ff.), or many names of Re in "The God and His Unknown Name of Power" (trans. J. A. Wilson in Pritchard 1955:12-14). Even if different names arose in connection with a deity in different periods, this indicates nothing about a particular document that employs these different names!

[32]So, e.g., P. J. Wiseman 1985:130; for Canaanite and Egyptian backgrounds, see pp. 130-32. Further on divine names, see Cassuto 1961:15-41. Elohim may appear consistently in the Joseph story (except in chap. 39) for genre reasons (cf. Redford 1970:130).

[33]For some characteristics, see, e.g., Soggin 1980:114-15.

[34]In fact, the predominance of *ani* in P may relate more to the editor's style for divine speech (*ani* is preferred in divine speech in roughly 97 percent of occurrences, but in the much rarer uses by other persons only 25 percent of the time). Some supposedly "late" words also appear as early as Ebla (centuries before Moses). Further, language and style often tell us only when a final revision occurred; spelling was modernized in copying, and language probably was as well (G. Wenham 1976:43). Many scholars think Deuteronomy includes many older traditions but was compiled in Josiah's time (Weinfeld 1967:262; Horsley 1995:197).

[35]Some defend some P material in Genesis (Emerton 1988), but what is distinctly "priestly" about redactional language like "genealogy" or "increased and multiplied"? There appears to be no genuine stylistic evidence for P in the patriarchal narratives, apart from the theory being read into the text (see Rendtorff 1990:136-70); "it is clear that a coherent P-narrative in the patriarchal story cannot be demonstrated" (Rendtorff 1990:156).

[36]Scholars continue to publish studies of P (recently, e.g., Coote and Ord 1991; Lohfink 1994). For a defense of P (against, e.g., F. M. Cross), see Nicholson 1988; as a source and not a redactional layer, Steck 1991; A. Campbell 1993; holding to P but modifying Wellhausen, Knohl 1987; for a linguistic study, Hurvitz 1988. Some find P material in Deuteronomy (Perlitt 1988). Yet the traditional theories tend to rely on slender evidence (see, e.g., Carmichael 1992:3-4), and no agreement remains on what constitutes P (Rendtorff 1990:104-5); some see layers in it, but the basic arguments largely derive from the nineteenth century (Rendtorff 1990:105-6).

[37]Thus, e.g., Cornelis Houtman (1989:196-97) admits that this is more difficult than was once thought. If one moves from the question of "sources" to developing "traditions," the problem of dating becomes virtually intractable: one must speak of at what *stage* a source incorporated a tradition.

[38]See especially Kline 1963:27-30, 43; LaSor, Hubbard and Bush 1996:112-17; Craigie 1976:22-29; Livingston 1974:153-62. Citing seventh-century parallels, Whybray (1995:21) suggests that the thirteenth-century Hittite parallels are no longer viewed as plausible. Yet the seventh-century parallels are far less adequate than the thirteenth-century ones, and covenants in Genesis fit those from the Middle Bronze era (see Kitchen 1989; Kitchen 1995:52-55; Weinfeld 1993). For sample early treaties, see Pritchard 1955:199-206; cf. Mendenhall 1954:58-60. Yahweh's "covenant" and the covenant lawsuit appear in the earliest-writing prophets (Hosea and Amos, each developing in his own way), earlier than the Deuteronomic history but surely dependent on a prior model.

[39]E.g., Mt. Ebal rather than Jerusalem appears to be Deuteronomy's designated "place the LORD will choose" (G. Wenham 1985b); moreover, an admonition to centralize the cult could have been ignored in practice as ancient legal collections often were, and could not in any case have been workable during the confused era of the judges. Thus the Deuteronomic editor of Samuel through Kings may reflect dependence on an earlier Deuteronomy rather than both Samuel through Kings and Deuteronomy stemming from the same period (G. Wenham 1985a, citing earlier parallels in Hosea and Amos and later ones in Neh 9:6-37 and Dan 9:4-19; for echoes of Deuteronomy's motifs in Joshua, see G. Wenham 1971).

[40]C. H. Gordon 1953:238-39. That a legal collection would fall into disuse is not improbable, since many paid them scant attention, even in court settings (see Otto 1994:160, following Landsberger 1939). Because Egyptian and Assyrian scribes in Josiah's era were appealing to older models and copying older texts, Joseph Blenkinsopp (1992:213-16) thinks D was probably drafted then, but could not this fact argue instead for the rediscovery of an existing book, as the biblical text suggests?

[41]C. H. Gordon 1953:239.

[42]G. Wenham 1979:13.

[43]Kitchen 1978:54. Wellhausen viewed law and institutionalization negatively largely due to his "own personal background" (Berquist 1995:5), and this view undoubtedly influenced his perspective on the dating of documents.

[44]Pentateuchal laws probably represent "autonomous forms" (unattached to J or E; Soggin 1980:159).

[45]The laws appear to belong to collections different from the narrative cycles. From cuneiform parallels, Raymond Westbrook (1994) has defended the unity of the legal code, though others have challenged him on literary (Morrow 1994) or social (V. Matthews 1994) grounds, and they are probably right about redactional development of traditions behind cuneiform texts as well (Levinson 1994a; Greengus 1994; Otto 1993 and 1994; on patterns, cf. Otto 1987). Probably no single model fits all the cuneiform texts, but a general unity prevails despite diversity (Lafont 1994).

[46]Albright 1979 and 1968:101-5. Because the laws appear old, Calum Carmichael (1992:20) thinks they were deliberately archaized; but could they not as easily appear old because they *are* old? Even the life setting of their editing seems premonarchical, agrarian and pretemple (Albright 1963:17-18).

[47]Scholars once dated JE to Solomon's reign, but no one view commands consensus today (Blenkinsopp 1992:26; cf., e.g., Schmitt 1985; Zwickel 1992 on J).

[48]B. Mazar 1986:50; Cornfeld and Freedman 1976:22; Rendsburg 1986:107-20.

[49]Also means by which God preserved the promise of the land, even through others' free choices (Gen 13:8-12; 36:6-8). The other primary emphasis of the early patriarchal narratives is the promise of the seed, demonstrated in opening infertile wombs, making Israel's very existence a miracle.

[50]That Israel later felt compelled to justify a conquest undertaken centuries before (as many argue) is not impossible, but in view of the more pressing concerns of a later period the dominance of the motif in Genesis seems improbable in a later period. In contrast to modern society, one is hard pressed to find many examples of ancient peoples, including Israel, seeking to *justify* past conquests (though they were quite willing to glorify them) in national epics.

[51]Van Seters (1983 and 1988) thinks the best comparison of the pentateuchal history matches the fifth-century B.C.E. writings of the Greek Herodotus. The differences, however, are far greater (Blenkinsopp 1992:39-41), and Israel may have anticipated the Greeks as Greeks anticipated others (Blenkinsopp 1992:42), or earlier models may have been rare and not preserved. (Even if the source in David's throne succession narrative and the annals behind Kings are Israel's first historical works—so Brongers 1989:140-41—they precede Herodotus.) We would find the works of 1 Samuel through 2 Kings, or 1—2 Chronicles, more analogous

to Herodotus. Patriarchal traditions in Genesis may have more in common *structurally* with the epic traditions of ancient heroes (some linked genealogically to later influential persons); Homer's sources are now unrecoverable but reflect some tradition from a period far prior to Herodotus. The comparison with Homer need not imply the inaccuracy of Genesis (see data below), but only that epics of origins can predate Herodotus. Cf. C. H. Gordon 1965b:104, who compares the narrative style of Genesis's patriarchal narratives with that of the Egyptian Tale of Sinuhe (twentieth century B.C.E.). Some events in Genesis (such as Abram's expulsion after plagues, 12:17-20, and Joseph's exaltation after slavery) prefigure Israel's experience in the exodus.

[52]See especially P. J. Wiseman 1985:59-73; DeWitt 1976.

[53]P. J. Wiseman 1985:20.

[54]On the historical context of the theory and subsequent modifications of it, cf. Harrison 1969:19-32, 351-441.

[55]Kitchen 1966:113-14.

[56]On Wellhausen's prejudice against legal material, see, e.g., Berquist 1995:5. The German climate shaped by Luther's revolt against Rome also infected New Testament scholarship's view of "late Judaism" and the hermeneutics of Rudolf Bultmann and others.

[57]Harrison 1978:29. Most extant legal collections—Hammurabi, Lipit-Ishtar, Eshnunna, Nuzi and others— precede the era of Moses; many ritual collections, such as in many Hittite texts, also stem from the second millennium B.C.E. Although these customs continued into a later period, one cannot argue for P's lateness on the basis of its content. (C. H. Gordon drew helpful parallels with Nuzi as early as 1940, but his redating of the patriarchs to the specific Nuzi era is less persuasive, despite his remarks on nomadic genealogies— Gordon 1965a:116; see the relevant critique of specific Nuzi parallels in Selman 1976. The first-millennium parallels of Van Seters 1968 are, however, still less likely.)

[58]The French physician Astruc believed that Moses used the older sources he believed he detected (Livingston 1974:220-24).

[59]Ibid., pp. 227, 229-30.

[60]Bernal 1987. Lefkowitz 1996:91-154 is correct to challenge the use of Masonic mythology. Articles in Lefkowitz and Rogers 1996 argue for weaknesses in Bernal's approach; though they focus especially on his overstatement of Egyptian evidence, some of his critique of scholarship's Eurocentric bias might also require readjustment (e.g., pp. 333-420). Such observations should not, however, distract from the correct observations of Martin Bernal and others: nineteenth-century Eurocentric scholarship was severely biased (cf., e.g., sources cited in Usry and Keener 1996:78-79).

[61]Whybray 1987:46-47. He elsewhere complains that the modern assumptions that drive the hypothesis ignore ancient literary methods (pp. 55, 130). Others have often critiqued the way the hypothesis ignores ancient Near Eastern evidence unknown at the time the hypothesis was composed (e.g., Harrison 1978:20-29).

[62]Levinson 1994b:10-11.

[63]See, e.g., A. Mazar 1990:225-26.

[64]On this genre, see Goldingay 1980. Thus we would regard as too skeptical, e.g., the conclusions of Noth 1960:121-27.

[65]For conservatives who allow for editing subsequent to writing, cf., e.g., Hill and Walton 1991:76-77.

[66]Kitchen 1995:94, with examples.

[67]Sarna 1977·8 is surely right that Van Seters proves that in some cases a late dating is possible (against overstatements by the Albright school), but that Van Seters never shows that it is *necessary*. One of my Old Testament colleagues was very impressed with a Hellenistic parallel Van Seters produced to a custom in Genesis until I pointed him toward Egyptian and Babylonian ones from the preceding millennium. We have not argued for dating on the basis of social customs (cf. Speiser 1970) because many of these continued over time (both first and second millennia—see Selman 1980); too many such parallels have been produced haphazardly to be useful until more careful work is done (Millard 1980:46-47).

[68]For one of the most recent, up-to-date and complete surveys of the case in favor of the narratives' historicity, see further Kitchen 1995; cf. also some data from Ebla in Millard 1992.

[69]Yamauchi 1972:30-31; see information there.

[70]Ibid., p. 25.

[71]E.g., Cassuto 1964:298-99.

[72]On archaeology's limitations, see Dever 1977 (Dever has been a primary critic of traditional biblical archaeology as a discipline as opposed to Syro-Palestinian archaeology). At the extreme, Giovanni Garbini (1988:8) derides Bright's approach as predominantly apologetic.

[73]Noted in Miller and Hayes 1986:59. The schematic in which the exodus occurs two-thirds of four thousand years after creation may be interesting, but placing the four-thousandth year at the temple's rededication in 164 B.C.E. (Miller and Hayes 1986:59) appears to go too far in late-dating the Pentateuch's chronology!

[74]Millard 1980:50-51.

[75]By one estimate, one thousand excavators moving 120,000 tons each year would take 124 years to move all nearly fifteen million tons at one of the mounds of Nineveh. At Yadin's rate of excavation at Hazor, the excavation of Babylon would have taken eight thousand years (Yamauchi 1972:153, following C. Thompson).

[76]Yamauchi 1972:146-62, esp. 156-57, noting also Paul Lapp's estimate in his note. For one example, reasonable data suggest that the Egyptians probably produced at least twenty-four million meters of temple records—of which only thirteen meters remain (p. 157).

[77]Rarely can archaeology "confirm the existence" of any "single individual" (Cornfeld and Freedman 1976:41).

[78]Malamat 1983:309.

[79]Much of the following material (except where cited otherwise) comes from LaSor, Hubbard and Bush 1996:41-43, who conveniently organize and update (in view of criticisms from Thompson, Van Seters and others) arguments often previously advanced by Albright and his school (where we omit citations on specific points, we depend especially on them). Where relevant, we have specifically cited the older arguments of Albright, Bright and others.

[80]"Abraham" fits all periods in West Semitic (Millard 1980:153; cf. Ahlström 1993:181).

[81]E.g., Albright 1963:3; C. H. Gordon 1965b:156; Bright 1981:77-78. Many of the names (including Laban, Milcah, Sarah and Terah) appear in the cult of the moon god of Ur and Haran, possibly suggesting an origin in that area (Bright 1981:90).

[82]Kitchen 1995:90, 92.

[83]Albright 1963:2, 6 and 1968:53, 65; Bright 1981:90; A. Mazar 1990:225. On Haran's significance in travel routes, cf., e.g., Beitzel 1978.

[84]Ahlström 1993:183, who nevertheless dates the mention of Haran to the exilic period, when it was also known (albeit probably less significant in its region).

[85]On the freedom of movement in this general period, cf. also Albright 1963:3; Dever 1977:118; Bright 1981:82. C. H. Gordon (1965a:117 n. 8) thinks this fits the fifteenth century better; he portrays Abraham as a merchant prince (from a different, northern Ur) in C. H. Gordon 1958.

[86]Middle Bronze II Egyptian execration texts in Ahlström 1993:172.

[87]See Bright 1981:82, 86; Millard 1980:70-75; A. Mazar 1990:225. Despite few excavated remains there (probably due to lack of a wall), nineteenth-century B.C.E. Egyptian texts mention Shechem (Albright 1968:66; Millard 1980:55); Bethel also appears in this period (Albright 1968.66-67). Some note the inadequacy of Negev and Transjordan evidence (Dever 1977:118), but whereas Genesis mentions the site of Beersheba, it mentions no town, which fits the current state of the evidence (Millard 1980:75-76).

[88]Some protest the lack of Middle Bronze II sites in the Negev, but erosion and other issues can obscure occupation patterns (Millard 1980:76-80; we suspect, however, that Millard dates Abraham too early); for a survey of known settlement patterns from Early Bronze to the Iron Age, see Cohen 1988. Thus Nelson Glueck's surveys (which though incomplete were mostly accurate—cf. Graf 1983) found Early Bronze but not Middle Bronze occupation of the Transjordan, but newer surveys have located Middle Bronze sites there (Sauer 1986). (The definition of Middle Bronze varies according to theory, and no demarcation fits all the evidence; newer chronologies of Middle Bronze IIB vary about fifty years from Albright's. The earlier Middle Bronze I suggestions for the patriarchs are untenable—Dever 1977:95-99.)

[89]See, e.g., Albright 1963:3; A. Mazar 1990:224; cf. Yeivin 1970. For Egypt's influence on Middle Bronze Palestine (mainly because it provided transit to Syria—Ahlström 1993:174), particularly in coastal areas, see, e.g., Ahlström 1993:160-74; B. Mazar 1970:176-80.

[90]Cf., e.g., G. E. Wright 1962:45, 47; Bright 1981:81; A. Mazar 1990:224, citing Mari texts, the Egyptian Tale of Sinuhe (twentieth century B.C.E.). Although pastoral nomadism has long characterized the Middle East (Eickelman 1989:73-94), tent-dwelling nomads may appear more in the second than in the first millennium B.C.E. (Kitchen 1978:58-59; D. J. Wiseman 1978). Middle Bronze II culture was apparently less nomadic than the earlier period and included both towns and connections with Egypt (Aharoni 1982:93-94; though cf. Weinstein 1975; for some evidence, see Wilson in Pritchard 1955:228-30; on urban centers, see Dever 1987). This was a prosperous and peaceful "golden age" for Egyptian culture (Bright 1981:52). On

links with Canaanite Phoenicia, see Kenyon 1965:162.

[91]Naturally if one does not on other grounds think the material early, one will dismiss the anachronisms as simply attesting a later date for the composition as a whole (e.g., B. Mazar 1986:54; Garbini 1988:77; Lemche 1988:60).

[92]Although ass nomads fit the period, Albright's picture of Abraham as a donkey caravaneer fits the wrong period (Millard 1980:61-62). On caravan routes in the ancient Near East, see von Wyrick 1988.

[93]On updating the language, see G. E. Wright 1962:40; Albright 1963:6-7; Bright 1981:81; on possible domestication, see Yamauchi 1972:42-43; Kitchen 1960:13 n. 56 and 1966:79-80; C. H. Gordon 1965a:124; Millard 1980:49-50. Camels were rare in the Nile Delta but are known as early as the First Dynasty (Montet 1968:6). Recently, see most fully Stone 1991 and 1992 (though more account should perhaps be taken of the difference between wild and domestic camels).

[94]Millard 1980:52-53, on Naram-Sin's reign.

[95]Kitchen 1995:94. On early manuscripts, see also Pritchard 1955:18-22.

[96]The titles fit the Late Bronze or Early Iron period (cf. W. M. Clark 1977:147). On anachronism, see above; in arguing for the antiquity of the traditions, we do not dispute their oral or written "updating" for later audiences.

[97]Hermann Gunkel (1994:103) thus avoids dating Genesis later than 900, though he does not push the current form of the stories much before that period.

[98]G. E. Wright 1962:51; C. H. Gordon 1965a:124; Kitchen 1966:155; Yamauchi 1972:43; Sarna 1970:167-69, citing Hittite (and some other) parallels (cf. Rabin 1968 for an allegedly Hurrian speech pattern). G. Tucker (1966) thinks the neo-Babylonian parallels are the strongest; later Israelites, unfamiliar with the customs, may have updated the language (cf. Reviv 1977). For various views, see Katzoff 1987-1988. The narrative's literary function in any case is to support Israel's possession of the land.

[99]See, e.g., C. H. Gordon 1953:109-10; Sarna 1977:9; Bright 1981:73-74; G. Wenham 1980; Fretheim 1996:69. Note also the absence of polemic against Baal and preponderance of El- names for the deity, possibly pointing to a period before 1500 B.C.E. (Crenshaw 1986:12, though holding the stories shrouded in legend).

[100]Yeivin 1970:207-8. Cultic practices differ considerably (Yeivin 1970:208-12; see also Haran 1970, though he overplays a distinction between J and E and denies the monotheism of the patriarchs).

[101]*Jubilees,* from the second century B.C.E., may offer some hard comparative evidence against the idea that a late P would read a nonsacrificial background (denying also differences between clean and unclean animals) into the early period that contrasts with J.

[102]In the second millennium B.C.E., kings often married off relatives to other kings to establish relations, which might relate to Abraham's strategy (cf. Hoffmeier 1992).

[103]See here Sarna 1970:110-15; Yamauchi 1972:24-25, 39-40; Albright 1963:7; Yeivin 1970:215-17. (On Sodom, see further Sarna 1970:137-51; the announcement of Sodom in the Ebla texts in Freedman 1978, however, proved premature.) J. M. Miller and J. H. Hayes (1986:64) concede the "ring of authenticity" but (technically correctly) deny this as positive proof.

[104]E.g., Kitchen 1995:56-57.

[105]Albright 1918 and 1961. I learned of these sources from Yamauchi 1972:174. See also Glueck 1970:22, 138-40 (for some updated information, see Sauer 1986).

[106]This section depends especially on sources in Sarna 1970:211-31, although we have again drawn from Yamauchi 1972 and LaSor, Hubbard and Bush 1996. Other matters also warrant exploration, e.g., customs relevant to the possibility that Joseph warranted the birthright from the start (Frymer-Kensky 1981), or perhaps the more prominent roles of Egyptian women in high positions (cf. Whitaker-da-Cunha 1976).

[107]Redford 1992:422; on compositional artistry, cf. Redford 1970:66-105; Humphreys 1988:15-131; Gunkel 1994:27-62; for common storytellers' motifs in the Pentateuch, see Miller and Hayes 1986:60. The cohesiveness argues against any mechanical combination of sources here (Dillard and Longman 1994:47); Donald Redford (who thinks the story later than J or E) doubts the presence of J and E in the story (1970:252-53).

[108]As argued by Redford 1992:422-23. From a purely literary (rather than historical) perspective, of course, many parallels with ancient fiction are possible and helpful; see Irvin 1977.

[109]From a literary perspective and by comparison with other ancient Israelite historiography, the pentateuchal narratives appear to be history (Dillard and Longman 1994:49-50).

[110]Kitchen 1995:92, 94.

[111] Not all well-told stories from the second millennium B.C.E. are novels; the Tale of Sinuhe may be embroidered, but it is probably the success story of someone who desired to boast in it.

[112] One may also compare information as far away as Babylon; cf. Kitchen 1995:52; Kitchen 1966:52-53; Yamauchi 1972:47; de Vaux 1961:84. The biblical accounts thus also fit contemporary prices in Exodus 21:32 and 2 Kings 15:20.

[113] See the Egyptian papyrus, c. 1740 B.C.E., in Yamauchi 1972:46-47. This detail would not, however, require unusual knowledge on the narrator's part; sale of minors was one of four major sources of slaves in antiquity (cf. Mendelsohn 1946:74-80).

[114] Some genuinely Egyptian names in the Joseph story (unlike in the Moses story) may represent later updating (G. E. Wright 1962:53; Montet 1968:14-15). This remains conjecture, however, given our limited evidence for the Delta region in this period (Yamauchi 1972:48, following Vergote 1959.147-48). (For Vergote's arguments in general, see more recently Vergote 1985.)

[115] The information in this paragraph depends especially on Sarna 1970.214-21, who provides more specific documentation, following especially Ward 1960 on Joseph's titles (with Vergote 1959; Jansen 1959:66-67); Lambdin 1953:146 and other sources on the loanwords; referring to Rowe 1962 for more data on On; Pritchard 1955:486 and other sources on the rise of Semitic foreigners in the Egyptian government; and Vergote 1959 on some other critical points. On the titles, see also C. H. Gordon 1953:125; G. E. Wright 1962:53; Pritchard 1955:212-14; for multiplication of titles, cf. Sinuhe in Pritchard 1955:18.

[116] Views on the identity of the Hyksos vary; for north Phoenicians, cf. Bietak 1984.

[117] E.g., A. Mazar 1990:225. Frequently "native pharaohs were far less lenient" (Montet 1968:10). The Hyksos were Asiatic, with Semitic and other elements; the title, however, is simply Egyptian for "foreigner" (Aharoni 1982:99; Kenyon 1965:187). Canaanite words also entered Egyptian in this period (Albright 1946:152). A close ethnic connection existed between the Hyksos (whose chieftains sometimes had names like Jacob) and the Hebrews, although our other Egyptian remains from this period are negligible (Albright 1963:10 and 1968:57). They were not all Israelites, however, despite Josephus *Against Apion* 1.75-91.

[118] Sarna 1970:230, following Albright 1954; Montet 1968:11.

[119] E.g., Blackman 1918:477; the impure were not admitted to the king's presence (Blackman 1918:482). The ability of Joseph and Pharaoh to converse concerning the one supreme God without explanation may reflect the Egyptian recognition in the patriarchal era (and other periods of abundant international contact) of a supreme god over all nations (C. H. Gordon 1965b:105, citing Sinuhe's report). (Other comparative details like the seven-year famine tradition, dream interpretation and cups for divination are too widespread to be linked even partly exclusively to Egypt.)

[120] The information in this paragraph depends especially on Sarna 1970:222-27, who includes more specific documentation, including Pritchard 1955:259 on descent to Egypt (a later example; cf. also Noth 1960:112); Steindorff and Seele 1963:88 and others on the land nationalization; Pritchard 1955:414 and Janssen 1950 on the ideal age for death. On nationalization, see also G. E. Wright 1962:58. Cf. the priests' exemption in other respects as early as the twenty-sixth century B.C.E. (Pritchard 1955:212); their exemption continued into the Roman period (Diodorus Siculus 1.28.1; 1.73.5; N. Lewis 1983:92).

[121] Herodotus thought the Egyptians were offended that Greeks ate cows (Herodotus *History* 2.41; cf. Diodorus Siculus 1.11.4). They reportedly shunned foreigners (Herodotus *History* 2.91), including Asiatic shepherds (G. E. Wright 1962:53). Athough later writers allegorized Israel's food taboos in Leviticus 11 (e.g., *Epistle of Barnabas* 10; Irenaeus *Adversus Haereses* 5.8.4), various other cultures also held food taboos; see Pritchard 1955:391; Herodotus *History* 2.41; 3.100; Diodorus Siculus 2.4.3; Schedl 1973:2:186; Artemidorus *Oneirocriticon* 1.8; Epictetus *Discourses* 1.11.12-13; in African societies, e.g., Mbiti 1970:65; in India, Fuchs 1964:133. (The Hittites, however, apparently did not; Moyer 1969:110.) Some thought the Jewish *kashrut* were formulated at least partly in opposition to Egyptian custom (Josephus *Against Apion* 1.239; Tacitus *Historiae* 5.4), though in some instances Israelite taboos parallel those of Egypt, e.g., abstention from camel (Albright 1968:179) or swine (Pritchard 1955:10; Herodotus *History* 2.47; Plutarch *Isis and Osiris* 7, *Moralia* 353F; Epictetus *Discourses* 1.22.4; Sextus Empiricus *Outlines of Pyrrhonism* 3.222-23; Josephus *Against Apion* 2.141; elsewhere, Lucian *Syrian Goddess* 54), though swine were used in other cults, especially for underworld deities (Pritchard 1955:351; Aristophanes *Peace* 1.372; Moyer 1969:96, 127; but even here, see Pritchard 1955:209; Moyer 1969:106 and 1983:29). Perhaps as their primary function, such laws historically kept Israel separate from other peoples (Schedl 1973:2:187); Albright 1968:177-80 also offers suggestions about some health factors in Leviticus 11 and suggests that this passage is more logical than surrounding cultures' lists. In any case, traditional cultures have an

appreciation for ritual purity and taboos that escapes us (see Douglas 1979; K. E. Schmidt 1964:144; Boyer 1964:409; Luzbetak 1976:74-75). Some ancients saw in the *kashrut* symbolism based on animals' moral significance (*Epistle of Aristeas* 144-60); perhaps most important in Leviticus 11, one cannot eat animals one cannot sacrifice.

[122] Albright 1946:152. For chariots in northern Canaan, see Rainey 1965b:19-21.

[123] On embalming, see, e.g., Youngblood 1988; Sarna 1970:226, following Frankfort 1948:92-93.

[124] E.g., Diodorus Siculus 19.99.3. Herodotus *History* 2.88 says the poor were embalmed for seventy days in Egypt.

[125] Cf. Pritchard 1955:414; G. E. Wright 1962:53; Montet 1968:13.

[126] E.g., T. L. Thompson 1977:154-55. Redford (1970:187-243) argues for errors in the story of Egypt and the correct background being late; W. Lee Humphreys (1988:154-75) thinks the Egyptian coloring is too general and the sense of cultural distance suggests the story derives from outside Egypt. But would not Israel even within Goshen be "outside" Egyptian society and less than concerned with minor nuancing of details? Redford (1970:242) doubts that the story fits the Ramesside era but incidentally concedes our great ignorance of the Hyksos era.

[127] Cf. later Jewish works on Ahiqar (adapting earlier material about an actual character) and Tobit.

[128] For details and documentation, see especially Sarna 1986:15-37, though we have also drawn material from other sources, including G. E. Wright 1962; Bright 1981. We offer specific citations below primarily where departing from or supplementing the information in these sources. Redford 1992:411 summarizes a number of minor individual details to which scholars have pointed (most of which we have not repeated here) but dismisses them as not requiring much familiarity with Egypt.

[129] See Albright 1963:22-23; Montet 1968:30, 32; Sarna 1986:25, citing sources including Albright 1954:229. "Pu'ah" appears in the Aqhat epic *(Pughat)*. Children of Asiatic slaves normally took Egyptian names (Montet 1968:11).

[130] If one reads all the data of Exodus literally, one might prefer a date under Merneptah (Montet 1968:19-20, who can better account for Pi-Ramesse in the reign of Ramses II).

[131] See Noth 1960:120; G. E. Wright 1962:56, 59; Montet 1968:19-22; cf. Pritchard 1955:252, 470-71. Probably Seti employed Semitic slaves even before Ramses' arrival in the days of Moses' childhood, but Ramses carried construction much further and gave the city its name reported in Exodus 1. After the eleventh century, however, Ramses was usually called Tanis, and later Israelite writers would probably not have used its thirteenth-century B.C.E. name had they been inventing the story (Bright 1981:121).

[132] Kitchen 1995:88, 90; cf. the later "Zoan" in Psalm 78:12, 43; Isaiah 19:11, 13; Ezekiel 30:14.

[133] His army remained famous, albeit through exaggeration, in the first century (Tacitus *Annals* 2.60); for his early reign, see Spalinger 1979; Murnane 1975. Considering his strength and the length of his reign, only his era explains how little he accomplished in Palestine (see Pritchard 1955:255-57); he made a treaty with the Hittites so he could turn his attention to the sea peoples (Pritchard 1955:199-201).

[134] For most information in this paragraph, see Sarna 1986:18-20, who cites many sources. Noth 1960:120 also places the labor of the Israelites in this period.

[135] See, e.g., Albright 1946:194-95; Cornfeld and Freedman 1976:35-36; LaSor, Hubbard and Bush 1996:59. This information apparently survived as late as Diodorus Siculus 1.56 (Sarna 1986:20). Egyptian scenes and texts depict Semitic slaves dragging stone for temples under Ramses II (Noth 1960:113; G. E. Wright 1962:58).

[136] For some Semitic (probably including Canaanite) slaves working for Egypt around the fifteenth century B.C.E., see, e.g., Colless 1990; proto-Sinaitic inscriptions, below. Southern Canaan maintained contacts with Egypt and Sinai's copper mines (Amiran 1988).

[137] For Semites in Egypt as late as the fifth century B.C.E., see T. L. Thompson 1977:156-57.

[138] See, e.g., Kitchen 1978:78 and sources he cites. Evidence suggests that the Semitic slaves retained their own language; see Albright 1969. Interestingly, "hundreds of Semitic words (Canaanite and Hebrew) occur in the native Egyptian literature of the period, especially in the thirteenth century, in which no literary composition failed to be sprinkled with them" (Albright 1963:14).

[139] Although the exact route remains disputed, the basic route taken by Israel corresponds to that later taken by two escaped slaves (*Papyrus Anastasi* 5.19.2ff., in Kitchen 1977:146).

[140] Bright 1981:122; John A. Wilson in Pritchard 1955:416 n. 17. Thus, for example, they tell little of the Hyksos until their expulsion (cf. Pritchard 1955:230-34). Later Egyptians had their own apocryphal response to the now-circulated Jewish exodus story (cf. Diodorus Siculus 1.28.2); their version was not flattering to

Israel (Tacitus *Historiae* 5.3).

[141]Bright 1981:120-21. The one possible historical exception (if their origin story is untrue) of which we are aware is the Meru (Mbiti 1970:60-61), and even here the parallels are limited.

[142]The Proto-Sinaitic inscriptions recurrently include *lb'lt*, "to [the] Lady," identifying the chief Canaanite goddess with Hathor, Egyptian deity of the mines (Aharoni 1982:146); for syncretism between Egyptian and Canaanite gods, see also Pritchard 1955.249-50, C. H. Gordon 1965b.127. "They had been living in Egypt so long that their divinities were partly Egyptianized" (Albright 1963:13). (The Canaanite/Hebrew *El* also appears; see Beit-Arieh 1984:46-47.) Later Jewish tradition also acknowledged Israel's idolatry in Egypt (*Mekilta Pisha* 5.39-40). Extant Hebrew script appears again only half a millennium after these inscriptions (cf. "Oldest Hebrew Letters" 1978:23-25, 28-30; Demski and Kochavi 1978).

[143]Sarna 1986:31, citing sources including Erman 1971:76.

[144]See, e.g., Sarna 1986:33-34 and sources he cites.

[145]See Kitchen 1976; Sarna 1986:22-24 and the sources he cites.

[146]Kitchen 1966:156-57.

[147]See Weinfeld 1987-1988; cf. Glueck 1970:21, 96, 98.

[148]See Zevit 1990. Snakes and magicians also fit emphases one might expect in Egypt (cf., e.g., Pritchard 1955:12-14, 326, 328).

[149]See, e.g., Hort 1957 and 1958 (the classic statement of the case, challenged appropriately in Sarna 1986:70-73); Duncan Hoyte 1993 (H. M. Duncan Hoyte is a parasitologist); Fretheim 1991 (resembling natural plagues but transformed to a cosmic level); Stieglitz 1987 (in their ancient setting, especially from Amarna, Mesopotamian and Ugaritic texts). On the Nile as a deity, Pritchard 1955:372-73; N. Lewis 1983:94. On heavy Egyptian influence in Exodus 1—15, see Niccacci 1987.

[150]One may compare, e.g., the long-standing tension between Aharoni and Yadin; on the lack of Late Bronze remains in the Negev, see Aharoni 1976.

[151]E.g., A. Mazar 1990:328-29.

[152]See Hess 1993. Glock 1970 offers historical support for Numbers 1—11.

[153]Cf. Bietak 1993; Albright 1963:38. It is less likely that Egypt is responsible for this widespread destruction in Palestine; even in an earlier period, they were probably not responsible for the widespread destruction in Middle Bronze IIC (Redford 1992:138-39). (On that earlier destruction, see further Hoffmeier 1989, 1990 and 1991, against Dever 1977:89 and 1990a, who attributes it to the expulsion of the Hyksos; Weinstein 1991. On the overthrow of the Hyksos, see Redford 1992:125-29.)

[154]Ahlström 1993:348.

[155]See, e.g., Dever 1977:91.

[156]Traditionally dated at 1220; some recent works (e.g., Kitchen 1995:50; LaSor, Hubbard and Bush 1996:59, but cf. LaSor, Hubbard and Bush 1996:56) have 1209.

[157]Pritchard 1955:378. Against a more natural reading of the stele, Pierre Montet (1968:25-27) thinks the Israelites were still in Egypt at this time, but perhaps through depending too heavily on biblical summaries of Moses' age.

[158]See Bright 1981:134.

[159]See Usry and Keener 1996:173 n. 123.

[160]Faiman 1989-1990. As noted below, we will not ultimately depend on this explanation; some would also argue that nursing practices may have limited multiplication (cf. Gruber 1989).

[161]Redford 1992:408.

[162]See Cornfeld and Freedman 1976:36-37 (following G. E. Mendenhall); J. Wenham 1993.

[163]See, e.g., Dever 1990b:39-84, who suggests a peaceful settlement.

[164]Ahlström 1993:345 (he doubts that archaeology supports any of the theories—p. 348).

[165]For a harsh critique, see Redford 1992:267-68.

[166]Ahlström 1993:359.

[167]A. Mazar 1990:353-55.

[168]Ibid., p. 354.

[169]Ahlström 1993:349. For data on the settlement, see also B. Mazar 1986:35-39.

[170]A. Mazar 1990:334-38.

[171]Ibid., pp. 338-47.

[172]Cf., e.g., Albright 1963:30-31; Bright 1981:130; A. Mazar 1990:332-34. On Lachish, see G. E. Wright 1962:82-83; Bright 1981:131; for Hazor, Bright 1981:132; Kitchen 1978:90; on Shechem, see also B. Mazar

1992:48; for another attempt to place Judges 9 in archaeological context, see E. Campbell 1983.

[173]E.g., Albright 1968:194-95. Continuing idolatry in Israel is attested both in the Bible and in the many female figurines, though archaeologists have surprisingly discovered extremely few attempts to make idols of Yahweh, in contrast to the vast numbers of Canaanite idols (G. E. Wright 1962:118; Bright 1981:160; Avigad 1980:35). Some ancients treated idols as the bodies of gods (cf. Pritchard 1955:5).

[174]Specific problems include insufficient data to support Canaanites in the Arad Valley or Transjordan (A. Mazar 1990:330).

[175]Summary lists of conquests, emphasizing only the positive points, constitute a common ancient literary type (cf., e.g., Merneptah's stele, including obvious exaggerations; Esarhaddon's campaign in Pritchard 1955:291).

[176]A. Mazar 1990:331, citing Jericho, Ai, Jerusalem and Hazor.

[177]Yamauchi 1972:59-60, following Kathleen Kenyon and others.

[178]The remains that have been found prevent the conclusion that Jericho was uninhabited in Joshua's time, but some suppose either that it was unwalled or that this Jericho was reusing the earlier period's fortifications (see G. E. Wright 1962:80; Bright 1981:130). "Perhaps, as at other sites, the massive Middle Bronze fortifications were reutilized" in this period (A. Mazar 1990:331).

[179]By contrast, some think a destruction layer fits an earlier exodus, c. 1400 B.C.E. (Crocker 1990b; Wood 1990a and 1990b), though most date this destruction layer to 1550 (Bienkowski 1990; see above). Bimson 1988 redates the massive destruction in Canaan to c. 1420 B.C.E., which could fit an earlier proposed date for the exodus (though Stiebing 1988 notes this dating still causes problems for the conquest narrative); but most date this layer to c. 1550 B.C.E. (Bietak 1988).

[180]Kitchen 1966:62-63.

[181]Yigael Yadin in Shanks 1983:17.

[182]A. Mazar 1990:331.

[183]The other main problem is Ai, which many assume is ahistorical or aetiological (A. Mazar 1990:331-32; Zevit 1985; cf. also Joseph Callaway in the inset, p. 68; for a critique of Noth's etiological position, see G. Wenham 1976:51). The other option, which allows us to take seriously the literary evidence without denying any other evidence, is that Ai simply has been mislocated, an easy possibility if its walls were torn down and it eroded away (Josh 8:28; Kitchen 1966:63-64; Yadin in Shanks 1983:18; Luria 1988-1989). Given the many points of correspondence between archaeological and literary data, the burden of proof should remain on those who argue against the narratives from silence.

[184]See further LaSor, Hubbard and Bush 1996:142 and studies they cite as early as Albright 1939 and G. E. Wright 1946; also A. Mazar 1990:334.

[185]On the frequent difference in structures, see G. E. Wright 1962:90; Bright 1981:177-78; cf. Callaway 1983; Beebe 1968:49. That this materially simpler and poorer culture settled in the land, usually immediately, might argue against the view that the "conquest" was merely the work of nomads or gradual infiltration. Although traditionally the hill-country people are viewed as Israel in line with the Bible (and absence of pig eating), some do explain the divergence as merely geographical (London 1989).

[186]G. E. Wright 1962:70. There was no strong power in the region in this period, including Egypt (cf. Pritchard 1955:25-29); even the Assyrians sent expeditions this far in the eleventh century B.C.E. (Pritchard 1955:274-75). Albright (1946:209) dates Joshua and Judges to the seventh century B.C.E. but thinks some of their contents "must have been put into writing as early as the tenth century." The recording of some traditions fits well into the period when David's scribes would have been consolidating his reign with pro-David propaganda—see for instance the opposing roles of Bethlehem and Gibeah (the respective birthtowns of David and Saul) in Judges 19—20 (cf. 12:8-10; 17:7-9; Ruth 1:1-2; 1:19—2:4). That the time spans of various judges may be concurrent rather than consecutive fits the way reigns of kings were added in Egypt (see Kitchen 1966:74 on Egypt's *Turin Papyrus of Kings*).

[187]We could take "grown" in 2:11 to mean closer to age sixty, but that, too, stretches the language; whatever age he was, he smote the Egyptian at that point. Some of the chronological problems, such as Jacob's likely age at marriage, were nevertheless accepted literally in some ancient sources (e.g., *Jubilees* 25:4).

[188]On the Pentateuch's apparent chronological and numerical improbabilities, see further Miller and Hayes 1986:60-61; LaSor, Hubbard and Bush 1996:44-45.

[189]Dillard and Longman 1994:23. They note principles of selectivity, emphasis, order and application (preaching, pp. 23-25) and warn against overhistoricizing by, e.g., neglecting the differences between Samuel-Kings and Chronicles, or genre questions regarding history in Job and Jonah (p. 23).

Bibliography

The main section of this bibliography includes secondary sources cited directly in this volume, plus twenty to twenty-five important entries not cited here. (Some of the most helpful contributions are asterisked.) Brief news reports without authors (some also without titles) are listed under the periodicals in which they appeared. Sources for ancient works cited appear in a separate list.

*Abanes, Richard
  1996   *American Militias: Rebellion, Racism and Religion.* Downers Grove, Ill.:
                                InterVarsity Press.
Abogunrin, S. O.
  1980   "The Modern Search of the Historical Jesus in Relation to Christianity in
                                Africa." *Africa Theological Journal* 9, no. 3 (1980): 18-29.
Abrahams, Israel
  1972   "Tabernacle." In *Encyclopedia Judaica,* 15:679-88. 16 vols. Jerusalem: Keter.

Abrahams, R. G.
  1973   "Some Aspects of Levirate." In *The Character of Kinship,* pp. 163-74. Edited
                                by Jack Goody. New York: Cambridge University Press.
**Adamo, David Tuesday
  1986   "The Place of Africa and Africans in the Old Testament and Its Environment."
                                Ph.D. dissertation, Baylor University.
Adams, Alice Dana
  1964   *The Neglected Period of Anti-slavery in America* (1808-1831). Radcliffe
                                College Monographs 14. Gloucester, Mass.: Peter Smith.
Adams, William Y.
  *1977   *Nubia: Corridor to Africa.* Princeton, N.J.: Princeton University Press.

  1978a   "Geography and Population of the Nile Valley." In *Africa in Antiquity 1: The
                                Arts of Ancient Nubia and the Sudan—The Essays,* pp. 16-25. Brooklyn, N.Y.:
                                Brooklyn Museum.

  1978b   "Medieval Nubia." In *Africa in Antiquity 1: The Arts of Ancient Nubia and
                                the Sudan—The Essays,* pp. 120-25. Brooklyn, N.Y.: Brooklyn Museum.
Africa News
  1992   July 6-19, p. 16.

*The African Heritage Study
  Bible*
  1993   Edited by Cain Hope Felder. Nashville: Winston-Derek.

Afshar, Haleh
  1984   "Muslim Women and the Burden of Ideology." *Women's Studies International
                                Forum* 7, no. 4 (1984): 247-50.

  1985   "The Legal, Social and Political Position of Women in Iran." *International
                                Journal of the Sociology of Law* 13, no. 1 (February 1985): 47-60.

Aharoni, Yohanan
1967   "The Negeb." In *Archaeology and Old Testament Study,* pp. 385-403. Edited
                             by D. Winton Thomas. Oxford: Clarendon.

1976   "Nothing Early and Nothing Late: Re-writing Israel's Conquest." *Biblical
                             Archaeologist* 39, no. 2 (May 1976): 55-76.

1982   *The Archaeology of the Land of Israel.* Translated by Anson F. Rainey.
                             Philadelphia: Westminster Press.
Ahlström, Gösta W.
1993   *The History of Ancient Palestine from the Palaeolithic Period to Alexander's
                             Conquest.* Edited by Diana Edelman. *Journal for the Study of the New Testament*
                             Supplement 146. Sheffield, U.K.: JSOT Press/Sheffield Academic Press.
Ahmed, Leila
1982   "Feminism and Feminist Movements in the Middle East—A Preliminary
                             Exploration: Turkey, Egypt, Algeria, People's Democratic Republic of
                             Yemen." *Women's Studies International Forum* 5, no. 2 (1982): 153-68.

1992   *Women and Gender in Islam: Historical Roots of a Modern Debate.* New
                             Haven, Conn.: Yale University Press.
Akano, Y.
1992   "The Ethical Teaching of Matthew 25:31-46." (In Japanese.) *Katorikku
                             Kenkyu* 31:141-65; *New Testament Abstracts* 37:352.
Akridge, Colin
1995   "Why I Cannot Be a Black Muslim." Newport, Penn.: Research and Education
                             Foundation, n.d. (P.O. Box 250, Newport, PA 17074.)
Aland, Kurt, ed.
1980-1982   *Synopsis of the Four Gospels: Greek-English Edition of the Synopsis Quattuor
                             Evangeliorum.* 4th/5th ed. New York: United Bible Societies.
Albright, William Foxwell
1918   "Historical and Mythical Elements in the Story of Joseph." *Journal of Biblical
                             Literature* 37:111-43.

1938   "What Were the Cherubim?" *Biblical Archaeologist* 1, no. 1 (February 1938):
                             1-3.

1939   "The Israelite Conquest of Canaan in the Light of Archaeology." *Bulletin of
                             the American Schools of Oriental Research* 74:11-23.

1943   "The Furniture of El in Canaanite Mythology." *Bulletin of the American
                             Schools of Oriental Research* 91 (October 1943): 39-44.

1946   *From the Stone Age to Christianity: Monotheism and the Historical Process.*
                             Baltimore: Johns Hopkins University Press.

1954   "Northwest Semitic Names in a List of Egyptian Slaves from the Eighteenth
                             Century B.C." *Journal of the American Oriental Society* 74:222-33.

1960   "Canaanite-Phoenician Sources of Hebrew Wisdom." In *Wisdom in Israel and
                             in the Ancient Near East: Presented to Professor Harold Henry Rowley for
                             His Sixty-fifth Birthday,* pp. 1-15. Edited by M. Noth and D. Winton Thomas.
                             Vetus Testamentum Supplements 3. Leiden, Netherlands: E. J. Brill.

1961a   "Abram the Hebrew: A New Archaeological Interpretation." *Bulletin of the
                             American Schools of Oriental Research* 163:36-54.

1961b   "What Were the Cherubim?" In *The Biblical Archaeologist Reader,* pp. 95-97. Edited by G. Ernest Wright and David Noel Freedman. Garden City, N.Y.: Doubleday.

1963   *The Biblical Period from Abraham to Ezra.* New York: Harper & Row.

1968   *Yahweh and the Gods of Canaan.* Jordan Lectures 1965 (School of Oriental and African Studies, University of London). Garden City, N.Y.: Doubleday.

1969   *Proto-Sinaitic Inscriptions and Their Decipherment.* Cambridge, Mass.: Harvard University Press.

1979   "The Antiquity of the Mosaic Law." In *The Bible in Its Literary Milieu,* pp. 148-55. Edited by Vincent L. Tollers and John R. Maier. Grand Rapids, Mich.: Eerdmans.

Alexander, T. D.
1989   "The Wife/Sister Incidents of Genesis: Oral Variants?" *Irish Biblical Studies* 11:2-22.

1992   "Are the Wife/Sister Incidents of Genesis Literary Compositional Variants?" *Vetus Testamentum* 42:145-53.

1993   "Genealogies, Seed and the Compositional Unity of Genesis." *Tyndale Bulletin* 44:255-70.

Allen, Richard
1960   *The Life Experience and Gospel Labors of the Rt. Rev. Richard Allen, to Which Is Annexed The Rise and Progress of the African Methodist Episcopal Church in the United States of America.* New York: Abingdon.

Allen, Willoughby C.
1977   *A Critical and Exegetical Commentary on the Gospel According to S. Matthew.* 3rd ed. International Critical Commentaries. Edinburgh: T & T Clark.

Al-Shaykh, Hanan
1992   *Women of Sand and Myrrh.* Translated by Catherine Cobham. Garden City, N.Y.: Doubleday/Anchor.

Amiran, Ruth
1988   "Un centre economique et culturel." *Le Monde de la Bible* 54 (May): 18-21.

Amnesty Action
1991a   January, p. 7.

1991b   November, p. 4.

1993   Fall, pp. 2, 4.

Anderson, Lisa
1983   "Qaddafi's Islam." In *Voices of Resurgent Islam,* pp. 134-49. Edited by John L. Esposito. New York: Oxford University Press.

Andezian, Sossie
1983   "Pratiques feminines de l'Islam en France." *Archives de Sciences Sociales des Religions* 28, no. 55 (January): 53-66.

Andrews, S. J.
1886   "The Worship of the Tabernacle Compared with That of the Second Temple." *Journal of Biblical Literature* 6 (June): 56-68.

Andrews, William L., ed.
1986   *Sisters of the Spirit: Three Black Women's Autobiographies of the Nineteenth*

220   **Defending Black Faith**

Century. Bloomington: Indiana University Press.

Anfray, F.
1981   "The Civilization of Aksum from the First to the Seventh Century." In *Ancient Civilizations of Africa*, pp. 362-80. Vol. 2 of *General History of Africa*. Edited by G. Mokhtar. UNESCO International Scientific Committee for the Drafting of a General History of Africa. Berkeley: University of California Press; London: Heinemann Educational; Paris: United Nations Educational, Scientific and Cultural Organization.

Applebaum, Shim'on
1974-1976   "Economic Life in Palestine." In *The Jewish People in the First Century: Historical Geography, Political History, Social, Cultural and Religious Life and Institutions*, pp. 631-700. Edited by S. Safrai and M. Stern with D. Flusser and W. C. van Unnik. 2 vols. Vol. 1: Assen, Netherlands: Van Gorcum, 1974. Vol. 2: Philadelphia: Fortress, 1976.

Armstrong, Karen
1992   Muhammad: *A Biography of the Prophet*. New York: HarperCollins.

Arowele, P. J.
1981   "This Generation Seeks Signs: The Miracles of Jesus with Reference to the African Situation." *African Theological Journal* 10, no. 3 (1981): 17-28.

Asante, Molefi Kete
1988   *Afrocentricity.* Rev. ed. Trenton, N.J.: Africa World Press.

1990   *Kemet, Afrocentricity and Knowledge.* Trenton, N.J.: Africa World Press.

Assaad, Marie Bassili
1980   "Female Circumcision in Egypt: Social Implications, Current Research and Prospects for Change." *Studies in Family Planning* 11, no. 1 (January): 3-16.

Astour, Michael C.
1966   "Tamar the Hierodule: An Essay in the Method of Vestigial Motifs." *Journal of Biblical Literature* 85, no. 2 (June): 185-96.

Aune, David E.
1983   *Prophecy in Early Christianity and the Ancient Mediterranean World.* Grand Rapids, Mich.: Eerdmans.

*1987   *The New Testament in Its Literary Environment.* Library of Early Christianity 8. Philadelphia: Westminster Press.

1988   "Greco-Roman Biography." In *Greco-Roman Literature and the New Testament: Selected Forms and Genres*, pp. 107-26. Edited by David E. Aune. Society of Biblical Literature Sources for Biblical Study 21. Atlanta: Scholars Press.

Avigad, Nahman
1980   *Discovering Jerusalem.* Nashville: Thomas Nelson.

Avi-Yonah, Michael
1978   *Hellenism and the East: Contacts and Interrelation from Alexander to the Roman Conquest.* Ann Arbor, Mich.: University Microfilms International/Hebrew University.

Bacon, Leonard
1846   *Slavery Discussed in Occasional Essays, from 1833 to 1846.* New York: Baker & Scribner. (Reprint New York: Arno/New York Times, 1969.)

Badawy, Alexander
1968   *A History of Egyptian Architecture: The Empire (1580-1085 B.C.).* Berkeley: University of California Press.

Bailey, Lloyd R.
1981   *The Pentateuch.* Interpreting Biblical Texts. Nashville: Abingdon.

*Bailey, Randall C.
1991   "Beyond Identification: The Use of Africans in Old Testament Poetry and
                              Narratives." In *Stony the Road We Trod: African American Biblical Interpre-
                              tation,* pp. 165-84. Edited by Cain Hope Felder. Minneapolis: Fortress.

Baker, D. W.
1980   "Diversity and Unity in the Literary Structure of Genesis." In *Essays on the
                              Patriarchal Narratives,* pp. 189-205. Edited by A. R. Millard and D. J.
                              Wiseman. Leicester, U.K.: Inter-Varsity Press.

Bamberger, Bernard J.
1962   *The Story of Judaism.* New York. Union of American Hebrew Congregations.

*Barnes, Gilbert Hobbs
1964   *The Antislavery Impulse 1830-1844.* New York: Harcourt Brace & World.
                              (Reprint of n.p.: American Historical Associations, 1933.)

Barnett, Paul
1986   *Is the New Testament Reliable? A Look at the Historical Evidence.* Downers
                              Grove, Ill.: InterVarsity Press.

Barrett, C. K.
1966   *The Holy Spirit and the Gospel Tradition.* London: S.P.C.K.

1978   *The Gospel According to St. John: An Introduction with Commentary and
                              Notes on the Greek Text.* 2nd ed. Philadelphia: Westminster Press.

Barton, John
1992   "Source Criticism (OT)." In *Anchor Bible Dictionary,* 6:162-65. Edited by
                              David Noel Freedman. New York: Doubleday.

Baumgarten, J. M.
1972   "The Exclusion of 'Netinim' and Proselytes in 4QFlorilegium." *Revue de
                              Qumran* 8, no. 1 (June): 87-96.

Bebbington, D. W.
1977   "William Wilberforce." In *Eerdmans Handbook to the History of Christianity,*
                              p. 561. Edited by Tim Dowley. Grand Rapids, Mich.: Eerdmans.

Bediako, Kwame
1994   "Jesus in African Culture: A Ghanaian Perspective." In *Emerging Voices in
                              Global Christian Theology,* pp. 93-121. Edited by William A. Dyrness. Grand
                              Rapids, Mich.: Zondervan.

Beebe, H. Keith
1968   "Ancient Palestinian Dwellings." *Biblical Archaeologist* 31, no. 2 (May):
                              38-58.

Beidelman, T. O.
1971   "Some Kaguru Notions About Incest and Other Sexual Prohibitions." In
                              Rethinking Kinship and Marriage, pp. 181-201. Edited by Rodney Needham.
                              Association of Social Anthropologists Monograph 11. New York: Tavistock.

Beit-Arieh, Itzhaq
1984   "Fifteen Years in the Sinai." *Biblical Archaeology Review* 10, no. 4 (July): 26-54.

Beitzel, Barry J.
1978   "From Harran to Imar Along the Old Babylonian Itinerary: The Evidence from
                              the *Archives Royales de Mari.*" In Biblical and Near Eastern Studies: Essays
                              in Honor of William Sanford LaSor, pp. 209-19. Edited by Gary A. Tuttle.
                              Grand Rapids, Mich.: Eerdmans.

Bell, Richard
1958   *Introduction to the Qur'an.* Edinburgh: Edinburgh University Press.

Ben-Jochannan, Yosef A. A.
1971   *Africa: Mother of Western Civilization.* N.p.: Alkebu-lan Books Associates.
                              (Reprint Baltimore: Black Classic, 1988.)

1991   *African Origins of the Major "Western Religions."* Baltimore: Black Classic.
                              (Reprint of n.p.: Alkebu-lan Books Associates, 1970.)
Benkheira, Mohammed Hocine
1983   "Allah, ses hommes et leurs femmes: Notes sur le dispositif de sexualité en
                              Islam." *Peuples Mediterraneens* 25 (October): 35-45.
**Bennett, Lerone, Jr.
1966   *Before the Mayflower: A History of the Negro in America, 1619-1964.* Rev.
                              ed. Baltimore: Penguin.
Bennett, Norman Robert
1971   *Mirambo of Tanzania, ca. 1840-1884.* New York: Oxford University Press.

Benoit, Pierre
1973-1974   *Jesus and the Gospels.* Translated by Benet Weatherhead. 2 vols. Vol. 1: New
                              York: Herder & Herder; London: Darton, Longman & Todd. Vol. 2: New York:
                              Seabury/Crossroad; London: Darton, Longman & Todd.
*Bernal, Martin
1987   *The Fabrication of Ancient Greece, 1785-1985.* Vol. 1 of *Black Athena: The
                              Afroasiatic Roots of Classical Civilization.* London: Free Association.

1991   *The Archaeological and Documentary Evidence.* Vol. 2 of *Black Athena: The
                              Afroasiatic Roots of Classical Civilization.* New Brunswick, N.J.: Rutgers
                              University Press.
Berquist, Jon L.
1995   *Judaism in Persia's Shadow: A Social and Historical Approach.* Minneapolis:
                              Fortress.
Best, Ernest
1977   *A Commentary on the First and Second Epistles to the Thessalonians.* Black's
                              New Testament Commentaries. London: Adam & Charles Black, 1977.
Betz, Hans Dieter
1976   "In Defense of the Spirit: Paul's Letter to the Galatians as a Document of Early
                              Christian Apologetics." In *Aspects of Religious Propaganda in Judaism and
                              Early Christianity,* pp. 99-114. Edited by Elisabeth Schüssler Fiorenza. Uni-
                              versity of Notre Dame Centre for the Study of Judaism in Antiquity 2. Notre
                              Dame, Ind.: University of Notre Dame Press.

1979   *A Commentary on Paul's Letter to the Churches in Galatia.* Hermeneia
                              Commentaries. Philadelphia: Fortress.
Bhatia, Shyam
1995   "A War's Human Booty." *World Press Review,* August 1995, p. 40. Reprinted
                              from *The Observer,* April 9, 1995.
Bianquis, T.
1988   "Egypt from the Arab Conquest Until the End of the Fatimid State (1171)."
                              In *Africa from the Seventh to the Eleventh Century,* pp. 163-93. Vol. 3 in
                              General History of Africa. Edited by M. El Fasi with I. Hrbek. UNESCO
                              International Scientific Committee for the Drafting of a General History of
                              Africa. Berkeley: University of California Press; London: Heinemann Edu-
                              cational Books; Paris: United Nations Educational, Scientific and Cultural
                              Organization.
Bienkowski, Piotr
1990   "Jericho Was Destroyed in the Middle Bronze Age, Not the Late Bronze Age."
                              Biblical Archaeology Review 16, no. 5: 45-46, 69.

Bietak, Manfred
1984   "Problems of Middle Bronze Age Chronology: New Evidence from Egypt."
American Journal of Archaeology 88:471-85.

1988   "Contra Bimson, Bietak Says Late Bronze Age Cannot Begin as Late as 1400
B.C." *Biblical Archaeology Review* 14, no. 4: 54.

1993   "The Sea Peoples and the End of the Egyptian Administration in Canaan." In
*Biblical Archaeology Today 1990: Proceedings of the Second International
Congress on Biblical Archaeology*, pp. 292-306. Edited by Avraham Biran and
Joseph Aviram. Jerusalem: Keterpress Enterprises.

Bimson, John J.
1988   "A Reply to Baruch Halpern's 'Radical Exodus Redating Fatally Flawed,' in *BAR*,
November/December 1987." *Biblical Archaeology Review* 14, no. 4: 52-55.

Biran, Avraham
1986   "An Incense-Altar and Other Discoveries at Dan." *Qadmoniot* 19:27-31. (In
Hebrew. Summarized in *Old Testament Abstracts* 11:117.)

Blackman, Aylward M.
1918   "Purification (Egyptian)." In *The Encyclopedia of Religion and Ethics*,
10:476-82. Edited by James Hastings. Edinburgh: T & T Clark.

Blassingame, John W., ed.
1977   *Slave Testimony: Two Centuries of Letters, Speeches, Interviews and Autobi
ographies.* Baton Rouge: Louisiana State University Press.

Blenkinsopp, Joseph
1971   "The Prophetic Reproach." *Journal of Biblical Literature* 90:267-78.

1985   "The Documentary Hypothesis in Trouble." *Bible Review* 1, no. 4: 22-32.

1992   *The Pentateuch: An Introduction to the First Five Books of the Bible.* Anchor
Bible Reference Library. New York: Doubleday.

Blidstein, Gerald
1974   "4QFlorilegium and Rabbinic Sources on Bastard and Proselyte." *Revue de
Qumran* 8, no. 3 (March). 431-35.

Bligh, John
1970   *Galatians: A Discussion of St. Paul's Epistle.* Householder Commentaries 1.
London: St. Paul.

Blockson, Charles L.
1981   *The Underground Railroad in Pennsylvania.* Jacksonville, N.C.: Flame International.

Blomberg, Craig
*1987   *The Historical Reliability of the Gospels.* Downers Grove, Ill.: InterVarsity Press.

1992   *Matthew.* New American Commentary 22. Nashville: Broadman.

Blumenthal, Elke
1992   "Vom Wesen der altägyptischen Religion." *Theologische Literaturzeitung*
117:889-96.

Boccaccini, Gabriele
1991   *Middle Judaism: Jewish Thought, 300 B.C.E. to 200 C.E.* Minneapolis: Fortress.

Bockmuehl, Klaus
1988   *The Unreal God of Modern Theology: Bultmann, Barth and the Theology
of Atheism—A Call to Recovering the Truth of God's Reality.* Translated by
Geoffrey W. Bromiley. Colorado Springs, Colo.: Helmers & Howard.

Bonsirven, Joseph
1964   *Palestinian Judaism in the Time of Jesus Christ.* New York: Holt, Rinehart &
                        Winston.
Borg, Marcus J.
1987   *Jesus: A New Vision (Spirit, Culture and the Life of Discipleship).* San
                        Francisco: Harper & Row.
Boring, M. Eugene, Klaus
   Berger and Carsten Colpe, eds.
1995   *Hellenistic Commentary to the New Testament.* Nashville: Abingdon.

Bowling, A.
1975   "Tell el Amarna." In *Zondervan Pictorial Encyclopedia of the Bible,* 5:614-21.
                        Edited by Merrill C. Tenney. 5 vols. Grand Rapids, Mich.: Zondervan.
Bowman, John
1975   *The Fourth Gospel and the Jews: A Study in R. Akiba, Esther and the Gospel
                        of John.* Pittsburgh Theological Monograph 8. Pittsburgh, Penn.: Pickwick.
Bowman, John, ed.
1977   *Samaritan Documents Relating to Their History, Religion and Life.* Pittsburgh
                        Original Texts and Translations Series 2. Pittsburgh, Penn.: Pickwick.
Boyd, Gregory A.
1995   *Cynic Sage or Son of God: Recovering the Real Jesus in an Age of Revisionist
                        Replies.* Wheaton, Ill.: BridgePoint/Victor.
Boyd, Paul C.
1991   *A Biblical and Historical Account.* Vol. 1 of *The African Origin of Christianity.*
                        London: Karia.
Boyer, L. Bryce
1964   "Folk Psychiatry of the Apaches of the Mescalero Indian Reservation." In
                        Magic, Faith and Healing: Studies in Primitive Psychotherapy Today, pp.
                        384-419. Edited by Ari Kiev. New York: Free Press/Macmillan.
Bradford, Sarah H.
1869   *Scenes in the Life of Harriet Tubman.* Auburn, Maine: W. J. Moses. (Reprinted
                        from a copy in the Fisk University Library Negro Collection: Freeport, N.Y.:
                        Books for Libraries, 1971.)
Bradley, David Henry, Sr.
1956-1970   *A History of the A.M.E. Zion Church.* 2 vols. Nashville: Parthenon.

Bradley, Keith R.
1986   "Wet-Nursing at Rome: A Study in Social Relations." In *The Family in Ancient
                        Rome: New Perspectives,* pp. 201-29. Edited by Beryl Rawson. Ithaca, N.Y.:
                        Cornell University Press.
Brander, Bruce
1996   "Sudan's Civil War: Silent Cries to a Deaf World." *World Vision,* June, pp. 1-7.

Breasted, James Henry
1906   *Ancient Records of Egypt.* New York: Russell and Russell.

Breckenridge, James, and
   Lillian Breckenridge
1995   *What Color Is Your God? Multicultural Education in the Church.* Wheaton,
                        Ill.: BridgePoint/Victor.
Bredero, Adriaan H.
1994   *Christendom and Christianity in the Middle Ages: The Relations Between
                        Religion, Church and Society.* Translated by Reinder Bruinsma. Grand Rapids,
                        Mich.: Eerdmans.

Briend, Jacques
    1989   "Megiddo et l'Égypte." *Le Monde de la Bible* 59 (May): 33-36.

    1992   "Lecture du Pentateuque et hypothèse documentaire." In *Le Pentateuque: Débats et recherches,* pp. 9-32. Edited by Pierre Haudebert. LD 151. Paris: Cerf.

Bright, John
    1981   *A History of Israel.* 3rd ed. Philadelphia: Westminster Press.

Brightman, Edgar Sheffield
    1918   *The Sources of the Hexateuch: J, E and P, in the Text of the American Standard Edition, According to the Consensus of Scholarship.* New York: Abingdon.

Brinsmead, Bernard
Hungerford
    1982   *Galatians—Dialogical Response to Opponents.* Society of Biblical Literature Dissertation Series 65. Chico, Calif.: Society of Biblical Literature.

Britten, Bruce
    1996   *We Don't Want Your White Religion.* 2nd ed. Roodepoort, South Africa: Word of Life.

Brock, S. P.
    1982   "Syriac Views of Emergent Islam." In *Studies on the First Century of Islamic Society,* pp. 9-21. Edited by G. H. A. Juynboll. Papers on Islamic History 5. Carbondale: Southern Illinois University Press.

Brock, William
    1854   "Slavery Not a Misfortune but a Crime." In *Autographs for Freedom,* 2:158. Edited by Julia Griffiths. Auburn, Maine: Alden, Beardsley; Rochester, N.Y.: Wanzer, Beardsley.

Brongers, H. A.
    1989   "The Literature of the Old Testament." In *The World of the Old Testament,* pp. 98-164. Edited by A. S. Van der Woude. Translated by Sierd Woudstra. Grand Rapids, Mich.: Eerdmans.

Brooklyn Museum
    1978   *Africa in Antiquity 1: The Arts of Ancient Nubia and the Sudan—The Essays.* Brooklyn, N.Y.: Brooklyn Museum.

Brooks, Geraldine
    1996   *Nine Parts of Desire: The Hidden World of Islamic Women.* Garden City, N.Y.: Anchor.

Brown, Antoinette L.
    1854   "The Size of Souls." In *Autographs for Freedom,* 2:41-43. Edited by Julia Griffiths. Auburn, Maine: Alden, Beardsley; Rochester, N.Y.: Wanzer, Beardsley.

Brown, Raymond E.
    1966-1970   *The Gospel According to John.* 2 vols. Anchor Bible Commentary 29-29A. Garden City, N.Y.: Doubleday.

    1994   *The Death of the Messiah: From Gethsemane to the Grave—A Commentary on the Passion Narratives in the Four Gospels.* 2 vols. New York: Doubleday.

Brownlow, Rev. W. G., and
Rev. A. Pryne
    1858   *Ought American Slavery to Be Perpetuated? A Debate Between Rev. W. G. Brownlow and Rev. A. Pryne Held at Philadelphia, September 1958.* Philadelphia: J. B. Lippincott. (Reprint from a copy in the Fisk University Library Negro Collection: Miami: Mnemosyne, 1969.)

Bruce, F. F.
    1951   *The Acts of the Apostles: The Greek Text with Introduction and Commentary.* Grand Rapids, Mich.: Eerdmans.

1963   *The Books and the Parchments: Some Chapters on the Transmission of the Bible.* 3rd rev. ed. Old Tappan, N.J.: Fleming H. Revell.

1974   *Jesus and Christian Origins Outside the New Testament.* Grand Rapids, Mich.: Eerdmans.

1978   *History of the Bible in English.* 3rd ed. New York: Oxford University Press.

*1980   *The New Testament Documents: Are They Reliable?* 5th ed. Grand Rapids, Mich.: Eerdmans.

1982   *1 and 2 Thessalonians.* Word Biblical Commentary 45. Waco, Tex.: Word.

Buber, Martin
1949   *The Prophetic Faith.* New York: Macmillan.

Bullard, Sara, ed.
1991   *The Ku Klux Klan: A History of Racism and Violence.* 4th ed. Montgomery, Ala.: Klanwatch/Southern Poverty Law Center.

Bultmann, Rudolf
1958   *Jesus and the Word.* New York: Charles Scribner's Sons.

Burkert, Walter
1985   *Greek Religion.* Translated by John Raffan. Cambridge, Mass.: Harvard University Press.

1987   *Ancient Mystery Cults.* Carl Newell Jackson Lectures. Cambridge, Mass.: Harvard University.

Burkett, Randall K., ed.
1978   *Black Redemption: Churchmen Speak for the Garvey Movement.* Philadelphia: Temple University Press.

Burkitt, F. C.
1932   *Church and Gnosis: A Study of Christian Thought and Speculation in the Second Century.* Morse Lectures for 1931. Cambridge: Cambridge University Press.

Burridge, Richard A.
1992   *What Are the Gospels? A Comparison with Graeco-Roman Biography.* Society for New Testament Studies Monograph 70. Cambridge: Cambridge University Press.

Buss, Martin J.
1969   "Mari Prophecy and Hosea." *Journal of Biblical Literature* 88:338.

Cadbury, Henry J.
1968   *The Making of Luke-Acts.* London: S.P.C.K.

Callaway, Joseph A.
1983   "A Visit with Ahilud." *Biblical Archaeology Review* 9, no. 5 (September): 43-53.

Callot, Olivier
1987   "Ougarit: Les temples." *Le Monde de la Bible* 48 (March): 34-35.

Campbell, Anthony
1993   "The Priestly Text: Redaction or Source." In *Biblische Theologie und gesellschaftlicher Wandel: Für Norbert Lohfink, S.J.,* pp. 32-47. Edited by George Braulik et al. Freiburg, Germany: Herder.

Campbell, Antony F., and
Mark A. O'Brien
1993   *Sources of the Pentateuch: Texts, Introductions, Annotations.* Minneapolis:
                Fortress.

Campbell, Edward F., Jr.
1983   "Judges 9 and Biblical Archaeology." In *The Word of the Lord Shall Go Forth:
                Essays in Honor of David Noel Freedman in Celebration of His Sixtieth
                Birthday,* pp. 263-71. Edited by Carol L. Meyers and M. O'Connor. Winona
                Lake, Ind.: Eisenbrauns/American Schools of Oriental Research.

Campbell, William
n.d.   *The Qur'an and the Bible in the Light of History and Science.* N.p.: Middle
                East Resources. (Available from Reasons to Believe, P.O. Box 5978,
                Pasadena, CA 91117-0978.)

Cannon, Katie Geneva
1995   "Slave Ideology and Biblical Interpretation." In *The Recovery of Black
                Presence: An Interdisciplinary Exploration—Essays in Honor of Dr. Charles
                B. Copher,* pp. 119-28. Edited by Randall C. Bailey and Jacquelyn Grant.
                Nashville: Abingdon.

Carcopino, Jérôme
1940   *Daily Life in Ancient Rome: The People and the City at the Height of the
                Empire.* Edited by Henry T. Rowell. Translated by E. O. Lorimer. New Haven,
                Conn.: Yale University Press.

Carmichael, Calum M.
1992   *The Origins of Biblical Law: The Decalogues and the Book of the Covenant.*
                Ithaca, N.Y.: Cornell University Press.

Carpenter, J. Estlin
1902   *The Composition of the Hexateuch.* London: Longmans, Green. (Appendices
                by George Harford, pp. 379-523.)

Carroll, Joseph Cephas
1938   *Slave Insurrections in the United States, 1800-1865.* N.p.: Chapman &
                Grimes, 1938. (Reprint from a copy in the New York Public Library: New
                York: New American Library, 1969.)

Carson, D. A.
1979   *The King James Version Debate: A Plea for Realism.* Grand Rapids, Mich.:
                Baker Book House.

1981   *Divine Sovereignty and Human Responsibility: Biblical Perspectives in Ten-
                sion.* New Foundations Theological Library. Atlanta: John Knox.

Carson, D. A., Douglas J. Moo
and Leon Morris
1992   *An Introduction to the New Testament.* Grand Rapids, Mich.: Zondervan.

Cassuto, Umberto
1942   "The Palace of Baal." *Journal of Biblical Literature* 61:51-56.

1961   *The Documentary Hypothesis and the Composition of the Pentateuch.* Trans-
                lated by Israel Abrahams. Jerusalem: Magnes/Hebrew University.

1964   *From Noah to Abraham, Genesis V19-XI32, with an Appendix: A Fragment
                of Part III.* Part 2 of *A Commentary on the Book of Genesis.* Jerusalem:
                Magnes/Hebrew University.

1967   *A Commentary on the Book of Exodus.* Translated by Israel Abrahams.
                Jerusalem: Magnes.

Ceresko, Anthony R.
1992   *Introduction to the Old Testament: A Liberation Perspective*. Maryknoll, N.Y.:
                     Orbis; London: Geoffrey Chapman.

Cerulli, E.
1988   "Ethiopia's Relations with the Muslim World." In Africa from the Seventh to
                     the Eleventh Century, pp. 575-85. Vol. 3 of General History of Africa. Edited
                     by M. El Fasi with I. Hrbek. UNESCO International Scientific Committee for
                     the Drafting of a General History of Africa. Berkeley: University of California
                     Press; London: Heinemann Educational Books; Paris: United Nations Educa-
                     tional, Scientific and Cultural Organization.

Chadwick, Henry
1967   *The Early Church*. Baltimore: Penguin.

Charlesworth, M. P.
1970   *Trade-Routes and Commerce of the Roman Empire*. 2nd rev. ed. New York:
                     Cooper Square.

Chaudhury, Rafiqul Huda
1977   "Marriage, Urban Women and the Labor Force: The Bangladesh Case." *Signs*
                     5, no. 1 (Autumn): 154-63.

Cheever, George B.
1857   *God Against Slavery: And the Freedom and Duty of the Pulpit to Rebuke It as
                     a Sin Against God. New York: Joseph H. Ladd. (Reprint Miami: Mnemosyne,
                     1969.)*

"Child Laborers"
1992   *World Press Review*, October, p. 33.

Childs, Brevard S.
1979   *Introduction to the Old Testament Scripture*. Philadelphia: Fortress.

Childs, John Brown
1980   *The Political Black Minister: A Study in Afro-American Politics and Religion*.
                     Reference Publications in Afro-American Studies. Boston: G. K. Hall.

Chirri, Mohamad Jawad
1965   *Inquiries About Islam*. Detroit: Islamic Center of Detroit.

Christensen, Duane L., and
    Marcel Narucki
1989   "The Mosaic Authorship of the Pentateuch." *Journal of the Evangelical
                     Theological Society* 32:465-71.

"Civil War Brings Suffering
    to Sudan"
1993   *Christianity Today*, May 17, p. 82.

Clark, Calvin Montague
1940   *American Slavery and Maine Congregationalists: A Chapter in the History of
                     the Development of Anti-slavery Sentiment in the Protestant Churches of the
                     North*. Bangor, Maine: Author.

Clark, W. Malcolm
1977   "The Biblical Traditions." In *Israelite and Judaean History*, pp. 120-48. Edited
                     by John H. Hayes and J. Maxwell Miller. Philadelphia: Westminster Press.

Clarke, Erskine
1979   *Wrestlin' Jacob: A Portrait of Religion in the Old South*. Atlanta: John Knox.

Clarke, John Henrik
1991   *Africans at the Crossroads: Notes for an African World Revolution*. Trenton,

N.J.: Africa World Press.

Clary, Johnny Lee
1995   *Boys in the Hoods: One Man's Journey from Hatred to Love—An Autobiographical Exposé of Racial Hatred, Racism and Redemption.* Bakersfield, Calif.: Pneuma Life.

Clifford, Richard J.
1971   "Tent of El and Israelite Tent of Meeting." *Catholic Biblical Quarterly* 33 (April). 221-27.

Clines, David J. A.
1978   *The Theme of the Pentateuch. Journal for the Study of the Old Testament* Supplement 10. Sheffield, U.K.: Department of Biblical Studies, Sheffield University Press.

Coffey, David M.
1970   "Natural Knowledge of God: Reflections on Romans 1:18-32." *Theological Studies* 31, no, 4 (December); 674-91.

Cogan, M.
1985-1986   " 'The City Which I Have Chosen'—The View of Jerusalem in Deuteronomic Literature." *Tarbiz* 55:301-9. (In Hebrew. Summarized in *Old Testament Abstracts* 10:101.)

Cohen, R.
1988   "Settlement in the Negev Highlands from the Fourth Millennium B.C.E. to the Fourth Century B.C.E." *Qadmoniot* 21:62 81. (Summarized in *Old Testament Abstracts* 12:247.)

Culless, Brian E.
1990   "The Proto-alphabetic Inscriptions of Sinai." *Abr Nahrain* 28:1-52.

Cone, James H.
1975   *God of the Oppressed.* New York: Seabury.

*1984   *For My People: Black Theology and the Black Church.* Maryknoll, N.Y.: Orbis.

Cone, James H., and
    Gayraud S. Wilmore, eds.
1993   *Black Theology: A Documentary History.* 2 vols. Maryknoll, N.Y.: Orbis.

Cook, Michael
1981   *Early Muslim Dogma: A Source-Critical Study.* Cambridge: Cambridge University Press.

1983   *Muhammad.* Past Masters Series. New York: Oxford University Press.

Coote, Robert B., and
    David Robert Ord
1991   *In the Beginning: Creation and the Priestly History.* Minneapolis: Fortress.

Cope, O. Lamar
1969   "Matthew xxv 31-46: 'The Sheep and the Goats' Reinterpreted." *Novum Testamentum* 11:32-44.

*Copher, Charles B.
1993   *Black Biblical Studies: An Anthology of Charles B. Copher—Biblical and Theological Issues on the Black Presence in the Bible.* Chicago: Black Light Fellowship.

Cornfeld, Gaalyah, and
    David Noel Freedman
1976   *Archaeology of the Bible Book by Book.* New York: Harper & Row.

Craghan, John F.
1975   "Mari and Its Prophets: The Contributions of Mari to the Understanding of Biblical Prophecy." *Biblical Theology Bulletin* 5:32-55.

Craig, William Lane
1980   "The Bodily Resurrection of Jesus." In *Studies of History and Tradition in the Four Gospels*, pp. 47-74. Vol. 1 of *Gospel Perspectives*. Edited by R. T. France and David Wenham. 6 vols. Sheffield, U.K.: JSOT Press.

1981   "The Empty Tomb of Jesus." In *Studies of History and Tradition in the Four Gospels*, pp. 173-200. Vol. 2 of *Gospel Perspectives*. Edited by R. T. France and David Wenham. 6 vols. Sheffield, U.K.: JSOT Press/University of Sheffield Press.

1985   "The Historicity of the Empty Tomb of Jesus." *New Testament Studies* 31:39-67.

1986   "The Problem of Miracles: A Historical and Philosophical Perspective." In *The Miracles of Jesus*, pp. 9-48. Edited by David Wenham and Craig Blomberg. Vol. 6 of *Gospel Perspectives*. Edited by R. T. France and David Wenham. 6 vols. Sheffield, U.K.: JSOT Press.

Craigie, Peter C.
1976   *The Book of Deuteronomy.* New International Commentary on the Old Testament. Grand Rapids, Mich.: Eerdmans.

1983   *Ugarit and the Old Testament.* Grand Rapids, Mich.: Eerdmans.

1986   *The Old Testament: Its Background, Growth and Content.* Nashville: Abingdon.

Crenshaw, James L.
1986   *Story and Faith: A Guide to the Old Testament.* New York: Macmillan; London: Collier Macmillan.

Crocker, P. T.
1986   "The City of Meroe and the Ethiopian Eunuch." *Buried History* 22:53-72.

1990a   "Archaeology, Mildew and Leviticus 14." *Buried History* 26:3-11.

1990b   "Joshua and the Walls of Jericho." *Buried History* 26:100-104.

Crone, Patricia
1987   *Meccan Trade and the Rise of Islam.* Princeton, N.J.: Princeton University Press.

Crone, Patricia, and Michael Cook
1977   *Hagarism: The Making of the Islamic World.* Cambridge: Cambridge University Press.

Cross, Frank Moore, Jr.
1947   "The Tabernacle: A Study from an Archaeological and Historical Approach." *Biblical Archaeologist* 10 (September): 45-68.

1961   "The Priestly Tabernacle." In *The Biblical Archaeologist Reader,* pp. 201-28. Edited by David Noel Freedman and G. Ernest Wright. Garden City, N.Y.: Doubleday.

Cross, Haman, Jr., and Donna E. Scott
1993   *Have You Got Good Religion? The Real Fruit of Islam.* Edited by Eugenie

Seals. Chicago: Moody Press; Detroit: Spoken Word.

Cullmann, Oscar
1963   *The Christology of the New Testament.* Philadelphia: Westminster Press;
                           London: SCM Press.

Culpepper, R. Alan
1975   *The Johannine School: An Evaluation of the Johannine-School Hypothesis
                           Based on an Investigation of the Nature of Ancient Schools.* Society of Biblical
                           Literature Dissertation Series 26. Missoula, Mont.: Scholars Press.

"Cupolas and Culture"
1990   *World Press Review,* September, p. 50.

Currid, John D.
1991   "An Examination of the Egyptian Background of the Genesis Cosmogony."
                           Biblische Zeitschrift 35:18-40.

Custance, Arthur C.
1975   *Noah's Three Sons: Human History in Three Dimensions.* Doorway Papers 1.
                           Grand Rapids, Mich.: Zondervan.

Dalman, Gustaf
1893   *Jesus Christ in the Talmud, Midrash, Zohar and the Liturgy of the Synagogue.*
                           Cambridge: Deighton, Bell. (Reprint New York: Arno, 1973.)

Danforth, Sandra C.
1984   "The Social and Political Implications of Muslim Middle Eastern Women's
                           Participation in Violent Political Conflict." *Women and Politics* 4, no. 1
                           (Spring): 35-54.

Daube, David
1956   *The New Testament and Rabbinic Judaism.* London: University of London,
                           1956. (Reprint New York: Arno, 1973; also Peabody, Mass.: Hendrickson,
                           n.d.)

Davidson, Basil
1968   *Africa in History: Themes and Outlines.* New York: Macmillan.

*Davidson, Basil, with
F. K. Buah
1966   *A History of West Africa to the Nineteenth Century.* Garden City, N.Y.:
                           Doubleday/Anchor.

Davies, G. Henton
1962   "Tabernacle." In *Interpreter's Dictionary of the Bible,* 4:498-506. Edited by
                           George A. Buttrick. 4 vols. New York: Abingdon.

Davies, W. D.
1967   "Reflexions on Tradition: The Aboth Revisited." In *Christian History and
                           Interpretation: Studies Presented to John Knox,* pp. 129-37. Edited by W. R.
                           Farmer, C. F. D. Moule and R. R. Niebuhr. Cambridge: Cambridge University
                           Press.

1980   *Paul and Rabbinic Judaism: Some Rabbinic Elements in Pauline Theology.*
                           4th ed. Philadelphia: Fortress.

Davies, W. D., and Dale C.
Allison
1988-1991   *A Critical and Exegetical Commentary on the Gospel According to Saint
                           Matthew.* International Critical Commentaries. 3 vols. Edinburgh: T & T
                           Clark.

Davis, David Brian
1975   *The Problem of Slavery in the Age of Revolution, 1770-1823.* Ithaca, N.Y.:
                           Cornell University Press.

Dawson, John
    1994   *Healing America's Wounds.* Ventura, Calif.: Regal.

Deedat, Ahmed
    n.d.   *Is the Bible God's Word?* Chicago: Kazi.

Deere, Jack
    1993   *Surprised by the Power of the Spirit.* Grand Rapids, Mich.: Zondervan.

De Kruijf, Th. C.
    1970   "The Glory of the Only Son (John i 14)." In *Studies in John: Presented to Professor Dr. J. N. Sevenster on the Occasion of His Seventieth Birthday,* pp. 111-23. Edited by W. C. van Unnik. Supplements to *Novum Testamentum* 24. Leiden, Netherlands: E. J. Brill.

Delaney, Carol
    1987   "Seeds of Honor, Fields of Shame." In *Honor and Shame and the Unity of the Mediterranean,* pp. 35-48. Edited by David D. Gilmore. American Anthropological Association 22. Washington, D.C.: American Anthropological Association.

Delaporte, L.
    1970   *Mesopotamia: The Babylonian and Assyrian Civilization.* New York: Barnes & Noble.

Demski, Aaron, and
    Moshe Kochavi
    1978   "An Alphabet from the Days of the Judges." *Biblical Archaeology Review* 4, no. 3 (September): 23-25, 28-30.

Denny, Frederick M.
    1987   *Islam and the Muslim Community.* San Francisco: HarperSanFrancisco.

Desanges, J.
    1981   "The Proto-Berbers." In *Ancient Civilizations of Africa,* pp. 423-40. Vol. 2 of *General History of Africa.* Edited by G. Mokhtar. UNESCO International Scientific Committee for the Drafting of a General History of Africa. Berkeley: University of California Press; London: Heinemann Educational Books; Paris: United Nations Educational, Scientific and Cultural Organization.

de Vaux, Roland
    1961   *Ancient Israel: Its Life and Institutions.* New York: McGraw-Hill.

Dever, William G.
    1974   "The MB IIC Stratifications in the Northwest Gate Area at Shechem." *Bulletin of the American Schools of Oriental Research* 216 (December): 43.

    1977   "Palestine in the Second Millennium B.C.E.: The Archaeological Picture." In *Israelite and Judaean History,* pp. 70-120. Edited by John H. Hayes and J. Maxwell Miller. Philadelphia: Westminster Press.

    1987   "The Middle Bronze Age: The Zenith of the Urban Canaanite Era." *Biblical Archaeologist* 50:148-77.

    1990a   " 'Hyksos,' Egyptian Destructions and the End of the Palestinian Middle Bronze Age." *Levant* 22:75-81.

    1990b   *Recent Archaeological Discoveries and Biblical Research.* Seattle: University of Washington Press.

DeWitt, Dale S.
1976   "The Generations of Genesis." *Evangelical Quarterly* 48, no. 4: 196-211.

Dibelius, Martin
1956   *Studies in the Acts of the Apostles.* London: SCM Press.

Dickerson, Dennis C.
1995   *Religion, Race and Region: Research Notes on A.M.E. Church History.* Nashville: AMEC Sunday School Union/Legacy. (Available from Dennis C. Dickerson, P.O. Box 301, Williamstown, MA 01267.)

Dillard, Raymond B., and
  Tremper Longman III
1994   *An Introduction to the Old Testament.* Grand Rapids, Mich.: Zondervan.

Diop, Cheikh Anta
1974   *The African Origin of Civilization.* Translated by Mercer Cook. Westport, Conn.: Lawrence Hill.

Dixon, Suzanne
1988   *The Roman Mother.* Norman: Oklahoma University Press.

Dodd, Brian J.
1996   *The Problem with Paul.* Downers Grove, Ill.: InterVarsity Press.

Dodd, C. H.
1967   *New Testament Studies.* Manchester, U.K.: Manchester University Press.

Domínguez, Jorge I.
1979   "Assessing Human Rights Conditions." In Jorge I. Domínguez et al., *Enhancing Global Human Rights,* pp. 21-116. 1980s Project/Council on Foreign Relations. New York: McGraw-Hill.

Donaldson, Stuart
1909   *Church Life and Thought in North Africa, A.D. 200.* Cambridge: Cambridge University Press.

Donaldson, Terence L.
1993   " 'Riches for the Gentiles' (Rom 11:12): Israel's Rejection and Paul's Gentile Mission." *Journal of Biblical Literature* 112, no. 1 (Spring): 81-98.

Donfried, Karl P.
1985   "The Cults of Thessalonica and the Thessalonian Correspondence." *New Testament Studies* 31, no. 3: 336-56.

Dorman, William A.
1979   "Iranian People v. US News Media: A Case of Libel." *Race and Class* 21, no. 1 (Summer): 57-66.

Douglas, Mary
1979   "The Abominations of Leviticus." In *Reader in Comparative Religion: An Anthropological Approach,* pp. 149-52. 4th ed. Edited by William A. Lessa and Evon Z. Vogt. New York: Harper & Row.

Douglass, Frederick
1968   *Narrative of the Life of Frederick Douglass: An American Slave.* New York: New American Library.

Downing, F. Gerald
1988   "Quite like Q—A Genre for 'Q': The 'Lives' of Cynic Philosophers." *Biblica* 69:196-225.

1991   "Actuality Versus Abstraction: The Synoptic Gospel Model." *Continuum* 1:104-20.

Dramani-Issifou, Z.
1988 "Islam as a Social System in Africa Since the Seventh Century." In *Africa from the Seventh to the Eleventh Century,* pp. 92-118. Vol. 3 of *General History of Africa.* Edited by M. El Fasi with I. Hrbek. UNESCO International Scientific Committee for the Drafting of a General History of Africa. Berkeley: University of California Press; London: Heinemann Educational Books; Paris: United Nations Educational, Scientific and Cultural Organization.

Draper, Jonathan
1984 "The Jesus Tradition in the *Didache.*" In *The Jesus Tradition Outside the Gospels,* pp. 269-87. Edited by David Wenham. Vol. 6 of *Gospel Perspectives.* Edited by R. T. France and David Wenham. 6 vols. Sheffield, U.K.: JSOT Press.

Driver, S. R.
1957 *An Introduction to the Literature of the Old Testament.* Cleveland, Ohio: Meridian/World.

Drower, E. S.
1962 *The Mandaeans of Iraq and Iran: Their Cults, Customs, Magic, Legends and Folklore.* Leiden, Netherlands: E. J. Brill.

Du Bois, W. E. B.
1980 *Prayers for Dark People.* Edited by Herbert Aptheker. Amherst: University of Massachusetts Press.

**1965 *The World and Africa: An Inquiry into the Part Which Africa Has Played in History.* Rev. ed. New York: International.

Duncan Hoyte, H. M.
1993 "The Plagues of Egypt: What Killed the Animals and the Firstborn?" *The Medical Journal of Australia* 158:706-8.

*Dunston, Bishop Alfred G., Jr.
1974 *The Black Man in the Old Testament and Its World.* Philadelphia: Dorrance.

Du Plessis, I. J.
1968 "Christ as the 'Only Begotten.' " *Neotestamentica* 2:22-31.

Dupont, Jacques
1964 *The Sources of Acts: The Present Position.* London: Darton, Longman & Todd.

1979 *The Salvation of the Gentiles: Essays on the Acts of the Apostle*s. Translated by John R. Keating. New York: Paulist.

Eastman, Carol M.
1984 "Waungwana na Wanawake: Muslim Ethnicity and Sexual Segregation in Coastal Kenya." *Journal of Multilingual and Multicultural Development* 5, no. 2: 97-112.

Edgerly, Adam, and Carl Ellis
1994 "Emergence of Islam in the African-American Community." *Reach Out* 7, nos. 3-4: 8-16.

Edwards, I. E. S., et al., eds.
1975 *History of the Middle East and the Aegean Region, c. 1380-1000 B.C.* Vol. 2, pt. 2 of *Cambridge Ancient History.* 12 vols. 3rd ed. Edited by J. B. Bury et al. Cambridge: Cambridge University Press.

Eickelman, Dale F.
1989 *The Middle East: An Anthropological Approach.* 2nd ed. Englewood Cliffs, N.J.: Prentice-Hall.

*El-Amin, Mustafa
1991 *The Religion of Islam and the Nation of Islam: What Is the Difference?*

Newark, N.J.: El-Amin Productions.

El Fasi, M., and I. Hrbek
1988a   "The Coming of Islam and the Expansion of the Muslim Empire." In *Africa from the Seventh to the Eleventh Century,* pp. 31-55. Vol. 3 of *General History of Africa.* Edited by M. El Fasi with I. Hrbek. UNESCO International Scientific Committee for the Drafting of a General History of Africa. Berkeley: University of California Press; London: Heinemann Educational Books; Paris: United Nations Educational, Scientific and Cultural Organization.

1988b   "Stages in the Development of Islam and Its Dissemination in Africa." In *Africa from the Seventh to the Eleventh Century,* pp. 56-91. Vol. 3 of *General History of Africa.* Edited by M. El Fasi with I. Hrbek. UNESCO International Scientific Committee for the Drafting of a General History of Africa. Berkeley: University of California Press; London: Heinemann Educational Books; Paris: United Nations Educational, Scientific and Cultural Organization.

El-Guindi, Fadwa
1981   "Veiling Infitah with Muslim Ethic: Egypt's Contemporary Islamic Movement." *Social Problems* 28, no. 4 (April): 465-85.

1983   "Veiled Activism: Egyptian Women in the Contemporary Islamic Movement." *Peuples Mediterraneens* 22 23:79 89.

Eliade, Mircea
1958   *Birth and Rebirth: The Religious Meanings of Initiation in Human Culture.* New York: Harper & Brothers.

Ellis, Carl F., Jr.
1993   *Malcolm: The Man Behind the X.* Chattanooga, Tenn.: Accord.

*1996   *Free at Last? The Gospel in the African-American Experience.* Downers Grove, Ill.: InterVarsity Press. (Revision of *Beyond Liberation.*)

El Sadaawi, Naal
1981   "Arab Women and Western Feminism: An Interview with Nawal El Sadaawi." *Race and Class* 22, no. 2 (Autumn): 175-82.

Emerton, J. A.
1988   "The Priestly Writer in Genesis." *Journal of Theological Studies* 39:381-400.

Epp, Eldon Jay
1975   "Wisdom, Torah, Word: The Johannine Prologue and the Purpose of the Fourth Gospel." In *Current Issues in Biblical and Patristic Interpretation: Studies in Honor of Merrill C. Tenney,* pp. 128-46. Edited by Gerald F. Hawthorne. Grand Rapids, Mich.: Eerdmans.

Erman, A.
1971   *Life in Ancient Egypt.* New York: Dover.

ESA Advocate
1992   October, p. 6.

Esposito, John L.
1991   *Islam: The Straight Path.* Rev. ed. New York: Oxford University Press.

Evans-Pritchard, E. E.
1951   *Kinship and Marriage Among the Nuer.* Oxford: Clarendon.

Ezeigbo, Joseph
1994   "A History of Early Christianity in Africa," *Reach Out* 7, nos. 3-4: 23-25.

Faiman, David
    1989-1990   "How Many Hebrews Left Egypt?" *Jewish Bible Quarterly* 18:230-33.

Falise, Thierry, and
    Christophe Loviny
    1994   "Child Soldiers of Myanmar." *World Press Review,* October, p. 25. (From
        Hong Kong's *Eastern Express.*)

Fanon, Frantz
    1963   *The Wretched of the Earth.* Translated by Constance Farrington. New York:
        Grove.

Farber, Bernard
    1968   *Comparative Kinship Systems: A Method of Analysis.* New York: John Wiley
        & Sons.

Fee, Gordon D.
    1987   *The First Epistle to the Corinthians.* New International Commentary on the
        New Testament. Grand Rapids, Mich.: Eerdmans.

    1994   *God's Empowering Presence: The Holy Spirit in the Letters of Paul.* Peabody,
        Mass.: Hendrickson.

Felder, Cain Hope
    *1989   *Troubling Biblical Waters: Race, Class and Family.* Bishop Henry McNeal
        Turner Studies in North American Black Religion 3. Maryknoll, N.Y.: Orbis.

    1993   "Cultural Ideology, Afrocentrism and Biblical Interpretation." In *Black The-*
        ology: A Documentary History, 2:184-95. Edited by James H. Cone and
        Gayraud S. Wilmore. 2 vols. Maryknoll, N.Y.: Orbis.

Ferguson, Everett
    1987   *Backgrounds of Early Christianity.* Grand Rapids, Mich.: Eerdmans.

Feuillet, André
    1980   "Le caractère universel du jugement et la charité sans frontières en Mt
        25,31-46." *Nouvelle Revue Théologique* 102:179-96.

Filler, Louis
    1960   *The Crusade Against Slavery, 1830-1860.* New York: Harper & Row.

Fischer, Michael M. J.
    1978   "On Changing the Concept and Position of Persian Women." In *Women in the*
        Muslim World. Edited by L. Beck and N. Keddie. Cambridge, Mass.: Harvard
        University Press.

    1983   "Imam Khomeini: Four Levels of Understanding." In *Voices of Resurgent Islam,*
        pp. 150-74. Edited by John L. Esposito. New York: Oxford University Press.

Flusser, David
    1988   *Judaism and the Origins of Christianity.* Jerusalem: Magnes/Hebrew Uni-
        versity.

Foakes Jackson, F. J., and
    Kirsopp Lake
    1979   "The Internal Evidence of Acts." In *The Beginnings of Christianity,* 2:121-204.
        5 vols. Grand Rapids, Mich.: Baker Book House.

Fogel, Robert William
    1989   *Without Consent or Contract: The Rise and Fall of American Slavery.* New
        York: W. W. Norton.

Fogel, Robert William, and
  Stanley L. Engerman
  1974   *Time on the Cross: The Economics of American Negro Slavery.* Boston: Little,
                          Brown.

Forbes, R. J.
  1966   *Studies in Ancient Technology.* 9 vols. Leiden, Netherlands: E. J. Brill.

Fordham, Monroe
  1975   *Major Themes in Northern Black Religious Thought, 1800-1860.* Hicksville,
                          N.Y.: Exposition.

"Forgotten Slaves"
  1991   *World Press Review,* January, p. 57.

Fortes, Meyer
  1950   "Kinship and Marriage Among the Ashanti." In *African Systems of Kinship
                          and Marriage,* pp. 252-84. Edited by A. R. Radcliffe-Brown and Daryll Forde.
                          New York: Oxford University Press.

Fowler, Mervyn D.
  1985   "Excavated Incense Burners: A Case for Identifying a Site as Sacred?"
                          Palestine Exploration Quarterly 117:25-29.

France, R. T.
  1970   "The Authenticity of the Sayings of Jesus." In *History, Criticism and Faith,*
                          pp. 101-43. Edited by Colin Brown. Downers Grove, Ill.: InterVarsity Press.

  1985   *Matthew.* Tyndale New Testament Commentaries. Grand Rapids, Mich.:
                          Eerdmans.

  1986   *The Evidence for Jesus.* Downers Grove, Ill.: InterVarsity Press.

Frankfort, H.
  1948   *Ancient Egyptian Religion: An Interpretation.* New York: Columbia Univer-
                          sity Press.

Freedman, David Noel
  1978   "The Real Story of the Ebla Tablets, Ebla and the Cities of the Plain." *Biblical
                          Archaeologist* 41, no. 4 (December): 143-64.

Fretheim, Terence E.
  1991   "The Plagues as Ecological Signs of Historical Disaster." *Journal of Biblical
                          Literature* 110:385-96.

  1996   *The Pentateuch.* Interpreting Biblical Texts. Nashville: Abingdon.

Freyne, Sean
  1988   *Galilee, Jesus and the Gospels: Literary Approaches and Historical Investi-
                          gations.* Philadelphia: Fortress.

Friedman, Richard E.
  1980   "The Tabernacle in the Temple." *Biblical Archaeologist* 43 (Fall): 241-48.

Fritz, Volkmar
  1987   "What Can Archaeology Tell Us About Solomon's Temple?" *Biblical Archae-
                          ology Review* 13, no. 4: 38-49.

Frymer-Kensky, Tikva
  1981   "Patriarchal Family Relationships and Near Eastern Law." *Biblical Archae-
                          ologist* 44, no. 4 (Fall): 209-14.

Fuchs, Stephen
  1964   "Magic Healing Techniques Among the Bahalis in Central India." In *Magic,*

238

Faith and Healing: Studies in Primitive Psychotherapy Today, pp. 121-38. Edited by Ari Kiev. New York: Free Press/Macmillan.

Fusco, V.

1983   "Le sezioni-noi degli Atti nella discussione recente." *Biblia e Oriente* 25:73-86.

Garbini, Giovanni

1988   *History and Ideology in Ancient Israel.* Translated by John Bowden. New York: Crossroad.

Gardner, Jane F.

1986   *Women in Roman Law and Society.* Bloomington: Indiana University Press.

Garrett, Duane

1991   *Rethinking Genesis: The Sources and Authorship of the First Book of the Pentateuch.* Grand Rapids, Mich.: Baker Book House.

Garvey, Marcus

1992   *Philosophy and Opinions of Marcus Garvey.* Edited by Amy Jacques-Garvey. New York: Atheneum. (Reprint of 1923-1925 edition.)

Gasparro, Giulia Sfameni

1985   *Soteriology and Mystic Aspects in the Cult of Cybele and Attis.* Études Préliminaires aux Religions Orientales dans l'Empire Romain 103. Leiden, Netherlands: E. J. Brill.

Gerhardsson, Birger

1961   *Memory and Manuscript: Oral Tradition and Written Transmission in Rabbinic Judaism and Early Christianity.* Acta Seminarii Neotestamentici Upsaliensis 22. Uppsala, Sweden: C. W. K. Gleerup.

1979   *The Origins of the Gospel Traditions.* Philadelphia: Fortress.

Gero, Stephen

1978   "Jewish Polemic in the Martyrium Pionii and a 'Jesus' Passage from the Talmud." *Journal of Jewish Studies* 29:164-68.

Gibert, Pierre

1992   "Vers une intelligence nouvelle du Pentateuque?" *Recherches de Science Religieuse* 80:55-80.

Gibson, J. C. L.

1977   *Canaanite Myths and Legends.* Edinburgh: T & T Clark.

Gill, David W. J.

1994   "Macedonia." In *Graeco-Roman Setting,* pp. 397-417. Edited by David W. J. Gill and Conrad Gempf. Vol. 2 of *The Book of Acts in Its First-Century Setting.* Grand Rapids, Mich.: Eerdmans; Carlisle, U.K.: Paternoster.

Glock, Albert E.

1970   "Early Israel as the Kingdom of Yahweh." In *A Symposium on Archaeology and Theology.* St. Louis: Concordia.

Gluckman, Max

1950   "Kinship and Marriage Among the Nozi of Northern Rhodesia and the Zulu of Natal." In *African Systems of Kinship and Marriage,* pp. 166-206. Edited by A. R. Radcliffe-Brown and Daryll Forde. New York: Oxford University Press.

Glueck, Nelson

1970   *The Other Side of the Jordan.* Cambridge, Mass.: American Schools of Oriental Research.

Goldingay, John

1980   "The Patriarchs in Scripture and History." In *Essays on the Patriarchal Narratives,* pp. 11-42. Edited by A. R. Millard and D. J. Wiseman. Leicester, U.K.: Inter-Varsity Press.

Good, Mary Jo DelVecchio
1980   "Of Blood and Babies: The Relationship of Popular Islamic Physiology to Fertility." *Social Science and Medicine* 14B, no. 3 (August): 147-56.

Goodell, William
1853   *The American Slave Code in Theory and Practice: Its Distinctive Features Shown by Its Statutes, Judicial Decisions and Illustrative Facts.* N.p.: American & Foreign Anti-slavery Society. (Reprint New York: Negro Universities Press/New American Library, 1969.)

Goodman, Martin
1983   *State and Society in Roman Galilee, A.D. 132-212.* Oxford Centre for Postgraduate Hebrew Studies. Totowa, N.J.: Rowman & Allanheld.

Goppelt, Leonhard
1981-1982   *Theology of the New Testament.* Edited by Jürgen Roloff. Translated by John E. Alsup. 2 vols. Grand Rapids, Mich.: Eerdmans.

Gordon, Cyrus H.
1940   "Biblical Customs and the Nuzu Tablets." *Biblical Archaeologist* 3, no. 1 (February): 1-12.

1953   *Introduction to Old Testament Times.* Ventnor, N.J.: Ventnor.

1958   "Abraham and the Merchants of Ura." *Journal of Near Eastern Studies* 17, no. 1 (January): 28-31.

1965a   *The Ancient Near East.* New York: W. W. Norton.

1965b   *The Common Background of Greek and Hebrew Civilizations.* New York: W. W. Norton.

Gordon, Dane R.
1985   *The Old Testament: A Beginning Survey.* Englewood Cliffs, N.J.: Prentice-Hall.

*Gordon, Murray
1989   *Slavery in the Arab World.* New York: New Amsterdam.

Gough, Kathleen
1973a   "Mappilla: North Kerala." In *Matrilineal Kinship,* pp. 415-42. Edited by David M. Schneider and Kathleen Gough. Berkeley: University of California Press.

1973b   "Variation in Preferential Marriage Forms." In *Matrilineal Kinship,* pp. 614-30. Edited by David M. Schneider and Kathleen Gough. Berkeley: University of California Press.

Goulder, M. D.
1964   *Type and History in Acts.* London: S.P.C.K.

Graf, David F.
1983   "The Nabateans and the Hisma: In the Footsteps of Glueck and Beyond." In *The Word of the Lord Shall Go Forth: Essays in Honor of David Noel Freedman in Celebration of His Sixtieth Birthday,* pp. 647-64. Edited by Carol L. Meyers and M. O'Connor. Winona Lake, Ind.: Eisenbrauns/American Schools of Oriental Research.

Graham, Lloyd
1991   *Deceptions and Myths of the Bible.* New York: Citadel/Carol.

Grant, Frederick C.
1953   *Hellenistic Religions: The Age of Syncretism.* Library of Liberal Arts. Indianapolis: Bobbs-Merrill/Liberal Arts.

Grant, George
1996   *Immaculate Deception: The Shifting Agenda of Planned Parenthood.* Chicago: Northfield.

Grant, Jacquelyn
1989   *White Women's Christ and Black Women's Jesus: Feminist Christology and Womanist Response.* American Academy of Religion Series 64. Atlanta: Scholars Press.

*1995   "Womanist Jesus and the Mutual Struggle for Liberation." In *The Recovery of Black Presence: An Interdisciplinary Exploration—Essays in Honor of Dr. Charles B. Copher,* pp. 129-42. Edited by Randall C. Bailey and Jacquelyn Grant. Nashville: Abingdon.

Grant, Robert M.
1986   *Gods and the One God.* Library of Early Christianity 1. Philadelphia: Westminster Press.

Grassi, Joseph A.
1965   *A World to Win: The Missionary Methods of Paul the Apostle.* Maryknoll, N.Y.: Maryknoll.

Gray, Edward McQueen
1923   *Old Testament Criticism, Its Rise and Progress from the Second Century to the End of the Eighteenth: A Historical Sketch.* New York: Harper & Brothers.

Gray, J.
1967   "Ugarit." In *Archaeology and Old Testament Study,* pp. 145-67. Edited by D. Winton Thomas. Oxford: Clarendon.

Gray, Sherman W.
1989   *The Least of My Brothers—Matthew 25.31-46: A History of Interpretation.* Society of Biblical Literature Dissertation Series 114. Atlanta: Scholars Press.

Grayzel, Solomon
1961   *A History of the Jews.* Philadelphia: Jewish Publication Society of America.

Green, Michael
1989   *I Believe in the Holy Spirit.* 2nd rev. ed. Grand Rapids, Mich.: Eerdmans.

Greengus, Samuel
1994   "Some Issues Relating to the Comparability of Laws and the Coherence of the Legal Tradition." In *Theory and Method in Biblical and Cuneiform Law: Revision, Interpolation and Development,* pp. 60-87. Edited by Bernard M. Levinson. *Journal for the Study of the Old Testament* Supplement 181. Sheffield, U.K.: Sheffield Academic Press.

Greenstone, Julius H.
1906   *The Messiah Idea in Jewish History.* Philadelphia: Jewish Publication Society of America.

Gregory, Joseph R.
1996   "African Slavery 1996." *First Things,* no. 63 (May 1996): 37-39.

Grimké, Rev. Francis J.
1973   *The Negro: His Rights and Wrongs, the Forces for Him and Against Him (Collected Sermons Delivered in Wash., D.C., at 15th St. Presbyt. Ch., Nov. 20th, 27, Dec. 4, 11).* Ann Arbor, Mich.: University Microfilms International.

Groenewegen-Frankfort,
  H. A., and Bernard Ashmole
1967   *The Ancient World.* Library of Art History 1. New York: New American Library.

Groothuis, Douglas
1994   "Understanding Diversity in the World's Religions." *Phi Kappa Alpha Jour-*

nal, Summer, p. 48.

1996   *Are All Religions One?* Downers Grove, Ill.: InterVarsity Press.

Groothuis, Rebecca Merrill
1994   *Women Caught in the Conflict: The Culture War Between Traditionalism and Feminism.* Grand Rapids, Mich.: Baker Book House.

Gross, G.
1964   "Die 'geringsten Brüder' Jesu in Mt 25,40 in Auseinandersetzung mit der neueren Ezegese." *Bibel und Leben* 5:172-80.

Gruber, Meyer I.
1989   "Breast-Feeding Practices in Biblical Israel and in Old Babylonian Mesopotamia." *Journal of the Ancient Near Eastern Society of Columbia University* 19:61-83.

Guillaume, Alfred
1956   *Islam.* 2nd rev. ed. New York: Penguin.

Gundry, Robert H.
1976   *Sōma in Biblical Theology: With Emphasis on Pauline Anthropology.* Cambridge: Cambridge University Press.

1982   *Matthew: A Commentary on His Literary and Theological Art.* Grand Rapids, Mich.: Eerdmans.

Gunkel, Hermann
1994   *The Stories of Genesis.* Translated by John J. Scullion. Edited by William R. Scott. Berkeley, Calif.: BIBAL Press.

Gurney, O. R.
1954   *The Hittites.* 2nd ed. Baltimore: Penguin.

1977   *Some Aspects of Hittite Religion.* Oxford: Oxford University Press/British Academy.

Guthrie, Donald
1970   *New Testament Introduction.* Downers Grove, Ill.: InterVarsity Press.

Guthrie, W. K. C.
1966   *Orpheus and Greek Religion: A Study of the Orphic Movement.* 2nd ed. New York: W. W. Norton.

Habel, Norman
1971   *Literary Criticism of the Old Testament.* Philadelphia: Fortress.

Habermas, Gary R.,
  and Antony G. N. Flew
1987   *Did Jesus Rise from the Dead? The Resurrection Debate.* Edited by Terry L. Miethe. San Francisco: Harper & Row.

Haeri, Shahla
1989   *Law of Desire: Temporary Marriage in Shi'i Iran.* Syracuse, N.Y.: Syracuse University Press.

Hagner, Donald A.
1995   *Matthew 14—28.* Word Biblical Commentary 33B. Dallas: Word.

Haim, Sylvia G.
1981   "The Situation of the Arab Woman in the Mirror of Literature." *Middle Eastern Studies* 17, no. 4 (October): 510-30.

Hakem, A. A., with I. Hrbek
  and J. Vercoutter
  1981   "The Civilization of Napata and Meroe." In *Ancient Civilizations of Africa*, pp.
                                    298-321. Vol. 2 of *General History of Africa*. Edited by G. Mokhtar. UNESCO
                                    International Scientific Committee for the Drafting of a General History of Africa.
                                    Berkeley: University of California Press; London: Heinemann Educational
                                    Books; Paris: United Nations Educational, Scientific and Cultural Organization.
Hale, Janice E.
  1995   "The Transmission of Faith to Young African American Children." In *The
                                    Recovery of Black Presence: An Interdisciplinary Exploration—Essays in
                                    Honor of Dr. Charles B. Copher*, pp. 193-207. Edited by Randall C. Bailey
                                    and Jacquelyn Grant. Nashville: Abingdon.
Hall, G.
  1987   "The Rhetorical Outline for Galatians: A Reconsideration." *Journal of Biblical
                                    Literature* 106:277-87.
Hallett, Robin
  1974   *Africa Since 1875: A Modern History*. University of Michigan History of the
                                    Modern World. Ann Arbor: University of Michigan Press.
Halpern, Baruch
  1992   "Kenites." In *Anchor Bible Dictionary*, 4:17-22. Edited by David Noel Freed-
                                    man. 6 vols. New York: Doubleday.
Hamerton-Kelly, R. G.
  1973   *Pre-existence, Wisdom and the Son: A Study of the Idea of Pre-existence in
                                    the New Testament*. Cambridge: Cambridge University Press.
Hamilton, Charles V.
  1972   *The Black Preacher in America*. New York: William Morrow.
Handy, James A.
  n.d.   *Scraps of African Methodist Episcopal History*. Philadelphia: A.M.E. Book
                                    Concern. (Probably published shortly after 1900. Reprint Ann Arbor, Mich.:
                                    University Microfilms, 1973.)
Haney, Marsha S.
  1994   "African American Muslims." *Reach Out* 7, nos. 3-4: 3-5. (Reprinted from
                                    Theology, News and Notes, March 1992.)
Hansberry, William Leo
  1981a   *Africa and Africans As Seen by Classical Writers*. William Leo Hansberry
                                    African History Notebook 2. Edited by Joseph E. Harris. Washington, D.C.:
                                    Howard University Press.
  *1981b   *Pillars in Ethiopian History*. Edited by Joseph E. Harris. William Leo
                                    Hansberry African History Notebook 1. Washington, D.C.: Howard Univer-
                                    sity Press.
Haran, Menahem
  1965   "The Priestly Image of the Tabernacle." *Hebrew Union College Annual*
                                    36:191-226.
  1970   "The Religion of the Patriarchs: Beliefs and Practices." In *Patriarchs*, pp.
                                    219-45. Edited by Benjamin Mazar. Vol. 2 of *The World History of the Jewish
                                    People*. New Brunswick, N.J.: Rutgers University Press.
  1978   *Temples and Temple-Service in Ancient Israel*. Oxford: Clarendon.
Hardesty, Nancy A.
  1984   *Women Called to Witness: Evangelical Feminism in the Nineteenth Century*.
                                    Nashville: Abingdon.

Hare, Douglas R. A.
1967   *The Theme of Jewish Persecution of Christians in the Gospel According to St. Matthew.* Cambridge: Cambridge University Press.

Harrelson, Walter
1969   *From Fertility Cult to Worship.* Garden City, N.Y.: Doubleday.

Harrington, Daniel J.
1982   *The Gospel According to Matthew.* Collegeville, Minn.: Liturgical.

Harris, B. F.
1962   "*Syneidēsis* (Conscience) in the Pauline Writings." *Westminster Theological Journal* 24, no. 2: 173-86.

Harrison, Roland Kenneth
1969   *Introduction to the Old Testament.* Grand Rapids, Mich.: Eerdmans.

1978   "The Historical and Literary Criticism of the Old Testament." In R. K. Harrison et al., *Biblical Criticism: Historical, Literary and Textual,* pp. 3-44. Grand Rapids, Mich.: Zondervan.

Hasan, Yusuf Fadl
1967   *The Arabs and the Sudan: From the Seventh to the Early Sixteenth Century.* Edinburgh: University of Edinburgh Press.

Hawting, G. R.
1982   "The Origins of the Muslim Sanctuary at Mecca." In *Studies on the First Century of Islamic Society,* pp. 23-47. Edited by G. H. A. Juynboll. Papers on Islamic History 5. Carbondale: Southern Illinois University Press.

Hayes, John H.
1967   "Prophetism at Mari and Old Testament Parallels." *Anglican Theological Review* 49:397-409.

1968   "The Usage of Oracles Against Foreign Nations in Ancient Israel." *Journal of Biblical Literature* 87:81-92.

1979   *An Introduction to Old Testament Study.* Nashville: Abingdon.

Haynes, Leonard L., Jr.
1953   *The Negro Community Within American Protestantism, 1619-1844.* Boston: Christopher.

Heer, D. M., and Nadia
  Youssef
1977   "Female Status Among Soviet Central Asian Nationalities: The Melding of Islam and Marxism and Its Implications for Population Increase." *Population Studies* 31, no. 1 (March): 155-73.

Heidel, Alexander
1963   *The Babylonian Genesis.* Phoenix ed. Chicago: University of Chicago Press.

Hendel, Ronald S.
1988   "The Social Origins of the Aniconic Tradition in Early Israel." *Catholic Biblical Quarterly* 50:365-82.

Hengel, Martin
1974   *Judaism and Hellenism: Studies in Their Encounter in Palestine During the Early Hellenistic Period.* Translated by John Bowden. 2 vols. Philadelphia: Fortress.

1985   *Studies in the Gospel of Mark.* Translated by John Bowden. Philadelphia: Fortress.

Henn, Jeanne K.
1984   "Women in the Rural Economy: Past, Present and Future." In *African Women South of the Sahara*, pp. 1-18. Edited by Margaret Jean Hay and Sharon Stichter. New York: Longman.

Herford, R. Travers
1903   *Christianity in Talmud and Midrash.* London: Williams & Norgate. (Reprint New York: KTAV, n.d.)

Herr, Larry G.
1988   "Tripartite Pillared Buildings and the Market Place in Iron Age Palestine." *Bulletin of the American Schools of Oriental Research* 272:47-67.

Herzog, Zev
1987   " 'Cult Stands' from the City of David—Incense Altars?" *Qadmoniot* 20:126. (In Hebrew. Summarized in *Old Testament Abstracts* 12:142.)

Heschel, Abraham J.
1962   *The Prophets.* New York: Harper & Row.

Hess, Richard S.
1993   "Early Israel in Canaan: A Survey of Recent Evidence and Interpretations." *Palestine Exploration Quarterly* 125:125-42.

Hill, Andrew E., and
John H. Walton
1991   *A Survey of the Old Testament.* Grand Rapids, Mich.: Zondervan.

Hill, David
1979   *New Testament Prophecy.* Atlanta: John Knox.

Hoffmeier, James K.
1989   "Reconsidering Egypt's Part in the Termination of the Middle Bronze Age in Palestine." *Levant* 21:181-93.

1990   "Some Thoughts on William G. Dever's 'Hyksos, Egyptian Destructions, and the End of the Palestinian Middle Bronze Age.' " *Levant* 22:83-89.

1991   "James Weinstein's 'Egypt and the Middle Bronze IIC/Late Bronze IA Transition': A Rejoinder." *Levant* 23:117-24.

1992   "The Wives' Tales of Genesis 12, 20 and 26 and the Covenants at Beer-Sheba." *Tyndale Bulletin* 43:81-99.

Hölbl, Gunther
1989   "Ägyptische Kunstelemente im phönikischen Kulturkreis des I: Jahrtausends v. Chr.—Zur Methodik ihrer Verwendung." *Orientalia* 58:318-25.

Holladay, Carl R.
1977   *Theios Aner in Hellenistic Judaism: A Critique of the Use of This Category in New Testament Christology.* Society of Biblical Literature Dissertation Series 40. Missoula, Mont.: Scholars Press.

Holladay, John S., Jr.
1970   "Assyrian Statecraft and the Prophets of Israel." *Harvard Theological Review* 63:29-51.

Holladay, William L.
1995   *Long Ago God Spoke: How Christians May Hear the Old Testament Today.* Minneapolis: Fortress.

Hollenweger, Walter J.
1988   *The Pentecostals.* Translated by R. A. Wilson. Peabody, Mass.: Hendrickson. (First English printing London: SCM Press, 1972.)

Holme, L. R.
1969   *The Extinction of the Christian Churches in North Africa.* New York: Burt Franklin. (Reprint of 1898 edition, no place or publisher given.)

Hood, Robert E.
1990   *Must God Remain Greek? Afro Cultures and God-Talk.* Minneapolis: Fortress.

Hooker, Morna
1960   "Adam in Romans I." *New Testament Studies* 6, no. 4 (July): 297-306.

Hopkins, Samuel
1854   *Timely Articles on Slavery.* N.p. (Reprinted from copy in the Negro Collection of Fisk University Library: Miami: Mnemosyne, 1969.)

Horsley, Richard A.
1995   *Galilee: History, Politics, People.* Valley Forge, Penn.: Trinity Press International.

Hort, Greta
1957   "The Plagues of Egypt" (pt. 1). *Zeitschrift für die Alttestamentliche Wissenschaft* 69:84-103.

1958   "The Plagues of Egypt" (pt. 2). *Zeitschrift für die Alttestamentliche Wissenschaft* 70:48-59.

Houssney, Georges
1989   "Unity: The Unfulfilled Dream of the Arabs." *Reach Out* 3, nos. 1-2 (June): 14-15.

Houtman, Cornelis
1989   "The Pentateuch." In *The World of the Old Testament,* pp. 166-205. Edited by A. S. Van der Woude. Translated by Sierd Woudstra. Grand Rapids, Mich.: Eerdmans.

1994   "Wie fiktiv ist das Zeltheiligtum von Exodus 25—40?" *Zeitschrift für die Alttestamentliche Wissenschaft* 106:107-13.

Huffmon, Herbert B.
1968   "Prophecy in the Mari Letters." *Biblical Archaeologist* 31:101-24.

Humphreys, W. Lee
1988   *Joseph and His Family: A Literary Study.* Studies on Personalities of the Old Testament. Columbia: University of South Carolina Press.

Hunter, Archibald M.
1966   *The Gospel According to St. Paul.* Philadelphia: Westminster Press.

Hunter, Emma
1900   Letter dated February 1900, Washington, D.C. Charles N. Hunter Papers, 1818-1931, Raleigh, North Carolina. Durham, N.C.: Duke University Manuscripts Collection.

Hurowitz, Victor (Avigdor)
1983-1984   "The Golden Calf and the Tabernacle." *Shnaton* 7/8:51-59. (In Hebrew. Summarized in *Religious and Theological Abstracts Database.*)

1985   "The Priestly Account of Building the Tabernacle." *Journal of the American Oriental Society* 105:21-30.

Hurvitz, Avi
1988   "Dating the Priestly Source in Light of the Historical Study of Biblical Hebrew a Century After Wellhausen." *Zeitschrift für die Alttestamentliche Wissenschaft* 100 (Supplement): 88-100.

Irvin, Dorothy
    1977   "The Joseph and Moses Stories as Narrative in the Light of Ancient Near
                            Eastern Narrative." In *Israelite and Judaean History*, pp. 180-203. Edited by
                            John H. Hayes and J. Maxwell Miller. Philadelphia: Westminster Press.
*Isaac, Ephraim
    1968   *The Ethiopian Church*. Boston: Henry N. Sawyer. (Includes chapter on the
                            traditional art of Ethiopia by Marjorie LeMay.)
**Isichei, Elizabeth
    1995   *A History of Christianity in Africa from Antiquity to the Present*.
                            Lawrenceville, N.J.: Africa World Press; Grand Rapids, Mich.: Eerdmans.
"Islam's Veiled Threat"
    1995   *World Press Review*, January, pp. 19-21.

Jackson, John G.
    1939   *Ethiopia and the Origin of Civilization: A Critical Review of the Evidence of
                            Archaeology, Anthropology, History and Comparative Religion According to the
                            Most Reliable Sources and Authorities*. N.p. (Reprint Baltimore: Black Classic
                            Press, n.d.)

    1970   *Introduction to African Civilizations*. New York: Carol.

Jacobs, Louis
    1973   *Jewish Biblical Exegesis*. New York: Behrman House.

Jakobielski, S.
    1988   "Christian Nubia at the Height of Its Civilization." In *Africa from the Seventh
                            to the Eleventh Century*, pp. 194-223. Vol. 3 of *General History of Africa*.
                            Edited by M. El Fasi with I. Hrbek. UNESCO International Scientific Com-
                            mittee for the Drafting of a General History of Africa. Berkeley: University
                            of California Press; London: Heinemann Educational Books; Paris: United
                            Nations Educational, Scientific and Cultural Organization.
James, George G. M.
    1954   *Stolen Legacy: Greek Philosophy Is Stolen Egyptian Philosophy*. New York:
                            Philosophical Library. (Reprint n.p.: African Publication Society, 1980;
                            Hampton, Va.: United Brothers Communications Systems, 1989.)
Janssen, J. M. A.
    1950   "On the Ideal Lifetime of the Egyptian." *Oudheidkundige Mededeelingen uit
                            het Rijksmuseum van Oudheden te Leiden, Netherlands* 31:33-44.

    1959   "Egyptological Remarks on the Story of Joseph in Genesis." *Jaarbericht . . .
                            Ex Orient Lux* 5:63-72.

Jensen, L. B.
    1963   "Royal Purple of Tyre." *Journal of Near Eastern Studies* 22, no. 2 (April):
                            104-18.

Jeremias, Joachim
    1954   "Zu Rm 1.22-32." *Zeitschrift für die Neutestamentliche Wissenschaft* 45, nos.
                            1-2: 119-21.

    1964   *The Prayers of Jesus*. Philadelphia: Fortress.

    1965   *The Central Message of the New Testament*. New York: Charles Scribner's Sons.

    1971   *New Testament Theology*. New York: Charles Scribner's Sons.

    1975   *Jerusalem in the Time of Jesus*. Philadelphia: Fortress. (Also London: SCM

Press, 1969.)

Johnson, Charles S., et al.
1947   *Into the Main Stream: A Survey of Best Practices in Race Relations in the
            South.* Chapel Hill: University of North Carolina Press.

Johnson, John L.
1993   *The Black Biblical Heritage.* Nashville: Winston-Derek.

Johnson, Luke T.
1986   *The Writings of the New Testament: An Introduction.* Philadelphia: Fortress.

1996   *The Real Jesus: The Misguided Quest for the Historical Jesus and the Truth
            of the Traditional Gospels.* San Francisco: HarperSanFrancisco.

Johnson, S. Lewis, Jr.
1972   "Paul and the Knowledge of God." *Bibliotheca Sacra* 129, no. 513 (January):
            61-74.

Johnstone, Patrick
1993   *Operation World.* 5th ed. Grand Rapids, Mich.: Zondervan.

Jones, A. M. H.
1970   *The Empire.* Vol. 2 of *A History of Rome Through the Fifth Century.* New
            York: Walker.

Jones, A. H. M., and
  Elizabeth Monroe
1955   *A History of Ethiopia.* Oxford: Clarendon. (First published in 1935 as *A
            History of Abyssinia.*)

Jones, Charles C.
1842   *The Religious Instruction of the Negroes in the United States.* Savannah:
            Thomas Purse. (Reprinted from copy in Fisk University Library Negro
            Collection: Freeport, N.Y.: Books for Libraries/Black Heritage Library Col-
            lection, 1971.)

Joshel, S. R.
1986   "Nurturing the Master's Child: Slavery and the Roman Child-Nurse." *Signs*
            12:3-22.

*Journal for the Study of
  the New Testament*
1994   Review of *Paul, Women and Wives. Journal for the Study of the New Testament*
            54:122-23.

1995   Review of *Paul, Women and Wives. Journal for the Study of the New Testament*
            58:121.

*Joyner, Charles
1984   *Down by the Riverside: A South Carolina Slave Community.* Urbana: Univer-
            sity of Illinois Press.

Julien, Charles-André
1970   *History of North Africa: Tunisia, Algeria, Morocco—From the Arab Conquest
            to 1830.* Edited and revised by R. Le Tourneau and C. C. Stewart. Translated
            by John Petrie. New York: Praeger.

Juster, Daniel
1995   *The Biblical World View: An Apologetic.* San Francisco: International Schol-
            ars.

Juynboll, G. H. A.
1982a   *Introduction to Studies on the First Century of Islamic Society,* pp. 1-7. Edited
            by G. H. A. Juynboll. Papers on Islamic History 5. Carbondale: Southern

                              Illinois University Press.

1982b   "On the Origins of Arabic Prose: Reflections on Authenticity." In *Studies on
                              the First Century of Islamic Society,* pp. 161-75. Edited by G. H. A. Juynboll.
                              Papers on Islamic History 5. Carbondale: Southern Illinois University Press.

Kaiser, Walter C., Jr.
1973   "The Ugaritic Pantheon." Ph.D. dissertation, Brandeis University.

1978   *Toward an Old Testament Theology.* Grand Rapids, Mich.: Zondervan.

Kamil, Jill
1990   *Coptic Egypt: History and Guide.* Rev. ed. Plans and maps by Hassan Ibrahim.
                              Cairo: American University in Cairo Press.

Kaplan, David A., et al.
1993   "Is It Torture or Tradition? The Genital Mutilation of Young African Girls Sparks
                              an Angry Intellectual Debate in the West." *Newsweek,* December 20, p. 124.

Karmon, Nira, and
  Ehud Spanier
1988   "Remains of a Purple Dye Industry Found at Tel Shiqmona." *Israel Explora-
                              tion Journal* 38:184-86, plates 27 B, C, D.

Katzoff, Louis
1987-1988   "Purchase of the Machpelah." *Dor le Dor* 16:29-31.

Kearney, Peter J.
1977   "Creation and Liturgy: The P Redaction of Ex 25—40." *Zeitschrift für die
                              Alttestamentliche Wissenschaft* 89:375-86.

Keck, Leander E.
1979   *Paul and His Letters.* Proclamation Commentaries. Philadelpia: Fortress.

Keddie, Nikki R., and
  Beth Baron, eds.
1992   *Women in Middle Eastern History: Shifting Boundaries in Sex and Gender.*
                              New Haven, Conn.: Yale University Press.

Kee, Howard Clark
1983   *Miracle in the Early Christian World: A Study in Sociohistorical Method.* New
                              Haven, Conn.: Yale University Press.

Keener, Craig S.
1991a   *. . . And Marries Another: Divorce and Remarriage in the Teaching of the New
                              Testament.* Peabody, Mass.: Hendrickson.

1991b   "The Function of Johannine Pneumatology in the Context of Late First-Cen-
                              tury Judaism." Ann Arbor, Mich.: University Microfilms International (Duke
                              University Ph.D. dissertation).

1992   *Paul, Women and Wives: Marriage and Women's Ministry in the Letters of
                              Paul.* Peabody, Mass.: Hendrickson.

1993a   "The Gospels as Historically Reliable Biography." *A.M.E. Zion Quarterly
                              Review* 105, no. 4 (October): 12-23.

*1993b   *The IVP Bible Background Commentary: New Testament.* Downers Grove,
                              Ill.: InterVarsity Press.

1995a   "A Critique of Burton Mack's *Lost Gospel of Q.*" Paper presented to the
                              Evangelical Theological Society, November 18, 1995, Philadelphia. (Avail-

	able from Theological Research Exchange Network, P.O. Box 30183, Portland, OR 97294-3183.)
1995b	"Slaves, Obey Your Masters: Ephesians 6:5." *A.M.E. Zion Quarterly Review* 107, no. 4 (October): 32-54.
1995c	"Subversive Conservative." *Christian History* 14, no. 3 (August): 35-37.
1996	*Three Crucial Questions About the Holy Spirit.* Grand Rapids, Mich.: Baker Book House.
1997a	"Husband of One Wife." *A.M.E. Zion Quarterly Review* 109, no. 1 (January 1997): 5-24.
1997b	*Matthew.* IVP New Testament Commentary. Downers Grove, Ill.: InterVarsity Press.
1997c	*The Spirit in the Gospels and Acts: Divine Purity and Power.* Peabody, Mass.: Hendrickson.

Kennedy, George A.

1980	*Classical Rhetoric and Its Christian and Secular Tradition from Ancient to Modern Times.* Chapel Hill: University of North Carolina Press.
1984	*New Testament Interpretation Through Rhetorical Criticism.* Chapel Hill: University of North Carolina Press.

Kenyon, Kathleen M.

1965	*Archaeology in the Holy Land.* 2nd ed. New York: Praeger.

Kerns, Phil, with Doug Wead

1979	*People's Temple, People's Tomb.* Plainfield, N.J.: Logos International.

Kister, M. J.

1982	"On 'Concessions' and Conduct: A Study in Early *Hadith*." In *Studies on the First Century of Islamic Society,* pp. 89-107. Edited by G. H. A. Juynboll. Papers on Islamic History 5. Carbondale: Southern Illinois University Press.

Kitchen, Kenneth A.

1960	"Some Egyptian Background to the Old Testament." *Tyndale Bulletin* 5, no. 16: 4-18.
*1966	*Ancient Orient and the Old Testament.* Downers Grove, Ill.: InterVarsity Press.
1976	"From the Brickfields of Egypt." *Tyndale Bulletin* 27:137-47.
1978	*The Bible in Its World: The Bible and Archaeology Today.* Downers Grove, Ill.: InterVarsity Press.
1989	"The Fall and Rise of Covenant, Law and Treaty." *Tyndale Bulletin* 40:118-35.
1995	"The Patriarchal Age: Myth or History?" *Biblical Archaeology Review* 21, no. 2: 48-57, 88, 90, 92, 94-95.

Klein, Herbert S.

1971	"Anglicanism, Catholicism and the Negro Slave." In *The Debate over Slavery: Stanley Elkins and His Critics,* pp. 137-90. Edited by Ann J. Lane. Urbana: University of Illinois Press.

Klein, William W., Craig L.
  Blomberg and Robert L.
  Hubbard Jr.
1993   *Introduction to Biblical Interpretation.* Dallas: Word.

Kline, Meredith G.
1963   *Treaty of the Great King—The Covenant Structure of Deuteronomy: Studies
                               and Commentary.* Grand Rapids, Mich.: Eerdmans.

Knohl, Israel
1987   "The Priestly Torah Versus the Holiness School: Sabbath and the Festivals."
                               Hebrew Union College Annual 58:65-117.

Kobishanov, Y. M.
1981   "Aksum: Political System, Economics and Culture, First to Fourth Century."
                               In *Ancient Civilizations of Africa,* pp. 381-400. Vol. 2 of *General History of
                               Africa.* Edited by G. Mokhtar. UNESCO International Scientific Committee
                               for the Drafting of a General History of Africa. Berkeley: University of
                               California Press; London: Heinemann Educational Books; Paris: United
                               Nations Educational, Scientific and Cultural Organization.

Koch, Klaus
1977   " '*Ōhel; 'āhal.*" In *Theological Dictionary of the Old Testament,* 1:118-30.
                               Rev. ed. Edited by G. Johannes Betterweck and Helmer Ringgren. Translated
                               by John T. Willis, Geoffrey W. Bromiley and David E. Green. 5 vols. Grand
                               Rapids, Mich.: Eerdmans.

Koester, Helmut
1982   *Introduction to the New Testament.* 2 vols. Hermeneia Foundations and Facets
                               Series. Philadelphia: Fortress.

*Koren, J., and Y. D. Nevo
1991   "Methodological Approaches to Islamic Studies." *Der Islam* 68:87-107.

Kroeger, Catherine Clark
n.d.   "Black History in the Early Church." Available from Christians for Biblical
                               Equality, 122 W. Franklin Ave., Suite 218, Minneapolis, MN 55404.

Kunjufu, Jawanza
1991   *Black Economics: Solutions for Economic and Community Empowerment.*
                               Chicago: African American Images.

Kuper, Hilda
1950   "Kinship Among the Swazi." In *African Systems of Kinship and Marriage,*
                               pp. 86-110. Edited by A. R. Radcliffe-Brown and Daryll Forde. New York:
                               Oxford University Press.

Kwapong, A. A.
1961   "Carthage, Greece and Rome." In *The Dawn of African History,* pp. 13-21.
                               Edited by Roland Oliver. London: Oxford University Press.

Ladd, George Eldon
1963   "The Resurrection and History." *Religion in Life* 32:247-56.

1964   "Israel and the Church." *Evangelical Quarterly* 36:206-13.

1974a   "The Parable of the Sheep and the Goats in Recent Interpretation." In *New
                               Dimensions in New Testament Study,* pp. 191-99. Edited by Richard N.
                               Longenecker and Merrill C. Tenney. Grand Rapids, Mich.: Zondervan.

1974b   *A Theology of the New Testament.* Grand Rapids, Mich.: Eerdmans.

Lafont, Sophie
1994   "Ancient Near Eastern Laws: Continuity and Pluralism." In *Theory and*

Method in Biblical and Cuneiform Law: Revision, Interpolation and Development, pp. 91-118. Edited by Bernard M. Levinson. *Journal for the Study of the Old Testament* Supplement 181. Sheffield, U.K.: Sheffield Academic Press.

Lake, Kirsopp, and
 Henry J. Cadbury
1979   *English Translation and Commentary.* Vol. 4 of *The Beginnings of Christianity.* Edited by F. J. Foakes Jackson and Kirsopp Lake. 5 vols. Grand Rapids, Mich.: Baker Book House.

Lalevée, Thierry
1993   "Tehran's New Allies in Africa: Exporting the Islamic Revolution." *World Press Review,* September, pp. 20-21 (from *Arabies*).

Lambdin, T. O.
1953   "Egyptian Loan Words in the Old Testament." *Journal of the American Oriental Society* 73:145-55.

Landsberger, B.
1939   "Die babylonischen Termini für Gesetz und Recht." In *Festschrift für P. Koschaker,* 2:219-34. Leiden, Netherlands: E. J. Brill.

Lapidus, I. M.
1982   "The Arab Conquests and the Formation of Islamic Society." In *Studies on the First Century of Islamic Society,* pp. 49-72. Edited by G. H. A. Juynboll. Papers on Islamic History 5. Carbondale: Southern Illinois University Press.

Lapoorta, Japie J.
1989   " '. . . Whatever You Did for One of the Least of These . . . You Did for Me' (Matt 25:31-46)." *Journal of Theology for Southern Africa* 68:103-9.

Larsen, David B., and
 Christopher A. Hall
1992   "Holy Health." *Christianity Today,* November 23, pp. 18-22.

Larson, Barbara K.
1984   "The Status of Women in a Tunisian Village: Limits to Autonomy, Influence and Power." *Signs* 9, no. 3 (Spring): 417-33.

LaSor, William Sanford,
 David Allan Hubbard and
 Frederick William Bush
1996   *Old Testament Survey: The Message, Form and Background of the Old Testament.* 2nd ed. Grand Rapids, Mich.: Eerdmans.

Lawrence, John M.
1980   "Ancient Near Eastern Roots of Graeco-Roman Sacrificial Divination." *Near East Archaeological Society Bulletin* 15-16 (Summer/Fall): 51-71.

Leclant, J.
1981   "The Empire of Kush: Napata and Meroe." In *Ancient Civilizations of Africa,* pp. 278-95. Vol. 2 of *General History of Africa.* Edited by G. Mokhtar. UNESCO International Scientific Committee for the Drafting of a General History of Africa. Berkeley: University of California Press; London: Heinemann Educational Books; Paris: United Nations Educational, Scientific and Cultural Organization

Lefkowitz, Mary R.
1976   "The Motivations for St. Perpetua's Martyrdom." *Journal of the American Academy of Religion* 44, no. 3 (September): 417-21.

1996   *Not out of Africa: How Afrocentrism Became an Excuse to Teach Myth as History.* New York: BasicBooks/HarperCollins.

Lefkowitz, Mary R., and
  Maureen B. Fant
1982   *Women's Life in Greece and Rome.* Baltimore: Johns Hopkins University
                             Press; London: Gerald Duckworth.

Lefkowitz, Mary R., and
  Guy MacLean Rogers, eds.
1996   *Black Athena Revisited.* Chapel Hill: University of North Carolina Press.

Lemche, Niels Peter
1988   *Ancient Israel: A New History of Israelite Society.* Sheffield, U.K.: JSOT
                             Press/Sheffield Academic Press.

Le Roux, J. H.
1990   "Sending en Pentateugkritiek." *Skrif en Kerk* 11:187-98. (Summarized in *Old
                             Testament Abstracts* 14:136.)

Levinson, Bernard M.
1994a   "The Case for Revision and Interpolation Within the Biblical Legal Corpora."
                             In *Theory and Method in Biblical and Cuneiform Law: Revision, Interpolation
                             and Development,* pp. 37-59. Edited by Bernard M. Levinson. *Journal for the
                             Study of the Old Testament* Supplement 181. Sheffield, U.K.: Sheffield
                             Academic Press.

1994b   Introduction to *Theory and Method in Biblical and Cuneiform Law: Revision,
                             Interpolation and Development,* pp. 1-14. Edited by Bernard M. Levinson.
                             Journal for the Study of the Old Testament Supplement 181. Sheffield, U.K.:
                             Sheffield Academic Press.

Lewis, Bernard
1975   *History Remembered, Recovered, Invented.* New York: Simon & Schuster.

**1990   *Race and Slavery in the Middle East: An Historical Enquiry.* New York:
                             Oxford University Press.

Lewis, C. S.
1946   *The Great Divorce.* New York: Macmillan.

Lewis, Naphtali
1983   *Life in Egypt Under Roman Rule.* Oxford: Clarendon.

Lieberman, Saul
1962   *Hellenism in Jewish Palestine: Studies in the Literary Transmission of Beliefs
                             and Manners of Palestine in the I Century B.C.E.—IV Century C.E.* 2nd ed. Texts
                             and Studies of the Jewish Theological Seminary of American 18. New York:
                             Jewish Theological Seminary of America Press.

*Lincoln, C. Eric
1994   *The Black Muslims in America.* 3rd ed. Trenton, N.J.: Africa World Press;
                             Grand Rapids, Mich.: Eerdmans, 1994. (Revised from the author's Ph.D.
                             dissertation, Boston University.)

Lincoln, C. Eric, and
  Lawrence H. Mamiya
1990   *The Black Church in the African American Experience.* Durham, N.C.: Duke
                             University Press.

Lindblom, J.
1962   *Prophecy in Ancient Israel.* Philadelphia: Fortress.

Liphshitz, Nili, and
  Gideon Biger
1991   "Cedar of Lebanon *(Cedrus libani)* in Israel During Antiquity." *Israel Explo-*

ration Journal 41:167-75.

Livingston, G. Herbert
1974   The Pentateuch in Its Cultural Environment. Grand Rapids, Mich.: Baker
                    Book House.

Lloyd, Seton
1978   The Archaeology of Mesopotamia. London: Thames & Hudson.

Loewenstamm, Samuel E.
1992   The Evolution of the Exodus Tradition. Translated by Baruch J. Schwartz. Perry
                    Foundation for Biblical Research. Jerusalem: Magnes/Hebrew University.

Lohfink, Norbert
1994   Theology of the Pentateuch: Themes of the Priestly Narrative and Deutero-
                    nomy. Translated by Linda M. Maloney. Minneapolis: Fortress.

London, Gloria
1989   "A Comparison of Two Contemporaneous Lifestyles of the Late Second
                    Millennium B.C." Bulletin of the American Schools of Oriental Research
                    273:37-55.

Long, Burke O.
1973   "The Effect of Divination upon Israelite Literature." Journal of Biblical
                    Literature 92:489-97.

Longenecker, Richard N.
1970   The Christology of Early Jewish Christianity. London: SCM Press.

1976   Paul, Apostle of Liberty. Grand Rapids, Mich.: Baker Book House.

Lowie, Robert H.
1968   "Relationship Terms." In Kinship and Social Organization: An Introduction
                    to Theory and Method, pp. 39-59. Edited by Ira R. Buchler and Henry A. Selby.
                    New York: Macmillan.

Lucas, A.
1962   Ancient Egyptian Materials and Industries. 4th ed. Rev. J. R. Harris. London:
                    Edward Arnold.

Luke, J. T.
1977   "Abraham and the Iron Age: Reflections on the New Patriarchal Studies."
                    Journal for the Study of the Old Testament 4:35-47.

Luria, Ben-Zion
1988-1989   "The Location of Ai." Dor le Dor 17:153-58.

Lurker, Manfred
1980   The Gods and Symbols of Ancient Egypt: An Illustrated Dictionary. London:
                    Thames & Hudson.

Luzbetak, Louis J.
1976   The Church and Cultures: An Applied Anthropology for the Religious Worker.
                    Pasadena, Calif.: William Carey Library.

Lyons, George
1985   Pauline Autobiography: Toward a New Understanding. Society of Biblical
                    Literature Dissertation Series 73. Atlanta: Scholars Press.

MacMullen, Ramsay
1980   "Women in Public in the Roman Empire." Historia 29:209-18.

MacShane, Denis
1991   "Captive Workers." World Press Review, May, p. 50. (From Far Eastern
                    Economic Review.)

Maddox, Robert
1982   The Purpose of Luke-Acts. Edinburgh: T & T Clark.

Mahjoubi, A.
1981   "The Roman Period." In *Ancient Civilizations of Africa*, pp. 465-99. Vol. 2 of
                       General History of Africa. Edited by G. Mokhtar. UNESCO International
                       Scientific Committee for the Drafting of a General History of Africa. Berkeley:
                       University of California Press; London: Heinemann Educational Books; Paris:
                       United Nations Educational, Scientific and Cultural Organization.

Maillot, A.
1978   "Quelques remarques sur la naissance virginale du Christ." *Foi et Vie* 77:30-44.

Majied, Atiyah (Lynn
2x Manning)
1994   *The Teachings of Both Holy Qur'an and Bible: As Taught by the Honorable
                       Elijah Muhammad Messenger of Allah (God) Master Fard Muhammad.*
                       Hampton, Va.: U.B. & U.S. Communications Systems.

Malamat, Abraham
1966   "Prophetic Revelations in New Documents from Mari and the Bible." In *Vetus
                       Testamentum Supplements*, 15:207-27. Leiden, Netherlands: E. J. Brill.

1983   "The Proto-history of Israel: A Study in Method." In *The Word of the Lord
                       Shall Go Forth: Essays in Honor of David Noel Freedman in Celebration of
                       His Sixtieth Birthday*, pp. 303-13. Edited by Carol L. Meyers and M. O'Con-
                       nor. Winona Lake, Ind.: Eisenbrauns/American Schools of Oriental Research.

Malcolm X, with Alex Haley
1965   *The Autobiography of Malcolm X*. New York: Grove.

Malherbe, Abraham J.
1970   " 'Gentle as a Nurse': The Cynic Background to I Thess ii." *Novum Testamen-
                       tum* 12, no. 2 (April): 203-17.

Mann, Thomas W.
1991   " 'All the Families of the Earth': The Theological Unity of Genesis." *Inter-
                       pretation* 45:341-53.

*Mannix, Daniel P., with
Malcolm Cowley
1962   *Black Cargoes: A History of the Atlantic Slave Trade, 1518-1865*. New York:
                       Viking.

Marcus, Ralph
1931-1932   "Divine Names and Attributes in Hellenistic Jewish Literature." *Proceedings
                       of the American Academy for Jewish Research* 3:43-120.

Marsh, Rev. Dr. William
1854   "The Law of Liberty." In *Autographs for Freedom*, 2:61-62. Edited by Julia
                       Griffiths. Auburn, Maine: Alden, Beardsley; Rochester, N.Y.: Wanzer, Beardsley.

Marshall, I. Howard
1990   *The Origins of New Testament Christology*. Rev. ed. Downers Grove, Ill.:
                       InterVarsity Press.

Marshall, Robert G., and
Charles A. Donovan
1991   *Blessed Are the Barren: The Social Policy of Planned Parenthood*. San
                       Francisco: Ignatius.

Martin, Clarice J.
1993   "Womanist Interpretations of the New Testament: The Quest for Holistic and
                       Inclusive Translation and Interpretation." In *Black Theology: A Documentary
                       History*, 2:225-44. Edited by James H. Cone and Gayraud S. Wilmore. 2 vols.
                       Maryknoll, N.Y.: Orbis.

Martin, Ralph P.
1982   *The Worship of God*. Grand Rapids, Mich.: Eerdmans.

Martin, Walter R.
1977   *The Kingdom of the Cults: An Analysis of the Major Cult Systems in the Present Christian Era.* 3rd rev. ed. Minneapolis: Bethany Fellowship.

Marx, A.
1967   "Y a-t-il une prédestination à Qumran?" *Revue de Qumran* 6, no. 2: 163-81.

**Masland, Tom, et al.
1992   "Slavery." *Newsweek,* May 4, pp. 30-39.

Matthews, Donald G.
1965   *Slavery and Methodism: A Chapter in American Morality, 1780-1845.* Princeton, N.J.: Princeton University Press.

Matthews, Victor H.
1994   "The Anthropology of Slavery in the Covenant Code." In *Theory and Method in Biblical and Cuneiform Law: Revision, Interpolation and Development,* pp. 119-35. Edited by Bernard M. Levinson. *Journal for the Study of the Old Testament* Supplement 181. Sheffield, U.K.: Sheffield Academic Press.

May, Herbert Gordon
1935   *The Material Remains of the Megiddo Cult.* Chicago: University of Chicago Press.

Mazar, Amihay
1973a   "Excavations at Tell Qasile, 1971-72: Preliminary Report." *Israel Exploration Journal* 23, no. 2: 65-67.

1973b   "A Philistine Temple at Tell Qasile." *Biblical Archaeologist* 36 (May): 42-48.

1990   *Archaeology of the Land of the Bible: 10,000-586 B.C.E.* Anchor Bible Reference Library. New York: Doubleday.

Mazar, Benjamin
1970   "Canaan in the Patriarchal Age." In *Patriarchs,* pp. 169-87. Edited by Benjamin Mazar. Vol. 2 of *The World History of the Jewish People.* New Brunswick, N.J.: Rutgers University Press.

1986   *The Early Biblical Period: Historical Studies.* Edited by Shmuel Ahituv and Baruch A. Levine. Jerusalem: Israel Exploration Society.

1992   *Biblical Israel: State and People.* Edited by Shmuel Ahituv. Jerusalem: Magnes/Hebrew University.

Mazar, Benjamin, et al., eds.
1959   *Views of the Biblical World.* 5 vols. New York: Arco.

*Mbiti, John S.
1970   *African Religions and Philosophies.* Garden City, N.Y.: Doubleday.

McCarter, P. Kyle, Jr.
1988   "A New Challenge to the Documentary Hypothesis." *Bible Review* 4, no. 2: 34-39.

McCloud, Aminah Beverly
1995   *African American Islam.* New York: Routledge.

McCown, Chester Carlton
1929   *The Genesis of the Social Gospel.* New York: Alfred A. Knopf.

*McCray, Walter Arthur
    1990   *The Black Presence in the Bible: Teacher's Guide.* Chicago: Black Light
                            Fellowship.
*McKissic, William Dwight, Sr.
    1990   *Beyond Roots.* Wenonah, N.J.: Renaissance Productions.

McKissic, William Dwight, Sr.,
    and Anthony T. Evans
    1994   *Beyond Roots II: If Anybody Ask You Who I Am—A Deeper Look at Blacks in
                            the Bible.* Wenonah, N.J.: Renaissance Productions.

Meeks, Wayne A.
    1983   *The First Urban Christians: The Social World of the Apostle Paul.* New
                            Haven, Conn.: Yale University Press.

Meier, John P.
    1991-1994   *A Marginal Jew: Rethinking the Historical Jesus.* 3 vols. Anchor Bible
                            Reference Library. New York: Doubleday.

*Mekouria, Tekle Tsadik
    1981   "Christian Aksum." In *Ancient Civilizations of Africa,* pp. 401-22. Vol. 2 of
                            General History of Africa. Edited by G. Mokhtar. UNESCO International
                            Scientific Committee for the Drafting of a General History of Africa. Berkeley:
                            University of California Press; London: Heinemann Educational Books; Paris:
                            United Nations Educational, Scientific and Cultural Organization.

    1988   "The Horn of Africa." In *Africa from the Seventh to the Eleventh Century,* pp.
                            558-74. Vol. 3 of *General History of Africa.* Edited by M. El Fasi with I. Hrbek.
                            UNESCO International Scientific Committee for the Drafting of a General
                            History of Africa. Berkeley: University of California Press; London: Heine-
                            mann Educational Books; Paris: United Nations Educational, Scientific and
                            Cultural Organization.

Mendelsohn, I.
    1946   "Slavery in the Ancient Near East." *Biblical Archaeologist* 9, no. 3 (Septem-
                            ber): 74-88.

Mendenhall, George E.
    1954   "Covenant Forms in Israelite Traditions." *Biblical Archaeologist* 17, no. 3
                            (September): 50-76.

Mernissi, Fatima
    1987   *Male-Female Dynamics in Modern Muslim Society.* Rev. ed. Bloomington:
                            Indiana University Press.

Metzger, Bruce M.
    1955   "Considerations of Methodology in the Study of the Mystery Religions and
                            Early Christianity." *Harvard Theological Review* 48:1-20.

    1968   *The Text of the New Testament: Its Transmission, Corruption and Restoration.*
                            2nd ed. New York: Oxford University Press.

Meyers, Eric M., and
    James F. Strange
    1981   *Archaeology, the Rabbis and Early Christianity.* Nashville: Abingdon.

Michaels, J. Ramsey
    1965   "Apostolic Hardships and Righteous Gentiles." *Journal of Biblical Literature*
                            84:27-38.

Michalowski, Kazimierz
    n.d.   *Art of Ancient Egypt.* New York: Harry N. Abrams.

    1981   "The Spreading of Christianity in Nubia." In *Ancient Civilizations of Africa,* pp.

326-40. Vol. 2 of *General History of Africa.* Edited by G. Mokhtar. UNESCO International Scientific Committee for the Drafting of a General History of Africa. Berkeley: University of California Press; London: Heinemann Educational Books; Paris: United Nations Educational, Scientific and Cultural Organization.

Mickelsen, A. Berkeley
1963   *Interpreting the Bible.* Grand Rapids, Mich.: Eerdmans.

Millard, Alan R.
1980   "Methods of Studying the Patriarchal Narratives as Ancient Texts." In *Essays on the Patriarchal Narratives,* pp. 43-58. Edited by A. R. Millard and D. J. Wiseman. Leicester, U.K.: Inter-Varsity Press.

1992   "Ebla and the Bible: What's Left (If Anything)?" *Bible Review* 8, no. 2: 18-31, 60, 62.

Miller, J. Maxwell, and
John H. Hayes
1986   *A History of Ancient Israel and Judah.* Philadelphia: Westminster Press.

Milligan, George
1908   *St. Paul's Epistles to the Thessalonians: The Greek Text with Introduction and Notes.* London: Macmillan.

Milson, David
1986   "The Design of the Royal Gates at Megiddo, Hazor and Gezer." *Zeitschrift des deutschen Palästina-Vereins* 102:87-92.

1988   "The Design of the Early Bronze Age Temples at Megiddo." *Bulletin of the American Schools of Oriental Research* 272:75-78.

Molyneux, Maxine
1985   "Legal Reform and Socialist Revolution in Democratic Yemen: Women and the Family." *International Journal of the Sociology of Law* 13, no. 2 (May): 147-72.

Mommsen, Theodor
1886   *The Provinces of the Roman Empire.* London: Bentley.

Monès, H.
1988   "The Conquest of North Africa and the Berber Resistance." In *Africa from the Seventh to the Eleventh Century,* pp. 224-45. Vol. 3 of *General History of Africa.* Edited by M. El Fasi with I. Hrbek. UNESCO International Scientific Committee for the Drafting of a General History of Africa. Berkeley: University of California Press; London: Heinemann Educational Books; Paris: United Nations Educational, Scientific and Cultural Organization.

Montefiore, C. G.
1979   "The Spirit of Judaism." In *The Beginnings of Christianity,* 1:35-81. Edited by F. J. Foakes Jackson and Kirsopp Lake. Grand Rapids, Mich.: Baker Book House.

Montet, Pierre
1968   *Egypt and the Bible.* Translated by Leslie R. Keylock. Philadelphia: Fortress.

Moran, William L.
1969   "New Evidence from Mari on the History of Prophecy." *Biblica* 50:15-56.

Morgenstern, Julian
1942-1943   "The Ark, the Ephod and the 'Tent of Meeting.'" *Hebrew Union College Annual* 17:153-265.

Morony, M. G.
1982   "Conquerors and Conquered: Iran." In *Studies on the First Century of Islamic Society,* pp. 73-87. Edited by G. H. A. Juynboll. Papers on Islamic History 5. Carbondale: Southern Illinois University Press.

Morrow, William
1994   "A Generic Discrepancy in the Covenant Code." In *Theory and Method in Biblical and Cuneiform Law: Revision, Interpolation and Development,* pp. 136-51. Edited by Bernard M. Levinson. *Journal for the Study of the Old Testament* Supplement 181. Sheffield, U.K.: Sheffield Academic Press.

Morton, A. Q., and G. H. C.
 MacGregor
1964   *The Structure of Luke and Acts.* New York: Harper & Row.

Mosley, A. W.
1965   "Historical Reporting in the Ancient World." *New Testament Studies* 12:10-26.

Moule, C. F. D.
1974   "An Unsolved Problem in the Temptation-Clause in the Lord's Prayer." *The Reformed Theological Review* 33:65-75.

Moyer, James Carroll
1969   "The Concept of Ritual Purity Among the Hittites." Ph.D. dissertation, Brandeis University.

1983   "Hittite and Israelite Cultic Practices: A Selected Comparison." Chap. 2 of *Scripture in Context II: More Essays on the Comparative Method.* Edited by William W. Hallo et al. Winona Lake, Ind.: Eisenbrauns.

Muhammad, Elijah
1992   *Message to the Blackman in America.* Newport News, Va.: United Brothers Communications Systems. (Based on the 3rd printing from the original copyright by Elijah Muhammad in 1965.)

Mukenge, Ida Rousseau
1983   *The Black Church in Urban America: A Case Study in Political Economy.* Lanham, Md.: University Press of America.

Munck, Johannes
1967a   *The Acts of the Apostles.* Revised by William F. Albright and C. S. Mann. Anchor Bible. Garden City, N.Y.: Doubleday.

1967b   *Christ and Israel: An Interpretation of Romans 9—11.* Philadelphia: Fortress.

Murnane, William J.
1975   "The Earlier Reign of Ramesses II and His Coregency With Sety I." *Journal of Near Eastern Studies* 34, no. 3 (July): 153-90.

Murray, Margaret A.
n.d.   *Egyptian Temples.* London: Sampson Law, Marston.

1963   *The Splendor That Was Egypt.* New York: Hawthorn.

Nadal, S. F.
1950   "Dual Descent in the Nuba Hills." In *African Systems of Kinship and Marriage,* pp. 333-59. Edited by A. R. Radcliffe-Brown and Daryll Forde. New York: Oxford University Press.

Nanan, Madame
1994   "The Sorcerer and Pagan Practices." In *Our Time Has Come: African Christian Women Address the Issues of Today,* pp. 81-87. Edited by Judy Mbugua. Grand Rapids, Mich.: Baker Book House; Carlisle, U.K.: Paternoster/World Evan-

gelical Fellowship.

Nash, Ronald
1994   *Is Jesus the Only Savior?* Grand Rapids, Mich.: Zondervan.

Nasr, Seyyed Hossein
1994   *Ideals and Realities of Islam.* Rev. ed. San Francisco: Aquarian/HarperCollins.
Nasrin, Taslima
1995   "Bengali Women: Tongues United." *World Press Review,* June, p. 48. (From
                       New Stateman and Society, February 17, 1995.)

Neill, Stephen
1964   *A History of Christian Missions.* Baltimore: Penguin.

Nelson, Harold H.
1961   "The Egyptian Temple." In *The Biblical Archaeologist Reader,* pp. 147-58.
                       Edited by G. Ernest Wright and David Noel Freedman. Chicago: Quadrangle.

Netland, Harold
1991   *Dissonant Voices: Religious Pluralism and the Question of Truth.* Grand
                       Rapids, Mich.: Eerdmans.

Neusner, Jacob
1984   *Judaism in the Beginning of Christianity.* Philadelphia: Fortress.

Nevo, Yehuda D., and
  Judith Koren
1990   "The Origins of the Muslim Descriptions of the Jahili Meccan Sanctuary."
                       Journal of Near Eastern Studies 49:23-44.

Newsweek
1992   October 12, p. 49.

Niccacci, Alviero
1987   "Yahweh e il Faraone: Teologia biblica ed egiziana a confronto." *Biblis-
                       cheNotizen* 38/39:85-102. (Summarized in *Old Testament Abstracts* 12:50-
                       51.)

Nicholson, E. W.
1988   "P as an Originally Independent Source in the Pentateuch." *Irish Biblical
                       Studies* 10:192-206.

1989   "The Pentateuch in Recent Research: A Time for Caution." In *Congress-
                       Volume: Leuven, 1989,* pp. 10-21. Edited by J. A. Emerton. *Vetus Testamentum*
                       Supplement 43. Leiden, Netherlands: E. J. Brill.

Nicol, George G.
1992   "Story-Patterning in Genesis." In *Text and Pretext: Essays in Honour of Robert
                       Davidson,* pp. 215-33. Edited by Robert P. Carroll. *Journal for the Study of
                       the Old Testament* Supplement 138. Sheffield, U.K.: JSOT PRESS.

Nilsson, Martin Persson
1948   *Greek Piety.* Translated by Herbert Jennings Rose. Oxford: Clarendon.

1951   *Cults, Myths, Oracles and Politics in Ancient Greece.* Skrifter Utgivna av
                       Svenska Institutet I Athen 8, no. 1. Lund, Sweden: C. W. K. Gleerup.

Nock, Arthur Darby
1933   "The Vocabulary of the New Testament." *Journal of Biblical Literature*
                       52:131-39.

1964   *Early Gentile Christianity and Its Hellenistic Background.* New York: Harper
                       & Row.

*Noll, Mark A.
1992   *A History of Christianity in the United States and Canada.* Grand Rapids,
                       Mich.: Eerdmans.
Noth, Martin
1960   *The History of Israel.* 2nd ed. New York: Harper & Row.

Nukunya, G. K.
1969   *Kinship and Marriage Among the Anlo Ewe.* London School of Economics
                       Monographs on Social Anthropology 37. New York: Humanities.
Ogot, Bethwell
1993   "The Muslim Trade." *World Press Review,* August, p. 23. (From *Daily Nation*
                       [Nairobi].)
"Oldest Hebrew Letters
  Found Near Tel Aviv"
1976   *Biblical Archaeology Review* 2, no. 4 (December): 6.

Oliver, Roland
1961   "The Riddle of Zimbabwe." In *The Dawn of African History,* pp. 53-59. Edited
                       by Roland Oliver. London: Oxford University Press.
Oliver, Roland, and J. D. Fage
1989   *A Short History of Africa.* New York: Facts on File.

Olmstead, A. T.
1959   *History of the Persian Empire.* Chicago: University of Chicago Press/Phoenix.

Oppenheim, A. Leo
1961   "The Mesopotamian Temple." In *The Biblical Archaeologist Reader,* pp.
                       158-69. Edited by G. Ernest Wright and David Noel Freedman. Chicago:
                       Quadrangle.
O'Reilly, Kenneth
1989   *"Racial Matters": The FBI's Secret File on Black America, 1960-1972.* New
                       York: Free Press/Macmillan.
O'Rourke, John J.
1961   "Romans 1,20 and Natural Revelation." *Catholic Biblical Quarterly* 23, no.
                       3 (July): 301-6.
Ott, Heinrich
1959   "Röm. 1,19ff. als dogmatisches Problem." *Theologische Zeitschrift* 15, no. 1
                       (January): 40-50.
Otto, Eckart
1987   "Rechtssystematik im altbabylonischen 'Codex Esnunna' und im altisraelitis-
                       chen 'Bundesbuch': Eine redaktionsgeschichtliche und rechtsvergleichende
                       Analyse von CE §§17; 18; 22-28 und Ex 21,18-32; 22,6-14; 23,1-3.6-8."
                       Ugarit-Forschungen 19:175-97.

1993   "Town and Rural Countryside in Ancient Israelite Law: Reception and Redac-
                       tion in Cuneiform and Israelite Law." *Journal for the Study of the Old
                       Testament* 57:3-22.

1994   "Aspects of Legal Reforms and Reformulations in Ancient Cuneiform and
                       Israelite Law." In *Theory and Method in Biblical and Cuneiform Law:
                       Revision, Interpolation and Development,* pp. 160-96. Edited by Bernard
                       M. Levinson. *Journal for the Study of the Old Testament* Supplement 181.
                       Sheffield, U.K.: Sheffield Academic Press.
Otto, Walter F.
1965   *Dionysus: Myth and Cult.* Translated by Robert B. Palmer. Bloomington:

Indiana University Press.

Owens, J. Garfield
1971   *All God's Chillun: Meditations on Negro Spirituals.* Nashville: Abingdon.

Palmer, Darryl W.
1993   "Acts and the Ancient Historical Monograph." In *The Book of Acts in its Ancient Literary Setting,* pp. 1-29. Edited by Bruce W. Winter and Andrew D. Clarke. Vol. 1 of *The Book of Acts in Its First-Century Setting.* Grand Rapids, Mich.: Eerdmans; Carlisle, U.K.: Paternoster.

**Pankhurst, Richard K. Y., ed.
1967   *The Ethiopian Royal Chronicles.* Addis Ababa: Oxford University Press.

Pannell, William
1993   *The Coming Race Wars? A Cry for Reconciliation.* Grand Rapids, Mich.: Zondervan.

Papanek, Hanna
1973   "Purdah: Separate Worlds and Symbolic Shelter." *Comparative Studies in Society and History* 15, no. 3 (June): 289-325.

Parrinder, Geoffrey
1980   *Sex in the World's Religions.* New York: Oxford University Press.

Parrot, André
1967   "Mari." In *Archaeology and Old Testament Study,* pp. 136-44. Edited by D. Winton Thomas. Oxford: Clarendon.

Pastner, Carroll McC.
1978   "Englishmen in Arabia: Encounters with Middle Eastern Women." *Signs* 4, no. 2 (Winter): 309-23.

Paul, Shalom M.
1971   "Prophets and Prophecy (in the Bible)." In *Encyclopaedia Judaica,* 13:1160-64. 16 vols. Jerusalem: Keter.

Payne, Bishop Daniel
Alexander
1969   *Recollections of Seventy Years.* Reprint ed. New York: Arno/New York Times.

Pelt, Owen D., and Ralph
Lee Smith
1960   *The Story of the National Baptists.* New York: Vantage.

Perkins, John
1976   *Let Justice Roll Down.* Ventura, Calif.: Regal.

1982   *With Justice for All.* Ventura, Calif.: Regal.

*Perkins, Spencer, and
Chris Rice
1993   *More Than Equals: Racial Healing for the Sake of the Gospel.* Downers Grove, Ill.: InterVarsity Press.

Perlitt, Lothar
1988   "Priesterschrift im Deuteronomium?" *Zeitschrift für die Alttestamentliche Wissenschaft* 100 (Supplement): 65-88.

Peters, F. E.
1994   *Muhammad and the Origins of Islam.* Albany: State University of New York Press.

Peterson, Thomas Virgil
1978   *Ham and Japheth: The Mythic World of Whites in the Antebellum South.*

262

American Theological Library Association Monograph 12. Metuchen, N.J.: Scarecrow/American Theological Library Association.

Petrie, W. M. Flinders
1910   *Arts and Crafts of Ancient Egypt.* New York: Attic.

Pettinato, Giovanni
1981   *The Archives of Ebla: An Empire Inscribed in Clay.* Garden City, N.Y.: Doubleday.

Pfeiffer, Charles F., ed.
1962   *Ras Shamra and the Bible.* Grand Rapids, Mich.: Baker Book House.
1966   *The Biblical World: A Dictionary of Biblical Archaeology.* Grand Rapids, Mich.: Baker Book House.

Pickthall, Mohammed
Marmaduke
n.d.   *The Meaning of the Glorious Koran: An Explanatory Translation.* New York: Mentor/New American Library.

Pierard, Richard V.
1976   "Social Concern in Christian Missions." *Christianity Today,* June 18, pp. 7-10.

Pierce, Larry
1993   "Where There's Faith, There's Hope for Boys." *Christianity Today,* September 13, p. 80.

Pilch, John J.
1991   "Sickness and Healing in Luke-Acts." In *The Social World of Luke-Acts: Models for Interpretation,* pp. 181-209. Edited by Jerome H. Neyrey. Peabody, Mass.: Hendrickson.

*Pobee, John S.
1979   *Toward an African Theology.* Nashville: Abingdon.

Pomeroy, Sarah B.
1975   *Goddesses, Whores, Wives and Slaves: Women in Classical Antiquity.* New York: Schocken.

Pope, Marvin H.
1987   "The Status of El at Ugarit." *Ugarit-Forschungen* 19:219-30.

Porter, Les
1994   "Will Your Church Become a Mosque?" *Reach Out* 7, nos. 3-4: 6-7.

Portnoy, Stephen L., and
David L. Petersen
1984   " 'Genesis, Wellhausen and the Computer': A Response." *Zeitschrift für die Alttestamentliche Wissenschaft* 96:421-25.

1991   "Statistical Differences Among Documentary Sources: Comments on 'Genesis: An Authorship Study.' " *Journal for the Study of the Old Testament* 50:3-14.

Pury, A. de, and T. Römer
1989   "Le Pentateuque en question." In *Le Pentateuque en question,* pp. 9-80. 2nd ed. Edited by A. de Pury. Le Monde de la Bible. Geneva: Labor et Fides.

Pyne, Robert A.
1994   Review of *Paul, Women and Wives. Bibliotheca Sacra* 151, no. 602 (April): 259.

Quarles, Benjamin, ed.
1968   *Frederick Douglass.* Great Lives Observed. Englewood Cliffs, N.J.: Prentice-Hall.

Rabe, Virgil W.
1976   "Origins of Prophecy." *Bulletin of the American Schools of Oriental Research* 221 (February): 125-28.

Rabin, C.
1968   "*L*- with Imperative (Gen. XXIII)." *Journal of Semitic Studies* 13:113-24.

**Raboteau, Albert J.
1978   *Slave Religion: The "Invisible Institution" in the Antebellum South.* New York: Oxford University Press.

Radcliffe-Brown, A. R.
1950   Introduction to *African Systems of Kinship and Marriage,* pp. 1-85. Edited by A. R. Radcliffe-Brown and Daryll Forde. New York: Oxford University Press.

Radday, Yehuda T., et al.
1982   "Genesis, Wellhausen and the Computer." *Zeitschrift für die Alttestamentliche Wissenschaft* 94:467-81.

Radday, Yehuda T., and
Haim Shore et al.
1985   *Genesis: An Authorship Study in Computer-Assisted Statistical Linguistics.* Rome: Biblical Institute Press.

Rainey, Anson F.
1965a   "The Kingdom of Ugarit." *Biblical Archaeologist* 28:102-25.

1965b   "The Military Personnel of Ugarit." *Journal of Near Eastern Studies* 24, no. 1 (January 1965): 17-27.

Ramsey, George W.
1977   "Speech-Forms in Hebrew Law and Prophetic Oracles." *Journal of Biblical Literature* 96:45-58.

Rankin, John
1838   *Letters on American Slavery Addressed to Mr. Thomas Rankin.* 5th ed. Boston: Isaac Knapp. (Reprint from copy in New York State Library: New York: Arno/New York Times, 1969.)

Rashad, Adib (James Miller)
1991   *The History of Islam and Black Nationalism in the Americas.* 2nd ed. Beltsville, Md.: Writers'.

Reach Out
1993   6, no. 1-2 (Spring), whole issue.

Redford, Donald B.
1970   *A Study of the Biblical Story of Joseph. Vetus Testamentum* Supplements 20. Leiden, Netherlands: E. J. Brill.

1992   *Egypt, Canaan and Israel in Ancient Times.* Princeton, N.J.: Princeton University Press.

Reitzenstein, Richard
1978   *Hellenistic Mystery-Religions: Their Basic Ideas and Significance.* Translated by John E. Steely. Pittsburgh Theological Monographs Series 15. Pittsburgh, Penn.: Pickwick.

Remus, H. E.
1984   "Authority, Consent, Law: *Nomos, Physis* and the Striving for a 'Given.' " *Studies in Religion/Sciences Religieuses* 13, no. 1: 5-18.

Rendsburg, Gary A.
1986   *The Redaction of Genesis.* Winona Lake, Ind.: Eisenbrauns.

1988   "The Egyptian Sun-God Ra in the Pentateuch." *Henoch* 10:3-15.

Rendtorff, Rolf
1990   *The Problem of the Process of Transmission in the Pentateuch.* Translated by John J. Scullion. *Journal for the Study of the Old Testament* Supplement 89. Sheffield, U.K.: JSOT Press/Sheffield Academic Press.

Reviv, Hanoch
1977   "Early Elements and Late Terminology in the Descriptions of the Non-Israelite Cities in the Bible." *Israel Exploration Journal* 27, no. 4: 189-96.

Reynolds, H. R.
1994   "Edesius." In *A Dictionary of Christian Biography and Literature to the End of the Sixth Century* A.D., *with an Account of the Principal Sects and Heresies,* p. 287. Edited by Henry Wace and William C. Piercy. Peabody, Mass.: Hendrickson.

Rice, Gene
1979   "The African Roots of the Prophet Zephaniah." *The Journal of Religious Thought* 36:21-31.

Richard, R. L.
1967   "Trinity, Holy." In *New Catholic Encyclopedia,* 14:293-306. 17 vols. Washington, D.C.: Catholic University of America.

Richardson, Don
1974   *Peace Child.* Ventura, Calif.: Regal.

Riesner, Rainer
1982   "Education élémentaire juive et tradition évangélique." *Hokhma* 21:51-64.

*Riggs, Marcia Y.
1994   *Awake, Arise and Act: A Womanist Call for Black Liberation.* Cleveland, Ohio: Pilgrim.

Ringgren, Helmer
1947   *Word and Wisdom: Studies in the Hypostatization of Divine Qualities and Functions in the Ancient Near East.* Lund, Sweden: Häkan Ohlssons Boktryckeri.

Roberts, J. Deotis
1974   *A Black Political Theology.* Philadelphia: Westminster Press.

1994   *The Prophethood of Black Believers: An African-American Political Theology for Ministry.* Louisville, Ky.: Westminster John Knox.

Roberts, R. L.
1973   "The Rendering 'Only Begotten' in John 3:16." *Restoration Quarterly* 16, no. 1: 2-22.

Robertson, Alexander, and
James Donaldson, eds.
1994   *Ante-Nicene Fathers: The Writings of the Fathers Down to* A.D. *325.* Revised by A. Cleveland Coxe. Peabody, Mass.: Hendrickson.

Robinson, Freddie
1993   *Errors in the Bible Revealed.* N.p.: Lee T. Robinson/Transfiguration Production.

Robinson, John A. T.
1962   *Twelve New Testament Studies.* Studies in Biblical Theology 34. London: SCM Press.

1977   *Can We Trust the New Testament?* Grand Rapids, Mich.: Eerdmans.

Ross, Fred A.
1857   *Slavery Ordained of God.* N.p.: J. B. Lippincott. (Reprint from copy in Fisk University Library Negro Collection: Miami: Mnemosyne, 1969.)

Ross, J. F.
1970
"Prophecy in Hamath, Israel and Mari." *Harvard Theological Review* 63:1-28.

Rossano, P.
1958
"Note arccheologiche sulla antica Tessalonica." *Rivista Biblica* 6, no. 3: 242-47.

Rowe, A.
1962
"The Famous Solar-City of On." *Palestine Exploration Quarterly* 94:133-42.

Ruchames, Louis
1964
The Abolitionists: A Collection of Their Writings. New York: Capricorn.

Safrai, S.
1976-1978a
"Education and the Study of the Torah." In *The Jewish People In the First Century: Historical Geography, Political History, Social, Cultural and Religious Life and Institutions,* pp. 945-70. Edited by S. Safrai and M. Stern with D. Flusser and W. C. van Unnik. 2 vols. Vol. 1: Assen, Netherlands: Van Gorcum, 1974. Vol. 2: Philadelphia: Fortress, 1976.

1974-1976b
"Home and Family." In *The Jewish People in the First Century: Historical Geography, Political History, Social, Cultural and Religious Life and Institutions,* pp. 728-92. Edited by S. Safrai and M. Stern with D. Flusser and W. C. van Unnik. 2 vols. Vol. 1: Assen, Netherlands: Van Gorcum, 1974. Vol. 2: Philadelphia: Fortress, 1976.

Sailhamer, John H.
1992
The Pentateuch as Narrative. Grand Rapids, Mich.: Zondervan.

Salama, P.
1981
"From Rome to Islam." In *Ancient Civilizations of Africa,* pp. 499-510. Vol. 2 of *General History of Africa.* Edited by G. Mokhtar. UNESCO International Scientific Committee for the Drafting of a General History of Africa. Berkeley: University of California Press; London: Heinemann Educational Books; Paris: United Nations Educational, Scientific and Cultural Organization.

Sanders, Cheryl Jeanne
1987
"Slavery and Conversion: An Analysis of Ex-Slave Testimony." Ann Arbor, Mich.: University Microfilms International. (Th.D. dissertation, Harvard University, 1985.)

*1995a
"Afrocentric and Womanist Approaches to Theological Education." In *Living the Intersection: Womanism and Afrocentrism in Theology,* pp. 157-75. Minneapolis: Fortress.

*1995b
"Black Women in Biblical Perspective: Resistance, Affirmation and Empowerment." In *Living the Intersection: Womanism and Afrocentrism in Theology,* pp. 121-43. Minneapolis: Fortress.

*1995c
Empowerment Ethics for a Liberated People: A Path to African American Social Transformation. Minneapolis: Fortress.

Sanders, E. P.
1977
Paul and Palestinian Judaism. Philadelphia: Fortress.

1993
The Historical Figure of Jesus. New York: Penguin.

Sandmel, Samuel
1978
Judaism and Christian Beginnings. New York: Oxford University Press.

*Sanneh, Lamin
1983   *West African Christianity: The Religious Impact.* Maryknoll, N.Y.: Orbis.

Sarna, Nahum M.
*1970   *Understanding Genesis.* New York: Schocken.

1977   "Abraham in History." *Biblical Archaeology Review* 4, no. 4 (November): 5-9.

*1986   *Exploring Exodus: The Heritage of Biblical Israel.* New York: Schocken.

Sasson, Jack M.
1966   "Circumcision in the Ancient Near East." *Journal of Biblical Literature* 85, no. 4 (December): 473-76.

"Saudi Arabia—Religious Intolerance"
1993   "Saudi Arabia—Religious Intolerance: The Arrest, Detention and Torture of Christian Worshippers and Shi'a Muslims." New York: Amnesty International, September 14.

Sauer, James A.
1986   "Transjordan in the Bronze and Iron Ages: A Critique of Glueck's Synthesis." *Bulletin of the American Schools of Oriental Research* 263:1-26.

Savage, W. Sherman
1938   *The Controversy over the Distribution of Abolition Literature, 1830-1860.* N.p.: Association for the Study of Negro Life and History.

Sawyer, George S.
1858   *Southern Institutes: Or, An Inquiry into the Origin and Early Prevalence of Slavery and the Slave-Trade, with an Analysis of the Laws, History and Government of the Institution in the Principal Nations, Ancient and Modern, from the Earliest Ages Down to the Present Time, with Notes and Comments in Defence of the Southern Institutions.* Philadelphia: J. B. Lippincott. (Reprint from copy in Fisk University Library Negro Collection: Miami: Mnemosyne, 1969.)

Schapera, Isaac
1950   "Kinship and Marriage Among the Tswana." In *African Systems of Kinship and Marriage,* pp. 140-65. Edited by A. R. Radcliffe-Brown and Daryll Forde. New York: Oxford University Press.

1966   *Married Life in an African Tribe.* Evanston, Ill.: Northwestern University Press.

Schedl, Claus
1973   *History of the Old Testament.* 5 vols. Staten Island, N.Y.: Alba House.

Scherer, Lester B.
1975   *Slavery and the Churches in Early America, 1619-1819.* Grand Rapids, Mich.: Eerdmans.

Schmidt, K. E.
1964   "Folk Psychiatry in Sarawak: A Tentative System of Psychiatry of the Iban." In *Magic, Faith and Healing: Studies in Primitive Psychotherapy Today,* pp. 139-55. Edited by Ari Kiev. New York: Free Press/Macmillan.

Schmidt, Ludwig
1988   "Jacob erschleicht sich den väterlichen Segen: Literarkritik und Redaktion von Genesis 27,1-45." *Zeitschrift für die Alttestamentliche Wissenschaft* 100:159-83.

Schmitt, Hans-Christoph
1985   "Die Hintergrunde der 'Neuesten Pentateuchkritik' und der Literarische Be-

fund der Josefsgeschichte Gen 37-50." *Zeitschrift für die Alttestamentliche Wissenschaft* 97:161-79.

Schofield, J. N.
1967   "Megiddo." In *Archaeology and Old Testament Study,* pp. 309-28. Edited by D. Winton Thomas. Oxford: Clarendon.

Scholem, Gershom
1973   *Sabbatai Sevi: The Mystical Messiah.* Princeton, N.J.: Princeton University Press.

"A School for Iqbal"
1995   *Amnesty Action,* Summer, pp. 5, 10.

Schultz, Joseph P.
1975   "Two Views of the Patriarchs: Noahides and Pre-Sinai Israelites." In *Texts and Responses: Studies Presented to Nahum N. Glatzner on the Occasion of His Seventieth Birthday by His Students,* pp. 43-59. Edited by Michael A. Fishbane and Paul R. Flohr. Leiden, Netherlands: E. J. Brill.

Schulz, Siegfried
1958   "Die Anklage in Röm. 1,18-32." *Theologische Zeitschrift* 14, no. 3 (May): 161-73.

Schweizer, Eduard
1975   *The Good News According to Matthew.* Translated by David E. Green. Atlanta: John Knox.

Scott, James M.
1994   "Luke's Geographical Horizon." In *Graeco-Roman Setting,* pp. 483-544. Vol. 2 of *The Book of Acts in Its First Century Setting.* Edited by David W. J. Gill and Conrad Gempf. Grand Rapids, Mich.: Eerdmans; Carlisle, U.K.: Paternoster.

Scott, John Atwood
1978   "The Pattern of the Tabernacle." Ann Arbor, Mich.: University Microfilms International. (Ph.D. dissertation, University of Pennsylvania, 1965.)

Scott, R. B. Y.
1954   *The Relevance of the Prophets.* New York: Macmillan.

Seabury, Rev. Samuel
1861   *American Slavery Distinguished from the Slavery of the English Theorists and Justified by the Law of Nature.* New York: Mason Brothers. (Reprint from copy in Fisk University Library Negro Collection: Miami: Mnemosyne, 1969.)

Selman, M. J.
1976   "The Social Environment of the Patriarchs." *Tyndale Bulletin* 27:114-36.

1977   "Comparative Methods and the Patriarchal Narratives." *Themelios* 3, no. 1: 9-16.

1980   "Comparative Customs and the Patriarchal Age." In *Essays on the Patriarchal Narratives,* pp. 93-138. Edited by A. R. Millard and D. J. Wiseman. Leicester, U.K.: Inter-Varsity Press.

*Sernett, Milton C.
1975   *Black Religion and American Evangelicalism: White Protestants, Plantation Missions and the Flowering of Negro Christianity, 1787-1865.* American Theological Library Association Monograph 7. Metuchen, N.J.: Scarecrow/American Theological Library Association.

Sernett, Milton C., ed.
1985   *Afro-American History: A Documentary Witness.* Durham, N.C.: Duke University Press.

Sevenster, J. N.
1961   *Paul and Seneca. Novum Testamentum* Supplements 4. Leiden, Netherlands:
                        E. J. Brill.

Shaaban, Bouthaina
1991   *Both Right and Left Handed: Arab Women Talk About Their Lives.* Bloom-
                        ington: Indiana University Press.

Shahid, Samuel
1992   " 'Rights' of Non-Muslims in an Islamic State." *Reach Out* 5, nos. 3-4 (April):
                        5-11.

Shanks, Herschel
1983   *"BAR* Interviews Yigael Yadin." *Biblical Archaeology Review* 9, no. 1 (Janu-
                        ary): 16-23.

Shapiro, Laura, with Daniel
  Pedersen and Marcus Mabry
1993   "The Fundamentals of Freedom." *Newsweek,* November 15, p. 87.

Sider, Ronald J.
1993   *One-Sided Christianity? Uniting the Church to Heal a Lost and Broken World.*
                        Grand Rapids, Mich.: Zondervan.

Sikes, Walter W.
1941   "The Anti-Semitism of the Fourth Gospel." *Journal of Religion* 21, no. 1
                        (January): 23-30.

Singer, Suzanne
1978   "From These Hills . . ." *Biblical Archaeology Review* 4, no. 2 (June): 16-25.

Skinner, Tom
1970   *Words of Revolution.* Grand Rapids, Mich.: Zondervan.

Slager, Donald J.
1992   "The Use of Divine Names in Genesis." *Bible Translator* 43:423-29.

Smillie, Gene R.
1995   "Adaptors to Foreign Cultures." *Mission Today* 95:4-5.

Smith, Edward D.
1988   *Climbing Jacob's Ladder: The Rise of Black Churches in Eastern American
                        Cities, 1740-1877.* Washington, D.C.: Smithsonian Institution.

Smith, H. Shelton
1972   *In His Image, But . . . : Racism in Southern Religion, 1780-1910.* Durham,
                        N.C.: Duke University Press.

Smith, Timothy L.
1980   *Revivalism and Social Reform: American Protestantism on the Eve of the Civil
                        War.* Baltimore: Johns Hopkins University Press.

Smith, William A.
1955   *Ancient Education.* New York: Philosophical Library.

Snowden, Frank M., Jr.
1970   *Blacks in Antiquity: Ethiopians in the Greco-Roman Experience.* Cambridge,
                        Mass.: Belknap/Harvard University Press.

**1983   *Before Color Prejudice: The Ancient View of Blacks.* Cambridge, Mass.:
                        Harvard University Press.

Soares Prabhu, George M.
1976   *The Formula Quotations in the Infancy Narrative of Matthew: An Enquiry
                        into the Tradition History of Matthew 1—2.* Rome: Biblical Institute Press.

Soggins, Alberto
 1980   *Introduction to the Old Testament from Its Origins to the Closing of the Alexandrian Canon.* Rev. ed. Translated by John Bowden. Philadelphia: Westminster Press.

Spalinger, Anthony
 1979   "Traces of the Early Career of Ramesses II." *Journal of Near Eastern Studies* 38, no. 4 (October): 271-86.

Sparks, Jack
 1979   *The Mind Benders: A Look at Current Cults.* 2nd ed. Nashville: Thomas Nelson.

Speight, R. Marston
 1989   *God Is One: The Way of Islam.* New York: Friendship.

Speiser, E. A.
 1970   "The Patriarchs and Their Social Background." In *Patriarchs,* pp. 160-68. Edited by Benjamin Mazar. Vol. 2 of *The World History of the Jewish People.* New Brunswick, N.J.: Rutgers University Press.

Spence, Jonathan D.
 1985   *The Memory Palace of Matteo Ricci.* Baltimore: Penguin.

Spieckermann, Hermann
 1992   "Stadtgott und Gottesstadt: Beobachtungen im Alten Orient und im Alten Testament." *Biblica* 73:1-31.

Stampp, Kenneth M.
 1978   *The Peculiar Institution: Slavery in the Ante-bellum South.* New York: Alfred A. Knopf.

Stanton, Graham N.
 1974   *Jesus of Nazareth in New Testament Preaching.* Cambridge: Cambridge University Press.

 1995   *Gospel Truth? New Light on Jesus and the Gospels.* Valley Forge, Penn.: Trinity Press International.

Steck, Odil Hannes
 1991   "Aufbauprobleme in der Priesterschrift." In *Ernten was man sät: Festschrift für Klaus Koch zu seinem 65 Geburstag,* pp. 287-308. Edited by Dwight R. Daniels et al. Neukirchen-Vluyn, Germany: Neukirchener.

Steindorff, G., and K. C. Seele
 1963   *When Egypt Ruled the East.* Chicago: University of Chicago Press.

Stephens, William N.
 1963   *The Family in Cross-Cultural Perspective.* New York: Holt, Rinehart & Winston.

*Sterling, Dorothy
 1984   *We Are Your Sisters: Black Women in the Nineteenth Century.* New York: W. W. Norton.

Stern, Ephraim
 1977   "A Late Bronze Temple at Tell Mevorakh." *Biblical Archaeologist* 40 (May): 89-91.

Stewart, Desmond
 1971   *The Pyramids and Sphinx.* New York: Newsweek.

Stiebing, William H., Jr.
 1988   "New Archaeological Dates for the Israelite Conquest: Part II. Proposals for an MB IIC Conquest." *Catastrophism and Ancient History* 10:61-71.

Stieglitz, Robert R.
1987   "Ancient Records and the Exodus Plagues." *Biblical Archaeology Review* 13, no. 6: 46-49.

Stone, Garry R.
1991   "The Camels of Abraham [pt. I]." *Buried History* 27:100-106.

1992   "The Camels of Abraham [pt. 2]." *Buried History* 28:3-14.

Stowasser, Barbara Freyer
1994   *Women in the Qur'an, Traditions and Interpretation.* New York: Oxford University Press.

Stowers, Stanley K.
1981   *The Diatribe and Paul's Letter to the Romans.* Society of Biblical Literature Dissertation Series 57. Chico, Calif.: Scholars Press/Society of Biblical Literature.

1986   *Letter Writing in Greco-Roman Antiquity.* Library of Early Christianity 5. Philadelphia: Westminster Press.

1988   "The Diatribe." In *Greco-Roman Literature and the New Testament: Selected Forms and Genres,* pp. 71-83. Edited by David E. Aune. Society of Biblical Literature Sources for Biblical Study 21. Atlanta: Scholars Press.

"Sudan"
1995   "Sudan: Caught in a Vicious Cycle of Human Rights Abuses, Poverty and Political Turmoil." *Amnesty Action,* Winter, pp. 1, 3.

"Sudan—The Ravages of War"
1993   "Sudan—The Ravages of War: Political Killings and Humanitarian Disaster." New York: Amnesty International, September 29.

*Sunderland, La Roy
1835   *The Testimony of God Against Slavery: Or, A Collection of Passages from the Bible Which Show the Sin of Holding Property in Man, with Notes.* Boston: Webster & Southard.

1837   *Anti Slavery Manual, Containing a Collection of Facts and Arguments on American Slavery.* New York: S. W. Benedict. (Reprint Detroit: Negro History Press, n.d. [P.O. Box 5129, Detroit, MI 48236]).

Sutton, Jane
1995-1996   "Child Labor: Robbing God's Cradle." *World Vision,* December/January, pp. 2-7.

Tabor, James D., and
  Eugene V. Gallagher
1995   *Why Waco? Cults and the Battle for Religion Freedom in America.* Berkeley: University of California Press.

Talbert, Charles H.
1974   *Literary Patterns, Theological Themes and the Genre of Luke-Acts.* Society of Biblical Literature Monograph Series 20. Missoula, Mont.: Scholars Press.

1977   *What Is a Gospel? The Genre of the Canonical Gospels.* Philadelphia: Fortress.

Talib, Y., with F. Samir
1988   "The African Diaspora in Asia." In *Africa from the Seventh to the Eleventh Century,* pp. 704-33. Vol. 3 of *General History of Africa.* Edited by M. El Fasi with I. Hrbek. UNESCO International Scientific Committee for the Drafting of a General History of Africa. Berkeley: University of California Press; London: Heinemann Educational Books; Paris: United Nations Educational,

Scientific and Cultural Organization.

*Tappan, Lewis
1854   "Disfellowshipping the Slaveholder." In *Autographs for Freedom*, 2:163-64. Edited by Julia Griffiths. Auburn, Maine: Alden, Beardsley; Rochester, N.Y.: Wanzer, Beardsley.

Tarrants, Tom
1992   "The Conversion of a Klansman." *Urban Family,* Spring, pp. 22-23.

*Taylor, John H.
1991   *Egypt and Nubia.* Cambridge, Mass.: Harvard University Press/Trustees of the British Museum.

Thalmann, Jean-Paul
1989   "Les temples de l'Age du Bronze." *Le Monde de la Bible* 59 (May): 16-19.

Theissen, Gerd
1991   *The Gospels in Context: Social and Political History in the Synoptic Tradition.* Translated by Linda M. Maloney. Minneapolis: Fortress.

Thompson, J. Alexander
1962   *The Bible and Archaeology.* Grand Rapids, Mich.: Eerdmans.

1975   "Incense." In *Zondervan Pictorial Encyclopedia of the Bible*, 3:274-76. Edited by Merrill C. Tenney. 5 vols. Grand Rapids, Mich.: Zondervan.

Thompson, T. L.
1974   *The Historicity of the Patriarchal Narratives; The Quest for the Historical Abraham.* Beihefte zur Zeitschrift für die Alttestamentliche Wissenschaft 133. Berlin: W. de Gruyter.

1977   "Historical Reconstructions of the Narratives." In *Israelite and Judaean History,* pp. 149-66. Edited by John H. Hayes and J. Maxwell Miller. Philadelphia: Westminster Press.

Thrall, Margaret E.
1967   "The Pauline Use of ΣΥΝΕΙΔΗΣΙΣ." *New Testament Studies* 14, no. 1 (October): 118-25.

Thurman, Howard
1949   *Jesus and the Disinherited.* New York: Abingdon. (Reprint Richmond, Ind.: Friends United, 1981.)

Torrey, C. C.
1916   *The Composition and Date of Acts.* Harvard Theological Studies 1. Cambridge, Mass.: Harvard University Press. (Reprint New York: Kraus Reprint, n.d.)

"Treasures from the Lands of the Bible"
1985   *Biblical Archaeology Review* 11, no. 2 (March): 26-38.

Trigger, Bruce G.
1978a   "The Ballana Culture and the Coming of Christianity." In *Africa in Antiquity 1: The Arts of Ancient Nubia and the Sudan—The Essays,* pp. 106-19. Brooklyn, N.Y.: Brooklyn Museum.

1978b   "Nubian, Negro, Black, Nilotic?" In *Africa in Antiquity 1: The Arts of Ancient Nubia and the Sudan—The Essays,* pp. 26-35. Brooklyn, N.Y.: Brooklyn Museum.

Tucker, Gene M.
1966   "The Legal Background of Genesis 23." *Journal of Biblical Literature* 85, no. 1 (March): 77-84.

Tucker, Judith E., ed.
1993   *Arab Women: Old Boundaries, New Frontiers.* Bloomington: Indiana University Press.

Tucker, Ruth A.
1983   *From Jerusalem to Irian Jaya: A Biographical History of Christian Missions.* Grand Rapids, Mich.: Zondervan.

Tuckett, Christopher M.
1988   "A Cynic Q?" *Biblica* 70:349-76.

Urbach, Ephraim E.
1979   *The Sages: Their Concepts and Beliefs.* Translated by Israel Abrahams. 2nd ed. 2 vols. Jerusalem: Magnes/Hebrew University Press.

Usry, Glenn, and
Craig S. Keener
1996   *Black Man's Religion: Can Christianity Be Afrocentric?* Downers Grove, Ill.: InterVarsity Press.

Ussishkin, D.
1977   In "Notes and News." *Israel Exploration Journal* 27, no. 1: 48-51.

Van Deburg, William S.
1975   "The Tragedy of Frederick Douglass." *Christianity Today,* January 31, pp. 7-8.

Vandermarck, William
1973   "Natural Knowledge of God in Romans: Patristic and Medieval Interpretation." *Theological Studies* 34, no. 1 (March): 36-52.

Van der Toorn, K.
1987   "L'oracle de victoire comme expression prophétique au Proche-Orient ancien." *Revue Biblique* 94:63-97.

Vandewiele, Michel
1983   "Perception of Women's Religious Status by Senegalese Adolescents." *Psychological Reports* 53:757-58.

Van Seters, John
1968   "The Problem of Childlessness in Near Eastern Law and the Patriarchs of Israel." *Journal of Biblical Literature* 87, no. 4 (December): 401-8.

1975   *Abraham in History and Tradition.* New Haven, Conn.: Yale University Press.

1983   *In Search of History: Historiography in the Ancient World and the Origins of Biblical History.* New Haven, Conn.: Yale University Press.

1988   "The Primeval Histories of Greece and Israel Compared." *Zeitschrift für die Alttestamentliche Wissenschaft* 100:1-22.

Ventura, Raphael
1988   "Bent Axis or Wrong Direction? Studies on the Temple of Serabit el-Khadim." *Israel Exploration Journal* 38:128-38, plates 23 C-D.

Vergote, Joseph
1959   *Joseph en Égypte.* Louvain: Publications Universitaires.

1985   " 'Joseph en Egypte': 25 ans après." In *Pharaonic Egypt: The Bible and Christianity,* pp. 289-306. Edited by Sarah Israelit-Groll. Jerusalem: Department of Egyptology, Hebrew University.

Vermaseren, Maarten J.
1977   *Cybele and Attis: The Myth and the Cult.* Translated by A. M. H. Lemmers. London: Thames & Hudson.

Vermes, Geza
1973   *Jesus the Jew: A Historian's Reading of the Gospels.* Philadelphia: Fortress.

Von der Mehden, Fred R.
1983   "American Perceptions of Islam." In *Voices of Resurgent Islam,* pp. 18-31.
                       Edited by John L. Esposito. New York: Oxford University Press.

Von Rad, Gerhard
1962   *Old Testament Theology.* Translated by D. M. G. Stalker. 2 vols. New York:
                       Harper & Row.

Von Wyrick, Stephen
1988   "Ancient Near East Caravans." *Biblical Illustrator* 14, no. 2: 56-58.

Vos, Geerhardus
1913   "The Range of the Logos-Title in the Prologue of the Fourth Gospel."
                       Princeton Theological Review 11:365-419, 557-602.

Wace, Henry
1994   "Tertullianus." In *A Dictionary of Christian Biography and Literature to the
                       End of the Sixth Century A.D., with an Account of the Principal Sects and
                       Heresies,* pp. 940-53. Edited by Henry Wace and William C. Piercy. Peabody,
                       Mass.: Hendrickson.

Wagner, Günter
1967   *Pauline Baptism and the Pagan Mysteries; The Problem of the Pauline
                       Doctrine of Baptism in Romans VI.1-11, in Light of Its Religio-historical
                       "Parallels."* Translated by J. P. Smith. Edinburgh: Oliver & Boyd.

Waines, David
1995   *An Introduction to Islam.* Cambridge: Cambridge University Press.

Wainwright, J. A.
1980   "Zoser's Pyramid and Solomon's Temple." *Expository Times* 91 (February):
                       137-38.

*Walker, David
1993   "David Walker's *Appeal.*" In *Witness for Freedom: African American Voices
                       on Race, Slavery and Emancipation,* pp. 42-46. Edited by C. Peter Ripley.
                       Chapel Hill: University of North Carolina Press, 1993.

Wallis, Richard T.
1974-1975   "The Idea of Conscience in Philo of Alexandria." *Studia Philonica* 3:27-40.

1975   *The Idea of Conscience in Philo of Alexandria.* Center for Hermeneutical
                       Studies in Hellenistic and Modern Culture Colloquy 13. Berkeley, Calif.:
                       Center for Hermeneutical Studies in Hellenistic and Modern Culture.

Walls, A. F.
1982   "Africa." In *New Bible Dictionary,* pp. 17-18. 2nd ed. Edited by J. D. Douglas.
                       Downers Grove, Ill.: InterVarsity Press.

Walls, William Jacob
1974   *The African Methodist Episcopal Zion Church, Reality of the Black Church.*
                       Charlotte, N.C.: A.M.E. Zion Publishing House.

Waltke, Bruce K.
1978   "The Textual Criticism of the Old Testament." In *Biblical Criticism: Histori-
                       cal, Literary and Textual,* pp. 47-82. Grand Rapids, Mich.: Zondervan.

Walton, John H.
1978   *Chronological Charts of the Old Testament.* Grand Rapids, Mich.: Zondervan.

Wansbrough, John
1977   *Quranic Studies: Sources and Methods of Scriptural Interpretation.* London
                       Oriental Studies 31 (School of Oriental and African Studies, University of

London). Oxford: Oxford University Press.

Ward, W. A.
1960   "The Egyptian Office of Joseph." *Journal of Semitic Studies* 5:144-50.

Washington, James Melvin, ed.
1986   *Frustrated Fellowship: The Black Baptist Quest for Social Power.* Macon,
                             Ga.: Mercer University Press.

1994   *Conversations with God: Two Centuries of Prayers by African Americans.*
                             New York: HarperCollins.

Washington, Raleigh, and
  Glen Kehrein
1993   *Breaking Down Walls: A Model for Reconciliation in an Age of Racial Strife.*
                             Chicago: Moody Press.

Waterman, G. Henry
1975   "The Sources of Paul's Teaching on the Second Coming of Christ in 1 and
                             2 Thessalonians." *Journal of the Evangelical Theological Society* 18:105-13.

Weems, Renita J.
1993   "Womanist Reflections on Biblical Hermeneutics." In *Black Theology: A
                             Documentary History*, 2:216-24. Edited by James H. Cone and Gayraud S.
                             Wilmore. 2 vols. Maryknoll, N.Y.: Orbis.

Weimar, Peter
1988   "Sinai und Schöpfung: Komposition und Theologie der Priesterschriftlichen
                             Sinaigeschichte." *Revue Biblique* 95:377-85.

Weinfeld, Moshe
1967   "Deuteronomy—The Present State of the Inquiry." *Journal of Biblical Litera-
                             ture* 86, no. 3 (September): 249-62.

1977   "Ancient Near Eastern Patterns in Prophetic Literature." *Vetus Testamentum*
                             27:178-95.

1987-1988   "The Traditions About Moses and Jethro at the Mountain of God." *Tarbiz*
                             56:449-60. (In Hebrew. Summarized in *Old Testament Abstracts* 12:170.)

1991   "What Makes the Ten Commandments Different?" *Bible Review* 7, no. 2:
                             34-41.

1993   "Covenant Making in Anatolia and Mesopotamia." *The Journal of the Ancient
                             Near Eastern Society of Columbia University* 22:135-39.

Weinstein, James M.
1975   "Egyptian Relations with Palestine in the Middle Kingdom." *Bulletin of the
                             American Schools of Oriental Research* 217 (February): 1-16.

1991   "Egypt and the Middle Bronze IIC/Late Bronze IA Transition in Palestine."
                             Levant 23:105-16.

Weisman, Ze'ev
1985   "Diverse Historical and Social Reflections in the Shaping of Patriarchal
                             History." *Zion* 50:1-13.

Wenham, David
1984   *The Rediscovery of Jesus' Eschatological Discourse.* Vol. 4 of *Gospel Per-
                             spectives.* Edited by R. T. France and David Wenham. 6 vols. Sheffield, U.K.:
                             JSOT Press.

Wenham, David, and
  Craig Blomberg, eds.
1986   *The Miracles of Jesus.* Vol. 6 of *Gospel Perspectives.* Edited by R. T. France,
                             David Wenham and Craig Blomberg. 6 vols. Sheffield, U.K.: JSOT Press.

Wenham, Gordon J.
1971   "The Deuteronomic Theology of the Book of Joshua." *Journal of Biblical Literature* 90, no. 2 (June): 140-48.

1976   "History and the Old Testament." In *History, Criticism and Faith,* pp. 13-75. Edited by Colin Brown. Downers Grove, Ill.: InterVarsity Press.

1979   *The Book of Leviticus.* New International Commentary on the Old Testament. Grand Rapids, Mich.: Eerdmans.

1980   "The Religion of the Patriarchs." In *Essays on the Patriarchal Narratives,* pp. 157-88. Edited by A. R. Millard and D. J. Wiseman. Leicester, U.K.: Inter-Varsity Press.

1985a   "The Date of Deuteronomy: Linch-Pin of Old Testament Criticism." *Themelios* 10, no. 3: 15-20.

1985b   "The Date of Deuteronomy: Linch-Pin of Old Testament Criticism, Part 2." *Themelios* 11, no. 1: 15-18.

1988   "Genesis: An Authorship Study and Current Pentateuchal Criticism." *Journal for the Study of the Old Testament* 42:3 18.

Wenham, John
1993   "The Large Numbers in the Bible." *Jewish Bible Quarterly* 21:116-20.

*West, Cornel
1993   *Race Matters.* Boston: Beacon.

Westbrook, Raymond
1994   "What Is the Covenant Code?" In *Theory and Method in Biblical and Cuneiform Law: Revision, Interpolation and Development,* pp. 15-36. Edited by Bernard M. Levinson. *Journal for the Study of the Old Testament* Supplement 181. Sheffield, U.K.: Sheffield Academic Press.

Whitaker-da-Cunha, Fernando
1976   "O feminismo politico." *Revista del Instituto de Ciencias Sociales* 27-28:259-68. (Summarized in *Sociofile Database.*)

White, Mel
1979   *Deceived.* Old Tappan, N.J.: Fleming H. Revell.

White, Ronald C., Jr.
1990   *Liberty and Justice for All: Racial Reform and the Social Gospel (1877-1925).* Rauschenbusch Lectures, New Series 2. San Francisco: Harper & Row.

Whybray, R. N.
1987   *The Making of the Pentateuch: A Methodological Study. Journal for the Study of the Old Testament* Supplement 53. Sheffield, U.K.: JSOT Press.

1995   *Introduction to the Pentateuch.* Grand Rapids, Mich.: Eerdmans.

"Wilberforce, William"
1992   In *The New Encyclopaedia Britannica,* 12:654. 15th ed. Chicago: University of Chicago Press.

Wilcox, Max
1988   " 'According to the Pattern *(tbnyt)* . . .': Exodus 25,40 in the New Testament and Early Jewish Thought." *Revue de Qumran* 13:647-56.

Wilkerson, David
  1974   *The Vision.* Old Tappan, N.J.: Fleming H. Revell.

*Williams, Chancellor
  1987   *The Destruction of Black Civilization: Great Issues of a Race from 4500 B.C. to 2000 A.D.* Illustrated by Murry N. DePillars. Chicago: Third World Press.

Williamson, H. G. M.
  1982   *1 and 2 Chronicles.* New Century Bible Commentary. Grand Rapids, Mich.: Eerdmans; London: Marshall, Morgan & Scott.

Willis, Geoffrey G.
  1975   "Lead Us Not into Temptation." *Downside Review* 93:281-88.

Willis, Rev. Dr.
  1854   "The Bible vs. Slavery." In *Autographs for Freedom,* 2:151-55. Edited by Julia Griffiths. Auburn, Maine: Alden, Beardsley; Rochester, N.Y.: Wanzer, Beardsley.

**Wilmore, Gayraud S.
  1983   *Black Religion and Black Radicalism: An Interpretation of the Religious History of Afro-American People.* 2nd rev. ed. Maryknoll, N.Y.: Orbis.

Wilson, Robert R.
  1978   "Early Israelite Prophecy." *Interpretation* 32:3-16.

Wilson, S.
  1979   "Anti-Judaism in the Fourth Gospel?" *Irish Biblical Studies* 1 (January): 28-50.

Wilson, Stephen G.
  1973   *The Gentiles and the Gentile Mission in Luke-Acts.* Society for New Testament Studies Monograph Series 23. Cambridge: Cambridge University Press.

Wimber, John, with
  Kevin Springer
  1986   *Power Evangelism.* San Francisco: Harper & Row.

Wiseman, D. J.
  1978   "They Lived in Tents." In *Biblical and Near Eastern Studies: Essays in Honor of William Sanford Lasor,* pp. 195-200. Edited by Gary A. Tuttle. Grand Rapids, Mich.: Eerdmans.

  1980   "Abraham Reassessed." In *Essays on the Patriarchal Narratives,* pp. 139-56. Edited by A. R. Millard and D. J. Wiseman. Leicester, U.K.: Inter-Varsity Press.

Wiseman, P. J.
  1985   *Ancient Records and the Structure of Genesis: A Case for Literary Unity.* Updated by D. J. Wiseman. Nashville: Thomas Nelson.

Witherington, Ben, III
  1984   *Women in the Ministry of Jesus: A Study of Jesus' Attitudes to Women and Their Roles As Reflected in His Earthly Life.* Society for New Testament Studies Monograph 51. Cambridge: Cambridge University Press.

  1988   *Women in the Earliest Churches.* Cambridge: Cambridge University Press.

  1990   *The Christology of Jesus.* Minneapolis: Fortress.

  1994   *Jesus the Sage: The Pilgrimage of Wisdom.* Minneapolis: Fortress.

  *1997   *The Jesus Quest: The Third Search for the Jew of Nazareth.* Revised edition.

Downers Grove, Ill.: InterVarsity Press.

Wolcott, Leonard T.
1976   "In Defense of Missions." *Christianity Today,* January 16, pp. 15-17.

Wolfson, Harry Austryn
1968   *Philo: Foundations of Religious Philosophy in Judaism, Christianity and
                Islam.* 4th rev. ed. 2 vols. Cambridge, Mass.: Harvard University Press.

Wood, Bryant G.
1990a   "Dating Jericho's Destruction: Bienkowski Is Wrong on All Counts." *Biblical
                Archaeology Review* 16, no. 5: 45, 47-49, 68.

1990b   "Did the Israelites Conquer Jericho?" *Biblical Archaeology Review* 16, no. 2:
                44-58.

Woolman, John
1754-1762   *Some Considerations on the Keeping of Negroes (1754); Considerations on
                Keeping Negroes (1762).* Philadelphia: James Chattin. (Reprint New York:
                Grossman/Viking, 1976.)

World Press Review
1989   March, pp. 28-29.

1991   June, p. 36.

1994   March, p. 31.

1996   January.

Wright, G. Ernest
1944   "The Significance of the Temple in the Ancient Near East." *Biblical Archae-
                ologist* 7, no. 3 (September): 41-44.

1946   "The Literary and Historical Problem of Joshua 10 and Judges 1." *Journal of
                Near Eastern Studies* 5:105-14.

1961   "The Temple in Palestine-Syria." In *The Biblical Archaeologist Reader,* pp.
                169-84. Edited by G. Ernest Wright and David Noel Freedman. Garden City,
                N.Y.: Doubleday.

1962   *Biblical Archaeology.* 2nd ed. Philadelphia: Westminster Press.

Wright, Jeremiah A., Jr.
1993   *What Makes You So Strong: Sermons of Joy and Strength.* Valley Forge, Penn.:
                Judson.

1995   *Africans Who Shaped Our Faith.* Chicago: Urban Ministries.

Wright, N. T.
1992   *Who Was Jesus?* Grand Rapids, Mich.: Eerdmans; London: S.P.C.K.

Yahuda, A. S.
1933   *The Language of the Pentateuch in Its Relation to Egyptian.* London: Oxford
                University Press.

1947   "Hebrew Words of Egyptian Origin." *Journal of Biblical Literature* 66:84-85.

Yamauchi, Edwin M.
1966a   "The 'Daily Bread' Motif in Antiquity." *Westminster Theological Journal* 28:145-56.

1966b   "The Present Status of Mandaean Studies." *Journal of Near Eastern Studies* 25, no. 2 (April): 88-96.

1972   *The Stones and the Scriptures: An Introduction to Biblical Archaeology.* Grand Rapids, Mich.: Baker Book House.

1973   *Pre-Christian Gnosticism: A Survey of the Proposed Evidences.* Grand Rapids, Mich.: Eerdmans.

1986   "Magic or Miracle? Diseases, Demons and Exorcisms." In *The Miracles of Jesus,* pp. 89-183. Edited by David Wenham and Craig Blomberg. Vol. 6 of *Gospel Perspectives.* Edited by R. T. France, David Wenham and Craig Blomberg. 6 vols. Sheffield, U.K.: JSOT Press.

1990   *Persia and the Bible.* Grand Rapids, Mich.: Baker Book House.

Yarbrough, Robert
1993   "New Light on Paul and Women?" *Christianity Today,* October 4, pp. 68, 70.

Yeivin, S.
1970   "The Patriarchs in the Land of Canaan." In *Patriarchs,* pp. 201-18. Edited by Benjamin Mazar. Vol. 2 of *The World History of the Jewish People.* New Brunswick, N.J.: Rutgers University Press.

Youngblood, Clark R.
1988   "The Embalming Process in Ancient Egypt." *Biblical Illustrator* 14, no. 2: 80-83.

Yoyotte, J.
1981   "Pharaonic Egypt: Society, Economy and Eulture." In *Ancient Civilizations of Africa,* pp. 112-35. Vol. 2 of *General History of Africa.* Edited by G. Mokhtar. UNESCO International Scientific Committee for the Drafting of a General History of Africa. Berkeley: University of California Press; London: Heinemann Educational Books; Paris: United Nations Educational, Scientific and Cultural Organization.

Zana, Mehdi
1995   "A Kurd's Tale of Turkish Prison." *World Press Review*, July, pp. 13-15. (From *Libération* [Paris], January 21-27, 1995.)

Zevit, Ziony
1985   "The Problem of Ai: New Theory Rejects the Battle As Described in the Bible but Explains How the Story Evolved." *Biblical Archaeology Review* 11, no. 2 (March): 58-69.

1990   "Three Ways to Look at the Ten Plagues." *Bible Review* 6, no. 3: 16-23, 42, 44.

1992   "Timber for the Tabernacle: Text, Tradition and *Realia.*" In *Avraham Biran Volume,* pp. 136-43. Edited by E. Stern and T. Levi. Eretz Israel 23. Jerusalem: Israel Exploration Society/Hebrew Union College.

Ziderman, I. Irving
1990   "Seashells and Ancient Purple Dyeing." *Biblical Archaeologist* 53:98-101.

Zwickel, Wolfgang
1992   "Der Altarbau Abrahams zwischen Bethel und Ai (Gen 12f)." *Biblische*

Zeitschrift 37:207-19.

Sources for Ancient Works Cited

2 Apocalypse of Baruch
1983   Translated by A. F. J. Klijn. In *The Old Testament Pseudepigrapha*, 1:615-52. Edited by James H. Charlesworth. 2 vols. Garden City, N.Y.: Doubleday.

Apocalypse of Moses
1983-1985   In *The Old Testament Pseudepigrapha*. Edited by James H. Charlesworth. 2 vols. Garden City, N.Y.: Doubleday.

Apuleius
1915   *Metamorphoses (The Golden Ass)*. Translated by W. Adlington. Revised by S. Gaselee. Loeb Classical Library. Cambridge, Mass.: Harvard University Press.

Aristotle
1935   *The Eudemian Ethics; On Virtues and Vices*. Translated by H. Rackham. Loeb Classical Library. Cambridge, Mass.: Harvard University Press.

Athenaeus
1927-1941   *The Deipnosophists*. Translated by C. B. Gulick. 7 vols. Loeb Classical Library. Cambridge, Mass.: Harvard University Press.

The Babylonian Talmud
1948   Edited by Isidore Epstein. London: Soncino.

2 Apocalypse of Baruch
1983   Translated by A. F. J. Klijn. In *The Old Testament Pseudepigrapha*, 1:615-52. Edited by James H. Charlesworth. 2 vols. Garden City, N.Y.: Doubleday.

The Book of the Dead
1974   *The Book of the Dead, or Going Forth by Day: Ideas of the Ancient Egyptians Concerning the Hereafter As Expressed in Their Own Terms*. Translated by Thomas George Allen. Oriental Institute of the University of Chicago Studies in Ancient Oriental Civilization 37. Chicago: University of Chicago Press.

Chariton
1939   *Chaereas and Callirhoe*. Translated by Warren E. Blake. Ann Arbor: University of Michigan Press; London: Oxford University Press. (Greek text: Oxford: Clarendon, 1938.)

Cicero   *Works*. 28 vols. Translated by Harry Caplan et al. Loeb Classical Library. Cambridge, Mass.: Harvard University Press (dates vary).

Corpus Inscriptionum Iudaicarum
1936-1952   *Corpus Inscriptionum Iudaicarum: Recueil des inscriptions juives qui vont du IIIe siècle avant Jesus-Christ au VIIe siècle de notre ere*. 2 vols. Edited by P. Jean-Baptiste Frey. Rome: Pontificio Istituto di Archeologia Cristiana.

Corpus Papyrorum Judaicarum
1957-1964   3 vols. Edited by Victor A. Tcherikover, with Alexander Fuks; vol. 3 edited by Victor A. Tcherikover, Alexander Fuks and Menahem Stern, with David M. Lewis. Cambridge, Mass.: Harvard University Press/Magnes/Hebrew University.

Cynic Epistles
1977   *The Cynic Epistles: A Study Edition*. Edited by Abraham J. Malherbe. Society of Biblical Literature Sources for Biblical Study 12. Missoula, Mont.: Scholars Press.

Diodorus Siculus
1933-1967   *The Library of History*. Translated by C. H. Oldfather et al. 12 vols. Loeb

                                    Classical Library. Cambridge, Mass.: Harvard University Press; London:
                                    Heinemann.

Diogenes Laertius
    1925   *Lives of Eminent Philosophers.* Translated by R. D. Hicks. 2 vols. Loeb
                                    Classical Library. Cambridge, Mass.: Harvard University Press.

Dionysius of Halicarnassus
    1937-1945   *The Roman Antiquities.* Translated by Earnest Cary. 5 vols. Loeb Classical
                                    Library. Cambridge, Mass.: Harvard University Press; London: Heinemann.

1 Enoch
    1978   *The Ethiopic Book of Enoch: A New Edition in the Light of the Aramaic Dead
                                    Sea Fragments.* Edited by Michael A. Knibb with Edward Ullendorff. 2 vols.
                                    Oxford: Clarendon.

    1983   Translated by E. Isaac. In *The Old Testament Pseudepigrapha,* 1:5-89. Edited
                                    by James H. Charlesworth. 2 vols. Garden City, N.Y.: Doubleday.

2 Enoch
    1983   Translated by F. I. Andersen. In *The Old Testament Pseudepigrapha,* 1:91-221.
                                    Edited by James H. Charlesworth. 2 vols. Garden City, N.Y.: Doubleday.

3 Enoch
    1983   Translated by P. Alexander. In *The Old Testament Pseudepigrapha,* 1:223-315.
                                    Edited by James H. Charlesworth. 2 vols. Garden City, N.Y.: Doubleday.

Epictetus
    1926-1928   *The Discourses As Reported by Arrian, the Manual and Fragments.* Translated
                                    by W. A. Oldfather. 2 vols. Loeb Classical Library. Cambridge, Mass.: Harvard
                                    University Press.

Epistle of Aristeas
    1951   *Aristeas to Philocrates: Letter of Aristeas.* Edited and translated by Moses
                                    Hadas. New York: Harper & Brothers/Dropsie College for Hebrew and
                                    Cognate Learning.

    1985   Translated by R. J. H. Shutt. In *The Old Testament Pseudepigrapha,* 2:7-33.
                                    Edited by James H. Charlesworth. 2 vols. Garden City, N.Y.: Doubleday.

Euripides
    1912   *Works.* Translated by Arthur S. Way. 4 vols. Loeb Classical Library. New York:
                                    G. P. Putnam's Sons.

Eusebius
    1926-1932   *The Ecclesiastical History.* Translated by Kirsopp Lake. 2 vols. Loeb Classical
                                    Library. New York: G. P. Putnam's Sons.

Ezekiel Exagoge
    1983-1985   In *The Old Testament Pseudepigrapha,* 2:808-19. Edited by James H. Char-
                                    lesworth. 2 vols. Garden City, N.Y.: Doubleday.

4 Ezra
    1983   Translated by B. M. Metzger. In *The Old Testament Pseudepigrapha,* 1:517-
                                    59. Edited by James H. Charlesworth. 2 vols. Garden City, N.Y.: Doubleday.

*The Fathers According to
    Rabbi Nathan*
    1955   Translated by Judah Goldin. Yale Judaica Series 10. New Haven, Conn.: Yale
                                    University Press.

    1975   *'Abot de Rabbi Nathan,* Version B. Translation and commentary by Anthony J.
                                    Saldarini. Studies in Judaism in Late Antiquity 11. Leiden, Netherlands: E. J. Brill.

Greek Magical Papyri
    1992   *The Greek Magical Papyri in Translation (Including the Demotic Spells).*
                                    Edited by Hans Dieter Betz. 2nd ed. Chicago: University of Chicago Press.

Herodotus
1920-1925   *History.* Translated by A. D. Godley. 4 vols. Loeb Classical Library. Cambridge, Mass.: Harvard University Press.

Horace
1914-1926   *Works.* Translated by C. E. Bennett and H. Rushton Fairclough. Loeb Classical Library. New York: G. P. Putnam's Sons.

Isocrates
1928-1961   *Orations.* Translated by George Norlin and Larue van Hook. 3 vols. Loeb Classical Library. London: Heinemann; New York: G. P. Putnam's Sons.

Josephus
1926-1965   *Works.* Translated by H. St. J. Thackeray et al. 10 vols. Loeb Classical Library. Cambridge, Mass.: Harvard University Press.

Jubilees
1985   Translated by Orval S. Wintermute. In *The Old Testament Pseudepigrapha.* 2:35-142. Edited by James H. Charlesworth. 2 vols. Garden City, N.Y.: Doubleday.

Juvenal
1940   *Satires.* Translated by G. G. Ramsay. Rev. ed. Loeb Classical Library. Cambridge, Mass.: Harvard University Press.

Life of Adam and Eve
1985   Translated by M. D. Johnson. In *The Old Testament Pseudepigrapha,* 2:249-95. Edited by James H. Charlesworth. 2 vols. Garden City, N.Y.: Doubleday.

Lucian
1913-1961   *Works.* Translated by A. M. Harmon, K. Kilburn and M. D. Macleod. 8 vols. Loeb Classical Library. Cambridge, Mass.: Harvard University Press.

Lucretius
1937   *De Rerum Natura.* 3rd rev. ed. Translated by W. H. D. Rouse. Loeb Classical Library. Cambridge, Mass.: Harvard University Press.

Marcus Aurelius
1916   *Meditations.* Translated by C. R. Haines. Loeb Classical Library. Cambridge, Mass.: Harvard University Press.

Mekilta de Rabbi Ishmael
1933-1935   Translated by Jacob Z. Lauterbach. 3 vols. Philadelphia: Jewish Publication Society of America.

The Midrash Rabbah
1977   Edited by Harry Freedman and Maurice Simon. 5 vols. New York: Soncino.

The Mishnah
1933   Translated by Herbert Danby. London: Oxford University Press.

1963   Pointed Hebrew text, introductions, translations, notes and supplements by Philip Blackman. 7 vols. New York: Judaica.

Palestinian Talmud
1982-   *Talmud of the Land of Israel: A Preliminary Translation and Explanation.* Edited by Jacob Neusner. Chicago: University of Chicago Press.

Pesikta de Rab Kahana
1975   *R. Kahana's Compilation of Discourses for Sabbaths and Festival Days.* Translated by William G. Braude and Israel J. Kapstein. Philadelphia: Jewish Publication Society of America.

Pesikta Rabbati
1968   Translated by William G. Braude. 2 vols. Yale Judaica Series 18. New Haven, Conn.: Yale University Press.

Philo of Alexandria
1929-1962   *Works.* Translated by F. H. Colson and G. H. Whitaker. Loeb Classical Library. New York: G. P. Putnam's Sons; London: Heinemann. (Supplementary vols. 1-2 translated by Ralph Marcus. Cambridge, Mass.: Harvard University Press, 1953.)

Philostratus
1912   *Life of Apollonus of Tyana.* Translated by F. C. Conybeare. 2 vols. Loeb Classical Library. Cambridge, Mass.: Harvard University Press.

Plato
1914-1926   *Works.* Translated by Harold North Fowler et al. 12 vols. Loeb Classical Library. Cambridge, Mass.: Harvard University Press.

Pliny
1938-1962   *Natural History.* Translated by H. Rackham, W. H. S. Jones and D. E. Echholz. 10 vols. Loeb Classical Library. Cambridge, Mass.: Harvard University Press.

Plotinus
1966-   *Works.* Translated by A. H. Armstrong. 6 vols. Loeb Classical Library. Cambridge, Mass.: Harvard University Press.

Plutarch
1914-   *Lives.* Translated by Bernadotte Perrin et al. 11 vols. Loeb Classical Library. New York: G. P. Putnam's Sons; London: Heinemann.

1927-1969   *Moralia.* Translated by Frank Cole Babbitt et al. 15 vols. Loeb Classical Library. New York: G. P. Putnam's Sons; London: Heinemann.

Polybius
1979   *The Rise of the Roman Empire.* Translated by Ian Scott-Kilvert. New York: Penguin.

Pritchard, James B., ed.
1955   *Ancient Near Eastern Texts Relating to the Old Testament.* 2nd ed. Princeton, N.J.: Princeton University Press.

Pseudo-Philo
1985   *Biblical Antiquities.* Translated by D. J. Harrington. In *The Old Testament Pseudepigrapha,* 2:297-377. Edited by James H. Charlesworth. 2 vols. Garden City, N.Y.: Doubleday.

Pseudo-Phocylides
1985   Translated by P. W. van der Horst. In *The Old Testament Pseudepigrapha,* 2:5656-82. Edited by James H. Charlesworth. 2 vols. Garden City, N.Y.: Doubleday.

Publilius Syrus
1935   In *Minor Latin Poets,* vol. 2. Translated by J. Wight Duff and Arnold M. Duff. 2 vols. Rev. ed. Loeb Classical Library. Cambridge, Mass.: Harvard University Press.

Quintilian
1920-1922   *The Institutio Oratoria.* Translated by H. E. Butler. 4 vols. Loeb Classical Library. Cambridge, Mass.: Harvard University Press.

Qumran texts
1971   *Die Texte aus Qumran.* Edited by Eduard Lohse. Munich: Kösel-Verlag.

Seneca
1928-   *Works.* Translated by John B. Basore et al. 10 vols. Loeb Classical Library. Cambridge, Mass.: Harvard University Press.

Sentences of Sextus
1981   Edited and translated by Richard A. Edwards and Robert A. Wild. Society of Biblical Literature Texts and Translations 22; Early Christian Literature Series 5. Chico, Calif.: Scholars Press.

Sextus Empiricus
1933-1949   *Works*. Translated by R. G. Bury. 4 vols. Loeb Classical Library. Cambridge, Mass.: Harvard University Press; London: Heinemann.

Sibylline Oracles
1902   *Die Oracula Sibyllina* (Greek text). Edited by Johannes Geffcken. Leipzig: n.p.

1983   Translated by J. J. Collins. In *The Old Testament Pseudepigrapha*, 1:317-472. Edited by James H. Charlesworth. 2 vols. Garden City, N.Y.: Doubleday.

Sifra to Leviticus
1988   *Sifra. An Analytical Translation*. Translated by Jacob Neusner. 3 vols. Brown Judaic Studies 138-40. Atlanta: Scholars Press.

Sifre to Deuteronomy
1987   *Sifre to Deuteronomy: An Analytical Translation*. Translated by Jacob Neusner. 2 vols. Brown Judaic Studies 98, 101. Atlanta: Scholars Press.

Sifre to Numbers
1986   *Sifre to Numbers: An American Translation and Explanation*. Translated by Jacob Neusner. 2 vols. Brown Judaic Studies 118-19. Atlanta: Scholars Press.

Tertullian
1931   *Apology*. Translated by T. R. Glover. Loeb Classical Library. Cambridge, Mass.: Harvard University Press.

Testament of Adam
1983   Translated by S. E. Robinson. In *The Old Testament Pseudepigrapha*, 1:989-95. Edited by James H. Charlesworth. 2 vols. Garden City, N.Y.: Doubleday.

Testament of Solomon
1922   Greek text. Edited by Chester Charlton McCown. Leipzig: J. C. Hinrichs'sche Buchhandlung.

1983   Translated by D. C. Duling. In *The Old Testament Pseudepigrapha*, 1:935-59. Edited by James H. Charlesworth. 2 vols. Garden City, N.Y.: Doubleday.

Testaments of the Twelve Patriarchs
1983   Translated by Howard Clark Kee. In *The Old Testament Pseudepigrapha*, 1:775-828. Edited by James H. Charlesworth. 2 vols. Garden City, N.Y.: Doubleday.

Theon
1989   *The Progymnasmata of Theon: A New Text with Translation and Commentary*. Translated by James R. Butts. Ann Arbor, Mich.: University Microfilms International.

The Tosefta
1977-1986   Translated by Jacob Neusner et al. 6 vols. New York: KTAV.

Index of Authors and Selected Topics

Index of Primary Sources

BIBLE

3:19-21 *197*
3:21 *53*

Colossians
1:15-18 *122*
2:18 *79*

1 Thessalonians
1:4-10 *115*
1:5 *190*
2:2 *99, 115*
2:5 *115*
2:7 *115*
2:13 *69, 190*
4—5 *197*
4:14 *115*
4:16 *115*

2 Thessalonians
2 *197*

Hebrews
book *194*
1:1-4 *122*
1:5 *73*
2:4 *190*
8:5 *143*

James
1:21-27 *40*
3:1 *129*
5:14-15 *190*

2 Peter
3:4 *133*
3:9 *133*
3:15 *133*

1 John
2:2 *120*
2:19-25 *120*
4:1-6 *84*
4:2-3 *120*
5:7 *7*
2
2 John
7-11 *120*

Revelation
1:5 *53*
1:6 *187*
2:14-16 *120*
2:20-23 *120*
5:9-10 *133*

9:20-21 *130*
12:11 *186*
12:17 *186*
14:12 *186*
16:6 *186*
17:6 *64, 186*
19:2 *186*
19:10 *186*
20:4 *186*

QUR'AN
2.31 *189*
2.37 *189*
2.124-30 *189*
2.136 *189*
2.285 *189*
3.47 *189, 192*
3.55 *193*
3.59 *189, 192*
3.64 *189*
3.83-84 *189*
4.48 *189*
4.157 *193*
4.159 *193*
4.164 *189*
4.171 *189, 192*
4.171-72 *189*
5.15 *191*
5.33 *198*
5.36 *198*
5.51 *198*
5.87 *170*
6.60 *193*
7.143-44 *189*
8.15-17 *198*
9.5 *198*
9.14 *198*
9.29-30 *198*
9.63 *198*
9.73 *198*
15.29 *189, 192*
19.19 *189*
19.20-22 *189, 192*
19.21 *189*
19.33-34 *193*
19.35 *189*
21.26 *189*
21.91 *189, 192*
26.10 *189*
27.8-12 *189*
28.30-35 *189*
41.39-40 *185*
41.43 *189*
41.50 *185*
46.9 *189*

48.29 *187*
66.12 *189, 192*

RABBINIC LITERATURE

'Abot de Rabbi Nathan, A
6 *194*
9 *199*
24 *196*
28 *180*
40 *199*

'Abot de Rabbi Nathan, B
12, §30 *200*
13, §31 *194*
16, §36 *199*
41, §116 *199*
48, §32 *180*

Babylonian Talmud
    'Aboda Zara
    2b *200*
    25a, bar. *194*
    64b, bar. *199*

    Beşa
    25b *200*

    Ketubot
    66b *194*

    Qiddušin
    49b *180*

    Sanhedrin
    43a *196*
    56ab, bar. *199*
    59a *199*
    107b *196*
    108b *171*

    Ta'anit
    19b-20a *194*

Mekilta
    Bahodesh
    5 *200*
    6.90ff. *199*

    Beshallah
    4.52ff *200*

    Pisha
    1.135-36 *196*
    5.39-40 *184, 215*